Diversity in Action
Local Public Management of Multi-ethnic Communities
in Central and Eastern Europe

C000156852

DIVERSITY IN ACTION

LOCAL PUBLIC MANAGEMENT OF MULTI-ETHNIC COMMUNITIES IN CENTRAL AND EASTERN EUROPE

Edited by

ANNA-MÁRIA BÍRÓ AND PETRA KOVÁCS

LGI Books

First edition published by
Local Government and Public Service Reform Initiative
Open Society Institute

Nador utca 11
H-1051 Budapest
Hungary
tel: (361) 327-3104
fax: (361) 327-3105
http: //www.osi.hu/lgi

Production by Tom Bass
Design by Arktisz Studio

ISBN 963 7316 70 1
ISSN 1586-1317

Printed in Hungary by Arktisz Studio

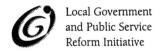 Local Government
and Public Service
Reform Initiative

Local Government and Public Service Reform Initiative (LGI), as one of the programs of the Open Society Institute (OSI), is an international development and grant-giving organization dedicated to the support of good governance in the countries of Central Eastern Europe (CEE) and Newly Independent States (NIS). LGI seeks to fulfill its mission through the initiation of research and support of development and operational activities in the fields of decentralization, public policy formation and the reform of public administration.

With projects running in countries covering the region between the Czech Republic and Mongolia, LGI seeks to achieve its objectives through:

- Development of sustainable regional networks of institutions and professionals engaged in policy analysis, reform-oriented training and advocacy;
- Support and dissemination of in-depth comparative and regionally applicable policy studies tackling local government issues;
- Support of country specific projects and delivery of technical assistance to implementation agencies;
- Assistance to local Soros foundations with the development of local government, public administration and/or public policy programs in their respective countries;
- Publishing of books, studies and discussion papers dealing with the issues of decentralization, public administration, good governance, public policy and lessons learnt from the process of transition in these areas;
- Development of curricula and organization of training programs dealing with specific local government issues;
- Support of policy centers and think-tanks in the region.

Apart from its own projects, LGI works closely with a number of other international organizations (Council of Europe, Department of International Development, USAID, UNDP and World Bank) and co-funds larger regional initiatives aimed at the support of reforms on the subnational level. Local Government Information Network (LOGIN) and Fiscal Decentralization Initiatives (FDI) are two main examples of this cooperation.

For additional information or specific publications, please contact:

Local Government and Public Service Reform Initiative
P.O. Box 519
H-1397 Budapest
Hungary
E-mail: lgprog@osi.hu · http://www.osi.hu/lgi
Tel: (361) 327-3104 · Fax: (361) 327-3105

CONTENTS

Acknowledgements

The editors would like to thank to Violetta Zentai, LGI Project Manager; Gábor Péteri, LGI Research Director; and Adrian Ionescu, LGI Program Director, for their continuous support and enthusiasm in making this project happen. We are grateful to our contributors for agreeing to undertake their tasks and for delivering the finished products in reasonable time. Thanks are also due to the expert-readers, Éva Heizer, Éva Orsós, Tamás M. Horváth, Metin Kazak, Teodora Noncheva, Dan Oprescu, Károly Tóth, Klara Orgovanova, Valentina Pavlenko, Martin Potůček, Tatjana Sisakova and Béla Varga, for providing careful critical comments on the various aspects of the chapters. We owe gratitude to Csilla Kató, Zsuzsa Katona and Judit Benke for carrying out administrative work for the book's completion. Tom Bass's advice, encouragement and patience in the production of the book were invaluable. Every publishing service that required in the course of bringing this book to press he provided. Alexandra Scacco, LGI Research Associate, helped us with her enormous commitment, expertise and patience in style, content-editing, compiling the glossary of terms and indices, fact-checking and final clarifications for which we remain indebted.

Contributors

Piotr Bajda is the Deputy Director of the Polish Institute in Bratislava, Slovakia. He holds an M.A. in Political and Social Science from the Academy of Catholic Theology in Warsaw. Previously, he worked on human and minority rights at the Helsinki Foundation for Human Rights in Poland and worked on promoting minority culture and Polish-Slovak relations at the Stefan Batory Foundation.

Anna-Mária Bíró is the Central and Eastern Europe Project Manager at the Budapest Co-ordination Office of Minority Rights Group International. She studied human rights and advocacy as an intern with the International Service for Human Rights near the United Nations in Geneva. She holds an M.Sc. in Public Administration and Public Policy from the London School of Economics and she is currently doing her Ph.D. at the Political Science Department of the Faculty of Law, University of Sciences (ELTE), Budapest. For two years, she was adviser on international relations to the President of the Democratic Alliance of Hungarians in Romania.

Ján Buček is researcher and lecturer at the Department of Human Geography, Comenius University in Bratislava. His primary research focus is political geography, with particular emphasis on public administration issues. His research interests reflect the new challenges and various problems of post-communist transformation at the local level. Since the mid-1990s, he has addressed issues of multi-ethnic co-existence at the local level. Buček received his Ph.D. from Comenius University in Bratislava in 1996. He has been a researcher in residence at the London School of Economics (1992) and Cambridge University (1997-1998).

István Horváth is a lecturer at the Sociology Department of Babes-Bolyai University in Cluj, Romania. He is Deputy Director of the Research Centre for Inter-Ethnic Relations in Cluj. He conducts research and teaches various courses on inter-ethnic relations and ethno-political evolution in Romania. He is also a Fellow of the New Europe College in Bucharest.

Jenő Kaltenbach is Parliamentary Commissioner for Minority Rights in Hungary, former chairman of the German Minority Self-Government and a constitutional lawyer. He was one of the initiators and later a spokesperson of the Roundtable of National and

Ethnic Minorities in Hungary. Kaltenbach has made great efforts to modernise the system of representation of minorities in the national decision-making process.

Petra Kovács is Researcher at the Local Government and Public Service Reform Initiative (LGI). Since 1997, she has directed the Managing Multi-ethnic Communities Project (MMCP). She holds an M.A. from the ELTE/UNESCO Ethnic and Minority Studies Program and a D.E.A. Degree in Public Policy from the University Paris 1 Pantheon-Sorbonne. She is a Ph.D. candidate in public policy at ELTE University in Budapest. Her main fields of interest are multi-ethnic community management, public policy analysis and minority access to public services.

Elena Gyurova has an M.A. in Sociology fromWarsaw University and has continued post-graduate studies in Society and Political Science at the Central European University, Prague, and completed an M.A. in European Integration at the New Bulgarian University. She has worked as a research fellow at the Institute of Culture, as the chief expert at the Ministry of Regional Development and Public Amenities in charge of local and regional development, social issues and groups in disadvantaged positions. She was also programme co-ordinator at the Inter-ethnic Initiative for Human Rights Foundation, Sofia. Her fields of interest include innovative democratic practices in managing local and regional development with the participation of civil society.

Laura Laubeová is a lecturer at the Institute of International Studies, Faculty of Social Sciences, Charles University, Prague. She is currently working on her Ph .D. in Public Policy, focusing on equal treatment policies and anti-discriminatory practices. She serves as a chairperson for the Globea Transborder Initiative for Tolerance and Human Rights. Previously, she was the Executive Director of the New School Foundation.

Alexandra Scacco is a Research Associate at the Local Government and Public Service Reform Initiative (LGI) at the Open Society Institute, Budapest, where she does research on multi-ethnic issues. She holds an M.Sc. in International Relations from the London School of Economics. She received her undergraduate degree from the Woodrow Wilson School of Public and International Affairs at Princeton University.

George Schöpflin is Jean Monnet Professor of Political Science and Director of the Centre for the Study of Nationalism at the School of Slavonic and East European Studies, University of London. He is the author of *Politics in Eastern Europe 1945-1992* (Oxford: Blackwell, 1993) and *Nations, Identity, Power* (London: Hurst, 2000) as well as of many other works, including numerous articles on ethnicity and nationhood. He is co-editor of and contributor to *Myths and Nationhood* (London: Hurst, 1997) and (with Stefano Bianchini) *State Building in the Balkans: the Dilemmas on the Eve of the 21ST Century* (Ravenna: Longo, 1998). His principal area of research is the relationship between ethnicity, nationhood and political power, with particular reference to post-communism.

Viktor Stepanenko received his Ph.D. from the University of Manchester in 1998. He is currently Senior Fellow at the Institute of Sociology in Kiev, Ukraine, where he has been working since 1992. Between 1992 and 1995 he took part in the international project, Neighbourhood of Cultures, established by Bielefeld and Warsaw Universities. During 1997-1998 he was a Fellow in the Ethnicity and Autonomy team in the framework of the Global Security Fellows Initiative at the University of Cambridge, UK. His fields of research include ethnic issues, political sociology and public policy analysis. His most recent publication is *Construction of Identity and School Policy in Ukraine* (Nova Science Inc., 1999).

Magdalena Syposz is the Europe and Central Asia Programme Co-ordinator at Minority Rights Group International. She holds an M.Sc. in Political Economy of Transition from the London School of Economics and Political Science. Previously, she did human rights research at the Jagiellonian University in Krakow, Poland, and worked on participation issues at the World Bank.

Patrick Thornberry is Professor of International Law, Keele University, and a faculty member at the University of Oxford and George Washington University Joint Programme in International Human Rights Law. He was appointed by the Foreign and Commonwealth Office to the list of six UK experts for the OSCE Human Dimension Mechanism and was Chairman of Minority Rights Group International from 1999. His publications include: *International Law and the Rights of Minorities* (Oxford University Press, 1991); *Minorities and Human Rights Law* (Minority Rights Group, 1987) revised in 1991. More recent publications include: 'In the Strongroom of Vocabulary', in: P. Cumper and S. Wheatley (eds.) *Minority Rights in the 'New' Europe* (Kluwer Law International, 1999). In December 2000 he was nominated by the UK government to membership of the Committee on the Elimination of Racial Discrimination (CERD) of the United Nations.

Tony Verheijen is currently working as a Chief Technical Adviser for the UNDP Good Governance Programme for the Europe and CIS region. He holds a Ph.D. in Law from Leiden University and M.A. degrees in International Relations (Free University of Brussels) and Public Administration (Erasmus University, Rotterdam). Previously he was a lecturer and director of the International Programme at Leiden University, Netherlands. He also worked for the SIGMA programme at OECD, the University of Limerick and the European Institute of Public Administration. He is the author of several books and articles on comparative public administration and European integration, including *Constitutional Pillars for New Democracies* (1995), *Innovations in Public Management* (1998) and *Civil Service Systems in Central and Eastern Europe* (1999).

Dariusz Wojakowski is an assistant to a professor at the Institute of Sociology of the Pedagogical University in Rzeszow. He holds an M.A. in Social Sciences from the Pedagogical University and in Religious Sciences from the Jagiellonian University, Krakow. He recently completed his doctoral dissertation, 'Ethnic-Cultural Pluralism in Local Communities in the Polish-Ukrainian Borderland' at the Jagiellonian University.

TABLES AND FIGURES

CASE STUDIES

PREFACE

DIVERSITY IN ACTION:
LOCAL PUBLIC MANAGEMENT OF MULTI-ETHNIC COMMUNITIES

Anna-Mária Bíró and Petra Kovács

Reform of Public Administration and Ethnic Identity Protection

The establishment of new political institutions and the reform of public administration are key events in the process of transition in the post-communist countries of Central and Eastern Europe (CEE). In this process, the effective management of multi-ethnic communities has become relevant at both the central and local levels of government. Minorities raised their voices for the protection of their rights and for their involvement in democratic state-building. In their view, meaningful democracies could only be based on consensual states incorporating all ethnic groups, whether majorities or minorities, on an equal footing. This inclusive legitimacy of the newly emerging states was thought to be a major guarantor of stability, a condition *sine qua non* of effective transition to market economies and the rule of law. Due to the legacy of nationalist-communist countries that discouraged and sanctioned public participation in policy-making in general and increasingly regarded the state as the ethnic property of the majority population, the aspirations of minorities for the preservation of their identity and effective participation have been resisted to various degrees throughout much of the region. Nevertheless, as a result of heated domestic debates under international pressure for peace and stability, it has been broadly recognised that the aspirations of minorities and indigenous peoples will not disappear and that there must be a systemic response to their needs.

The protection of minority rights and the political, economic and social inclusion of minorities have also been urged by various intergovernmental organisations. These organisations include the United Nations (UN), the Organisation for Security and Cooperation in Europe (OSCE), the Council of Europe (CoE) and the European Union (EU), which have developed a number of politically and legally binding instruments regulating and guiding the domestic treatment of minorities. The international community has declared that the welfare of minorities is no longer an exclusively internal affair of the state but a legitimate concern of the entire community.

As a consequence of domestic and international events, post-communist countries have established various forms of legal and institutional frameworks for the protection of minorities. But it has become increasingly clear that an exclusively rights-based approach in the spirit of effective protection defined by international minimum standards may not necessarily provide for a broader inclusion of minorities at all levels of government. Thus, the development of participatory systems of governance responsive to the special needs of diverse minorities has become key to stable and functioning democracies of this multi-ethnic region. The establishment of inclusive systems of local governance in general and from an ethnic perspective in particular, is an important first step towards building participatory systems overall.

The bulk of the minority rights and multi-ethnic policies are implemented by local authorities. In addition, special measures and services are truly effective only if designed and carried out at the closest level to those affected. In many countries, as a result of public administration reforms and decentralisation, local authorities gained competencies to design policies responsive to ethnic diversity through the representation or direct involvement of minorities. In some countries, autonomous arrangements in the field of culture were set. Yet the effective implementation of these policies is often hindered by central government control, skewed administration of law, insufficient technical expertise and inadequate resources. There is, therefore, an urgent need to develop methods to overcome these barriers and to enhance local government capacity to meet the specific needs of diverse communities.

Experience shows that, on one hand, effective decentralisation can often be delayed by central government fears of secession by territorially compact ethnic groups. On the other hand, even if the centre is co-operative on ethnic issues, nationalist local authorities may block the implementation of decentralised minority policies. Whilst decentralisation and the principle of subsidiarity can be very effective, domestic supervision and international monitoring are also needed to improve minority protection in the region. In addition, the building of a political culture acceptant of a multi-ethnic public administration should supplement the legal and institutional reforms. A multi-disciplinary approach to public administration reform coupled with the application of multiple tools of reform, including training, is key to the establishment of pluralist democracies in Central and Eastern Europe.

The Project

In the fall of 1996, the Local Government and Public Service Reform Initiative (LGI) of the Open Society Institute launched a project to identify and disseminate useful information on the effective management of multi-ethnic communities and development of multi-ethnic politics in Central and Eastern Europe (Managing Multi-ethnic Communities Project (MMCP) http://lgi.osi.hu/ethnic). As of January 2001, more than 160 relevant cases of local policy innovation had been identified, and a network comprised of more than 300 local experts and civil servants was established. (As of spring of 2000, LGI Managing Multiethnic Communities Project and the Center for European Migration and Ethnic Studies (CEMES) have engaged in a partnership to update and maintain the database of case studies on innovative practices.)

As a result of this project, LGI understood the urgent need for support of local government capacity-building and multi-disciplinary training of public officials to address problems related to the governance of multi-ethnic communities. In November 1998 LGI began the production of this textbook for schools of public administration in the region in order to provide public officials with a solid knowledge of the relevant legal, political and administrative issues related to the effective governance of multi-ethnic communities of the region. As most country chapters were submitted before the summer 2000, important political events which have since occured in the region are not addressed in the book.

Consonant with the Managing Multi-ethnic Communities Project, LGI has already published a book with similar focus covering the countries of former Yugoslavia. (Nenad Dimitrijevic (ed.), *Managing Multiethnic Local Communities in Countries of Former Yugoslavia*, LGI: Budapest, 2000.) Another book on the Newly Independent States is forthcoming. (LGI Managing Multi-ethnic Communities Project and the Network of Ethnological Monitoring and Early Warning of Conflict in Moscow are expected to publish *Democratic Governance of Multi-ethnic Communities in the Newly Independent States,* edited by Valery Tishkov, in 2001.)

Substance and Methodology

Due to the lack of relevant literature and research in this field, this textbook intends to fill the gap by providing information and 'food for thought' for public officials and relevant professionals and practitioners. It is not intended to be an exhaustive comparative study of local management of multi-ethnic communities in the region; it does not establish theories and models that identify commonalties and differences in inter-community management at the local level across all relevant countries in a systematic way. Such a task would exceed the introductory intentions of the book. The major objective of this book is to set the ground for basic multi-disciplinary knowledge in this field, to provide a regional overview of the major issues that were identified across the countries in question and to collect and share strategies for addressing these issues through the case studies of good practice. It is hoped that this book will invite creative criticism and further research and debate that can inform the everyday work of those concerned.

The textbook covers the following countries of Central and Eastern Europe: Bulgaria, the Czech Republic, Hungary, Poland, Romania, Slovakia and Ukraine. These countries share commonalties that make them suitable for comparative research. All of them are post-communist and in a period of political, economic and social transition; they have all experienced peaceful transition processes; each of them opted for accession to the European Union and integration into Euro-Atlantic structures; and all of them are historically multi-ethnic and have undertaken significant institutional reforms, including public administration reform.

This volume analyses the management of multi-ethnic communities from a multi-disciplinary perspective, attempting to briefly map out the broader context of the issue together with a focus on particular in-country situations and practices. It also combines a more detached view of comprehensive expert analyses with the perspective of local authors focusing on local particularities. The book is divided into two major parts.

Part One introduces the political, legal and administrative environment of the management of multi-ethnic communities.

The political science chapter is structured around the basic concepts of state, ethnicity and civil society, and the conditions for their effective functioning under modernity and globalisation. Related issues such as legitimacy, state integrity and state collapse, citizenship, ethnicity and cultural reproduction, multi-ethnicity and multi-culturalism are re-assessed critically in a comparative framework of examples from Western and Eastern Europe. The question of post-communism and the special role of ethnicity in these states are also addressed.

The chapter on public administration gives an overview of institutional reforms carried out in the last ten years at both central and local levels in the relevant countries of Central and Eastern Europe. In the section discussing the initial constitutional and institutional reforms in post-communist states, the two major competing constitutional settlements, parliamentarism and presidentialism, are presented and analysed. The following part provides a critical survey of the central government reforms, including the civil service and administrative structures and the issue of the training of public officials. A number of problems related to the development of the new administrations are analysed from historic, economic, political and legal perspectives. The overview of local government reform incorporates key elements including size, competencies and property as well as central/local relations.

The overview of the existing legislative framework on the protection of minorities presents the international law background and context and the leading global and European texts. Its analysis focuses on four key texts: Article 27 of the International Covenant on Civil and Political Rights, the United Nations Minority Rights Declaration, the Charter for Regional and Minority Languages and the Framework Convention for the Protection of Minorities of the Council of Europe. The interpretative complexities of each text are addressed, and an explanation of what these instruments mean and how they can be used is provided. The focus on legal analysis is combined with a broader focus on political issues, 'diplomatic' approaches to conflict prevention and redress, and the benefits of inter-cultural and multi-cultural education.

Part Two identifies the relevant historic legacy, legislation and institutional structures, major political debates in minority protection and public administration reform, with particular reference to local government on a country by country basis. Innovative local practices in this subject area are included. Policy analysis is combined with demographic and sociological surveys, and rights-based assessments are combined with inquiries from a public policy perspective. To lay the foundation for a more or less systematic comparative review, the editors suggested some guidelines to the authors containing a set of issues for analytic consideration. These issues include: various characteristics/qualifiers of multi-ethnicity, the legal and political position of minorities, public administration and local government reform with reference to the representation and participation of minorities, and policy recommendations. Some authors chose to structure their analyses according to the guidelines. Others shaped them according to what was considered as most important from their perspective in the field. For instance, some authors focused on the analysis of one or two minority situations instead of a more comprehensive overview of inter-ethnic issues in their states.

Authors identified various types of minorities and minority policies. It seems that the number/size, geographical location, pre-communist history and institutional memory, elites (skilled, organised), available local resources (spiritual and material), and external resources proved to be decisive factors in designing minority policies. Part Two emphasises that various ethnic groups in a given country may have very different aspirations, claims and needs. Different groups also enjoy very different levels of social and political integration. This kind of information, it is hoped, may help public officials and civil servants to better understand the nature of the region's ethnic diversity and to design policies according to the needs of various ethnic groups.

Each country chapter includes an in-depth analysis of the legislative and institutional frameworks for the protection of minorities. Chapters discuss differences between *de jure* and *de facto* provisions of legal and institutional guarantees. Conflicts between international law and domestic legislation are discussed in all chapters. While Central and Eastern European countries have become parties to various international and European legal instruments, these guarantees sometimes contradict domestic legislation. Sometimes international standards are stronger than domestic laws, while in other cases domestic law can exceed international norms. Harmonisation of international and domestic legislation, however, should not be used as a means of lowering or disrupting existing domestic standards.

There are various forms of constitutional recognition of minorities throughout the region. The outcomes of political debates on these forms of recognition can be assessed along a broad constitutional spectrum. At one end of the spectrum, minorities are recognised in constitutions, and may be granted state-constituent status. At the other end, their constitutional recognition may be denied altogether. This lack of recognition can prevent effective minority protection. However, nonrecognition of minorities at a constitutional level may be the price for some *de facto* provisions for identity protection at the local level.

In the emerging democracies of Central and Eastern Europe, new institutions in civil society have emerged to design and implement various types of public policy. Nonprofit or civic organisations have been established to respond to new challenges or to provide adequate services for particular groups. Due to their autonomy, these organisations are often more creative in developing new models and means to provide specialised services. On the basis of the experience of these NGOs, successful innovations might be translated and adapted in other localities. The civil sector can fill in gaps in government policy and practice, and can work in partnership with local government to meet minority needs.

Some other major issues identified across the chapters are the following: representation and/or direct involvement of minorities in local governments, use of minority languages in public administration, financial guarantees for cultural autonomy, financial and political support for minority education, and minority access to local public services. Almost all of these topics have emerged in each of the seven countries. However, institutional arrangements and policy responses have varied to a great degree. Further, political debates that marked the introduction of new policies both at the central and the local level crystallised around different issues: language, education, territorial autonomy or property restitution, citizenship, and distributive justice. The textbook presents a set of innovative approaches and policy programmes that have attempted to address these issues.

The country analyses are supplemented by case studies of innovative practices coming from various multi-ethnic localities in the region. Case studies are intended to raise awareness among public officials and practitioners of the many old and new strategies for the promotion of local multi-ethnic harmony across the region. These case studies were included to illustrate local experiences in concrete detail so that they can be adapted and used under different circumstances.

Special attention was paid to ensure that multiple ethnic perspectives were reflected in each country chapter. Expert readers from diverse ethnic groups were invited to provide comments and advice to the authors that were subsequently integrated into the text. Because of the pilot nature and multi-ethnic character of the book, the editors did not opt for a rigid structure and uniform style and terminology across chapters. On the contrary, they tried to respect the individual perspective, methodology, style and language present in each chapter to celebrate what is the major topic of this book: diversity.

Key Features of the Book

Each of the chapters is designed to be easy to read with a number of learning aids including:

- **Abstracts.** A brief summary of the main points is provided at the beginning of each country chapter.
- **Boxed Case Studies.** Important cases of good practice and innovative thinking are contained in boxes.
- **Appendices and Annexes.** These provide useful information to supplement the text.
- **Further reading.** Each chapter provides a brief list of further reading on the subject covered.
- **Consolidated bibliography.** At the end of the book a detailed list of sources is provided chapter by chapter.
- **Glossary.** A selection of key concepts is briefly explained at the end of the book.

PART ONE

THE CONTEXT:

POLITICAL, ADMINSTRATIVE AND LEGAL PERSPECTIVES

MINORITIES AND DEMOCRACY

George Schöpflin

Contents

MINORITIES AND DEMOCRACY

George Schöpflin

The central issue is this—how can the modern democratic state come to terms with its own diversity, with the very diversity that democracy produces, and not fall apart while simultaneously providing for the expression of that diversity?

Democracy

There are various answers. In the first place, democracy is made democratic by basing its rule on the consent of those governed. The means for articulating that consent and feeding into the system of governance is the concept of popular sovereignty. There must also be a system of institutions for transmitting the will of the people to the rulers, together with a readiness on the part of the rulers to translate popular aspirations into policy. These might be termed inclusive means. Equally, there are instruments for excluding certain ideas, options, actions and pressures. Some of these instruments are explicit, like legal regulation, and others are implicit and informal, encoded in cultural givens. And some are physical, material, technological, economic, etc.

Language is one of the most self-evident ways of including and excluding. People who speak the same language and share the same culture will automatically be closer to one another and have the sense that they can rely on fellow members of the language community to understand them without further explanation. But language is seldom enough on its own. There have to be factors like shared history, memory and ways of life for communities of solidarity to come together. Note that speakers of the same language in the philological sense do not automatically constitute a community of solidarity. Thus speakers of English understand each other more readily, but their communities of solidarity are quite different—English, American, Irish, etc.

Under conditions of modernity, which in politics means continuous change, expanding choice and increasing complexity, the central institution for sustaining order and coherence is the state. The state comprises the entire set of institutions controlled by the elected authorities, the machinery of administration, central, regional and local levels of government, plus various state and semi-state agencies, as well as the judiciary, procuracy and other bodies involved in the administration of justice. Parliaments and elected local councils are notionally semi-autonomous of the state; in practice, they are in continuous interaction with it. Government agencies may be also semi-autonomous of it, in that they depend for their legality and legitimacy, as well as their budgets, on the state, but can act with extensive discretion. Nongovernmental organisations (NGOs) are notionally fully independent of the state, but will normally be in continuous interaction with it and will be structured by that interaction; NGOs which receive some or all of their funding from the state may also have a status that is more autonomous than that of government agencies.

Then, there is an important distinction to be made between democracy and consent to be ruled. A system may be consensual in the sense that its rulers are elected democratically, meaning that the electorate has consented to their being in power. But if the rulers' power is not exercised according to the principles of democracy—self-limitation, commitment, moderation, compromise, responsibility—it will not be democratic. This split between democratic sanction for power, which is often exercised undemocratically or semi-democratically, is characteristic of many of the post-communist states.

The State

It is vital to recognise a number of real, as distinct from formal, features of the state. In the first place, the state, like any other political actor, operates by adhering to a set of rules and does so supposedly in strict terms, thereby ensuring transparency, consistency and accountability. Hence following procedures and accounting for budgets are essential in maintaining a responsive relationship between the citizens and the state. The professionalism of the administrators, their training and socialisation, is another safeguard against the exercise of arbitrary power. Respect for the rule of law is vital.

However, given the complexity and extent of the tasks that the state has to resolve, it is impossible to make advance provision for all the contingencies that the state administration must deal with. Hence the agents of the state are entrusted with a considerable degree of discretion and they are supposed to exercise this within their formal and informal terms of reference. This requires them to act according to the doctrine of self-limitation, to accept feedback and to recognise a wider public good in acting in conformity to the dictates of consistency. In real political terms, the result is that the agencies of the state can arrogate power to themselves, leaving the citizen with only few resources to resist, particularly when judicial remedies are restricted.

The agencies of the state and their personnel are, therefore, political actors, even when their power is relatively restricted, and should act in a democratic way, guided by democratic values. When they do not, that power is to some extent discredited. Citizens will be reluctant to rely on it and will prefer to make their own private arrangements with it. This can take the form of various types of informality like corruption or the personalisation of power, when individuals prefer to deal with agents of the state known to them, rather than rely on the impersonal norms by which the state is supposed to abide.

True democracy, then, requires that there be a widely acknowledged sense of public good and an impersonal public sphere, impersonal in the sense that all citizens are treated evenhandedly by it and there are clear and effective remedies against abuses of power. But this desirable state of affairs is hard to establish and demands constant vigilance by all political actors, inside the state machinery and outside it (i.e. civil society), to monitor such abuses. And all actors have to accept that they may themselves stray into arbitrariness.

There is a particularly complex problem of the interlocking nature of the relationship between the state, language and modernity. Under conditions of modernity, the state is the pivotal agency of establishing and maintaining coherence and stability. All societies aim to create coherence; coherence provides a stable moral order and the set of shared meanings that lets individuals feel that they are members of a collectivity rather than mere individuals disconnected from the world they live in.

At the same time, modernity also demands very high levels of successful communication in order to secure state-driven coherence. This creates an expectation for the state to be monolingual. This means, further, that there is a qualitative difference between 'language' in general and the 'language of the state'. The language of a state has the prestige and power that the state has created. All languages have the potential to be developed into state languages and thus acquire the political power that is encoded in such a language, but comparatively few actually succeed in this. Crucially, it is vital to distinguish between the philological quality of language and the political. This distinction is frequently overlooked and ignoring it can contribute materially to the disempowerment of linguistic minorities.

Arbitrariness

The arbitrary power of the state is a worldwide phenomenon, and the institutions, instruments and culture of democracy are notionally the most effective means of making the state responsive to the aspirations of the citizens. In this connection, however, it should be clearly understood under modernity that the state itself has an interest in being responsive to society. If the state pursues a largely arbitrary course and ignores public opinion, it will generate both active and passive opposition or, in extreme cases, violent resistance. Furthermore, all the evidence points in the direction of the proposition that the central *raison d'etre* of the state, the maintenance of a monopoly of coercion and taxation, are achieved most efficiently when the citizens consent to this monopoly. Without such consent, therefore, the state is captured by its own bureaucratic norms and becomes incapable of discharging its tasks of sustaining order and coherence, because it cannot cope with simultaneous change and complexity. This, in effect, was the fate of the ultra-bureaucratic and hyper-etatistic communist systems. They collapsed under the weight of their own disorder and incoherence.

Order and Diversity

Thus the modern democratic state has, in effect, two irreconcilable tasks—to sustain order and to permit the articulation of ever more fragmented, disparate, differentiated aspirations; the integration of these two tasks is the criterion of success. In this context, there will never be a perfect solution to the key political issues of democracy at this time, only more or less acceptable ones. Hence it becomes vital to provide space for remedies, and that, in turn, requires that the state and those exercising power should have the necessary self-awareness and flexibility to respond to pressure. Equally, while the power of the state must be circumscribed, it should neither be excessively constrained nor fragmented. Crucial in this connection is that the state should be perceived as legitimate, a process that is sustained both by the actions of the state and that of society.

Legitimacy

Legitimacy is not automatic. All political actors, the state included, have to earn legitimacy by being responsive to the needs of the citizens; citizens as actors have to abide by the law and apply self-limitation to their activities. This is a counsel of perfection, of course, because it is impossible for all actors, especially the state, to meet the individual demands of each and every citizen.

The solution is to create predictability by following routines and procedures and to exercise discretion with care. Accountability must also be made clear, balanced and predictable. There must be proper procedures for calling political actors to account for their decisions and equally actors must be protected from trivial or frivolous attacks on their work. Note that both 'trivial' and 'frivolous' are culturally determined and will differ in time and place.

If a system is generally disliked by the bulk of the population and if that dislike is expressed in the open, then over time the self-confidence of political actors is eroded. The severe criticism of the public sector in the United Kingdom in the 1980s, coupled with far-reaching privatisation, clearly lowered the morale of those working there. In the longer term, a ruler who no longer feels that he has the support of the population will find it difficult to discharge his tasks or to do it very effectively, with the result that the self-legitimation of the entire system may be called into a question and a process of erosion will be under way. The institution in question, and it may be a state, will be seen as irrelevant or as a distraction; what it says will be ignored. Russia was in this situation for much of the 1990s.

State Collapse

There is, furthermore, a particular and generally undiagnosed problem with respect to the post-communist state. When communism collapsed in 1989-1991, it was not merely communism as an ideology that disintegrated, but so too did the communist state. Whatever the legitimacy of that state, it was a real entity in as much as it did provide a degree of order and coherence that was seen as 'normal and natural' by the bulk of the population. Its institutions may have been regarded as facades, and the levels of arbitrariness and informality that they sustained were certainly incompatible with anything remotely resembling democracy.

Nevertheless, they had established themselves, had become routinised and were to that extent accepted. The collapse of communism eliminated the key principle on which these states rested and on which their integrative power depended. Hence the end of communism brought into being political formations that had to re-establish their authority and to find new raw materials for their *raison d'etre*. Classically in Europe, as we have seen, this is derived from the state, from civil society and from ethnicity. Given the absence of civil society (destroyed under communism) and the weakness of the state (disintegrated after the collapse), the purposiveness of politics and social-cultural coherence came to depend heavily on ethnicity.

Ethnicity

Ethnicity is a widely used (and abused) term. In essence, it refers to a group that defines itself as a community of solidarity and identity, with a sense of its past and future, a shared set of meanings and a web of symbolic and mythic markers. Ethnic communities mark themselves off from other groups by various boundary mechanisms, of which language, territory and religion are the most significant, though not sufficient conditions. Ethnicity functions both at the explicit, overt level of meanings, and equally at the tacit, implicit level through the encoding of assumptions that members of a community accept without further questioning. While the codes of solidarity that ethnic groups generate vary enormously, the actual fact of ethnicity is universal. All human beings share in these codes at some level—the language they speak ensures this—and to that extent they all have ethnicity.

Although many in the West deny that their actions are in any way affected by ethnicity, this denial does not have to be taken at face value. Rather, the denial is a part of the assumption that European values are universal, something that has been one of the central tenets of European thought since the Enlightenment. In this perspective, what are defined as universal human values are regarded as ethically superior to those seen as particularistic. In reality, all universalisms are coloured to a greater or lesser extent by codes of ethnic solidarity. In this sense, French civic values are not only civic but also French and so on. The problem of ethnic exclusion or violence, therefore, is not ethnicity as such, but the presence or absence of other, countervailing ideas, values and institutions, like civil society and civic values, that delimit the exclusivist functioning of ethnicity

Modernity

With the coming of modernity in the 18TH century, and the steady growth of the reordering and integrative power of the modern state, ethnicity has become politicised. Ethnic groups have concluded that in order to ensure their uninterrupted cultural reproduction—the ultimate purposiveness of all groups—they must gain access to political power. Most commonly, this is the state, which thereby becomes the nation-state. However, various types of arrangements short of state independence also exist, which can—at any rate for a period of time—satisfy the needs and aspirations of ethnic communities. The autonomous arrangements for Catalonia, Scotland and the different regions of Belgium illustrate this.

One particular quality of ethnicity that has to be addressed is that when it functions without strong institutions and impersonal norms that are accepted by both rulers and ruled, negotiations between one ethnic group and another become extremely problematic. When a group concludes that its survival is challenged, it will be most reluctant to make the compromises that are a necessary element of democratic politics.

Different Meanings of Ethnicity

A further complication is that the term 'ethnicity' is currently used with a variety of different, and not necessarily complementary, meanings. Thus the word can refer to the identity of Third World immigrants to Western Europe, in which case its resonance is positive; to the salient ways of expressing identity under post-communism, in which case it is viewed as negative; and to the ethnic identities to the well-established democratic states of the West, in which case the existence of ethnicity is denied. This results in the kinds of absurdity that gives high value to the ethnicity of, say, Turkish immigrants in Germany but denies that German ethnicity has any value at all. This confusion is relevant to any discussion of issues of multi-ethnicity and multi-culturalism. In broad terms, the ethnicities of long-settled, established European communities tend to be regarded as negative, because they are regarded as sources of majority power and thus, in the eyes of those promoting this kind of discourse, inherently undesirable. This approach is based on the misconception that such disapproval will diminish attachment to majority ethnicity; a more effective way forward is to accept it and make political provision for it.

Multi-culturalism and Multi-ethnicity

There is a considerable amount of confusion about these terms and they tend to be used interchangeably, which adds to the confusion. In reality, they refer to different sociological and political situations. In multi-culturalism, one is dealing with the identities of recently settled populations in another country and the problems of integrating them into the dominant majority. In other words, multi-culturalism applies to immigrants, possibly immigrants of different racial origins, who by immigrating are signalling that in the long term, they or their descendants are ready to adopt the cultural norms of the majority. Crucially, under multi-culturalism there is not expected to be any long-term persistence of the languages that the immigrants bring with them.

Certain cultural traits, like religion, may well be conserved, but the intensity of acculturation and, correspondingly, the degree of separateness between majority and minority is likely to be small. Indeed, the concept of multi-culturalism contains a serious challenge for white majorities—will they be prepared to accept the demand that will certainly arrive on the cultural agenda, that non-whites can be fully accepted as members of the dominant community? For the time being, the answers differ. In some states, like France, the answer is notionally yes, but the terms of full acceptance are harsh—complete acculturation, including the abandonment of all previous cultural traits. Elsewhere, the answers are more ambiguous, as in Britain, roughly implying that the white majority has yet to face up to the question.

Multi-lingualism and multi-ethnicity are qualitatively different, in as much as they explicitly reject the idea of full acculturation and assume that the different language groups will live in the same state and sustain their different languages and cultures. This is a far more difficult state of affairs and requires quite different solutions from multi-cultural-ism. Above all, it will demand a level of sensitivity and accommodation by both (all) groups to the demands of the others and a readiness to compromise one's own moral and cultural agendas that some will not find palatable. In political terms, this means forms of power sharing, along the lines defined by consociationalism, which accepts and relies on the collective identities of groups as a key political building block (see below).

In practice, it is inconceivable that well-established ethnic minorities, like the Hungarians of Romania or the Russians of Latvia will abandon their languages and moral norms in order to merge into the majority. Nor is it certain that the majority would wel-come this. Hence these ethno-linguistic groups constitute separate societies that live in the same political space. The consequence is that the traffic between majority and minor-ity has to be regulated by clear and transparent rules, ones that both accept and, where necessary, challenge. Communication between them is likely to operate at the elite level, and in this context effective elite communication is vital for political stability, while at the street level mutual respect and acceptance of the other are generally sufficient.

Civil Society

The concept of civil society also demands further examination. Currently, 'society' when it is invested with the term 'civil' is widely seen as a possessing the moral high ground, even while it is perfectly clear that certain forms of social activity are evidently immoral (e.g. the oppression of minorities). Hence any analysis of civil society has to be refined to resolve the contradiction. The key here is the role of the state in establishing order and maintaining the rule of law. Where these processes are weak or absent or the state is not trusted, as in many of the post-communist states, society will not be very civil; it will not have any sense of operating under an even-handed set of rules and will, therefore, prefer personal to institutional forms of operation. This makes access to power uneven and bears particularly hard on minorities, social as well as ethnic.

Political actors will not necessarily act by the yardstick of democratic values, but— where the state is not strong enough to enforce the law—will rely instead on clientilistic networks, personal (rather than institutional) trust, favours and hierarchies of power. All these usually overlapping, informal institutions do, indeed, provide an alternative to the civic state and create a restricted security and order that people need in their encounters with power. But such a system is not very efficient or reliable: it perpetuates arbitrariness. Power is opaque and people will see abuses of power whether they are there or not; nor will they see remedies, resulting in frustration and a sense of injustice. Under moderni-ty, there is no adequate alternative to the impersonal state.

Ethnic (and other) minorities will tend to have poorer access to these informal net-works because they are in a minority and thus inherently weaker; their negative reaction to the exercise of power will be correspondingly stronger. They will be inclined to see power as being directed against them and will not recognise that the rulers (from the majority) may also be dealing with the majority ethnic group poorly. A case in point was the Slovak language law of the mid-1990s passed by the Meciar government, which the Hungarian minority saw as aimed at itself and would not accept that the law bore hard on some of the Slovak majority as well.

Post-communism

It should be noted that the present weakness of the state in the post-communist world is exacerbated by an unexpected phenomenon. The current discourse of civil society has evolved out of a Western context, from a need to challenge the strong, well-grounded Western welfare state of the post-1945 era. This discourse tends to see the relationship between civil society and the state as, at best, a zero-sum game and, vitally, it has no theory of the state.

The discourse does not, therefore, try to understand what the state is for, what its positive features and functions are and why sizeable sections of society continue to depend on it materially and culturally. Nor does this attitude like to recognise that civil society and the state are in a mutual relationship—each needs the other to operate effectively. Instead, this discourse dismisses the state as an obstacle to emancipation and does what it can to delegitimate it. This state of affairs tends to perpetuate the weakness and ineffectiveness of the state, even while the state has extensive tasks to discharge, which it consequently does much less well than it should.

The importing of this discourse into the post-communist world, aided as it was by the pre-1989 democratic opposition's anti-etatist perspectives, has resulted in the paradox noted above: that the post-communist state is not strong enough to provide the stabilising framework for civil society; hence society operates along a pattern of informalism, thereby weakening itself. Thus the pattern so common in post-communist societies: they have no pronounced civic sense and are not well able to exercise democratic control over the state and the government. The system is partly consensual, established and self-reproducing; there is no reason to expect any change in this area in the foreseeable future.

Ethnicity and Post-communist Systems

The foregoing should begin to provide an explanation for why ethnicity has come to play such a significant role in the running of post-communist states. It is the preeminent resource for the maintenance of order and coherence and will remain so until the state has acquired the requisite authority to provide the framework for the functioning of civil society. In the interim, where multi-ethnic relations are involved, these can raise questions that go beyond the capacity of the existing conflict resolution mechanisms. When the state and its institutions are not regarded as neutral by all the actors, for example, the police is seen as ethnically biased, minority ethnic groups will find themselves forced to create their own, potentially divergent forms of self-protection, which can come to be seen by the majority as threatening to the integrity of the state.

This has several outcomes. The weakness of the agreed mechanisms for conflict resolution tends to lead to rapid escalation in majority-minority relations; each is inclined to see the activities of the other in the worst light; each sees the other as a single, solid—and, therefore, threatening—block, which then leads them to listen only to the extremists and disregard the diversity of the other. Thereby, it is easy to understand the negative cycles from which it is difficult to escape. However, escape is not impossible, merely difficult. No community actually wants to live in a state of tension and if the elites can find an effective minimum basis for communication, de-escalation is feasible. Northern Ireland is a case where accommodation has proved all but impossible; Estonia offers a more positive picture.

Moral Worth

Central to any community's sense of itself in the modern world is that it is accepted by others, especially by its direct competitors, as a community of moral worth. While others may not share its particular combination of values and ideals, let alone its symbolic system, it is vital for collective self-esteem that a community be accepted by others on equal terms. What is very significant in this connection in the modern world is that all cultures seek acceptance as high cultures; indeed, there is a close nexus between political power and possessing a high culture, with all the necessary paraphernalia of language, vocabulary and density of meanings that allows a cultural community to compete on equal terms. Crucially, political demands—whether within a state or internationally—have to be articulated in a universally acceptable form. This means possessing the right kind of high cultural vocabulary that modernity demands.

However, when two cultures are competing for power within the same state, the majority will find such political contests very difficult to tolerate, given the close association between cultural power, state power and political power. It is this collision that makes the rights of ethnic minorities so difficult to regulate in a democratic way. Probably the most successful form of such regulation is consociationalism, which provides the necessary political power for all the cultural communities in the same etatic space and the means for resolving political contests.

Consociational systems explicitly recognise that the power of the state depends on all the ethnic groups that live there. Power has to be shared and exercised proportionately between them. In practical terms, consociational systems (Belgium, Switzerland, Finland, South Tyrol) depend on the idea of a coalition in which all groups are represented, on elite cooperation, on proportional access to the material and symbolic goods of the state by all groups, on the right of veto by all groups on matters that affect their most vital interests and, it should be added, that all the ethnic communities are committed to the territorial integrity of the state.

It is crucial in such systems that contests for political power, which are a normal part of every political system, can be expressed in such a way as to avoid ethnic polarisation, which spills very readily into ethnicisation, a situation where everything—all initiatives, moves and decisions—are read in ethnic terms and only in ethnic terms. In such situations, the 'public good' or civic sphere, that ought to attach to the state and transcend ethnicities, does not do so. Switzerland is an illustration of a successful case, as is Finland; Northern Ireland is an example of the opposite.

State Integrity

The problem of the integrity of the state is not as straightforward as it appears at first sight. On the face of it, this concept refers to the integrity of state territory and seeks to impose a general interdict on the fragmentation or disintegration of states. It implies that once a state has come into being, it is there forever—that there is a moral purposiveness in state integrity—and, hence, anything that threatens it is to be condemned and may, therefore, be combated. However, in the real world of politics, the configuration of states undergoes constant change and it is only from the unusual perspective of 1945-1989, when state boundaries remained extraordinarily stable, that this appearance of changelessness arose. Most European states have been involved in some kind of major or minor boundary change in the 20TH century. At the same time, such change is deeply disliked by states and thus by the international order, which has adopted this position.

There are several factors which help to explain this conservatism. In the first place, the state has a tacit function as the final repository of rationality, so that the questioning of the state is a challenge to rationality itself. Second, when a state is rearranged, this causes far-reaching upheaval, as the new state—the state within its new frontiers—has to impose its particular order on the newly acquired territory. Germany after reunification is a good example. Third, new states give rise to greater complexity in the international order, which is disliked by the existing beneficiaries of the system, as it means accepting new entrants. Foreign ministries, which have established their own routines, networks of information, contacts and other forms of cultural capital, are reluctant to accept that their hard-won knowledge has become useless in the new circumstances. This conservatism was acutely visible during the crisis that led to the disintegration of Yugoslavia, when Western states were most uneasy with the idea that Yugoslavia as a state and as an aspiration had lost the consent of the majority of the people who lived there. Indeed, the hesitations of the West contributed to the ensuing chaos. Fourth, given the foregoing, reconfiguring the state order (new states, new frontiers) is generally difficult and is often the outcome of upheaval. While it is usually the outcome of upheaval and not necessarily the cause of it, in popular perceptions the two are often confounded. Fifth, as the modern state has been entrusted with the maintenance of order and coherence, any challenge to it is deeply disturbing—when states are faced with collapse or fragmentation, it as if a part of the natural world had suddenly changed, it seems inexplicable and is profoundly threatening. If an alternative source of order is not available, those affected will be vulnerable to extremist mobilisation, as happened to the Serbs of Bosnia in 1992.

Ethnic Minorities

All this inevitably impacts on ethnic minorities, because majorities can seek to present their claims for political power as a threat to the international order and the territorial integrity of the state and find a ready audience. On the other hand, the evolution of the European order in the 1990s has to some extent confronted this problem by giving minorities an international audience, a space within which they can articulate their demands, without the automatic assumption that they are seeking secession. Through the Council of Europe, the High Commissioner on National Minorities of the Organisation for Security and Cooperation in Europe (OSCE), as well as a host of international NGOs, ethnic minorities have acquired the space to address international public opinion directly, while simultaneously there is a consensus that the classical, strict definition of state has been considerably diluted. The international community has in effect declared that the welfare of ethnic minorities is the concern of the entire community.

Territory

Particular attention should be paid in this connection to the role of territory. Historically, there was a direct equation between territory and power; the more territory a state controlled, the more powerful it was thought to be. Elements of this kind of thinking survive, although in power terms, territory is far less important than it was. Power nowadays resides in information, in ideas, in ability to manipulate concepts and to persuade others to act, rather than force them to do so. The consensual exercise of power, which this shift betokens, is far more effective—far better at condensing and accumulating power—than the power that grows out of the barrel of a gun.

Nevertheless, this does not signify that territory has lost all significance in the exercise of power and especially in the context of power in inter-ethnic relations. Despite globalisation and despite the loss of power by the state (as traditionally measured), territory continues to play a key role at the concrete level, as well as at the symbolic one. Communities structure their identities around myths of territory and project this onto a concrete piece of land. In this sense, territory has a dual function in the politics of identity—it establishes and expresses a particular community and it gives it wider recognition, as well as endowing it with the space in real terms that it can regard as its own.

In an indirect way, communities weigh one another's worth by their being communities of territory. This makes it especially difficult for nonterritorial groups, like the Roma, to gain the recognition they are seeking. Equally, when two or more groups share the same territory and invest it with special symbolic significance, the arrangement of inter-ethnic relations will be highly intractable, though not completely so.

This points to another facet of the role of territory in inter-ethnic relations. Each community tends to regard its territory—its mythic territory—as its monopoly possession. When the mythic territory coincides with the boundaries of the state, there is no serious difficulty; but when there is no such coincidence, the conflict of concrete and mythic can become very complex indeed to negotiate. Inter-ethnic relations in Romania, where both Romanians and Hungarians invest Transylvania with a mythic function of this nature, is an example of this kind of contest.

Myths and Symbols

All this raises the thorny issue of the role of myths and symbols in politics in general and in the politics of inter-ethnic relations in particular. In a good deal of the literature on this area, there is no serious analysis of the role of symbols; reference may be made to that role, but it is not examined in any depth. This can result in the underestimation of the impact and importance of symbolic-mythic processes. The most persuasive way of looking at these processes, then, is to see the concrete and the symbolic as being in a continuous, interactive relationship, that when the institutional and procedural forms of power are well grounded, the role of symbols stays in the background, though it would be a mistake to imagine that they disappear entirely.

All communities—ethnic, civic, other—depend on myth and symbol to screen in certain ideas, propositions, meanings and to exclude others. By doing so, communities create an order, a way of seeing the world that is particular and proper to them and them alone. These meanings are then made 'normal and natural' by that particular community.

Communities construct narratives about themselves as a way of responding to the bewildering variety of experience that the world is and to make sense of what would otherwise be chaos. The meanings so created are then transformed into the particular world of the community concerned and are seen as the norm, as central to its sense of self and its aspiration to live on, engaging in cultural reproduction. The myths and symbols on which communities rely also act as a boundary towards the external world and control the boundary traffic—certain ideas are screened in, while others are screened out. These processes are not necessarily conscious; nor are they manipulative, but constitute the normal means of community maintenance.

Cultural Reproduction

The continuity of communities, their reproduction, the capacity of their members to recognise one another and to establish boundaries towards nonmembers all depend in part on the web of symbolic meanings that are generated and used to sustain solidarity. Furthermore, once a community is established at the symbolic level, it will necessarily sacralise the bases of its founding assumptions, meaning that they will be placed in the realm of doxa, where the 'normal and natural' is encoded and where implicit meanings reside; this means that for the members of that community, the assumptions so encoded will be beyond ordinary scrutiny. Nonmembers of the community can quite often see these assumptions—certainly, the symbolic and ritual forms that they take will be quite visible—but they will not identify with them. Thus at the most everyday level, people will identify themselves with their flag, but for others, the particular colours of someone else's flag will generate no resonance.

Globalisation

In the last 10-15 years, however, a new phenomenon has appeared with far-reaching consequences for identity formation. This is globalisation. Globalisation should be seen as a series of overlapping and interconnected processes, not just economic and fiscal, but also informational, technological and a whole range of other activities. There is a causal nexus operating here, so that globalisation in one area can reinforce it in another. The crucial result of globalisation is that established tradition is rapidly fragmented, the denseness of meanings is diluted and coherence feels threatened. Communities feel that they have lost control over their destinies. The loss is too rapid to be easily replaced—something that could be done in the past—and the outcome is a bewilderment, a fear, a sense that both individual and collective security, faith in the future, transparency and predictability are being destroyed.

Consequently, we feel that we can no longer devise viable life strategies, that our cultural meanings are differently interpreted by different members of the community, so that solidarity is waning. We find it difficult to respond to these challenges, we do not necessarily even have the language for doing so, and the most that we can do is to retreat into the thickets of our cultural norms, underpinned by a stronger insistence on our symbols and myths. The problem is that much as we would like to do this, the sheltered quality of our cultural norms is in danger, there is or there seems to be no safe area because of the impact of globalisation. Our endeavours to recreate tradition, through the packaging of history and memory in theme parks, for example, do not work too well when our self-awareness is constantly reinforced by the flood of information about ourselves. This is the phenomenon known as reflexivity and reflexivity does not make for an easy world.

In Europe, we tend to see globalisation as having its roots in the United States. When we resent its effects on us, it is the intrusion of US values that we dislike and above all, we dislike it that what we regard as US norms are presented to us as universal norms, whereas we know that they are not so. How do we know? Because we have our culture, our distinctive cultural norms, that are not respected by what we perceive as those of the United States. We do not seem to have consented to them, there has been no negotiation, they just arrive and we take them or else. In this sense, globalisation directly erodes our sense of moral worth and produces defensive reactions—identities are changing and our control of that change seems weak.

Conclusion

Broadly, there are both positive and negative trends in inter-ethnic relations in Europe and it is far too easy to concentrate on the pathology, as many do, and to ignore the success stories. The war in Kosovo in 1999 and the ensuing ethnicisation of the territory were, indeed, a major catastrophe, but success stories are generally less conspicuous and much less sensational. The central proposition is that there are indeed successful ways of managing inter-ethnic conflict, but these demand long, slow and often tedious negotiations that are much less visible—the extremely lengthy negotiations that resulted in the relatively relaxed state of affairs in the South Tyrol is a case in point.

Second, although the process of European integration via the European Union is like-wise slow, cumbersome and bureaucratic, it has resulted in the rise of a European iden-tity that for certain purposes transcends the nation, the state and ethnicity. European inte-gration is a very long-term project and its outcome remains unclear. But what is indubitable is that for the generations born after the 1960s, it has become the norm and they accept that their European identities bring them closer to one another than before.

Third, the rise of the discourse of human rights has a direct bearing on the fate of minorities—they are very much included in human rights normativity as a matter of prin-ciple. The radical nature of this turn is frequently underestimated. Before 1989, the treat-ment of ethnic minorities was overwhelmingly seen as an issue for the sovereign state. As argued, this is no longer the case and the process is far from over. Both politically and legally, minorities have acquired a protection that is denser and more effective than at any time in the past.

Fourth, the adoption of democracy throughout Europe, even where its functioning is imperfect, establishes far greater space for innovation than before. New forms of knowl-edge and power can create institutions for minorities—give them voice—at both the local and the state-wide levels that can in itself be helpful. Besides, democracy helps to ensure that neither the majority nor the minority defines itself as homogeneous and the conse-quent heterogeneity creates spaces where inter-ethnic cooperation can take root. The emphasis here is on 'can'; there is no automatic guarantee of success, but the potential is significantly greater than before 1989.

Further reading

Bauman, Zygmunt (1998) *Globalization: the Human Consequences,* Cambridge: Polity.

Berger, Peter (1967) *The Sacred Canopy: Elements of a Sociological Theory of Religion,* New York: Doubleday.

Douglas, Mary (1986) *How Institutions Think,* Syracuse NY: Syracuse University Press.

Lal, Deepak (1998) *Unintended Consequences: the Impact of Factor Endowments, Culture, and Politics on Long-Run Economic Performance,* Cambridge MA: MIT Press.

Schöpflin, George (2000) *Nations, Identity, Power,* London: Hurst.

Urry, John (2000) *Sociology beyond Societies: Mobilities for the Twenty-first Century,* London: Routledge.

PUBLIC ADMINISTRATION REFORM: A MIXED PICTURE

Tony Verheijen

Contents

PUBLIC ADMINISTRATION REFORM: A MIXED PICTURE

Tony Verheijen

Introduction

An analysis of progress in institutional development and public administration reform in Central and Eastern Europe, more than 10 years after the start of the transition, yields a mixed picture of success and failure.

Assessments of central government systems by the European Union (EU) and in academic publications continue to paint a dire picture of public administration. This may come as a surprise if one considers the overall achievements in Central and East European (CEE) states in building new political institutions. With the exception of some of the successor states of ex-Yugoslavia and a few states in the European part of the former Soviet Union (fSU), the states in the region have created generally accepted constitutions, built the political institutions provided for in these constitutions and undergone one or more peaceful changes of government and leadership. Progress in the development of democratic systems of local self-government is generally acknowledged, even though in most Central and East European states several questions regarding the status, functions and financial management of local self-governing authorities remain to be addressed.

In this chapter a brief review is made of progress on both central and local government reform in Central and Eastern Europe. The chapter starts with a brief comparative overview of the institutional frameworks put in place. Then it focuses on a comparative analysis of success and failures of public administration reform at central and local government level in order to contextualise a discussion on governance in multi-ethnic states later on in this volume.

Institutional Reform and Constitutionalism

The overall governance framework can be considered settled in most states in the Central and East European region.[1] The states in the region went through a period of institutional flux, the duration of which varied strongly. Scenarios ranged from a short transitional period in Hungary (2-3 years), which ended with a fundamental revision of the previous constitution and institutional framework, to a prolonged political battle over the consti-

---

[1] With the exception of Federal Republic of Yugoslavia; Belarus, where further institutional transformation seems to be inevitable if democratic systems of governance are to emerge; and possibly Bosnia-Herzegovina—once an indigenous fully operational system of governance will start to function.

tutional framework, in Poland, where it took until 1997 before a final constitutional settlement was reached.[2]

The Debate on Parliamentarism vs. Presidentialism

The debate on presidentialism vs. parliamentarism focused on the relative merits of different
types of institutional models. In pure presidential models, such as in the US, the government
depends fully on the president for its appointment and dismissal, while in pure parliamentary
models the government depends fully on the confidence of the parliament.

The arguments of those advocating systems based on strong, directly elected presidents, with
wide-ranging powers was that this model:

1. Would provide a combination of direct democracy and strong leadership.
2. Safeguard the new democracies against the woes of coalition politics.

Those advocating the creation of parliamentary system of government argued that:

1. Giving too much power in the hands of one politician, whether directly elected or not, would
   stifle the development of truly democratic systems of government.
2. There are tried and tested methods to limit potential instability arising from parliamentarist
   systems, such as constructive no-confidence votes, in which a government cannot be dis-
   missed unless parliament also agrees on the appointment of a new prime minister.

In the early years of the transition to democracy there was a strong academic and political debate on the suitability of institutional models for the new democracies of Central
and Eastern Europe, a debate on the relative merits of presidentialism versus parliamentarism (see above).[3] In the end, most Central and East European states have opted for
some form of a *semi-presidential system* (for an in-depth discussion, see Elgie 1999). Slovakia
joined the long list of states with semi-presidential systems with the direct election of
President Schuster in Spring 1999; it represented a compromise between the two extremes
outlined above. Interestingly, this form of government previously was quite rare in
European states, with Finland, France and Iceland the only examples until the transition
in Central and Eastern Europe.

Semi-presidential systems with strong presidential offices have been created, for
instance, in Russia and the Ukraine. The semi-presidential systems of Poland and Romania
have strong presidents in legal terms, but their real strength depends on the extent to
which they can count on a clear and supportive majority in parliament. Bulgaria and
Slovakia have created semi-presidential systems in which presidents have very limited
powers, even though at times presidents have played a crucial role in forging political stability.[4]

---

[2] Even more radical examples include the attempted coup in Russia, which also resulted from a
conflict between institutions.
[3] See for a summary of the debate: Verheijen (1995) chapter 1.
[4] Verheijen (1995).

> *The Role of Presidents in Stabilizing Political Systems*
> *President Zhelev in Bulgaria 1990-1996*
>
> The case of Bulgaria provides an interesting illustration of how a directly-elected president managed to play an important role in stabilizing a polarized political system in the early years of the transition to democracy. Zhelev used his limited powers, such as the ability to submit legislation to the constitutional court, in a way as to try to prevent a 'dictatorship of small majorities' (a term coined by the American political scientist Jon Elster). Zhelev did not make himself popular with any of the political forces in the country by playing this role, especially not with the Union of Democratic Forces, the party that had nominated him. However, by being a president above party politics he did play a crucial role in preventing an escalation of the political conflicts that marred the early years of the transition in Bulgaria (see also Verheijen 1995, chapter 5).

The experience of the states that have opted for semi-presidential systems has been one of gradually finding a balance of power between president, prime minister and parliament. This balance has generally been achieved, even if there have been in many states turbulent periods in political development and even lengthy political stalemates between president and legislature, in particular on the issue of the appointment of a prime minister. The cases of Russia, Poland and, in more recent times, Lithuania highlight such conflicts.

Fewer states in the region have opted for creating parliamentary constitutional systems, often including a weak presidential office, the incumbent of which is generally elected by the parliament, for instance, in Hungary and the Czech Republic. The latter systems give much more formal power to parliament, as the government depends fully on the confidence of the parliament, with the president having very limited influence over the appointment and dismissal of the government.

Pure presidential systems do not exist in any European state at the current time, even though the Russian system has de facto leaned towards this model.[5]

The institutional compromises which have led to the prevalence of semi-presidential systems of government in Central and Eastern Europe have not created the much feared instability associated by some with such systems. Regardless of the initial political turmoil surrounding the creation of semi-presidential systems in several states (see Elgie 1999), a balance of power between the main state institutions has gradually emerged, allowing for a stabilisation of the political system in the overwhelming majority of Central and East European states.

---

[5] Some states not discussed in this volume, but nevertheless often considered 'European', such as Azerbaijan and Georgia can be considered presidential in real terms, even if from a formal constitutional point of view they are not.

Central Government Reform—Continued Limited Achievements

In contrast to the development of the overall constitutional and institutional system, where important achievements have been made, the level of progress in the reform of public administration at the central government level remains incomplete. The following section will provide a comparative analysis of progress in several key areas, as well as an explanation why this particular area of reform has proven to be so problematic.

Key indicators of the limited progress in central government administrative reform include:

1. Academic publications on public administration in Central and Eastern Europe continue to focus on the need to address some of the classical issues in public administration.

   A comparison of academic work on central government reform written early on in the transformation process (for instance, Hesse 1993) with more recent publications[6] would lead one to conclude that little progress has been made in addressing the *key issues* in public administration development, such as *structuring politico-administrative relations, creating a system of employment conditions which allows the civil service to attract and retain highly qualified staff, defining a new accountability system and developing management and policy-making capacities.* A review of the last five issues of the proceedings of the Annual Conferences of the Network of Institutes and Schools of Public Administration in Central and Eastern Europe (NISPAcee) leads to a similar conclusion[7]

2. Negative assessments in European Commission Opinions and Progress Reports.

   A second indicator of the limited progress in administrative reform in Central and Eastern Europe are the Commission Opinions and Progress Reports.[8] The 1997 Commission Opinions highlighted serious deficiencies in the administrative systems of the candidate states (European Commission 1997 and Fournier 1998). Whereas the Opinions are moderately positive on the development of the overall institutional system, the central public administration is singled out as a weak link in this system. *What is reflected in the opinions are fragmented, politicised administrations, rife with allegations of corruption, underpaid staff and a resulting high degree of staff turnover. Policy-making capacities are evaluated as weak and the lack of personnel development strategies is frequently pointed out.*

   The 1998 and 1999 Commission Progress Reports again evaluated public administration capacities as weak in most of the candidate states, with progress in administrative capacity development assessed as mixed at best.

3. High disapproval ratings in public opinion polls.

   A further indication of the weak administrative capacities at central government level is the continuing high level of citizens' distrust in central administrations

---

[6] Verheijen and Coombes (1998); Hesse (1998); Verheijen (1999).

[7] The NISPAcee Annual Conference provides one of the main platforms for academic discussion on developments in public administration in Central and Eastern Europe (see http://www.nispa.sk for further reference). Jabes and Vintar (1996); Jabes (1997, 1998, 1999); and Jabes and Caddy (2000).

[8] http://www.europa.int/comm/enlargement/index.html.

Levels of Trust in Central Public Administration

A. *Confidence levels*

In a comparative study on Civil Service Systems in Central and Eastern Europe (Verheijen 1999), the general picture of levels of trust in public administration was dismal. In the nine states dealt with in the study, the number of citizens expressing trust in the public administration never exceeded 40%, with a low of 10% in Russia (based on material from Estonia, Latvia, Lithuania, Poland, Slovakia, Hungary, Bulgaria, Russia and Yugoslavia).

B. *Perception of behaviour: comparison with the previous regime*

A study by Miller, Grodelund and Koshechkina on corruption in Central and Eastern Europe includes the following discussion on relative appreciation of behaviour of officials:[9]

Two out of three citizens in the Czech Republic said most of their politicians now behaved worse than they did under communism, so did 82 percent in Slovakia and 87 percent in Ukraine, though much less in Bulgaria. People in Bulgaria and the Czech Republic were evenly divided on whether officials who deal with ordinary people and their problems now behaved better or worse than they did under communism; but 66 percent in Slovakia and 89 percent in Ukraine claimed such officials behaved worse.

---

4. The widely acknowledged link between inadequate administrative capacities and failure in economic reforms.

Finally, the low quality of administrations is considered an important explanatory factor for the economic downturns and crises that several Central and Eastern European states have experienced in recent years. In Bulgaria, failure and corruption in the administration were considered a major factor in the severe economic crisis of 1996-1997 (Dimitrova and Verheijen 1998). In the same period these conditions also held for Romania (International IDEA 1997). In the Czech Republic, the economic downturn of 1997-1998 gave rise to a debate on the need for administrative reform which had been a neglected issue until that time (see Vidlakova *in* Jabes 1999). In 1999 in Lithuania, serious criticism of the government planning capacity and budgetary patterns resulted in the creation of a 'Sunset Commission' which examined ways to downsize the administration and improve its effectiveness and efficiency.

The following comparative section on reform in three key areas—civil service reform, the development of training systems and structural reform—provides an illustration.

---

[9] Miller, Grodelund and Koshechkina (1999) *Are the People Victims or Accomplices? The Uses of Presents and Bribes to Public Officials,* Discussion Papers No. 6, Budapest: LGI. See also: http://www.osi.hu/lgi/publications/dp/index.html.

Civil service reform

Civil service reform has in most states been limited to the development and adoption of civil service legislation—considered the *main reform tool for addressing problems like politicisation, fragmentation and instability*. Regardless of the adoption of civil service laws in an increasing number of states in the region, the problems of instability and politicisation have not been resolved in most states, and in no case has the adoption of laws led to the development of a well-working system of long-term career development.

In Hungary, where a civil service law was adopted as early as 1992, the development of a well-balanced recruitment and promotion system has still not evolved. Furthermore, politicians have made extensive use of loopholes in the law, such as the fact that the civil service law does not make it mandatory to advertise vacancies. Hungary, however, at the same time constitutes the most positive example of administrative stabilisation. Staff turnover has been reduced significantly since the adoption of the civil service law. The question that remains, and on which there is an ongoing debate in Hungary, is how the impact of the civil service law can be taken beyond stabilisation.

In Poland, the incoming government in Autumn 1997 halted the implementation of the 1996 civil service law and adopted a new law in 1998. The incoming government was reluctant to work with civil servants in office and with management structures created and staffed by the previous government, thus the scuttling of the law. Under the previous communist regime, Poland was the only state in Central and Eastern Europe to have a civil service law; it continues to use the old 1982 law in conjuction with implemented elements of the new civil service law, which mostly apply to higher level civil servants.

Civil service laws were adopted in Estonia, Latvia and Lithuania within a relatively short time span. Even though in all three cases the laws were based on continental European tradition, the impact of civil service legislation has been very different from case to case. In Latvia and Lithuania, the adopted civil service laws were never fully implemented. In Latvia, the revision of the law is still not complete, while, in Lithuania, a new civil service law was adopted in 1999. In Estonia, the civil service law, adopted in 1995, entered into force in January 1996. Unlike in the other two Baltic States, the Estonian civil service law has been implemented. However, since the implementation of the civil service law was not enshrined in a clear public administration reform concept (the development of which was completed only in 1998), the overall impact of the law has remained limited.

In Bulgaria, a new civil service law was adopted in August 1999 and its implementation has just started. The Romanian government adopted new civil service regulations by decree in late 1999.

In three of the EU candidate states, Slovenia, the Czech Republic and Slovakia, civil service laws are still pending. In these three states there has been neither the political will nor the political consensus necessary to pass a civil service law.

In conclusion, from the perspective of adopting relevant legislation, the positive picture is really a false impression. *Civil service laws seldom have had the impact they were expected to have: to be a catalyst for the stabilisation, de-politicisation and professionalisation of the central administration.* They have in many cases been reconsidered even before the implementation process was completed or have not been fully implemented at all.

Reform of administrative structures:
An underestimated element of administrative development?

The redesign of administrative structures is a core element of administrative reform. Even if a professional civil service is constituted, this will have a limited impact as long as they are not embedded in well-designed administrative structures. Well-designed administrative structures should be based on: *(1) functioning horizontal and vertical co-ordination systems, (2) a clear definition of responsibility and accountability and (3) provide civil servants with the necessary freedom of action.*

The development of new administrative structures has legal as well as cultural aspects. The redefinition of the role and position of ministries, their subordinated organisations and the core executive unit[10] in the administration is a crucial aspect of the administrative development process. This element is of particular importance in Central and East European states, since the core executive units of the administration used to 'shadow' line ministries under the previous regime and played a dominant role in the process of policy co-ordination. Policy processes were therefore 'top heavy', based on co-ordination at the top. Core executive units also tended to manage large numbers of subordinated institutions. Accountability lines were directed towards the leading political party.

The reform of policy-making and implementation structures and systems could have been expected to be one of the most difficult elements of the administrative development process in Central and Eastern Europe. Nevertheless, little or no attention was given to this element of reform until recently. Policy-making and implementation processes still show many features of the previous systems, as discussed above. Even in new states, such as the Baltic States, the division of labour between ministries and the core executive unit in the policy process still shows some of the features of the former system. The SIGMA Centre of Government Profiles[11] provide a clear illustration of this point.

Main Issues Hindering the Developments of Effective Policy-making Processes

1. Lack of delegation in the administration;
2. Lack of 'filtering mechanisms' in the policy process, needed to separate routine issues from the core political issues for debate at government level;
3. Lack of strategic planning capacities in the centre of government offices.

In some states attempts have been made to redefine the role of the different components of the central administration in the policy process. Poland has carried out a substantial reform of the administration of the Council of Ministers, with the objective to create a small core Prime Minister's Office, among others, by 'pushing down' co-ordination tasks into the administration. In Hungary, attempts have also been made previously to

---

[10] For instance, chancelleries, prime ministers' offices, cabinet offices or councils of ministers.

[11] http://www.oecd.org/puma/sigmaweb/acts/cogprofiles/

'slim down' the Prime Minister's Office, though the current government has again expanded the number of substantive shadow units in the office (Meyer-Sahling 2000).

A thorough and sustained reform effort will be required for policy-making systems to
start working more effectively, in particular a comprehensive redefinition of the role of the
different units in the administration and the relations between these units. This is an issue
that has not featured on the administrative development agenda until quite recently.

During the last few years initiatives have been taken in several states to adopt laws to
regulate the role and function of the different institutions in the administration and to
rationalise the way in which the administration works. In Bulgaria, the Law on Public
Administration was adopted in 1998, which defines the type of institutions that can exist
in the state administration, how these relate to one another and what the role and function of different types of institutions can be. Other states have also taken initiatives of this
kind in recent years, such as Latvia, Lithuania and the Republic of Macedonia. The adoption of such laws is a tentative step in the direction of a rationalisation of the policy process
in these states; however, one should pose the question to what extent these laws can and
will be enforced. In the drafting process there has been a great resistance among line ministries to what is considered to be the limitation of their ministerial autonomy. It therefore remains to be seen to what extent such laws are enforceable.

The development of a new administrative culture will be even more difficult to achieve.
Under the previous regimes the operation of administrative systems was based on secre-
cy and suspicion, both in relations with citizens and in relations between the different
elements of the administration. Adopting laws cannot change these types of attitudes. The
potential to bring about change in the administrative culture depends heavily on the willingness of politicians to allow and stimulate co-operation between civil servants working
at different administrative units and to encourage officials to adopt a client-friendly
approach towards citizens. So far there is little evidence of a decentralisation of responsibility inside the administration or of co-ordination being 'pushed down' to lower levels
in the administration. Even if formally more co-ordination structures are set up at the
lower levels of the administration, this has often not led to real changes in policy-making
practises.[12] The development of a different administrative culture depends on the adoption of enabling legislation and procedural rules in the administration and on a clarification of accountability relations.

In view of the discussion above on civil service legislation, it seems doubtful that much
progress can be made on this second core element of administrative development. The
definition of the framework structure of the central administration should have been an
issue at the start of the administrative development process, not at the end. Obviously it
takes time to bring about changes in administrative culture, but it seems that lack of trust
between politicians and civil servants remains a feature of many Central and East European
administrations. The development of a new legislative framework for the administration
and the development of a less centralised administrative culture are therefore elements in

---

[12] As an example, reviews of European Integration policy co-ordination systems in three Central
and East European states, carried out by SIGMA, confirmed that there is still a high degree of
reluctance among politicians to 'decentralise' policy co-ordination.

the administrative development process in Central and Eastern Europe on which most of the work remains to be done.

Training: the problems in developing new training systems

Training can play an important role in the development of new administrative systems. Whereas civil service legislation can set the framework for the development of a stable and professional civil service, training can be used as an instrument to fill in the substance of the framework. Training can also make a contribution to the development of a coherent administration. Joint pre- or post-entry training of new recruits can help in creating a sense of community among new civil servants. This sense of community could play a role in reducing the still universally high degree of fragmentation in Central and East European administrations. Joint training of top level officials can have a similar effect.

In order for training to have a positive impact on the way administrations work, training efforts should be underpinned by a well-defined human resource policy and training strategy. Furthermore, pre- or post-entry training for new recruits should be carried out in parallel to in-service training to bring about changes in attitudes and work practises among existing staff. In Central and East European administrations the method of training high quality young graduates and inserting them into the administrations as 'change managers' was unlikely to work on its own, in view of the very fundamental changes to be introduced in work practises, in attitudes and in relations with citizens and politicians.

Training—if implemented in the right way, combining a sustained effort at in-service training with the development of high-quality initial training programmes for new recruits—could have had a significant impact on Central and East European administrations. Instead, the lack of developed human resource development policies, in tandem with a lack of progress in creating suitable new training structures in Central and Eastern Europe, can be considered key elements of the failure to develop new administrations.

The Fate of Training Institutions in Central and Eastern Europe

In the early years of the transition, there were numerous attempts to develop new government *initial training institutions* in a number of Central and East European states. The National School of Public Administration in Poland provides the most interesting example of this 'first generation' of initiatives. The Polish school was created as an integrated element of the administration, based on the French model of the *École National d'Administration*/National School of Administration (ENA) . The concept of the Polish school was based on the assumption that by inserting highly qualified graduates in top positions in the administration, it would be possible to create a 'multiplier effect' and bring about rapid change. This high level training of young promising staff would have to be accompanied by in-service training for those already in the administration to achieve the desired effect. However, the parallel in-service training system was never made fully operational, which limited the impact of the institution. However, unlike other similar institutions created in the early 1990s, the Polish school is still working; its graduates are still guaranteed a position in the administration and have the obligation to work for the administration for a defined number of years.

Two other training schools created in the early 1990s—the Slovak School of Public Administration at Academia Istropolitana and the Romanian National School of Public Administration—were either closed down (Slovakia) or progressively marginalised for political reasons (Romania).

The experience in developing government-run or -funded *in-service training institutions* has been slightly more positive. The Latvian School of Public Administration was given a central role in the training of civil service candidates. However, when the implementation of the civil service law was halted by the government in 1997, the role of training in the civil service development process was reduced significantly. In some other states in-service training institutions have also been established. In Slovenia, Estonia and Lithuania, government and semi-government in-service training institutions are among the most important providers of in-service training. In other states the creation of such institutions is planned. The problem with these training institutions is that very often they are little more than managers of training programmes and do not actually have a core body of permanent trainers in the staff, which in practise has often made them overly reliant on training supplied by foreign institutions.

The problem of using training as a reform tool has two aspects in the Central and East European context.

First, governments have generally been reluctant to use training as an element of reform programmes. The emphasis has generally been put on the adoption of legislation rather than on the application of more complex reform tools like training. As a result of this most governments have no training policy or programme. The general scepticism among politicians about the usefulness of training as a reform has thus become a self-fulfilling prophecy.

Second, training capacities in Central and East European states are generally not well developed. A lot of training is 'imported'. 'Imported' training might have been useful in the early stages of the reform process, as an information and awareness raising tool, but is now of much less value, unless it is tailor-made and aimed at the transfer of specific, job-related skills. The training capacities of national institutions are still too limited and for budgetary reasons most governments have not been willing to invest in their development. Thus there is a stalemate situation, which makes it difficult to use training as a reform tool at the current time. Only sustained support of the development of local capacities might provide a solution to this problem.

Explaining Problems in Administrative Development

The following section addresses five important factors explaining the limited progess of administrative development in Central and Eastern Europe. They are: the legacy of history, economic pressures, political polarisation, the lack of a balanced 'package' of reform instruments and the changing and often contradictory signals of external organisations.

The legacy of history

The legacy of history remains one of the most important potential explanations for the problems in administrative development in Central and Eastern Europe. Whereas before WW II the development of administrative systems in Central and Eastern Europe was more or less in line with continental European tradition.[13] The divergence which have occurred between the adminstrative systems of the Soviet block and the West of Europe in the period 1945-1990, explains much of the difficulties of the process of adminstrative reform in Central and Eastern Europe. From the perspective of Western bureacracies, there are three major factors which make the two systems differ significantly. These are: full politicisation, the abolition of the distinction between civil servants and other workers in terms of labour relations and fragmentation brought about by communism.

Under the former communist system public administration tasks were more or less divided between the Party and the state administration. The state administration only fulfilled a part of the traditional functions of the public administration. The previous regimes in Central and Eastern Europe created an administrative apparatus which worked according to the principle of subordination of the administration to political power and priorities. A parallel Party bureaucracy was created, consisting of Party members, which developed policies, gave orders and controlled the state bureaucracy at each hierarchical level. The part of the systems which was considered most similar to a traditional state administration was in reality a subordinated mechanical organisation. The state administration carried out its tasks without giving professional input or feedback to the policies developed by the party bureaucracy. Giving feedback or professional inputs was punished rather than rewarded. The administrative side of the political administrative process was fully politicised, creating a so-called 'Politbürokratie' (Josza 1988 and 1989). Politicisation of the public administration was common practise under the previous regime and supported by ideological considerations.

The public administration was an *important instrument of suppression* for the state in the politico-administrative systems of Central and East European countries before 1989. Therefore there was a need to rapidly depoliticise the administration after the change of regime. However, the impact of forty years of institutionalised and ideologically supported politicisation of the general perception of public administration has made the depoliticisation of the administration a difficult issue.

The system of employment conditions in place under the previous regime made it easier for politicians to continue the tradition of politicisation. Where specific legislation governing the employment conditions had been in place before the establishment of the communist regimes, this legislation was abolished; under communism employment conditions were regulated under the Labour Code. The idea of a civil service, distinct from other sectors of the economy in function, tasks and position, vanished with the 'privatisation' of the administration.

The third part of this legacy is the fragmentation of the administration. Public administration previously consisted of ministries subordinated to the government. The central office of government, the Council of Ministers, was often substantially larger than cabinet

---

[13] With the obvious exception of the USSR.

offices or departments of general affairs in Western Europe. Constitutionally, the Council of Ministers was controlled by the parliament.[14] In reality, however, it was politically subordinated to the Central Committee of the Communist Party, while the top layers of the administrative structure were controlled by the Party bureaucracy. This rather straightforward governmental system often complicated the creation of a State Council. The State Council was a kind of collective head of state to which the parliament delegated certain powers (often foreign and defence policy). The relation between State Council and Council of Ministers was often not defined clearly.[15] Initially the State Councils lacked the administrative apparatus needed to prepare and implement decisions in an efficient way. The State Councils developed their own bureaucracy soon after they had been created. *Four different types* of bureaucracies co-existed in Central and Eastern Europe before 1989, all highly politicised and in competition with one another: Communist Party Bureaucracy, Council of Ministers administration, State Council administration and the ministries. Public administrations were characterised by an iota of co-operation and co-ordination.

In conclusion, the previous regimes left a cursed legacy in terms of public administration. The previously existing civil service tradition was supplanted by the direct subordination of officials to political parties in a system characterised by horizontal and vertical institutional fragmentation.

Economic pressures: working against administrative development

Economic pressure could have been a potential catalyst for the initiation of administrative reform processes. *Efficient and effective administrations are needed to attract foreign investment, to ensure state income from taxation and to perform a number of other tasks crucial to the often still-fragile economic recovery process.* The weakness of administrations has been considered an important factor in the economic crises, which have plagued several Central and East European states in recent years. Therefore there appear to be several strong economic arguments for the prioritisation of administrative development. However, even though economic conditions, at first glance, constitute a potential incentive to politicians to move administrative development forward, the specific nature of the administrative problems in Central and Eastern Europe has so far created the reverse effect.

The nature of administrative 'reform' in Central and Eastern Europe is often misunderstood. The use of the word 'reform' in itself would mean that the objective of the process would be to change an existing administration. However, Central and East European states did not have a 'public administration' as it is generally understood in 'Western Europe'. This has important implications for the nature of the processes under way in Central and Eastern Europe—processes of developing new administrative systems, not of reforming established systems.

It is important to note that building a professional, stable and impartial administration is costly and requires a considerable investment, even if one opts for the creation of

---

[14] See the analysis of the institutional systems of Central and Eastern European countries under the Communist regimes in F.J.M. Feldbrugge (ed.) (1987) *The Distinctiveness of Soviet Law*, Dordrecht: Martinus Nijhoff Publishers, pp. 5-33.

[15] *Ibid.*

a 'career' civil service with a limited scope.[16] The cost of recruitment, training and the employment conditions associated with a career civil service are considerable, both in the immediate term and for the future.[17] The notion of administrative reform as used in Western Europe and other OECD states—the main objective of which is usually saving money—therefore does not apply to Central and East European states. The economic conditions in these states make the implementation of reform strategies more difficult.

Political polarisation and a lack of continuity

Central and East European voters have virtually thrown out the government in office on every occasion.. This affects administrative development policies in particular, since these are not 'vote-winning policies'. Governments mainly concerned with framing popular policies to keep the allegiance of a volatile electorate are unlikely to 'invest' in administrative capacity development, which is generally an issue that does not 'speak' to the voters.

As an aggravating factor, political party systems remain highly polarised, which further reduces the potential for continuity in policies. Interestingly, this appears to affect economic policies, where there is a certain degree of continuity even when governments change, much less than administrative development. However, the reversal of administrative development measures, strategies and even laws remains common practise throughout the region, including in states which were considered to have overcome the high level of adversity deemed characteristic for states in transition or in the early stages of consolidation. The absence of long-term policies to stimulate administrative development therefore does not need to come as a surprise.

The 'legal bias'

Politicians in Central and Eastern European states often appear to have mistaken the term 'Rule of Law' as 'Rule by Law', especially where public administration development is concerned. The adoption of laws has so far been the main and sometimes the only administrative development tool. Where administrative development strategies have been adopted, they are often little more than a framework for a package of laws. The problems with this type of approach to administrative development is that the value of law as a reform instrument depends heavily on the quality of their implementation and that laws do not change mentalities. These implementation problems have certainly reduced the value of law as a reform instrument.

The overreliance on laws as reform instruments would not come as a surprise to those who have studied the Central and East European administrative tradition. Most states in the region have a strong legalistic tradition stemming from the pre-World War II period, based either on the German, Austrian or, to a lesser degree, on the French model. The approach of the previous regime (creating legitimacy through law) has strengthened, rather

---

[16] Under consideration, for instance, in Latvia, where the number 'civil service' posts is unlikely to be higher than 200.

[17] Considering, for instance, the cost of pensions.

than weakened the legalistic bias. The EU, which also focuses very much on legal requirements for membership, has, perhaps involuntarily, strengthened this bias towards using
legal instruments in administrative development. It is important that advisers to Central
and Eastern European governments put more emphasis on the development of a multi-
instrument approach to administrative development, stressing the importance of law as
one but not the only reform instrument. The formation of multi-disciplinary reform teams
would be an important step in this direction.[18] The expert team which carried out the
review of the Slovak state administration, is one rare example of such a multi-disciplinary
team, including economists, lawyers as well as public administration specialists. The recommendations of the expert team, which were endorsed by the government in August
2000, have created the basis for a comprehensive reform of the structure and management of the state administration.

Contradictory signals from international actors

At first glance, external pressure to carry out administrative reform seems to be considerable. The EU is the main organisation to have important political leverage in the region.
EU membership conditions include the creation of stable, professional and accountable
administrations,[19] which should provide incentives to Central and Eastern European governments. However, the EU has been far from consistent in the signals it has sent to the
candidate states. The re-orientation of PHARE assistance towards the development of sectoral administrative capacities—through twinning arrangements between candidate states
and member states—could be interpreted by governments of the candidate states as an
indication that general administrative capacities are of less importance than the creation
of technical capacities to implement and enforce the *acquis communautaire*. The
Commission recognises the potential dangers inherent in this approach and has continued to put pressure on candidate states to create a stable and professional civil service.
However, if some financial support for general administrative development is not continued, there is a strong likelihood that the concerns about the development of sectoral
capacities will move the development of a professional and coherent administration further down the political agenda.

Other institutions, in particular the World Bank and the International Monetary Fund
(IMF), have also increasingly put pressure on Central and Eastern European governments
to give more priority to administrative development. The interest of the World Bank, and
to a lesser degree the IMF, in promoting public administration development is still quite
recent and it is too early to predict to what degree these institutions will be able to have a
significant impact in this area. However, the work of the World Bank has generally focused
on improving management in public administration, rationalising central government structures[20] and the development of fair and sustainable reward systems in the region. These are

---

[18] I owe this point to Michal Ben-Gera, Formerly Head of Policy-Making, Co-ordination and
Regulation at SIGMA.
[19] As defined in the so-called SIGMA baseline criteria (SIGMA, 1999).
[20] In particular in Latvia.

some of the core issues identified earlier on as crucial to the success of public administration development. In this respect the work of the World Bank has the potential to become a catalyst for administrative development in years to come.

Viable Alternatives?

The complex reasons why administrative reform has failed to produce good results are difficult to address. It is clear that politicians need to be convinced, one could even say 'converted', to the idea of a professional administration. This remains one of the keys to a process of successful development of professional and impartial central administrations. However, even if one could address the issue for the politicians currently in government and parliament by means of training and information provision, the considerable turnover among parliamentarians would still make it difficult to find a long-term solution to this problem. Building a 'political culture' which accepts the idea of an impartial public administration has taken decades in most European states. Re-introducing the concept to societies which have had impartial administrations in the past (at least to some degree) might take less time, but still more than ten years. This problem is aggravated by the fact that there are few indications of a possible decrease in political polarisation.[21]

Alternative Approaches to Central Government Reform

Three possible methods can be proposed to improve levels of achievement in public administration, taking into account the complexities of the Central and East European situation:
1. Investing in the development of a political culture that accepts the idea of an impartial and professional public administration by convincing politicians and mobilising public opinion.
2. Using a different approach to reform, applying multiple reform instruments rather than focusing almost solely on legislative reform.
3. Using the potential leverage of the academic community.

A change in reform instruments, a second measure to be considered, might be easier to bring about, at least at first glance. However, for a variety of reasons it is unlikely that there will be a considerable change in the use of reform instruments. First, the European Union (EU) membership requirements, which potentially have a high degree of influence at least in the candidate states, have focused primarily on the adoption of laws and regulations. Second, whereas the adoption of laws is relatively 'cheap', the investment required to develop sustainable training capacities would be considerable. This also explains, in part, why the adoption of laws, as such, has not led to significant changes: implementing laws does require budgetary means, which very often are not made available.

---

[21] The attempts of incoming governments in Bulgaria (admittedly a special case), Poland and Hungary in 1997 and 1998 to 'convert' administrations by means of dismissals, using loopholes in laws, etc., shows the still deeply-seated sense of suspicion among political forces.

Whereas there might be viable alternatives in terms of strategy and the use of reform instruments, a combination of reluctant politicians, political polarisation and the 'confirmation' of the current approach by potentially influential external actors like the EU, make it very difficult to bring about a real change in approach. The academic community, another potential 'change agent' with 'privileged access' to politicians is still often dominated by lawyers, which currently limits the potential role of the academic community in this respect. Unless one of the above potential sources of influence could and would bring about a change in approach, it may take a generation before professional and impartial administrations will be in place in Central and East European states.

Local government: a successful start

Public administration reform at the central government level emerges as a problematic, complex and contentious issue. But analyses of local government reform yield a rather different and more mixed result. Whereas there are many issues that remain to be addressed, at the same time significant progress has been made, especially when considering the *legacy of dual subordination and democratic centralism* that characterised the previous communist system of local governance.

The creation of local self-governing authorities, often with rather broad competencies, has been completed in virtually all Central and East European states at least on one level of government (see Bennet 1994, Coulson 1995, Verheijen and Coombes 1998). Even though these authorities have encountered serious difficulties, due to problems of size[22] and budget, they remain popular with citizens (see Baka on Hungary and Bercik and Kuklis on Slovakia in Verheijen and Coombes 1998). Popular affinity with the newly created democratic structures at the grass-roots level has stifled moves towards a recentralisation of self-government, at least in Hungary and Slovakia.

The above development is highly important for the creation of sustainable democratic systems of governance. The development of participatory approaches to local governance is extremely important in this region in particular. The previous regime discouraged and even penalised public participation in policy-making. The development of a culture of local governance that stimulates and facilitates participation could play an important role in reversing the trend of alienation and disaffection. The development of inclusive systems of local governance is an important first step towards building participatory systems of government overall. Obviously, this first step is easiest to make at the local level, where a number of instruments can be applied to promote broad participation such as:

· local elections,
· local referenda,

---

[22] The creation of local self-governing authorities was in most Central and East European states guided by the principle that each community should have the right to create its own self-governing authority, which has led to the establishment of large numbers of very small authorities in many states (e.g. Hungary, Czech Republic and Slovakia). The lack of a second level of self-government which could co-ordinate the first level has created serious problems.

· public hearings,
· citizens' initiatives, such as petitions.

Laws on local elections can be designed in such a way to make it easy for citizens to vote as well as to stand for elections, for instance, by requiring only small numbers of nominations for the registration of candidates. In Poland, only 20 signatures are required in smaller municipalities. Provisions on local referenda can facilitate citizens' initiatives by allowing for groups of voters to initiate referenda as well as by making results binding for the local council. In Hungary, a variety of systems are in place in municipalities that allow groups of voters to initiate referenda, requiring 10 per cent of eligible voters' signatures in some cases, up to 25 per cent in others. The right of citizens to call public meetings, participate in public hearings and submit petitions to local politicians are further instruments that can be applied much more easily at local government level than at central government level. Provisions to facilitate participation have been included in various ways in the legal frameworks that regulate local government. Local government laws in most states, including Hungary, Slovakia and the Czech Republic, include provisions on local referenda. The overall level of popularity of local governments, which is higher than that of central governments in virtually all states, indicates that local government indeed has the potential to help building the foundations for the further development of pluralist democracies in Central and Eastern Europe.

In *terms of democracy*, this element of public administration reform has been a success, at least in a majority of the Central and East European states.

In *terms of effectiveness and efficiency*, further measures need to be taken to ensure effective service delivery to citizens, for example, through co-ordination and co-operation in delivery between small self-governing authorities. In terms of sustainability, local self-governing authorities need to be put on a sounder financial basis. However, in general, local government reform in Central and Eastern Europe has so far delivered good results. Democratic self-governing structures at the grass-roots level have been set up and a basis for the further development of a sustainable system of local self-government has been established.

The following is a comparative discussion of some key elements of local government reform and an illustration of how these are being addressed in Bulgaria, Hungary and Slovakia, drawn from research work carried out between 1995-1998.

Reform of Local-Central Government: Some Key Issues

1. The definition of the ideal size of basic units of self-government.
2. Division of labour between central government and self-governments.
3. The separation of county/municipal property from state property.
4. Local government finances: How to strike a balance between financial independence and control of public deficits.
5. Definition of the relations between local state government and local self-government.
6. Finding a new equilibrium in relations between central government and local self-government

Source: based on Verheijen and Coombes (1998) chapter 10.

Definition of the size of basic self-government units

Decisions on the size of basic self-government units generally are *a trade-off between effi-ciency and democracy*. Giving self-government status to each identifiable settlement is obvi-ously the most democratic form of self-government, but this can create substantial prob-lems of *sustainability and quality of service delivery*, unless a higher tier unit of self-government is created to which some functions can be transferred. In Hungary and Slovakia, the prin-ciple of self-government was applied in a way that granted the right of self-government to even the smallest settlements. A large number of self-governments were thus created, some with numbers of inhabitants lower than 500. In Hungary, a higher tier of local self-gov-ernment was created to fulfil some of the functions small local self-government units were unlikely to be able to cope with. In both countries the smallest self-government units are experiencing considerable problems. They lack the financial means to provide adequate services and have as a consequence become financially dependent on central government. In addition, it is more difficult for such units to attract qualified staff. Furthermore the duplication of administrations makes the system expensive to run. However, at the same time, there is widespread popular support for the small municipalities, which makes it dif-ficult for central governments to abolish the local government system.

In Bulgaria, the principle of *sustainability* was given preference over giving rights of self-government to each unit; the territory of self-governing units was determined in a way as to ensure that the smallest basic self-government units would still have at least 5,000 inhabitants. However, smaller settlements inside municipalities were given repre-sentation in the form of *executive mayors*, who manage lower tier administrative units. In this way a solution was found for the problems of sparsely populated municipalities dot-ted throughout mountain areas. However, the system of executive mayors has generally not worked well. This has given the population of more remote settlements the feeling of being too far removed from local decision-making, a situation that does not help local self-governments in their attempts to increase their level of legitimacy.

Possible alternatives, such as using *single or multi-purpose joint councils* to deliver cer-tain types of public services, as is practised in France and Italy, have so far not been used extensively in the region.

The above cases show the difficulties involved in deciding on the size of the basic self-governing units, which constitutes a difficult trade-off between democracy and efficien-cy. It is therefore likely that it will take more time before a more permanent self-govern-ment system will emerge in most Central and East European states.

Functions, finances and property

The unambiguous definition of functions, financial means and self-government proper-ty is a basic condition to be fulfilled to allow self-governments to function independent-ly. This issue has been resolved to a varying degree in the three cases discussed here.

In Hungary, a clear separation of municipal and state property was carried out early on in the reform process. The tasks of municipalities and counties are considered finalised. Financial independence of local self-governments is guaranteed in principle, though local governments depend to a large degree on fluctuating levels of central government funding.[23] However, this is counterbalanced by *their practically unlimited right to take out loans*, even from foreign banks, which provides them with an important bargaining tool with a central government bent on reducing the public deficit in the context of EU accession.[24] Furthermore the predominant proportion of central government transfers are not earmarked, which further increases the freedom of local self-governments to determine their own expenditures.

In Bulgaria, local government tasks are also clearly defined. The system of financial relations between local and central government has also been defined quite clearly, even though the system as it works is rather disadvantageous for local self-governments. Bulgarian local governments do not have similar revenue raising and borrowing rights like their Hungarian counterparts, but, like in Hungary, the main portion of *central government transfers are not earmarked* (even though more or less binding 'directions' are sometimes issued), which gives local self-governments some degree of freedom in expenditure management. The provisions of the law providing the basis for separating state and municipal property in Bulgaria were implemented only in the last few years. For a long time local self-governing authorities were thus deprived of important potential income and had no incentive to try to use property on their territory in the most profitable way.

In Slovakia, the discussion on the division of tasks between the state and local self-government has not yet reached its conclusion. A number of 'expensive' policy areas, such as health and education, were transferred from local government to state control in 1990. The central government intends to transfer many of these competencies to local government control over the next years. However, the previous experience of other institutions, such as health insurance companies, which received inadequate compensation for functions they had taken over from the state in the mid-1990s, have made local governments reluctant to accept any transfer of functions—unless a transparent financing system will be created. The definition of municipal property was finalised early on in the reform process.

Relations between local state administration and local self-government

The relationships between local self-government and local state government in Bulgaria, Hungary and Slovakia are characterised by a high degree of separation. They therefore more closely resemble the *dual system* of local-central government relations that exists in the United Kingdom and in Ireland, rather than *the fused system* in place in most continental European states. In fused systems, central government appointees work together with elected representatives in managing self-governing structures, whereas dual systems rely on regulations and instructions as the main instrument for steering policy delivery by local authorities. The rather strict separation between local state government and local self-government in the former cases can be explained as a reaction to the high level of integration under the previous regime. Similarly, the preference for small basic units of self-government can be explained as a reaction to the high level of centralisation.

---

[23] The proportion of transferred income tax has varied between 100% in the first year after the adoption and 5% at the current time.

[24] The risk involved with municipalities taking out loans has been limited by the provisions of the law on municipal bankruptcy.

Figure 1. Middle-Level Local Government Tiers in Central European Countries 1999		
Countries with Dominantly Governing Mid-level Tiers	Direction of Change	Countries with Dominantly Self-Administrative Mid-level Tiers
Latvia	(→)?	
		Lithuania
		Estonia
Poland ← (1 Jan 1999)		
	←	Czech Republic
	(←)?	Slovakia
Hungary		
	←	Slovenia

Source: Tamás M. Horváth (ed.) (2000) *Decentralisation: Experiments and Reforms,* LGI: Budapest, p. 49

It is still difficult to predict how the relationship between local state government and local self-government will evolve. The two main elements of the relationship that need clarification are the nature of the supervisory role of local state government and the form that methodological assistance from local state government to local self-government will take.

In relation to *the supervisory role*, institutions of local state government should, in theory, only have the right to contest the legality of local self-government decisions in the courts, except when local self-governments are performing certain functions on behalf of the central government. Due to the existence of a rather extensive system of local state government in Bulgaria, Hungary and Slovakia, the number of tasks self-governments actually perform on behalf of the central government is rather limited, so direct supervision should appear rather rarely. In reality, however, local authorities often appear to be under significant informal pressure from local state government authorities,[25] which indicates that there is a difference between the relations as regulated by law and the real character of the relations between local state government and local self-government. Such informal pressures can significantly limit the real independence of local self-government.

The second aspect of the relationship between local state-government and local self-government that needs further clarification is the provision of *'methodological assistance'* by local state government institutions. This methodological assistance usually consists of advice on the organisation and management of local self-governments. In the early stages of the development of self-governments, small self-government units, in particular, do need assistance from local state government officials. However, some ten years after the start of the development of local self-government institutions in Bulgaria, Hungary and Slovakia, there is now a less apparent need for methodological assistance. There is a risk that local state government institutions will use their right to provide methodological assistance to extend their influence over the management of self-government institutions. It may, therefore, be

---

[25] Research in other CEE states indicates a similar pattern.

worth considering whether the provision of methodological assistance should remain an explicit part of the tasks of local state government institutions.

Finding a new equilibrium between central government and local self-government

The position of self-governments vis à vis central government in the three Central and East European countries discussed here varies significantly. Two main factors can be singled out which largely determine whether self-governments are able to act independently and stand up to central governments in defence of their interests. The first factor is the extent to which self-governments really use the powers which legislation assigns to them. The second factor is the extent to which local self-governments are able to develop a coherent interest group structure to counterbalance the power of central governments.

The results of the research work referred to above show that there is a marked difference between Bulgaria, Hungary and Slovakia as regards the attitude of local self-government towards central government. Whereas in Bulgaria local government officials still suffer from a mentality of subordination, self-governments in Hungary, and to a lesser extent in Slovakia, show a high level of self-confidence. As a result Bulgarian local governments have not managed to make the best use of their relatively extensive competencies. Local governments take few initiatives and often look for approval by central government bodies before doing so. As a result, local self-governments have failed to gain high levels of legitimacy with local citizens. Local governments in Hungary and Slovakia have managed to gain much more support from local residents. The reluctance of central government in Hungary to reduce some of the extensive powers of local government and the lack of a decision on amalgamation of local self-government units in Slovakia can, in part, be explained by the fear of an electoral backlash.

The development of a *coherent interest group structure* can help local self-governments to improve their position vis à vis central governments. Notably, among the three states discussed here, the only country in which local self-governments managed to develop a common interest group is Slovakia.[26] In Hungary and Bulgaria, local government interest groups are divided along political lines, leaving local governments open to 'divide and rule' tactics from above. The Slovak local government association ZMOS has cross-party membership and therefore is able to put pressure on the central government to take local government interests into consideration as it makes relevant policy decisions. Even though ZMOS still finds it difficult to influence central government policy, it still has much better chance of helping local government reach its objectives than the divided interest groups in Hungary and Bulgaria.

A preliminary balance

Progress in the development of local self-government and the redefinition of relations between central and local government in the early stages of the transition to democracy was impres-

---

[26] ALAL in Lithuania is a further example of a unified and rather influential local government association.

sive, particularly when compared with progress in central government reform. However, the results of field research carried out in Bulgaria, Hungary and Slovakia indicate much work remains to be done in this area, as in many other states in the region. By the year 2000, Hungary was the only country among these three, and generally one of the few states in the region, to have fully established a system of both local self-government and local state government, closely modelled on the German system. A more permanent system of relations between state and self-governments remains to be put in place in the near future in all three countries. Progress in the still less politically controversial area of local government reform therefore remains considerably more impressive than in the area of central government reform. Political polarisation also seems to play a much less significant role.

Conclusion

A comparative review of institutional reform in Central and Eastern Europe reveals a highly contrasting picture of achievements and failures. While the basic institutional framework for policy-making has been created in virtually all states, with few well-known exceptions, progress in public administration reform at central government level remains unsatisfactory. At the same time, the roots for any democratic system of governance— local self-governing institutions—have been created in most states of the region, providing a good foundation for further development.

The reasons for the uneven development of governance structures in the region are complex. Though the creation of core governance institutions and an agreement on accepted basic 'rules of the game' in the form of constitutions or constitutional laws is a condition *sine-qua-non* for states to function at all, the impact of deficient systems of public administration is felt only after a longer period of time. Only in recent years has the link between weak systems of public administration and weak economic performance has become an issue of concern to policy-makers, spurred by the growing importance of administrative capacity requirements as a condition for EU membership. A complex set of factors—the legacy of the previous regime, weak design of the reform process, political polarisation, factors, as well as a lack of consistent external pressure—explains the disappointing results in public administration development. There are no easy remedies for this problem, making it likely that in many Central and East European states policy-making and, in particular, policy implementation will remain serious bottlenecks in the operation of the institutional system.

The prevailing picture of the development of new administrative structures, especially the creation of local self-governing institutions, is more positive. Even if the process of developing new administrative structures cannot be considered finalised in virtually any of the states of the region, the problems to be addressed seem more easily resolvable. A discussion of three representative case studies has highlighted some five to six key areas where work remains to be done to complete the development of local government systems, and in particular local-central government relations. In general, the development of structures for grass-root's democracy appears to be much more advanced than the creation of modern central administrations. This reflects the clear wish to break with the past system early on in the transition process, the less politicised nature of local government reform, and, perhaps most importantly, a much higher degree of citizens' interest.

More than ten years after the start of the post-communist transition, the process of institutional transformation in Central and Eastern Europe is by no means complete, even though significant progress has been made on the creation of core political institutions and, to a lesser degree, on local government reform. For a diverse set of reasons, the development of new systems of public administration at the central government level has proven to be the most complex element of the reform of governance systems. This imbalance in the institutional reform process in Central and Eastern Europe must be addressed, so that systems of governance in the region can help foster rather than hinder economic development, social progress and EU integration.

Further Reading

Coulson, A. (1995) *Local Government in Eastern Europe*, Cheltenham: Edward Elgar Publishers.

Hesse, J. J. (1993) 'From Transformation to Modernization: Administrative Change in Central and Eastern Europe', *Public Administration*, Vol. 71, No. 1/2.

Hesse, J .J. (1998) 'Rebuilding the State, Administrative Reform in Central and Eastern Europe', in: *Preparing Public Administrations for the European Administrative Space.* Paris: OECD, SIGMA Papers, No. 23.

Packer, John (2000) 'The Origin and Nature of the Lund Recommendations on the Effective Participation of National Minorities in Public Life', *Helsinki Monitor*, Vol. 11, No. 4, pp. 29-61.

Verheijen, T. and D. Coombes (1998) *Innovations in Public Management, Experiences from East and West Europe*, Aldershot: Edward Elgar Publishers.

Verheijen, T. (1999) *Civil Service Systems in Central and Eastern Europe*, Aldershot: Edward Elgar Publishers.

AN UNFINISHED STORY OF MINORITY RIGHTS

Patrick Thornberry

Contents

An Unfinished Story of Minority Rights

Patrick Thornberry

Introduction

Contemporary interest in identity and ethnicity throughout a range of scholarly disciplines parallels the concern of international law. The 'philosophical' interest has been conditioned by political and legal 'events' and in turn has the capacity to shape them. Threads in the great tapestry of 'events' involve the dismantling of communism in Eastern Europe and the former Soviet Union, accelerated processes of globalisation, the development of an international civil society particularly in the fields of environment and human rights, and the emergence of indigenous peoples' and other subaltern movements. Liberals, communitarians and republicans,[1] cultural relativists and agnostics,[2] idealists, hegemonists, merchants of astonishment,[3] sentimentalists,[4] postmodernists and religious fundamentalists have all devoted attention in recent years to ethnic and nationality questions.

Some of the ferment has infused the staid institutions of law and government; most of those who deal therein with minority issues are involved or should be in 'a hermeneutical process mediated by international documents'.[5] It is tolerably clear that international law has been subjected to a considerable process of ethnicity-sensitisation, particularly in the course of the last decade.[6] As philosophers have turned their attention to identity and self-determination in a battle of the books, organisations have moved, some with all the

---

[1] For a spectrum of 'philosophy', see: W. Kymlicka (ed.) (1995) *The Rights of Minority Cultures*, Oxford University Press. The term 'Republicans' is employed in: P. Pettit (1997) *Republicanism: A Theory of Freedom and Government*, Oxford University Press.

[2] A distinction made by Makau wa Mutua (2000) 'Politics and Human Rights: An Essential Symbiosis', in: M. Byers (ed.) *The Role of Law in International Politics*, Oxford University Press, pp. 149-75.

[3] C. Geertz (2000) *Available Light*, Princeton University Press—he means anthropologists.

[4] The implied reference is to that 'sentimental education' which Richard Rorty urges as a non-foundationalist basis of human rights: 'Human Rights, Rationality and Sentimentality', in: S. Shute and S. Hurley (eds.) *On Human Rights: The Oxford Amnesty Lectures 1993*.

[5] W. Barbieri (1999) 'Group Rights and the Muslim Diaspora', *21 Human Rights Quarterly*, pp. 907-26, 913.

[6] P. Thornberry (1999) 'In the Strongroom of Vocabulary', in: P. Cumper and S. Wheatley (eds.) *Minority Rights in the 'New' Europe*, The Hague: Martinus Nijhoff Publishers, pp. 1-14.

inertia at their command, to shake out texts on the table. The world of human rights texts is opulent, while categories of resistance to their implementation are legion and the texts are often only paper tigers.[7]

The present chapter is a short guide through the babble of international instruments. Within this compass it is possible to catalogue only the main legal 'events', a little 'philosophy' and a few reflections. We pick out the leading global and European texts only,[8] suggesting what they mean and what they import, bearing in mind that this is a personal reading with which others will differ. Within the canon of human rights, minority rights raise difficult issues. It is relatively easy—give or take a few anthropologists—to agree that torture is wrong and interpretation of anti-torture laws is directed to the question of how to stop the torturers plying their trade.[9] Minority rights are not like that, but raise issues about the kind of society we have and want, the principles which do or should animate it, and the means by which we should achieve it, keeping in mind that means cannot always be detached from ends.

It is not accurate to suggest that the 'underpinnings' of human rights are the main or only controversy;[10] that the texts are lucid. Such philosophical disorder as there is infuses the texts, adding to interpretive complexities. We discuss the international law background and context; the spectrum of instruments and processes; four key texts: two 'global' and two emanating from the Council of Europe, with the longest analysis reserved to the Framework Convention for the Protection of National Minorities. The leading questions raised by the texts are then set out, with intimations of possible answers. The point of doing it this way is that while general principles can be extracted from the panoply of texts, the application of a human rights instrument starts with that text and may or may not subsume principles from elsewhere.

International Law: Comings and Goings

Minority rights have a long if ambivalent history in European international law. In the twentieth century, the League of Nations protected particular groups through specific instruments, covering the States of Eastern and Central Europe[11] and even Iraq[12] with a

---

[7] Broad assessments of human rights 'performance' are made in: P. Alston and J. Crawford (eds.) (2000)*The Future of UN Human Rights Treaty Monitoring,* Cambridge: Cambridge University Press.

[8] I use the term 'global' to indicate geographical scope: I am aware of the distinction between the 'merely global' and 'the universal'. Readers will decide whether the texts underlined contain 'universal' principles, timeless truths or simply the latest historical consequences. For an elaboration of the distinction see T. Asad (1997) 'On Torture, or Cruel, Inhuman and Degrading Treatment', in: R. A. Wilson (ed.) *Human Rights, Culture and Context,* London and Chicago: Pluto Press, pp. 111-33, 128.

[9] Asad, *supra*: I do not attribute this view to the author.

[10] Barbieri, *supra*.

[11] The States and territories covered were Austria, Poland (including Upper Silesia), the Serb-Croat-Slovene State, Czechoslovakia, Bulgaria, Romania, Hungary, Greece, the Free City of Danzig, the Aaland Islands, Albania, Estonia, Lithuania, Latvia, Turkey and the Memel.

[12] Iraq made a Declaration to the Council of the League of Nations on becoming independent in 1932.

carpet of treaties or declarations to the League Council for the benefit of 'racial, religious or linguistic' minorities. The system described but did not define minorities. A limit on the authority of States to define at will is implied in the Permanent Court of International Justice's observation on the Greco-Bulgarian Convention of 1919 that: 'The existence of communities is a question of fact; it is not a question of law ...'[13] What this means is that 'minority' carries an autonomous meaning in international law, and claims by States that they have no minorities will be judged on the facts in the light of international standards. The minority regime collapsed with the League itself. In 1945, the 'new world order' embodied in the UN Charter and later in the Universal Declaration of Human Rights (UDHR), omitted reference to minority rights, focusing instead on individual rights coupled with a principle of nondiscrimination. Critical reaction to the League experience was tinted with the wisdom of hindsight and dyed with a new philosophical individualism which superficially opposed individuals to groups.

The political version of Occam's Razor which excised minorities from the *corpus* of international law never completed its cut. The setting up of the UN Sub-Commission on the Prevention of Discrimination and the Protection of Minorities in the 1940s,[14] and the drafting of Article 27 of the Covenant on Civil and Political Rights (ICCPR) were pointers to an eventual re-emergence of minority rights on the international agenda. In Europe, bilateral and domestic law arrangements provided codes of minority rights; the European Convention on Human Rights (ECHR) included 'association with a national minority' among prohibited grounds of discrimination. In the UN era, international law gradually moved in the direction of greater complexity, supplementing the simple notion of 'rights for all without discrimination'. The founding concepts of the 'age of rights'[15] have been 'stretched' to recognise the specific claims of refugees, migrant workers, children, women, indigenous peoples, adherents of religions, the stateless and myriad other groups through dedicated international instruments.[16]

Principles of nondiscrimination are still axiomatic, but function in the context of a widening range of rights specifically addressed to multiple human groups. In line with the American heritage, early UN era human rights were potentially conducive to a melting-pot of cultures. The total effect of the newer prescriptions is an increased validation of diversity as opposed to sameness; integration as opposed to assimilation of groups; lightness, quickness and multiplicity of communities as the heaviness of state-building lifts off and nations redefine themselves in pluralist terms.

A Range of Instruments and Mechanisms

International organisations have now delivered up basic principles on minority rights which enshrine respect for the complexities of human community and resistance to the

---

[13] P.C.I.J. Series B, No. 17, 31 July 1930, 19, 21, 22 and 33.

[14] Now the Sub-Commission on the Promotion and Protection of Human Rights.

[15] N. Bobbio (1996) *The Age of Rights*, London: Polity Press.

[16] For a snapshot, see: I. Brownlie (1992) *Basic Documents on Human Rights*, Oxford: Clarendon Press, 3RD edition.

notion that States are single communities in all important senses. Apart from the ICCPR, most other texts were drafted in late 1980s and in the 1990s, responding at various speeds to the recrudescence of ethnic consciousness in Eastern Europe and elsewhere. At the level of the United Nations, Article 27 of the ICCPR continues to function as the minimum global treaty standard, and the most important non-treaty text specifically devoted to minority rights is the UN Declaration on the Rights of Persons Belonging to National or Ethnic, Religious and Linguistic Minorities.[17] The application of this instrument is now in the hands of a Working Group of the UN Sub-Commission on the Promotion and Protection of Human Rights.

At the specifically European level, the 'politically binding' instruments of the CSCE (now OSCE) contained the earliest set of specific principles in European space. The broadest spectrum of minority rights in the OSCE canon is provided by the Document of the Copenhagen Meeting of the Human Dimension 1990; the OSCE created the office of the High Commissioner on National Minorities in 1992.[18] The Council of the Baltic Sea States followed this by establishing the post of CBSS Commissioner on Democratic Institutions and Human Rights including the Rights of Persons Belonging to National Minorities in 1994. The Council of Europe has produced two treaties which incorporate the term 'minority': the Charter on Regional or Minority Languages, 1992, and the Framework Convention for the Protection of National Minorities in 1995. The former is pro-minority languages ad cultural diversity, not explicitly pro-minority rights; the latter is claimed by the Council of Europe to be the first multilateral treaty of its kind. Non-treaty standards from the Council of Europe may also be brought into consideration—notably Recommendation 1201 (1993) of the Parliamentary Assembly,[19] a document which gained an additional 'force' in being part of 'admission requirements' to the Council of Europe in the case of some States.[20]

In addition to these, the Central European Initiative produced an instrument in 1994,[21] as did the Commonwealth of Independent States (CIS).[22] The CEI text is strong on the international character of minority rights—'issues concerning ... minorities are matters of legitimate international concern and ... do not constitute exclusively an internal affair of the respective State'.[23] It is however restrictive on citizenship, the preamble asserting that 'the protection of national minorities concerns only citizens of the respective State'; this is coupled with a definition in Article 1 referring to members of minorities as 'nationals of the State'. CEI States also recognise the treatment of the Roma as a human rights

---

[17] General Assembly resolution 47/135, 18 December 1992.

[18] The setting up of the office of High Commissioner on National Minorities (HCNM) at the Helsinki Meeting in 1992 is of major significance to the development of minority rights. A selection of his speeches and recommendations may be obtained from the OSCE site on the internet.

[19] See generally, P. Thornberry and M. Amor Martin Estebanez (1994) *The Council of Europe and Minorities*, Strasbourg: Council of Europe.

[20] F. Benoit-Rohmer (1996) *The Minority Question in Europe: Texts and Commentary*, Strasbourg: Council of Europe Publishing.

[21] Text on CEI website: http://www.ceinet.org/minority.htm.

[22] 21 October 1994.

[23] Preamble.

issue, promising measures to preserve and develop Roma identity and facilitate their social integration.[24] The CIS text describes minorities as both citizens and permanent residents; the document is flawed in purporting to restrict some rights in the name of 'national legislation',[25] and by insisting that minorities fulfil unspecified 'obligations' to the State. States of Eastern and Central Europe have also concluded a range of bilateral treaties and declarations among themselves, wholly or partially devoted to minority rights.[26] Some of these have the effect of transforming 'soft law' into legally binding standards to be applied within States. The Dayton Agreement[27] and the Stability Pact for South-East Europe also incorporate minority rights standards.[28]

The European Union has not developed an instrument on minority rights, but treaty references to culture and education, to European cultural and linguistic diversity, and principles further reflected in Article 22 of the European Charter on Fundamental Freedoms agreed at the EU Summit at Nice are significant.[29] Europe Agreements', and 'Association Agreements' with potential members effectively enshrine minority rights. The European Bureau for Lesser Used Languages, largely financed by the European Commission, watches over the autochthonous linguistic heritage of EU members. Despite the limited attention given to minority questions within the EU, one writer summarises the EU approach as insisting:

> ... that East European minority nations must be recognised as legitimate groups within their respective societies, and must be accorded group rights ... (whereas) in Western Europe, within the EU, minority nations have self-evidently not been protected through the granting of group rights.[30]

There is now a wealth of texts relevant to the concerns of minorities in contemporary international law. For pedagogical purposes they can be classified into instruments of 'undifferentiated' human rights (for all persons), and 'differentiated' texts (or parts thereof) for minorities in particular. The United Nations has acted on the concerns expressed at the time of the Universal Declaration of Human Rights in 1948—when the General Assembly declared that the UN could not remain indifferent to the fate of minorities;[31] other international organisations have also taken up the cry.

---

[24] Article 7.

[25] Articles 6 and 8. Such restrictions contradict the basic principle that in the event of conflict between international and domestic law, the former prevails.

[26] See: A. Bloed and P. van Dijk (eds.) (1999) *Protection of Minority Rights through Bilateral Treaties: The Case of Central and Eastern Europe*, The Hague: Kluwer Law International.

[27] J. Mertus (1999) 'The Dayton Peace Accords: Lessons from the Past and for the Future', in: Wheatley and Cumper, pp. 261-83.

[28] Cologne, 10 June 1999; text at: http://www.seerecon.org/KeyDocuments/

[29] M. Amor Martin Estebanez (1996) *International Organisations and Minority Protection in Europe*, Turku/Abo: Abo Akademi University, Part III, and various references in: P. Alston, M. Bustelo and J. Heenan (eds.) (1999) *The EU and Human Rights*, Oxford University Press.

[30] A. Biscoe (1999) 'The European Union and Minority Nations', in: Wheatley and Cumper, *supra*,, 89-103, 98.

[31] Resolution 217C (III).

Key International Texts

The brunt of the analysis below relates to the differentiated minority rights instruments. For comparison, a short account of the European Convention on Human Rights is included: the attraction of that Convention for minority rights activists lies mostly in its implementation mechanism, based on individual applications to the (former Commission and) Court of Human Rights alleging violation of the provisions. In passing, it may be observed that while 'individualisation' of implementation mechanisms plays an important role in securing human rights, mechanisms with a systemic and preventive focus also have their place. While an adverse finding by the European Court of Human Rights is intended to deter, the judgment is still only a reaction to a violation which may have given rise to uncompensable harm to individuals. UN treaties tend to combine overview reporting procedures with procedures for individual claims; European instruments usually detach these functions in practice if not in theory. The focus on legal interventions should not lead us to underestimate 'diplomatic' approaches to conflict prevention and redress, the potential of intercultural and multicultural education, and the benefits of a complementarity of approaches in attempts to resolve particular cases.

Article 27 of the International Covenant of Civil and Political Rights (ICCPR)

The ICCPR's implementing body, the Human Rights Committee, has been exercised by this brief, weight-bearing article on many occasions:

> In those States in which ethnic, religious or linguistic minorities exist, persons belonging to such minorities shall not be denied the right, in community with the other members of their group, to enjoy their own culture, to profess and practice their own religion, or to use their own language.[32]

The right to identity represents in many ways the essence of the case for minorities within the *corpus* of human rights. The elements of that identity can be ethnic, religious or linguistic, or more than one in combination. Article 27 appears tentative in its affirmations. The opening phrase 'In those States in which ... minorities exist' almost invites States to declare that they have no minorities., but only France has recorded an 'official' statement to that effect, declaring that 'Article 27 is not applicable so far as the French Republic is concerned'.[33] Following this example, reservations and declarations on Article

---

[32] Cf. Article 30 of the Convention on the Rights of the Child, which adapts Article 27 to provide for rights of minority and indigenous children.

[33] *Human Rights Status of International Instruments* (1987) New York: United Nations, pp. 35. The Federal Republic of Germany has interpreted the declaration by France (*ibid.*, 88) to mean that 'the Constitution of the French Republic already fully guarantees the individual rights protected by Article 27'. France as reaffirmed this position on many occasions. For its reiteration before a European human rights body, see the European Commission Against Racism and Intolerance (ECRI), *Second Report on France*, Council of Europe Doc. CRI (2000) 31, Adopted 10 December

30 of the UN Convention on the Rights of the Child have been made upon signature confirmed on ratification by France, Venezuela, and upon signature by Turkey.[34]

However, according to General Comment No. 23 of the Human Rights Committee:[35] 'The existence of an ethnic, religious or linguistic minority in a given State party ... requires to be established by objective criteria'.[36] In the language of the General Comment and following the line in *Greco-Bulgarian* case of the PCIJ (*supra*) 'existence' 'does not depend upon a decision by (a) State party ...'.[37] Article 27 does not contain a definition of 'minority' and the General Comment does not offer one. In *Ballantyne, Davidson and McIntyre v. Canada*,[38] a majority of the Committee decided that members of the majority Anglophone community in Canada could not be considered as a minority even when they were a minority in a Province (Quebec): Article 27 'refers to minorities in States; this refers ... to ratifying States ... the minorities ... are minorities within such a State, and not minorities within any Province'.[39] Other Members of the Committee dissented.[40] Confining the meaning of 'minority' to exclude members of a majority in a minority situation in provinces or autonomous areas distances the approach of the Committee from that found in some of the 'European' texts.[41]

Minority rights have been 'admitted' into the contemporary canon of human rights as rights of individuals, not as 'collective' or 'group' rights. The terms are ambiguous and conceal two truisms: that 'the individual' is an abstraction as much as 'the group', and that all rights are 'collective' in that they apply to a class of persons.[42] Of the contested conceptions, we should distinguish between collective rights of individuals in virtue of belonging to or being perceived as member of a particular group (collective as adjective); and rights of a 'collective'—a corporate conception implying rights for the group as such, against the world and even against its 'members'.

Article 27 clearly eschews the corporate conception: rights are for: 'persons belonging to ... minorities'. There is no indication as to how membership ('belonging') is to be defined. In *Lovelace v. Canada*,[43] the Human Rights Committee stated, in relation to a

---

1999. 'Observations' on the report by the French authorities reaffirm the validity of France's 'Republican principles'.

[34] UN Doc. CRC/C/2 (22 August 1991) 10, 16, 17.

[35] 26 April 1994.

[36] General Comment, para. 5.2.

[37] Paragraph 5.2.

[38] UN Doc. CCPR/C/47/D/359/1989 and 385/1989/Rev.1 (31 March 1993).

[39] Paragraph 11.2.

[40] Individual opinion by Mrs. Elizabeth Evatt, co-signed by Messrs. Ando, Bruni Celli and Dimitrijevic, 23.

[41] For example, Recommendation 1201 (1993) of the Parliamentary Assembly of the Council of Europe (Article 1) defines 'national minority' to include groups 'smaller in number than the rest of the population of that State or of a region of that State'.

[42] Barbieri, pp. 916-18.

[43] Human Rights Committee (1985) *Selected Decisions Under the Optional Protocol* (2nd to 16th sessions), UN Doc. CCPR/C/OP/1, 10 (admissibility); 37 (interlocutory decision); 83 (views of the Human Rights Committee).

woman denied membership in the Tobique Band of Indians through marriage to a non-Indian, that: 'Persons who are born and brought up on a reserve, who have kept ties with their community and wish to maintain these ties must normally be considered as belonging to that minority ...'. The general 'membership' criteria to be extracted from this laconic statement are those of fact, intention or desire: the use of 'normally' indicates that these may not always be decisive. So while a certain threshold weight may be accorded to 'self-definition as a member of a minority', that criterion is not absolute. Article 27 exhibits a further collective dimension in that members of minorities 'enjoy the rights in community with the other members of their group'. The Human Rights Committee has also indicated that in the enjoyment of rights under Article 27, the right of individuals to participate in aspects of community life may be restricted, but only if the restricting legislation reflects the legitimate aim of minority group survival and well-being, and the restriction on the right of an individual is not disproportionate to that aim.[44]

Following *Lovelace*, the Human Rights Committee stated in *Kitok v. Sweden*,[45] that 'a restriction upon the right of an individual member of a minority must be shown to have a reasonable and objective justification and to be necessary for the continued viability and welfare of the minority as a whole'. The significance of this is that, despite the 'individualist' phrasing of Article 27, continued group existence and character is assumed to have value in itself, a factor which may be 'weighed' against the desires of individuals.

If the principle of survival of minority cultures and religions in the face of assimilationist pressures is to have meaning, States should take measures to the extent necessary to ensure that the disadvantages of minority status do not result in the denial of the right. Protective State action will be required for as long as minority status persists. Article 27 does not specify the modalities of action to be taken. The General Comment on Article 27 insists on the positive nature of the Article despite its negative language, and on its 'horizontal' effect[46]:

> Positive measures of protection are ... required not only against the acts of the State party itself, whether through its legislative, judicial or administrative authorities, but also against the acts of other persons within the State party.[47]

Finally, we may note that within the confines of the ICCPR, minority rights are served by the ensemble of other articles, some of which impact intimately on questions of identity. In cases where for one reason or another Article 27 may not be applied, the Human Rights Committee has been creative in its utilisation of other articles to secure ends analogous to those of Article 27.[48] The message is that human rights strategies need not be narrowly focused: the full text is there to be quarried for relevant principles, article by article, and interpreted as a whole.

---

[44] *Lovelace*, paragraph 17.

[45] UN Doc. CCPR/C/33/D/197/1985; Views of the Committee adopted on 27 July 1988.

[46] Where the State is held responsible for violations of rights by other individuals, not just by the State authorities.

[47] Paragraph 6.1.

[48] UN Doc. CCPR/C/60/D/549/1993, Views of the Committee adopted on 29 July 1997.

The UN Minority Rights Declaration[49]

This non-treaty instrument (the UNDM) was adopted by the consensus of the UN General Assembly in 1992. Despite the paragraph in its preamble claiming 'inspiration' from Article 27, the Declaration represents a fresh start and is not simply an 'expansion' of the ICCPR. The text took some fourteen years to emerge from the bowels of the UN, in which time ideological and political configurations had changed enormously. The Declaration was the UN's response to changes which by 1992 had already begun to reveal their dark side in the former Yugoslavia and the former USSR. The drafters were obviously aware of distinctions between individual and collective rights. Rights are consistently for 'persons belonging to' minorities. On the other hand, Article 1.1. of he Declaration transcends the tentative phrasing of Article 27 and explicitly describes identity and existence as fundamental attributes of groups. The obligation to protect existence and identity is set out as mandatory.

A meagre diet of rights is set out in article 2, which begins brightly by replacing the 'shall not be denied the right' of Article 27 with the positive 'have the right'. While the textual limitations of Article 27 have not prevented the Human Rights Committee from declaring that 'positive measures of protection are ... required'.[50] The explicitly positive approach of the Declaration removes some intellectual doubts about the international community's reception of minority rights: the Article 27 formulae suggests a kind of 'aggrieved hospitality' was at work,[51] but not a welcome. The Declaration makes an important departure from Article 27 in its wide-ranging specification of participation rights— minority rights 'to participate effectively in cultural, religious, social, economic and public life', and the right to participate effectively in decisions affecting them. Modalities of participation remain unspecified but the development of mediating organisations to facilitate participation is legitimate since the article sets out a right to establish and maintain minority associations. The own associations right is supplemented by rights to establish and maintain free and peaceful contacts including 'contacts across frontiers with citizens of other States to whom they (the members of minorities) are related by national or ethnic, religious or linguistic ties'. Article 3 provides for the exercise of rights individually 'as well as 'collectively—in case States should be tempted to 'decide' that culture, religion, etc., are to be carried on only in private.

The measures set out in the qualified language of Article 4 confront important aspects of group life and should, by analogy with measures in the International Covenants, be 'deliberate, concrete and targeted as clearly as possible towards meeting the obligations recognised ...'.[52] Mandatory language extends to members of minorities the promise that

---

[49] Two relevant commentaries (the second is in draft only) are: P. Thornberry (1995) 'The UN Declaration on the Rights of ... Minorities: Background, Analysis, Observations, and an Update', in: A. Phillips and A. Rosas (eds.) *Universal Minority Rights*, London and Abo: Minority Rights Group and Abo Akademi University, pp. 13-76; A. Eide, *Commentary to the Declaration ... A Working Paper*, UN Doc. E/CN.4/Sub.2/AC.5/2000/WP.1.

[50] UN Doc. CCPR/C/21/Rev.1/Add.5, paragraph 6.1.

[51] Barbieri, pp. 910.

[52] See General Comment No. 3 of the Committee on Economic, Social and Cultural Rights entitled 'The Nature of States Parties Obligations', in UN Doc. HRI/GEN/1, 43.

they may 'fully and effectively' exercise all their human rights without discrimination and on a basis of equality. Measures are not defined, but the term is appropriate to cover both legislative and non-legislative measures.[53] Article 4.2. indicates that States must facilitate the expression and development of minority culture, traditions and customs, etc., 'except where specific practices are in violation of national law and international standards.' The qualification is necessary and meets an objection sometimes placed against minorities and indigenous peoples: that group traditions may incorporate *practices* inconsistent with human rights.

The provisions on learning and instruction in mother tongue are qualified and ambiguous. The intended contrast in the references to 'learning' and 'instruction' is between learning through the medium of one's own language, and being taught the rudiments of that language. The words in the text convey this contrast only in dim fashion. The 'philosophical' point of Article 4—expressed in its fourth paragraph—is to promote self-knowledge on the part of minorities, and their awareness of the wider world, while informing society at large of the cultural and other contributions of minorities to the nation as a whole. Accordingly, the culture, history, traditions, etc., of minority groups should be the subject of positive valuations and not of the kind of distorted representations which produce low self-esteem in the groups and negative stereotypes in the wider community. Reciprocally, minority doctrines of ethnic exclusiveness are discouraged.

Article 8 sets minority rights in their universal context and 'balances' their exercise with the rights of others, implying that measures for minorities are generally compatible with equality, though this also suggests that they should not be pushed too far to the detriment of others. Article 8.4. connects with the fear of some States that minority rights may lead to self-determination. To the extent that a secessionist 'threat' exists, it must be in virtue of other principles of international law, and this applies equally to the converse argument that the Declaration 'protects' territorial integrity from valid claims to self-determination. The Declaration has nothing to say about self-determination. The General Comment on Article 27 goes to great pains to eliminate any 'confusion' between the two rights, and notes in analogous fashion to the Declaration that: 'enjoyment of the rights to which Article 27 relates does not prejudice the sovereignty and territorial integrity of a State party'.[54] Article 9 points to contributions from the United Nations to the realisation of the purposes of the text. The language is such as to implicate all the relevant organs of the UN system. The follow-up to the Declaration proceeded slowly. The Commission on Human Rights adopted, on 3 March 1995, resolution 1995/24 authorising the Sub-Commission to establish a Working Group on Minorities. The Working Group met for the sixth time in 2000, and now enjoys an 'indefinite' mandate.[55]

---

[53] Cf. Article 1.

[54] General Comment, paragraph 3.2. See also paragraphs 2 and 3.1.

[55] The background to the establishment of the Working Group and its mandate are set out in *Report of the Fifth Session*, UN Doc. E/CN.4/Sub.2/1999/21, 24 June 1999.

European Instruments

Virtually all European States (however we define 'Europe') are parties to the main UN human rights treaties, or have joined in the consensus which validates the UN Declaration. As noted, the standards of the OSCE were 'first in line' to meet the challenge of the melt-down of communism in Europe, on democracy and rule of law questions as well as human rights, minorities, environment—the manifold forms of human security. The OSCE Copenhagen Document is important primarily as a commitment made by States re-validating minority rights in the new *ordo rerum*. It represents an early contemporary 'codification' of minority rights in Europe, setting out the essential standards of group recognition, promotion of culture, participation, etc., recognising also the positive contribution of autonomy to the resolution of ethnic conflicts. The Copenhagen document influenced the drafting of the UN Declaration and subsequent exercises in setting standards at the Council of Europe and elsewhere. The OSCE continues to develop minority rights through the instrumentalisation of Copenhagen principles and the work of the HCNM. Attempts have also been made under the aegis of the HCNM to consolidate minority rights principles in the fields of education, language and participation.[56]

The major treaty-promoting human rights organisation in Europe is the Council of Europe, dedicated to the holy trinity of human rights, democracy and the Rule of Law. The European Convention on Human Rights of 1950 remains the organisation's 'flagship'. The text deals only with human rights for all persons and not minority rights; it is in our terminology 'undifferentiated', although Article 14 forbids discrimination on the grounds of 'association with a national minority'. The ECHR underpins many rights which, while they concern 'all persons', have particular relevance to minorities. Accordingly, the Convention's focus on pluralist democracy,[57] nondiscrimination, respect for private life, family life and ways of life,[58] the attention paid to issues of human dignity,[59] and the protection offered to freedom of expression,[60] freedom of association,[61] and profession of religion,[62] all offer vital safeguards to minority groups while not formally visualising minorities through its 'optic'.

---

[56] The reference here is to three sets of recommendations on minority rights prepared by the Foundation on Inter-Ethnic Relations under the guidance of the HCNM: the Hague Recommendations regarding the Education Rights of National Minorities 1996; the Oslo Recommendations on the Linguistic Rights of National Minorities 1998; and the Lund Recommendations on the Effective Participation of National Minorities in Public Life 1999.

[57] Among many cases, see: *Socialist Party and Others v. Turkey*, 20/1997/804/1007, Judgment of 25 May 1998.

[58] *G. and E. v. Norway*, Application Nos. 9278/81 and 9415/81, D.R. 35 (1983), pp. 30-45.

[59] *Assenov and Others v. Bulgaria*, Application No. 24760/94, Judgment of 28 October 1998.

[60] Again, in a plethora of case law, see *Arslan v. Turkey*, Application No. 23462/94, Judgment of 8 July 1999. Judgments on twelve other cases with similar facts were issued against Turkey on the same day.

[61] *Stankov and United Macedonian Association 'ILINDEN' v. Bulgaria*, Application Nos. 29221/95 and 29225/95, admissibility decision 29 June 1998.

[62] *Serif v. Greece*, Application No. 38178/97, Judgment of 14 December 1999.

There is evidence that, like undifferentiated instruments at the global level, the ECHR is undergoing gradual 'sensitisation' to minority questions in a number of fields, although doubts remain as to whether the bodies of the ECHR always treat 'ethnic' issues with sufficient *gravitas*.[63] The prospects for an 'opening out' of the Convention to minority issues are enhanced by the adoption of Protocol 12 on nondiscrimination in general.[64]

The Charter for Regional or Minority Languages of the Council of Europe

The Charter for Regional or Minority Languages is the first treaty essay by the Council of Europe in the field of minorities.[65] Although it has 'minority' in the title and operative articles, it is not *per se* an instrument on minority rights. The Charter works for the benefit of speakers of minority *languages*. As the *Explanatory Report* makes clear:

> The Charter sets out to protect and promote regional or minority languages, not linguistic minorities. For this reason emphasis is placed on the cultural dimension and the use of a regional or minority language in all the aspects of the life of its speakers. The Charter does not establish any individual or collective rights for the speakers ... Nevertheless, the obligations of the parties with regard to the status of these languages and the domestic legislation which will have to be introduced in compliance with the Charter will have an obvious effect on the situation of the communities concerned ....[66]

Its validation of these languages contributes to the Council of Europe's overall conception of a diversified and culturally pluralist Europe where lesser used languages have enhanced capacity for survival and flourishing. The Charter adopts a 'menu' approach to State undertakings in the area of minority languages. Positively, this allows for flexible accommodation to particular circumstances and is less potentially confrontational than a platform of strongly asserted group rights. The limitation is the perceptible dilution (*infra*,

---

[63] See, for example: *Buckley v. UK*, Judgment of 25 September 1996.

[64] Protocol No. 12 was adopted by the Committee of Ministers of the Council of Europe on 26 June 2000, and will be opened for signature by member States on 4 November 2000; entry into force requires ten ratifications. Whereas Article 14 of the ECHR forbids discrimination in relation only to the rights set out in the Convention, Protocol 12 provides that 'enjoyment of *any right set forth by law* shall be secured without discrimination ...' (present author's emphasis). The *Explanatory Report* to the Protocol states (paragraph 24) that 'while ... positive obligations cannot be excluded altogether, the prime objective of Article 1 (of the Protocol) is to embody a negative obligation for the parties: the obligation not to discriminate against individuals'. The *Report* also observes (paragraph 29) that the word 'law' in 'set forth by law' 'may also cover international law, but this does not mean that this provision entails jurisdiction for the European Court of Human Rights to examine compliance with rules of law in other international instruments'.

[65] Opened for signature on 5 November 1992; in force 1 March 1998. At the time of writing, the Charter has been ratified by nine States: Croatia, Finland, Germany, Hungary, Liechtenstein, the Netherlands, Norway, Sweden and Switzerland.

[66] *Ibid.*, paragraph 11.

concluding lecture) of State obligations through the range of options offered to States. The Charter should not therefore be understood as proposing a complete alternative to standard minority rights but as a project to foster the creation of detailed national regimes for the support of minority languages with points of guidance to States which concentrate and highlight essential areas of action.

The supervision mechanism is essentially a reporting procedure through a Committee of Experts. The major normative limitation is its focus on the 'traditional' languages of Europe and not on the newer arrivals. Migrants are, however, a part of European society, and the Charter's focus on languages traditionally used may alienate. In conceptual terms there are possibilities of 'slippage' between the 'traditional' and the 'new'. Conceptions of languages of European 'tradition' to be safeguarded are subject to change: further exploration of this point by the Committee of Experts over the life of the instrument will be welcome. However, de minimis, the Romany language is covered by key provisions.

The stance of the Charter is broadly comparable with that of minority rights texts, in that it seeks an improving relationship between the 'public' and 'official' languages, and the living languages of European minorities. While some States remain resolutely opposed to minority rights, ratification of the Charter may represent an avenue to realise some minority rights objectives. From its own perspective, the Charter goes beyond other instruments in interlacing the 'public' space with a complex of language requirements. Its flexibility is capable of meeting the resource constraints on human rights programmes, though it is important that the application of the Charter should not be unduly 'minimalist'. Perhaps the principal concern for civil society is that the Charter should be worked through in as transparent a manner as possible and not be perceived as only 'intergovernmental—the relative lack of NGO input into the drafting may be accounted as a loss.[67]

The Framework Convention for the Protection of National Minorities[68]

In the drafting of the ECHR, unavailing suggestions were made for the adoption of a specific provision on minority rights; more recently the Council of Europe laboured in vain to produce and additional minority rights (and even cultural rights) protocol to the ECHR.[69] The lack of a binding 'differentiated' instrument in the Council of Europe was remedied in 1995, when the Framework Convention was opened for signature by the Committee of Ministers. The Convention distils, elaborates, applies—and possibly dilutes—propositions in OSCE and UN texts. The present chapter concentrates on some of the principles therein which give the Convention its particular colour. The strength of the Framework Convention lies in its character as a binding treaty backed up by a standing implementation mechanism.

---

[67] Crnic-Grotic and Bucci, 'The View of the Authors of the Charter', in: *Implementation*, pp. 76-77, 77.

[68] The text was opened for signature by the Committee of Ministers of the Council of Europe on 1 February 1998, entering into force in 1 February 1998. At the time of writing thirty-one States have ratified the Convention. More than half of these States have submitted their initial reports.

[69] Benoit-Rohmer, *op.cit.*

i) A Framework

The incorporation of the notion of a 'framework' into the title of a legally binding Convention has attracted critical comment, to the general effect that the terminology represents the softening of an otherwise 'hard law' treaty.[70] The nature of State obligation takes colour from two paragraphs in the preamble, the first of which expresses the resolution of the signatories 'to define the principles to be respected and the obligations which flow from them, in order to ensure ... the effective protection of national minorities ...';[71] and the second, describing the signatories as 'Being determined to implement the principles set out in this Framework Convention through national legislation and appropriate government policies'.[72] One author considers that the 'framework' idea 'seems to impose upon States only an obligation to endeavour to put ... vague and imprecise descriptions of rights into effect',[73] which, along with other 'defects', renders the Convention 'almost worthless'.[74]

This last remark assumes too much. All human rights instruments are in essence open and developmental, only imprecisely dispositive of disagreements, so that the task of discovering meanings in the human rights canon is a constant in the work of the implementing 'treaty-bodies'. Irrespective of the precise form, it should not be forgotten that the Convention creates obligations in international law; it cannot be treated as somehow less binding on account of its structure.[75] The *Explanatory Report* on the Convention observes that it 'contains mostly programme-type provisions setting out objectives which the parties undertake to pursue', and that the provisions 'will not be directly applicable'.[76] However, certain provisions of the Framework Convention look appropriate for 'direct application', including articles which 'track' or 'parallel' obligations under the ECHR; Article 3 would also be a strong candidate. Some States appear to have committed themselves to a programme of 'direct application'.[77]

---

[70] Strong language emanated from the Parliamentary Assembly of the Council of Europe in their overall assessment that the Convention 'is weakly worded' and 'formulates a number of vaguely defined objectives and principles, the observation of which will be an obligation of the contracting States but not a right which individuals may invoke. Its implementation machinery is feeble and there is a danger that, in fact, the monitoring procedure will be left entirely to governments'—Recommendation 1255 (1995), text adopted by the Assembly on 31 January 1995.

[71] 12TH preambular paragraph.

[72] 13TH preambular paragraph.

[73] G. Gilbert (1999) 'Minority Rights under the Council of Europe', in: P. Cumper and S. Wheatley (eds.) *Minority Rights in the 'New' Europe*, The Hague: Martinus Nijhoff Publishers, pp. 53-70, at 63.

[74] *Ibid.* For more nuanced views, see the same author's 'The Council of Europe and Minority Rights' (1996) *18 Human Rights Quarterly,* pp. 160-89.

[75] See A. Spiliopoulou-Akermark (1997) *Justifications of Minority Protection in International Law,* Uppsala: Iustus Forlag, pp. 229, n. 114. Note also her remark that 'the contracting parties cannot avoid the legal implementation of a treaty by calling it "framework Convention" or "convention specifying principle"'.—*Ibid.,* pp. 227.

[76] *Explanatory Report*, paragraph 11.

[77] Consider Article 15 (4) (a) of the Hungarian-Slovak treaty on Good-Neighbourliness, etc., wherein the parties declare 'that as regards the rights and obligations of persons belonging to minori-

ii) National Minorities

Section I makes important points on the integration of minority rights with human rights more explicitly than in UN texts, restating the UN and OSCE principles of freedom of choice of every person belonging to a national minority to be treated as such without disadvantage,[78] and the individual as well as communal exercise of the rights.[79] The *Explanatory Report* offers the opinion that 'no collective rights of minorities are envisaged',[80] and that 'choice of belonging' 'does not imply a right for an individual to choose arbitrarily to belong to any national minority. The individual's subjective choice is inseparably linked to objective criteria relevant to the person's identity'.[81] There is no explicit reference in the Convention to State denial of the existence of minorities.

Despite the relative openness of the text, a number of States have provided restrictive definitions of minorities,[82] while others are more generous, addressing the existence of minorities as a factual situation.[83] In cases of exemption of noncitizens from the 'national minority', the objection of the Russian Federation, which considers that no State 'is entitled to include unilaterally in reservations or declarations ... a definition of the term 'national minority',[84] is noteworthy. Further,

> ... attempts to exclude from the scope of the ... Convention ... persons who permanently reside in the territory of State parties ... and previously had a citizenship but have been arbitrarily deprived of it, contradict the purpose of the ... Convention ....[85]

The Russian declaration raises an issue of the validity of the various readings of the term 'national minority', particularly the narrower versions. The statement is close to claiming that the restrictions *ratione personae* contradict, in the language of the Vienna Convention on the Law of Treaties—the 'object and purpose ' of the Convention.[86] Such objections raise delicate legal issues on the application of the treaty between objector and reserving States.[87] The Human Rights Committee offers the helpful advice in such situa-

---

ties living within their respective territories they shall apply the Framework Convention ... unless their domestic legal systems provide for broader protection of rights of persons belonging to national minorities ...'—treaty in force 6 May 1996, text in: A. Bloed and P. van Dijk (eds.) (1999) *Protection of Minority Rights through Bilateral Treaties*, The Hague: Kluwer Law International, pp. 370-75.

[78] Article 3.1.

[79] Article 3.2.

[80] Paragraph 31.

[81] Paragraph 35.

[82] See, for example, the statements on signature/ratification and initial reports of Estonia, Denmark, Germany and Slovenia.

[83] Finland, *Initial Report*, 5.

[84] Declaration made on ratification, 21 August 1998—*Council of Europe Information*, 21 January 2000.

[85] *Ibid.*

[86] Article 19 (c).

[87] See, in general: F. G. Jacobs, and R. C. A. White (1996) *The European Convention on Human Rights*, Oxford: Clarendon Press, 2ND edition, chapter 22.

tions that 'an objection to a reservation made by States may provide some guidance … in … interpretation as to … compatibility with the object and purpose …' of the treaty in question.[88]

iii) Culture and its Limitations

The preamble to the Convention refers to respecting the ethnic, cultural, etc., identity of each person and to creating conditions for the expression of this identity. The text implies that identity may have multiple aspects, so that the nuances of expressing identity will vary with the person. According to Article 5.1., the parties undertake to promote the conditions necessary for persons belonging to minorities 'to maintain and develop their culture, and to preserve the essential elements of their identity, namely their religion, language, traditions and cultural heritage'. The reference to 'essential elements of their identity' appears to be a narrower formulation than that in the UNDM, which speaks simply of 'identity'.[89] The *Explanatory Report* comments that 'reference to 'traditions' is not an endorsement or acceptance of practices which are contrary to national law or international standards. Traditional practices remain subject to limitations arising from the requirements of public order'.[90]

Thus interpreted, the limits of cultural expression in the Convention are narrower than elsewhere. The UNDM implies—in careful language—that cultural practices must not violate international human rights standards *and* national law. The *Report* would allow wider scope for restrictive national legislation.[91] In this instance, the provisions of Article 19 of the Convention become relevant—allowing only for limitations, etc., 'which are provided for in international legal instruments', in particular the ECHR.[92] The Convention also recognises that culture and identities are mutable through employing terms such as 'express, preserve and develop'. There is no question within its terms of 'locking in' minorities to an unchangeable corpus of traditional lifestyles and practices before allowing access to the norms of international law—this coheres with the case law of the ICCPR.[93]

iv) Language and Education

For many minority groups, the provisions on language and education represent core issues. Language and education are at the centre of ancient and modern exercises in minority rights. The Convention's provisions are replete with 'qualifiers'. Their chief innovation is to introduce the concept of a minority 'area', within the (indeterminate but protected)[94] boundaries of which some minority rights are enhanced.[95] Article 10 recognises the right

---

[88] General Comment No. 24 (52), CCPR/C/21/Rev.1/Add.6, 11 November 1994, paragraph 17.

[89] Article 1.1.

[90] Paragraph 44.

[91] See remarks in the report of Slovakia on 'value modification' in relation to Roma through education: *Initial Report*, p. 27.

[92] See: *Jacobs and White*, ch. 19—'Limitations'.

[93] *Ilmari Lansman v. Finland*, Views of the Committee in UN Doc. A/50/40, pp. 66-76.

[94] Article 16 imparts a measure of integrity to minority areas.

[95] Finland refers to Aland and the Sami Homeland as relevant 'areas'—*Initial Report*, pp. 19-20.

to use a minority language freely and without interference, in public or in private, 'perfecting' the freedom of expression set out in Articles 7 and 9.[96]

Paragraph 2 of Article 10 is directed towards the possibility of using minority languages in dealings with administrative authorities. Not all relations with public authorities are dealt with: the reference is to 'administrative authorities', though 'the latter must be broadly interpreted' (the *Explanatory Report* specifically mentions Ombudsmen).[97] The 'area' where the right applies is one inhabited by minority members 'traditionally or in substantial numbers'. For the right to be activated, there must be a request and the minority request should correspond 'to a real need'. If this is the case, the parties are only committed to the thin obligation 'to endeavour to ensure, as far as possible, the conditions which would make it possible' to use the minority language in relations with administrative authorities.

The provision imports a lexicon of qualifiers: traditional or substantial inhabitation, real need, and the various vocabularies of possibility, before the right is activated. The right struggles to escape, gripped even more tightly by the *Explanatory Report* which suggests that the existence of a real need 'is to be assessed by the State on the basis of objective criteria',[98] and that the financial resources of the State must also be taken into consideration in applying the article. The issue of need can hardly be in the exclusive domain of the State—simply to be 'assessed' by State agencies. If need is subject to 'objective criteria', as the *Report* suggests, the question of a minority input to the assessment cannot be discounted.[99] The 'good-faith' provisions of Article 2 are also relevant. In as far as resources are concerned, all human rights consume resources—even the elimination of official torture requires education (re-education) and training for aberrant officials, as well as continuous vigilance against recurrence.

The first paragraph of Article 11 sets out a right to use names in the minority language 'and the right to official recognition of them, according to modalities provide for in their legal system'. This is followed by the right to display minority language 'signs, inscriptions and other information of a private nature visible to the public';[100] and the second 'minority area' provision,[101] whereby the State 'shall endeavour' 'to display traditional local names, street names and other topographical indications intended for the public also in the minority language ...'.[102] According to the *Explanatory Report*, the first paragraph

---

[96] Paragraph 3 of Article 10—which provides a right to be informed of reasons for arrest, etc.,—adds little or nothing to the body of minority rights. The paragraph is satisfied by proceedings in the language understood by a person arrested, etc., not necessarily a minority language. Compare Articles 5 and 6 ECHR, and Article 9 of the Charter on Regional or Minority Languages.

[97] *Report*, paragraph 64.

[98] Paragraph 65.

[99] Article 15 supports this view.

[100] Paragraph 2.

[101] In this case dependent on being 'traditionally inhabited by substantial numbers' of persons belonging to minorities—unlike Article 10.2., inhabitation and numbers are cumulative requirements.

[102] Paragraph 3.

of Article 11, providing for official recognition of minority names, allows these to be transcribed into the alphabet of the official language in their phonetic forms.[103] Relying largely on Article 11, the OSCE Oslo Recommendations interpret this requirement to mean additionally that the phonetic rendering 'must be done in accordance with the language system and tradition of the national minority'.[104] This will be the case even if the minority linguistic system sits uneasily with the forms of the official language.[105] Paragraph 68 of the *Explanatory Report* also states that Article 11 means that persons who have been forced to change their names—perhaps under policies of forced assimilation—should have the right to revert to them. It must be supposed that in such cases any costs incurred in securing a reversion will fall on the authorities and not on the victims.

The question of minority language signs visible to the public draws the comment from the *Explanatory Report* that the right does not prevent the individual being required to use the official language in addition to the minority language.[106] As a blanket proposition, this cannot be right. While particular issues may be raised under health and safety, or signs using offensive language, these can be addressed by specific State legislation. On the other hand, many private signs (the name of a house, a poster in the window) are 'visible to the public', and there are clearly cases where there is no conceivable State interest in adding the official or other language. Some States reporting on this article indicate that the freedom to display is not subject to restriction.[107] Different issues are raised by paragraph 3, where the question is the public allocation of street names, etc., if there is sufficient demand. In this case, it is appropriate that the official or State language enters the equation. What is 'sufficient' will vary with the case;[108] questions of visibility of the respective language components of any signage will also be raised.[109] Erasing minority 'footprints' through changing names of towns, villages and historical sites can be part of a process of assimilation against the will of a minority.

---

[103] Paragraph 68. See also R. Hoffman (1999) 'A Presentation of the Framework Convention ... and its Contribution to the Protection of Minority Languages', in: *Implementation of the European Charter for Regional or Minority Languages*, Strasbourg: Council of Europe, pp. 21-24, 23.

[104] Oslo Recommendation 1 and Explanatory Report.

[105] This applies for example to non-Slovak female suffixes. Thus, the 'female surname of a person other than Slovak nationality is written without the grammatical ending of Slovak declination'— in the event of various requests to that effect; *Initial Report of Slovakia*, 23. This is a question relating to 'linguistic systems'.

[106] Paragraph 69.

[107] See, *Report of Finland,* 22; *Report of Hungary*, 99.

[108] Estonia requires place names in Estonian, unless an exception is 'justified historically'—*Report*, 50; Finland adopts the lowest percentage rule for a minority population in a municipality to trigger bilingual signage rules—8% minority inhabitation—as well as all municipalities where over 3,000 inhabitants speak the other official language—*Report*, 22-23; Romania opts for 20% habitation—*Report*, 38; Slovakia also operates a 20% minority settlement rule for road signs— *Report*, 24; Ukraine appears to require a majority in a locality of members of a national minority—*Report*, 26; UK rules are generally permissive and devolve to local bodies (in Northern Ireland, adding a language implicates the agreement of 'the occupiers of a street')—*Report*, 37.

[109] Among reporting States, Denmark uniquely raises the issue of road safety for bilingual signs; *Report*, 37.

Article 12 provides that parties 'shall, where appropriate, take measures in the fields of education and research to foster knowledge of the culture, history, language and religion of their national minorities and of the majority'. This is the Framework Convention's account of 'intercultural education'. Analogous provisions are found in the human rights canon.[110] The aim, in the words of the *Explanatory Report* is to 'create a climate of tolerance and dialogue'.[111] Provisions on intercultural education require balancing with provisions to strengthen the minority's sense of itself. Accordingly, the Convention makes provision in Article 13 for the setting up private educational establishments, and learning minority languages—Article 14. Apart from the general right 'to learn his or her minority language',[112] the parties shall endeavour to ensure, in minority 'areas' and within the framework of their education systems, that minorities 'have adequate opportunities for being taught the minority language or for receiving instruction in this language', without prejudice to learning or teaching in the official language.[113]

The education provisions look tentative and ambiguous. The draconian statement in Article 13.2. that the right to set up private institutions 'shall not entail any financial obligation' for the parties may be incorrect for many practical situations. As the *Explanatory Report* notes in respect of para. 1, the principle of nondiscrimination enters the equation when considering minority education.[114] It can be argued that, in conformity with this principle, when States subsidise the education of some groups, they would be obliged to consider subsidising others.[115] The wording of the language learning provisions appears to visualise (a) being taught the minority language as any language; or (b) being taught through the medium of the minority language'. In which case, like its equivalent in the UNDM, it is inexpertly drafted, since the provision for learning through the minority language comes across as a vague injunction concerning 'instruction'. Assuming that alternatives (a) and (b) are indicated, there appears to be no obligation to support education through the medium of a minority language. The *Explanatory Report* observes in para-

---

[110] See, for example: Article 4 of the UNDM, paragraph 34 of the OSCE Copenhagen Document, and Articles 27 and 31 of ILO Convention No. 169 on Indigenous and Tribal Peoples.

[111] Paragraph 71.

[112] Article 14.1.

[113] Article 14.2. and 14.3. The *Explanatory Report* (paragraph 78) observes that 'knowledge of the official language is a factor of social cohesion and integration'.

[114] Paragraph 72. For recent experience of the UN Human Rights Committee, see *Waldman v.Canada*, UN Doc. CCPR/C/67/D/694/1996, Views of the Committee on 3 November 1999; and *Tadman et al. v. Canada*, UN Doc. CCPR/C/67/D/816/1998, Views of the Committee on 29 October 1999.

[115] Here, the Hague Recommendations make two pertinent points: (i) the setting up of private schools should not be inhibited by unduly burdensome regulations (Recommendation 9); (ii) minority education institutions (or promoters) are entitled to seek funding from the State or elsewhere (Recommendation 10). A number of States report that they subsidise private minority education—Czech Republic, *Report*, 35-36; Denmark, *Report*, 40; Hungary, *Report*, 120-22; Slovakia, *Report*, 29; UK, *Report*, 32. For a broad review, see: *Report on the Linguistic Rights of Persons belonging to National Minorities in the OSCE Area* (1999) The Hague: OSCE High Commissioner on National Minorities.

graph 77 that there is nothing to prevent a State from implementing (a) and (b), perhaps through the medium of bilingual instruction.[116]

The assumption of the Convention seems to be that minority and official languages stand opposed; that capabilities in one diminish the standards of the other. The Hague Recommendations attempt to countermand this perception by suggesting a scheme whereby being comfortable in the minority language leads to confidence in mastering the State language. The Hague approach is partly grounded in an interpretation of the Framework Convention, but reaches out to 'relevant international norms' interpreted in the light of educational research.[117] The Framework Convention makes no comment on levels of education. Nor does it comment on the drafting of curricula which particularly concern minorities—including the general curriculum to the extent that minority cultures are 'represented' therein. However, the participation provisions of Article 15 suggest, de minimis, that minorities should have input into curricula, making education more responsive to their interests and concerns.

In minority affairs, education issues are often delicately balanced between integration and separation.[118] If integration is pushed too far, the result is assimilation and the disappearance of the minority as a distinct culture; a policy of separation, on the other hand, can lead to a ghetto culture of withdrawal from society.[119] Education is a powerful instrument for the achievement of social engineering. The Convention suggests ways and means through which a balance is to be achieved between the 'separate domain' reserved to the flourishing of minority culture, and the 'common domain' of shared rights and responsibilities.[120] The Convention's premises are that identity is shaped through interaction with others and that identity is multiple or hybrid:[121] that each person may be touched by a

---

[116] The fact that there is a general provision on language learning in paragraph 1 of Article 14 suggests that the provisions in paragraphs 2 and 3 of that article, which are restricted to minority 'areas', must add something significant to the 'basic right' in paragraph 1. This should mean the right to have education (instruction) through the medium of the minority language, subject to the conditions in paragraphs 2 and 3. We may call this the strong conclusion. The distinction between paragraphs cannot imply, as the Report appears to suggest (paragraph 74), that the State under paragraph 1 is in effect obliged to nothing. The Report does not draw the strong conclusion in respect of paragraphs 2 and 3.

[117] Hague Recommendations 11-18 and Explanatory Report.

[118] N. Dimitrov (1999) The Framework Convention, Skopje and Melbourne: Matica Makedonska, pp. 173.

[119] The anxieties of governments—and the need for balance—are reflected in the Romanian Law on Education (1995, as amended in 1995), Article 12 (2) of which provides that the 'organisation and content of education shall not be structured according to exclusivist and discriminatory criteria of an ideological, political, religious or ethnic nature ...'. Such provisions can result in the disablement of institutions of minority education. Accordingly, the provision (necessarily) adds that 'Educational units and institutions established for religious or linguistic reasons in which education is provided in accordance with the choice of pupils' parents or legal guardians shall not be regarded as structured according to exclusivist or discriminatory criteria'—Initial Report, 42.

[120] A. Eide (1993) Possible Ways and Means of Facilitating the Peaceful and Constructive Solution of Problems involving Minorities, UN Doc. E/CN.4/Sub.2/1993/34, section II.

[121] C. Taylor (1991) The Ethics of Authenticity, Cambridge, MA and London: Harvard University Press.

complex of influences, from family to neighbourhood, through ethnic group, religion and the wider society of the State—as well as the cosmopolitan ideals of human rights.[122] The education (and other) provisions should be seen as opening up possibilities of individual self-authorship in conjunction with community survival and the aspirations of States to a coherent and functioning democratic polity.

v) Obligations of Minorities
While it does not elaborate a special principle to promote the 'loyalty' of minority members to their 'host-State', the Convention approaches the question of 'duties' in Article 20:

> In the exercise of the rights and freedoms … in the present Framework Convention, any person belonging to a national minority shall respect the national legislation and the rights of others, in particular those of persons belonging to the majority or to other national minorities.

The loyalty of minorities has not been an explicit demand of international human rights law.[123] Duties are expressed in general phrases in the Universal Declaration of Human Rights—Article 29 of which states that 'everyone has duties to the community', and in general citizenship legislation. Loyalty-type provisions tend to 'appear' in instruments on minority rights because of sensitivities about self-determination, secession, etc., despite the often separation of the issues in international discourse.[124] While no objection may be taken to members of minorities respecting the rights of others, respect for 'national legislation' as a treaty demand raises questions. What if the national legislation does not respect the rights of members of minorities? Are minorities placed under an obligation to 'respect' when others are not? The rights in the Convention are in no sense 'conditional' on respecting the 'national legislation'.

The *Explanatory Report* offers limited guidance to the application of the provision, noting that 'this reference to national legislation clearly does not entitle Parties to ignore the provisions of the … Convention'.[125] Thus far, few States have reported explicitly on Article 20, which perhaps indicates that they do not perceive any pressing problems. For example, Ukraine reports that its 'citizens of all nationalities … are obliged to observe the Constitution and laws of Ukraine, to defend its State sovereignty and territorial integrity, to respect languages, cultures, traditions, customs, religious originality of the Ukrainian people and all national minorities'[126] a provision not directed specifically at minorities.

---

[122] Cf. Article 26 (2) of the Universal Declaration of Human Rights: 'Education shall be directed to the full development of the human personality and to the strengthening of respect for human rights and fundamental freedoms. It shall promote tolerance and friendship among all nations, racial or religious groups ….'

[123] For an appreciation of the issues, see various references in J. Jackson Preece (1998) *National Minorities and the European Nation-States System*, Oxford: Clarendon Press.

[124] See, for example, the opening paragraphs of General Comment 23 of the Human Rights Committee, *supra,*.

[125] Paragraph 89.

[126] *Initial Report,* 35.

vi) Implementation[127]

The Convention sketches an outline of an implementation mechanism.[128] Article 25.1. provides that, within one year from the Convention coming into force for the Contracting Party, State reports are to be transmitted to the Secretary-General of the Council of Europe, who will transmit them to the Committee of Ministers (COM). Further information of relevance to the implementation of the Convention will be transmitted 'on a periodical basis' and 'whenever the Committee of Ministers so requests'.[129] The COM is assisted by an Advisory Committee (AC), 'the members of which shall have recognised expertise in the field of protection of national minorities'.[130] *Ex facie*, the supervision of the Convention is entrusted to the political wisdom of the COM, with the AC playing a subordinate role. These heavily criticised arrangements were developed in less ostensibly political directions through a set of rules adopted by the COM in 1997 on the basis of preparatory work by an ad hoc committee (CAHMEC) with a significant input from the Parliamentary Assembly and expert opinion. While the rules augment the transparency and impartiality of the mechanism, its 'success' will be assessed on the basis of its eventual 'track record'.

Essential points in the rules concern publicity and NGO input. The provisions on publicity for reports state that they can be made public on receipt by the Secretary-General of the Council of Europe and that opinions of the AC can be made public at the same time as recommendations of the Committee of Ministers. According to the provisions for consultation with NGOs—the AC may *receive* information from other sources than state reports, and can *invite* information from other sources unless 'otherwise directed' by the COM; however, the AC must obtain a specific mandate if it wishes to *hold meetings* with other sources for purposes of ascertaining information.[131] Additionally, the AC can call on the COM to mandate an ad hoc report, and be involved in monitoring 'follow-up' to the conclusions and recommendations as instructed by the COM. The rules also gave the Advisory Committee the responsibility of drawing up its own rules of procedure[132] these were adopted by the Committee in October 1998.[133] The AC may seek the assistance of outside experts and consultants, and co-operate, etc., with other Council of Europe bodies. The AC is to be kept aware of cases of non-submission of reports, and can propose measures. Outlines for reports have been adopted by the Committee of Ministers;[134] the Advisory Committee emphasises that these are for initial reports only.[135]

---

[127] For a review of the initial working of the Convention mechanism, consult the *First Activity Report of the Advisory Committee, 1 June 1998-31 May 1999*, ACFC/INF (99) 1def., 15 September 1999.

[128] The Convention and associated documents are brought together in *Framework Convention for the Protection of National Minorities: Collected Texts* (1999) Strasbourg: Council of Europe Publishing.

[129] Article 25.2.

[130] Article 26.1.

[131] Rule 32. Such meetings shall be held in closed session.

[132] Rule 37.

[133] *Collected Texts*, 64-71.

[134] 642ND meeting of Ministers' Deputies, 30 September 1998.

[135] *First Activity Report*, paragraph 11.

The first year of operation of the Advisory Committee saw the setting up of various procedures and processes. In general, the Committee observes that in almost all cases, additional information has been sought from the country concerned—data which mainly relates to the application of norms in practice.[136] In-country meetings have been held.[137] The Committee argues the usefulness of involving NGOs and minority groups in processes leading to State reports, and decided that contacts with independent sources should be a regular feature of its work. Information is sought from nongovernmental sources as well as official reports, and meetings have been held with concerned groups.[138] The Committee of Ministers is not informed on every occasion about NGO contacts; instead a 'blanket' notification to the Committee of Ministers covers the monitoring cycle. 'Parallel' reports from various NGOs have been submitted to the Advisory Committee.[139] Initially at least, and in the interests of consistency, the Committee decided to group together a set of opinions on the country reports, rather than submit separate single opinions.[140] The President of the Advisory Committee has argued that the Committee is under-resourced: a Secretariat of three administrators 'is clearly inadequate and needs to be augmented as a matter of urgency'.[141] He issued the following warning:

'The recent events in Kosovo and elsewhere demonstrate all too clearly the high costs that result from ignoring minority protection. If we do not provide consistent, vigorous monitoring, a human rights problem may develop into a full-blown crisis, and by then it is already too late for the monitoring mechanism … to intervene effectively'.

Minority Rights: An Unfinished Story

The above sketch of minority rights is limited in scope. It has not been possible to say enough about the abiding importance of nondiscrimination as an essential first step in protecting minorities. Many practical problems of minority rights can be 'solved' (in a technical sense) by the application of non-discrimination without more. But there are cases where groups ask for explicit 'recognition' in law and practice, for sensitivity to their voices, and opportunities to promote their character and culture—not merely to be tolerated by others. These demands and desiderata are the stuff of minority rights instruments, symbols of that recognition and care. In a longer work, the relationship between minorities and genocide would be a subject of concern, and the relevance of basic freedoms for all, and of democracy. The reader may also wish to know more about the relationship between minorities and indigenous peoples, and the adaptation of principle that

---

[136] *First Activity Report*, paragraph 17.

[137] *Ibid.*, paragraphs 19-20—in Finland, Hungary and Slovakia.

[138] *Ibid.*, paragraph 20.

[139] Speech by the President of the Advisory Committee, Prof. R. Hoffman, to the Committee on Legal Affairs and Human Rights of the Parliamentary Assembly of the Council of Europe, 6 April 2000..

[140] *Activity Report*, paragraph 21.

[141] Hoffman speech.

being indigenous requires, in Europe as elsewhere.[142] The boundaries of any outline of minority rights are contestable. Whether we take it from the angle of lightening oppression or domination of groups, or their right to self-gathering and self-development, the range of human rights which potentially affect minorities is indeterminate.

Despite the range of possibilities, contemporary minority rights texts are broadly similar (a 'family of resemblances'), and work with a limited palette. The texts are very general, addressing the complex taxonomies of minorities with norms of general guidance. They focus on definition, existence and membership in only slightly different ways, while the absence of common definitions is noticeable. There are indeed definitions: 'scientific' and 'official',[143] but the major instruments avoid them. A possible reason is that governments may be tempted to define narrowly, as if they are not convinced about pluralism, and can more easily manage (or think they can) a 'homogeneous' nation, even if it is only homogeneous in their ideology. Definitions abound at the domestic and community levels. Their absence at the level of international law is partly accounted for by the nature of the system, which remains essentially dynamic and fluid, allowing for development, change and adaptation. Another reason is something to do with people having the capacity to define themselves, to say who they are as persons and collectives. The legal point is that all definitions are open to international scrutiny, and that the 'resolution' of a definition puzzle is conceived as a dialogic exercise. It is also the case that, while self-identification as a private exercise is unassailable, when it engages the responsibilities and resources of the State, the latter is also entitled to a view.

The instruments suggest reflection on individual and collective rights. The question exercises the Liberals, Communitarians, and the rest of the motley crew. 'Differentiated' texts of minority rights employ the formula of individual rights collectively exercised, making it clear that the rights belong to persons. *Ex facie*, they do not deal with group rights in the corporate sense. There are three basic reasons. The first is that the corporate conception challenges State monopoly on power and loyalty, purporting to create an 'entity' with a legal and moral existence, capable of reaching international law directly over the heads of governments. The second is self-determination: it is sensed that reifying the group will contribute to the intensification of its potential for separatism. This also affects perceptions of the legitimacy of autonomy—applauded but not mandated by interna-

---

[142] The present author is in the course of writing a book on '*International Law and Indigenous Rights*' to be published by Manchester University Press in 2001. European indigenous peoples include the Sami of Fennoscandia and Russia. There are many more such groups, particularly in the area of the former USSR.

[143] The most famous is by Capotorti, who defined a minority for the purposes of Article 27 of the ICCPR as: 'A group numerically inferior to the rest of the population of a State, in a non-dominant position, whose members—being nationals of the State—possess ethnic, religious or linguistic characteristics differing from those of the rest of the population and show, if only implicitly, a sense of solidarity, directed towards preserving their culture, traditions, religion or language'—*Study on the Rights of Persons Belonging to ... Minorities* (1991) (New York: United Nations, paragraph 568. The UN Human Rights Committee has not accepted the need for members of a minority to be nationals of the State in order to claim Article 27 rights—General Comment 23, *supra*.

tional law.[144] The third is cultural—the literature is full on 'cultural relativism', often and unfairly carrying the assumption that minorities are peculiarly oppressive of women, dissidents, etc. All this washes over minority rights with insinuations of inadmissible practices. There is even a literature on 'the minority within the minority'—a much theorised oppression, as if no government ever oppressed its people.[145]

The formal absence of group rights does not mean that the group goes unregarded. In cases on Article 27 of the ICCPR, the Human Rights Committee has attempted to balance questions of group survival against individual choice. The shade of group rights haunts the text; efforts to exorcise it look doomed to fail. Dealing with minority rights through relentless insistence that they are rights not of minorities but of persons belonging to minorities has its limitations. Other instruments are bolder: UNESCO declares that cultures have a value; treaties and declarations on indigenous peoples address indigenous peoples as holders of rights.

A further point is that minority rights—with difficulty—have penetrated the public realm. The texts are at their most grudging when minority language meets the government office, when minorities challenge for resources, when they claim participation in decision-making, when they claim to mark the landscape with their names and their history. On the other hand, to 'privatise' minority rights would be the end. The texts have made small moves in the direction of pluralising the public domain so that it comes to represent the social and cultural pluralism of the people. Minority rights are anti-totalitarian, and against mega-projects of social or other engineering unless the ethnic dimension is seriously addressed, or just against mega-projects. The stress on participation skirts the notion of deliberative democracy, listening to subaltern voices tell the story of the nation.

While in the nature of things, minorities may have more need of the world's attention than the comfortable, the world's oppression is not unique to minorities. Derrida paints a dramatic picture:

> Never have violence, inequality, exclusion, famine, and ... economic oppression affected as many human beings in the history of the earth and humanity ... let us never neglect this macroscopic fact, made up of innumerable singular sites of suffering: no degree of progress allows one to ignore that never before, in absolute figures, have so many men, women and children been subjugated, starved or exterminated.[146]

In this theatre of cruelty, the provisions of minority rights instruments can appear 'light', frothy, superficial, dealing with superstructural questions of culture and language. Derrida's macroscopic drama can be set alongside Eagleton who writes that:

---

[144] Cf. M. Suksi (ed.) (1998) *Autonomy: Applications and Implications*, The Hague: Kluwer.

[145] Among many contributions, see: L. Green (1994) 'Internal Minorities and their Rights', in: J. Baker (ed.), *Group Rights*, Toronto, Buffalo, London: Toronto University Press, pp. 100-17.

[146] J. Derrida (P. Kamuf, trans.) (1994) *Specters of Marx*, p. 85, cited in: S. Marks (1997) 'The End of History? Reflections on Some International Legal Theses', 3 *E.J.I.L.*, 449-77, at 457.

Culture is not only what we live by. It is also, in great measure, what we live for. Affection, relationship, memory, kinship, place, community, emotional fulfilment, intellectual enjoyment, a sense of ultimate meaning.[147]

There is also the point that ethnicity may not be 'light' to others. Ethnicity and the perception of 'otherness' are distinctive bases of oppression and underprivilege. Poverty results from cultural disintegration. Subordinate groups need cultural confidence. The Roma are only one such case. Cultural self-determination, in negotiation with the norms of the broader community, is a mode of resistance to the narratives and stereotyping of others and of engaging their respect. We should nevertheless be cautious about overvaluing those like 'ourselves'—Eagleton again:

Yet culture can also be too close for comfort. This very intimacy is likely to grow morbid and obsessional unless it is set in an enlightened political context, one which can temper these intimacies with more abstract, but also in a way more generous, affiliations.[148]

It may be that in time the intensity of contemporary focus on minority rights will lessen. If the forces of nation-building and other totalising ideologies are weaker, then hitherto oppressed cultures will flourish again. Forms of domination vary, and the role of States is ambivalent. If threats to minorities emanate from the State, minority groups and a supportive civil society will appeal and resist. If threats emanate from transnational corporations, the continuing support of the State is vital. In the working through of international standards on minority rights, governments have modified their behaviour, if somewhat unevenly: the glass is half-empty and half-full. Identity politics is not the only politics, is more than merely reactive, and looks set to endure. Identities are strategic, but also primordial: the paradigm of the self-inventing cosmopolitan does not address the sheer quiddity of things, the burden of materiality that presses the lives of many people.

Rights talk is not the only avenue for cultural groups. Rights are necessary now, but can be confrontational, egotistic, a kind of *Kulturkampf*. Other languages—duty, *agape*, virtue—may eventually come to illuminate the politics. The 'communitarians' already speak of the need for a Copernican turn to duties; the religious concur. Education is a key, including 'education of the sentiments'.[149] But it seems that the language of human rights will not easily be discounted. It is effectively the only transnational language for the negotiation of values that we possess. Even in a distorted, imperfect way, a spectrum of nations or 'civilisations' has already contributed to its development. If 'rights' are to continue to hold emotional sway, it is salutary to remember from where they came: from the sense of right not as weapons but as rightness, right ordering, just states of being. If it is to this justice that we aspire, minority rights are a means to that end, not the end in itself.

---

[147] T. Eagleton (2000) *The Idea of Culture*, Oxford: Blackwell Publishers, pp. 131.
[148] *Ibid.*
[149] Rorty, *supra*, n. 4.

Further reading

Benoit-Romer, F. (1996) *The Minority Question in Europe: Texts and Commentary,* Strasbourg: Council of Europe Publishing.

Biscoe, A. (1999) 'The European Union and Minority Nations', in: P. Cumper and S. Wheatley (eds.) *Minority Rights in the 'New Europe',* The Hague: Martinus Nijhoff Publishers.

Estebanez, M. Amor Martin (1996) *International Organizations and Minority Protection in Europe,* Turko/Abo: Abo Akademi University.

Kymlicka, W. (ed.) (1995) *The Rights of Minority Cultures,* Oxford: Oxford University Press.

Spiliopoulou-Akermark, A. (1997) *Justifications of Minority Protection in International Law*, Uppsala: Iustus Forlag.

Appendix A
Framework Convention for the Protection
of National Minorities

Adopted by the Committee of Ministers of the Council of Europe on 10 November 1994. It was opened for signature on 1 February 1995.

See: http://www.dhdirhr.coe.fr/Minorities/index.htm

The member States of the Council of Europe and the other States, signatories to the present framework Convention,

Considering that the aim of the Council of Europe is to achieve greater unity between its members for the purpose of safeguarding and realising the ideals and principles which are their common heritage,

Considering that one of the methods by which that aim is to be pursued is the maintenance and further realisation of human rights and fundamental freedoms;

Wishing to follow-up the Declaration of the Heads of State and Government of the member States of the Council of Europe adopted in Vienna on 9 October 1993;

Being resolved to protect within their respective territories the existence of national minorities;

Considering that the upheavals of European history have shown that the protection of national minorities is essential to stability, democratic security and peace in this continent;

Considering that a pluralist and genuinely democratic society should not only respect the ethnic, cultural, linguistic and religious identity of each person belonging to a national minority, but also create appropriate conditions enabling them to express, preserve and develop this identity;

Considering that the creation of a climate of tolerance and dialogue is necessary to enable cultural diversity to be a source and a factor, not of division, but of enrichment for each society;

Considering that the realisation of a tolerant and prosperous Europe does not depend solely on co-operation between States but also requires transfrontier co-operation between local and regional authorities without prejudice to the constitution and territorial integrity of each State;

Having regard to the Convention for the Protection of Human Rights and Fundamental Freedoms and the Protocols thereto;

Having regard to the commitments concerning the protection of national minorities in United Nations conventions and declarations and in the documents of the Conference on Security and Co-operation in Europe, particularly the Copenhagen Document of 29 June 1990;

Being resolved to define the principles to be respected and the obligations which flow from them, in order to ensure, in the member States and such other States as may become Parties to the present instrument, the effective protection of national minorities and of the rights and freedoms of persons belonging to those minorities, within the rule of law, respecting the territorial integrity and national sovereignty of states;

Being determined to implement the principles set out in this framework Convention through national legislation and appropriate governmental policies;

Have agreed as follows:

Section I

Article 1

The protection of national minorities and of the rights and freedoms of persons belonging to those minorities forms an integral part of the international protection of human rights, and as such falls within the scope of international co-operation.

Article 2

The provisions of this framework Convention shall be applied in good faith, in a spirit of understanding and tolerance and in conformity with the principles of good neighbourliness, friendly relations and co-operation between States.

Article 3

1. Every person belonging to a national minority shall have the right freely to choose to be treated or not to be treated as such and no disadvantage shall result from this choice or from the exercise of the rights which are connected to that choice.

2. Persons belonging to national minorities may exercise the rights and enjoy the freedoms flowing from the principles enshrined in the present framework Convention individually as well as in community with others.

Section II

Article 4

1. The Parties undertake to guarantee to persons belonging to national minorities the right of equality before the law and of equal protection of the law. In this respect, any discrimination based on belonging to a national minority shall be prohibited.

2. The Parties undertake to adopt, where necessary, adequate measures in order to promote, in all areas of economic, social, political and cultural life, full and effective equality between persons belonging to a national minority and those belonging to the majority. In this respect, they shall take due account of the specific conditions of the persons belonging to national minorities.

3. The measures adopted in accordance with paragraph 2 shall not be considered to be an act of discrimination.

Article 5

1. The Parties undertake to promote the conditions necessary for persons belonging to national minorities to maintain and develop their culture, and to preserve the essential elements of their identity, namely their religion, language, traditions and cultural heritage.

2. Without prejudice to measures taken in pursuance of their general integration policy, the Parties shall refrain from policies or practices aimed at assimilation of persons belonging to national minorities against their will and shall protect these persons from any action aimed at such assimilation.

Article 6

1. The Parties shall encourage a spirit of tolerance and intercultural dialogue and take effective measures to promote mutual respect and understanding and co-operation among all persons living on their territory, irrespective of those persons' ethnic, cultural, linguistic or religious identity, in particular in the fields of education, culture and the media.

2. The Parties undertake to take appropriate measures to protect persons who may be subject to threats or acts of discrimination, hostility or violence as a result of their ethnic, cultural, linguistic or religious identity.

Article 7

The Parties shall ensure respect for the right of every person belonging to a national minority to freedom of peaceful assembly, freedom of association, freedom of expression, and freedom of thought, conscience and religion.

Article 8

The Parties undertake to recognise that every person belonging to a national minority has the right to manifest his or her religion or belief and to establish religious institutions, organisations and associations.

Article 9

1. The Parties undertake to recognise that the right to freedom of expression of every person belonging to a national minority includes freedom to hold opinions and to receive and impart information and ideas in the minority language, without interference by public authorities and regardless of frontiers. The Parties shall ensure, within the framework of their legal systems, that persons belonging to a national minority are not discriminated against in their access to the media.

2. Paragraph 1 shall not prevent Parties from requiring the licensing, without discrimination and based on objective criteria, of sound radio and television broadcasting, or cinema enterprises.

3. The Parties shall not hinder the creation and the use of printed media by persons belonging to national minorities. In the legal framework of sound radio and television broadcasting, they shall ensure, as far as possible, and taking into account the provisions of paragraph 1, that persons belonging to national minorities are granted the possibility of creating and using their own media.

4. In the framework of their legal systems, the Parties shall adopt adequate measures in order to facilitate access to the media for persons belonging to national minorities and in order to promote tolerance and permit cultural pluralism.

Article 10

1. The Parties undertake to recognise that every person belonging to a national minority has the right to use freely and without interference his or her minority language, in private and in public, orally and in writing.

2. In areas inhabited by persons belonging to national minorities traditionally or in substantial numbers, if those persons so request and where such a request corresponds to a real need, the Parties shall endeavour to ensure, as far as possible, the conditions which would make it possible to use the minority language in relations between those persons and the administrative authorities.

3. The Parties undertake to guarantee the right of every person belonging to a national minority to be informed promptly, in a language which he or she understands, of the reasons for his or her arrest, and of the nature and cause of any accusation against him or her, and to defend himself or herself in this language, if necessary with the free assistance of an interpreter.

Article 11

1. The Parties undertake to recognise that every person belonging to a national minority has the right to use his or her surname (patronym) and first names in the minority language and the right to official recognition of them, according to modalities provided for in their legal system.

2. The Parties undertake to recognise that every person belonging to a national minority has the right to display in his or her minority language signs, inscriptions and other information of a private nature visible to the public.

3. In areas traditionally inhabited by substantial numbers of persons belonging to a national minority, the Parties shall endeavour, in the framework of their legal system, including, where appropriate, agreements with other States, and taking into account their specific conditions, to display traditional local names, street names and other topographical indications intended for the public also in the minority language when there is a sufficient demand for such indications.

Article 12

1. The Parties shall, where appropriate, take measures in the fields of education and research to foster knowledge of the culture, history, language and religion of their national minorities and of the majority.

2. In this context the Parties shall inter alia provide adequate opportunities for teacher training and access to textbooks, and facilitate contacts among students and teachers of different communities.

3. The Parties undertake to promote equal opportunities for access to education at all levels for persons belonging to national minorities.

Article 13

1. Within the framework of their education systems, the Parties shall recognise that persons belonging to a national minority have the right to set up and to manage their own private educational and training establishments.

2. The exercise of this right shall not entail any financial obligation for the Parties.

Article 14

1. The Parties undertake to recognise that every person belonging to a national minority has the right to learn his or her minority language.

2. In areas inhabited by persons belonging to national minorities traditionally or in substantial numbers, if there is sufficient demand, the Parties shall endeavour to ensure, as far as possible and within the framework of their education systems, that persons belonging to those minorities have adequate opportunities for being taught the minority language or for receiving instruction in this language.

3. Paragraph 2 of this article shall be implemented without prejudice to the learning of the official language or the teaching in this language.

Article 15

The Parties shall create the conditions necessary for the effective participation of persons belonging to national minorities in cultural, social and economic life and in public affairs, in particular those affecting them.

Article 16

The Parties shall refrain from measures which alter the proportions of the population in areas inhabited by persons belonging to national minorities and are aimed at restricting the rights and freedoms flowing from the principles enshrined in the present framework Convention.

Article 17

1. The Parties undertake not to interfere with the right of persons belonging to national minorities to establish and maintain free and peaceful contacts across frontiers with persons lawfully staying in other States, in particular those with whom they share an ethnic, cultural, linguistic or religious identity, or a common cultural heritage.

2. The Parties undertake not to interfere with the right of persons belonging to national minorities to participate in the activities of non-governmental organisations, both at the national and international levels.

Article 18

1. The Parties shall endeavour to conclude, where necessary, bilateral and multilateral agreements with other States, in particular neighbouring States, in order to ensure the protection of persons belonging to the national minorities concerned.

2. Where relevant, the Parties shall take measures to encourage transfrontier co-operation.

Article 19

The Parties undertake to respect and implement the principles enshrined in the present framework Convention making, where necessary, only those limitations, restrictions or derogations which are provided for in international legal instruments, in particular the Convention for the Protection of Human Rights and Fundamental Freedoms, in so far as they are relevant to the rights and freedoms flowing from the said principles.

Section III

Article 20

In the exercise of the rights and freedoms flowing from the principles enshrined in the present framework Convention, any person belonging to a national minority shall respect the national legislation and the rights of others, in particular those of persons belonging to the majority or to other national minorities.

Article 21

Nothing in the present framework Convention shall be interpreted as implying any right to engage in any activity or perform any act contrary to the fundamental principles of international law and in particular of the sovereign equality, territorial integrity and political independence of States.

Article 22

Nothing in the present framework Convention shall be construed as limiting or derogating from any of the human rights and fundamental freedoms which may be ensured under the laws of any Contracting Party or under any other agreement to which it is a Party.

Article 23

The rights and freedoms flowing from the principles enshrined in the present framework Convention, in so far as they are the subject of a corresponding provision in the Convention for the Protection of Human Rights and Fundamental Freedoms or in the Protocols thereto, shall be understood so as to conform to the latter provisions.

Section IV

Article 24

1. The Committee of Ministers of the Council of Europe shall monitor the implementation of this framework Convention by the Contracting Parties.

2. The Parties which are not members of the Council of Europe shall participate in the implementation mechanism, according to modalities to be determined.

Article 25

1. Within a period of one year following the entry into force of this framework Convention in respect of a Contracting Party, the latter shall transmit to the Secretary General of the Council of Europe full information on the legislative and other measures taken to give effect to the principles set out in this framework Convention.

2. Thereafter, each Party shall transmit to the Secretary General on a periodical basis and whenever the Committee of Ministers so requests any further information of relevance to the implementation of this framework Convention.

3. The Secretary General shall forward to the Committee of Ministers the information transmitted under the terms of this article.

Article 26

1. In evaluating the adequacy of the measures taken by the Parties to give effect to the principles set out in this framework Convention the Committee of Ministers shall be assisted by an advisory committee, the members of which shall have recognised expertise in the field of the protection of national minorities.

2. The composition of this advisory committee and its procedure shall be determined by the Committee of Ministers within a period of one year following the entry into force of this framework Convention.

Section V

Article 27

This framework Convention shall be open for signature by the member States of the Council of Europe. Up until the date when the Convention enters into force, it shall also be open for signature by any other State so invited by the Committee of Ministers. It is subject to ratification, acceptance or approval. Instruments of ratification, acceptance or approval shall be deposited with the Secretary General of the Council of Europe.

Article 28

1. This framework Convention shall enter into force on the first day of the month following the expiration of a period of three months after the date on which twelve member States of the Council of Europe have expressed their consent to be bound by the Convention in accordance with the provisions of Article 27.

2. In respect of any member State which subsequently expresses its consent to be bound by it, the framework Convention shall enter into force on the first day of the month following the expiration of a period of three months after the date of the deposit of the instrument of ratification, acceptance or approval.

Article 29

1. After the entry into force of this framework Convention and after consulting the Contracting States, the Committee of Ministers of the Council of Europe may invite to accede to the Convention, by a decision taken by the majority provided for in Article 20.d of the Statute of the Council of Europe, any non-member State of the Council of Europe which, invited to sign in accordance with the provisions of Article 27, has not yet done so, and any other non-member State.

2. In respect of any acceding State, the framework Convention shall enter into force on the first day of the month following the expiration of a period of three months after the date of the deposit of the instrument of accession with the Secretary General of the Council of Europe.

Article 30

1. Any State may at the time of signature or when depositing its instrument of ratification, acceptance, approval or accession, specify the territory or territories for whose international relations it is responsible to which this framework Convention shall apply.

2. Any State may at any later date, by a declaration addressed to the Secretary General of the Council of Europe, extend the application of this framework Convention to any other territory specified in the declaration. In respect of such territory the framework Convention shall enter into force on the first day of the month following the expiration of a period of three months after the date of receipt of such declaration by the Secretary General.

3. Any declaration made under the two preceding paragraphs may, in respect of any territory specified in such declaration, be withdrawn by a notification addressed to the Secretary General. The withdrawal shall become effective on the first day of the month following the expiration of a period of three months after the date of receipt of such notification by the Secretary General.

Article 31

1. Any Party may at any time denounce this framework Convention by means of a notification addressed to the Secretary General of the Council of Europe.

2. Such denunciation shall become effective on the first day of the month following the expiration of a period of six months after the date of receipt of the notification by the Secretary General.

Article 32

The Secretary General of the Council of Europe shall notify the member States of the Council, other signatory States and any State which has acceded to this framework Convention, of:

a. any signature;

b. the deposit of any instrument of ratification, acceptance, approval or accession;

c. any date of entry into force of this framework Convention in accordance with Articles 28, 29 and 30;

d. any other act, notification or communication relating to this framework Convention.

In witness whereof the undersigned, being duly authorised thereto, have signed this framework Convention. Done at Strasbourg, this 1st day of February 1995, in English and French, both texts being equally authentic, in a single copy which shall be deposited in the archives of the Council of Europe. The Secretary General of the Council of Europe shall transmit certified copies to each member State of the Council of Europe and to any State invited to sign or accede to this framework Convention.

Appendix B
Declaration on the Rights of Persons Belonging to National, Ethnic, Religious or Linguistic Minorities

Adopted by United Nations General Assembly resolution 47/135 of 18 December 1992.

See: http://www.unhcr.ch/html/menu3/b/d_minori.htm

The General Assembly,

Reaffirming that one of the basic aims of the United Nations, as proclaimed in the Charter, is to promote and encourage respect for human rights and for fundamental freedoms for all, without distinction as to race, sex, language or religion,

Reaffirming faith in fundamental human rights, in the dignity and worth of the human person, in the equal rights of men and women and of nations large and small,

Desiring to promote the realization of the principles contained in the Charter, the Universal Declaration of Human Rights, the Convention on the Prevention and Punishment of the Crime of Genocide, the International Convention on the Elimination of All Forms of Racial Discrimination, the International Covenant on Civil and Political Rights, the International Covenant on Economic, Social and Cultural Rights, the Declaration on the Elimination of All Forms of Intolerance and of Discrimination Based on Religion or Belief, and the Convention on the Rights of the Child, as well as other relevant international instruments that have been adopted at the universal or regional level and those concluded between individual States Members of the United Nations,

Inspired by the provisions of article 27 of the International Covenant on Civil and Political Rights concerning the rights of persons belonging to ethnic, religious or linguistic minorities,
Considering that the promotion and protection of the rights of persons belonging to national or ethnic, religious and linguistic minorities contribute to the political and social stability of States in which they live,

Emphasizing that the constant promotion and realization of the rights of persons belonging to national or ethnic, religious and linguistic minorities, as an integral part of the development of society as a whole and within a democratic framework based on the rule of law, would contribute to the strengthening of friendship and cooperation among peoples and States,

Considering that the United Nations has an important role to play regarding the protection of minorities,

Bearing in mind the work done so far within the United Nations system, in particular by the Commission on Human Rights, the Subcommission on Prevention of Discrimination and Protection of Minorities and the bodies established pursuant to the International Covenants on Human Rights and other relevant international human rights instruments in promoting and protecting the rights of persons belonging to national or ethnic, religious and linguistic minorities,

Taking into account the important work which is done by intergovernmental and non-governmental organizations in protecting minorities and in promoting and protecting the rights of persons belonging to national or ethnic, religious and linguistic minorities,

Recognizing the need to ensure even more effective implementation of international human rights instruments with regard to the rights of persons belonging to national or ethnic, religious and linguistic minorities,

Proclaims this Declaration on the Rights of Persons Belonging to National or Ethnic, Religious and Linguistic Minorities:

Article 1

1. States shall protect the existence and the national or ethnic, cultural, religious and linguistic identity of minorities within their respective territories and shall encourage conditions for the promotion of that identity.
2. States shall adopt appropriate legislative and other measures to achieve those ends.

Article 2

1. Persons belonging to national or ethnic, religious and linguistic minorities (hereinafter referred to as persons belonging to minorities) have the right to enjoy their own culture, to profess and practise their own religion, and to use their own language, in private and in public, freely and without interference or any form of discrimination.
2. Persons belonging to minorities have the right to participate effectively in cultural, religious, social, economic and public life.
3. Persons belonging to minorities have the right to participate effectively in decisions on the national and, where appropriate, regional level concerning the minority to which they belong or the regions in which they live, in a manner not incompatible with national legislation.
4. Persons belonging to minorities have the right to establish and maintain their own associations.
5. Persons belonging to minorities have the right to establish and maintain, without any discrimination, free and peaceful contacts with other members of their group and with persons belonging to other minorities, as well as contacts across frontiers with citizens of other States to whom they are related by national or ethnic, religious or linguistic ties.

Article 3

1. Persons belonging to minorities may exercise their rights, including those set forth in the present Declaration, individually as well as in community with other members of their group, without any discrimination.
2. No disadvantage shall result for any person belonging to a minority as the consequence of the exercise or non-exercise of the rights set forth in the present Declaration.

Article 4

1. States shall take measures where required to ensure that persons belonging to minorities may exercise fully and effectively all their human rights and fundamental freedoms without any discrimination and in full equality before the law.
2. States shall take measures to create favourable conditions to enable persons belonging to minorities to express their characteristics and to develop their culture, language, religion, traditions and

customs, except where specific practices are in violation of national law and contrary to international standards.

3. States should take appropriate measures so that, wherever possible, persons belonging to minorities may have adequate opportunities to learn their mother tongue or to have instruction in their mother tongue.

4. States should, where appropriate, take measures in the field of education, in order to encourage knowledge of the history, traditions, language and culture of the minorities existing within their territory. Persons belonging to minorities should have adequate opportunities to gain knowledge of the society as a whole.

5. States should consider appropriate measures so that persons belonging to minorities may participate fully in the economic progress and development in their country.

Article 5

1. National policies and programmes shall be planned and implemented with due regard for the legitimate interests of persons belonging to minorities.

2. Programmes of cooperation and assistance among States should be planned and implemented with due regard for the legitimate interests of persons belonging to minorities.

Article 6

States should cooperate on questions relating to persons belonging to minorities, inter alia, exchanging information and experiences, in order to promote mutual understanding and confidence.

Article 7

States should cooperate in order to promote respect for the rights set forth in the present Declaration.

Article 8

1. Nothing in the present Declaration shall prevent the fulfilment of international obligations of States in relation to persons belonging to minorities. In particular, States shall fulfil in good faith the obligations and commitments they have assumed under international treaties and agreements to which they are parties.

2. The exercise of the rights set forth in the present Declaration shall not prejudice the enjoyment by all persons of universally recognized human rights and fundamental freedoms.

3. Measures taken by States to ensure the effective enjoyment of the rights set forth in the present Declaration shall not prima facie be considered contrary to the principle of equality contained in the Universal Declaration of Human Rights.

4. Nothing in the present Declaration may be construed as permitting any activity contrary to the purposes and principles of the United Nations, including sovereign equality, territorial integrity and political independence of States.

Article 9

The specialized agencies and other organizations of the United Nations system shall contribute to the full realization of the rights and principles set forth in the present Declaration, within their respective fields of competence.

Appendix C
Lund Recommendations on the Effective Participation
of National Minorities in Public Life

Published by the Foundation on Inter-ethnic Relations, a nongovernmental organisation established in 1993 to carry out specialised activities in support of the OSCE High Commissioner on National Minorities in September 1999.

See: http://www.osce.org/hcnm/recommendations

Introduction

In its Helsinki Decisions of July 1992, the Organisation for Security and Co-operation in Europe (OSCE) established the position of High Commissioner on National Minorities to be 'an instrument of conflict prevention at the earliest possible stage'. This mandate was created largely in reaction to the situation in the former Yugoslavia which some feared would be repeated elsewhere in Europe, especially among the countries in transition to democracy, and could undermine the promise of peace and prosperity as envisaged in the Charter of Paris for a New Europe adopted by the Heads of State and Government in November 1990.

On 1 January 1993 Mr. Max van der Stoel took up his duties as the first OSCE High Commissioner on National Minorities (HCNM). Drawing on his considerable personal experience as a former Member of Parliament, Foreign Minister of The Netherlands, Permanent Representative to the United Nations, and long-time human rights advocate, Mr. van der Stoel turned his attention to the many disputes between minorities and central authorities in Europe which had the potential, in his view, to escalate. Acting quietly through diplomatic means, the HCNM has become involved in over a dozen States, including Albania, Croatia, Estonia, Hungary, Kazakhstan, Kyrgyzstan, Latvia, the Former Yugoslav Republic of Macedonia, Romania, Slovakia and Ukraine. His involvement has focused primarily on those situations involving persons belonging to national/ethnic groups who constitute the numerical majority in one State but the numerical minority in another State, thus engaging the interest of governmental authorities in each State and constituting a potential source of inter-State tension if not conflict. Indeed, such tensions have defined much of European history.

In addressing the substance of tensions involving national minorities, the HCNM approaches the issues as an independent, impartial and cooperative actor. While the HCNM is not a supervisory mechanism, he employs the international standards to which each State has agreed as his principal framework of analysis and the foundation of his specific recommendations. In this relation, it is important to recall the commitments undertaken by all OSCE participating States, in particular those of the 1990 Copenhagen Document of the Conference on the Human Dimension which, in Part IV, articulates detailed standards relating to national minorities. All OSCE States are also bound by United Nations obligations relating to human rights, including minority rights, and the great majority of OSCE States are further bound by the standards of the Council of Europe.

Through the course of more than six years of intense activity, the HCNM has identified certain recurrent issues and themes which have become the subject of his attention in a number of States in which he is involved. Among these are issues of minority education and use of minority languages, in particular as matters of great importance for the maintenance and development of the identity of persons belonging to national minorities. With a view to achieving an appropriate and coherent application of relevant minority rights in the OSCE area, the HCNM requested the Foundation on Inter-Ethnic Relations—a nongovernmental organisation established in 1993 to carry out specialised activities in support of the HCNM—to bring together two groups of internationally recognised independent experts to elaborate two sets of recommendations: The Hague Recommendations regarding the Education Rights of National Minorities (1996) and the Oslo Recommendations regarding the Linguistic Rights of National Minorities (1998). Both sets of recommendations have subsequently served as references for policy- and law-makers in a number of States. The recommendations are available (in several languages) from the Foundation on Inter-Ethnic Relations free of charge.

A third recurrent theme which has arisen in a number of situations in which the HCNM has been involved is that of forms of effective participation of national minorities in the governance of States. In order to gain a sense of the views and experiences of OSCE participating States on this issue and to allow States to share their experiences with each other, the HCNM and the OSCE's Office for Democratic Institutions and Human Rights convened a conference of all OSCE States and relevant international organisations entitled 'Governance and Participation: Integrating Diversity', which was hosted by the Swiss Confederation in Locarno from 18 to 20 October 1998. The Chairman's Statement issued at the end of the conference summarised the themes of the meeting and noted the desirability of 'concrete follow-up activities, including the further elaboration of the various concepts and mechanisms of good governance with the effective participation of minorities, leading to integration of diversity within the State'. To this end, the HCNM called upon the Foundation on Inter-Ethnic Relations, in co-operation with the Raoul Wallenberg Institute of Human Rights and Humanitarian Law, to bring together a group of internationally recognised independent experts to elaborate recommendations and outline alternatives, in line with the relevant international standards.

The result of the above initiative is The Lund Recommendations on the Effective Participation of National Minorities in Public Life—named after the Swedish city in which the experts last met and completed the recommendations. Among the experts were jurists specialising in relevant international law, political scientists specialising in constitutional orders and election systems, and sociologists specialising in minority issues. Specifically, under the Chairmanship of the Director of the Raoul Wallenberg Institute, Professor Gudmundur Alfredsson, the experts were:

- · Professor Gudmundur Alfredsson (Icelandic), Director of the Raoul Wallenberg Institute of Human Rights and Humanitarian Law, Lund University;
- · Professor Vernon Bogdanor (British), Professor of Government, Oxford University;
- · Professor Vojin Dimitrijevic (Yugoslavian), Director of the Belgrade Centre for Human Rights;

· Dr. Asbjørn Eide (Norwegian), Senior Fellow at the Norwegian Institute of Human Rights;
· Professor Yash Ghai (Kenyan), Sir YK Pao Professor of Public Law, University of Hong Kong;
· Professor Hurst Hannum (American), Professor of International Law, Fletcher School of Law and Diplomacy, Tufts University;
· Mr. Peter Harris (South African), Senior Executive to the International Institute for Democracy and Electoral Assistance;
· Dr. Hans-Joachim Heintze (German), Director of the Institut für Friedenssicherungsrecht und Humanitäres Völkerrecht, Ruhr-Universität Bochum;
· Professor Ruth Lapidoth (Israeli), Professor of International Law and Chairman of the Academic Committee of the Institute for European Studies, The Hebrew University of Jerusalem;
· Professor Rein Müllerson (Estonian), Chair of International Law, King's College, University of London;
· Dr. Sarlotta Pufflerova (Slovak), Director, Foundation Citizen and Minority/Minority Rights Group;
· Professor Steven Ratner (American), Professor of International Law, University of Texas;
· Dr. Andrew Reynolds (British), Assistant Professor of Government, University of Notre Dame;
· Mr. Miquel Strubell (Spanish and British), Director of the Institute of Catalan Socio-Linguistics, Generalitat de Catalunya;
· Professor Markku Suksi (Finnish), Professor of Public Law, Åbo Akademi University;
· Professor Danilo Türk (Slovene), Professor of International Law, Ljubljana University;
· Dr. Fernand de Varennes (Canadian), Senior Lecturer in Law and Director of the Asia-Pacific Centre for Human Rights and the Prevention of Ethnic Conflict, Murdoch University;
· Professor Roman Wieruszewski (Polish), Director of the Poznan Human Rights Centre, Polish Academy of Sciences.

Insofar as existing standards of minority rights are part of human rights, the starting point of the consultations among the experts was to presume compliance by States with all other human rights obligations including, in particular, freedom from discrimination. It was also presumed that the ultimate object of all human rights is the full and free development of the individual human personality in conditions of equality. Consequently, it was presumed that civil society should be open and fluid and, therefore, integrate all persons, including those belonging to national minorities. Moreover, insofar as the objective of good and democratic governance is to serve the needs and interests of the whole population, it was presumed that all governments seek to ensure the maximum opportunities for contributions from those affected by public decision-making.

The purpose of the Lund Recommendations, like The Hague and Oslo Recommendations before them, is to encourage and facilitate the adoption by States of specific measures to alleviate tensions related to national minorities and thus to serve the ultimate conflict prevention goal of the HCNM. The Lund Recommendations on the Effective Participation of National Minorities in Public Life attempt to clarify in relatively straightforward language and build upon the content of minority rights and other standards generally applicable in the situations in which the HCNM is involved. The standards have been interpreted specifically to ensure the coherence of their application in open and democratic States. The Recommendations are divided into four subheadings which group the twenty-four recommendations into general principles, participation in decision-making, self-governance, and ways of guaranteeing such effective participation in public life. The basic conceptual division within the Lund Recommendations follows two prongs: participation in governance of the State as a whole, and self-governance over certain local or internal affairs. A wide variety of arrangements are possible and known. In several recommendations, alternatives are suggested. All recommendations are to be interpreted in accordance with the General Principles in Part I. A more detailed explanation of each recommendation is provided in an accompanying Explanatory Note wherein express reference to the relevant international standards is found.

I. General Principles

1. Effective participation of national minorities in public life is an essential component of a peaceful and democratic society. Experience in Europe and elsewhere has shown that, in order to promote such participation, governments often need to establish specific arrangements for national minorities. These Recommendations aim to facilitate the inclusion of minorities within the State and enable minorities to maintain their own identity and characteristics, thereby promoting the good governance and integrity of the State.

2. These Recommendations build upon fundamental principles and rules of international law, such as respect for human dignity, equal rights, and nondiscrimination, as they affect the rights of national minorities to participate in public life and to enjoy other political rights. States have a duty to respect internationally recognised human rights and the rule of law, which allow for the full development of civil society in conditions of tolerance, peace and prosperity.

3. When specific institutions are established to ensure the effective participation of minorities in public life, which can include the exercise of authority or responsibility by such institutions, they must respect the human rights of all those affected.

4. Individuals identify themselves in numerous ways in addition to their identity as members of a national minority. The decision as to whether an individual is a member of a minority, the majority or neither rests with that individual and shall not be imposed upon her or him. Moreover, no person shall suffer any disadvantage as a result of such a choice or refusal to choose.

5. When creating institutions and procedures in accordance with these Recommendations, both substance and process are important. Governmental authorities and minorities should pursue an inclusive, transparent and accountable process of consultation in order to maintain a climate of confidence. The State should encourage the public media to foster intercultural understanding and address the concerns of minorities.

II. Participation in Decision-Making

A. Arrangements at the Level of the Central Government

6. States should ensure that opportunities exist for minorities to have an effective voice at the level of the central government, including through special arrangements as necessary. These may include, depending upon the circumstances:

   · special representation of national minorities, for example, through a reserved number of seats in one or both chambers of parliament or in parliamentary committees; and other forms of guaranteed participation in the legislative process;

   · formal or informal understandings for allocating to members of national minorities cabinet positions, seats on the supreme or constitutional court or lower courts, and positions on nominated advisory bodies or other high-level organs;

·   mechanisms to ensure that minority interests are considered within relevant ministries, through, e.g., personnel addressing minority concerns or issuance of standing directives; and

·   special measures for minority participation in the civil service as well as the provision of public services in the language of the national minority.

B. Elections

7. Experience in Europe and elsewhere demonstrates the importance of the electoral process for facilitating the participation of minorities in the political sphere. States shall guarantee the right of persons belonging to national minorities to take part in the conduct of public affairs, including through the rights to vote and stand for office without discrimination.

8. The regulation of the formation and activity of political parties shall comply with the international law principle of freedom of association. This principle includes the freedom to establish political parties based on communal identities as well as those not identified exclusively with the interests of a specific community.

9. The electoral system should facilitate minority representation and influence.

   ·   Where minorities are concentrated territorially, single-member districts may provide sufficient minority representation.

   ·   Proportional representation systems, where a political party's share in the national vote is reflected in its share of the legislative seats, may assist in the representation of minorities.

   ·   Some forms of preference voting, where voters rank candidates in order of choice, may facilitate minority representation and promote inter-communal cooperation.

   ·   Lower numerical thresholds for representation in the legislature may enhance the inclusion of national minorities in governance.

10. The geographic boundaries of electoral districts should facilitate the equitable representation of national minorities.

C. Arrangements at the Regional and Local Levels

11. States should adopt measures to promote participation of national minorities at the regional and local levels such as those mentioned above regarding the level of the central government (paragraphs 6-10) The structures and decision-making processes of regional and local authorities should be made transparent and accessible in order to encourage the participation of minorities.

D. Advisory and Consultative Bodies

12. States should establish advisory or consultative bodies within appropriate institutional frameworks to serve as channels for dialogue between governmental authorities and national minorities. Such bodies might also include special purpose committees for addressing such issues as housing, land, education, language and culture. The composition of such bodies should reflect their purpose and contribute to more effective communication and advancement of minority interests.

13. These bodies should be able to raise issues with decisionmakers, prepare recommendations, formulate legislative and other proposals, monitor developments and provide views on proposed governmental decisions that may directly or indirectly affect minorities. Governmental authorities should consult these bodies regularly regarding minority-related legislation and administrative measures in order to contribute to the satisfaction of minority concerns and to

the building of confidence. The effective functioning of these bodies will require that they have adequate resources.

III. Self-Governance

14. Effective participation of minorities in public life may call for non-territorial or territorial arrangements of self-governance or a combination thereof. States should devote adequate resources to such arrangements.

15. It is essential to the success of such arrangements that governmental authorities and minorities recognize the need for central and uniform decisions in some areas of governance together with the advantages of diversity in others.

   · Functions that are generally exercised by the central authorities include defense, foreign affairs, immigration and customs, macroeconomic policy and monetary affairs.

   · Other functions, such as those identified below, may be managed by minorities or territorial administrations or shared with the central authorities.

   · Functions may be allocated asymmetrically to respond to different minority situations within the same State.

16. Institutions of self-governance, whether non-territorial or territorial, must be based on democratic principles to ensure that they genuinely reflect the views of the affected population.

A. Non-Territorial Arrangements

17. This section addresses non-territorial autonomy—often referred to as 'personal' or 'cultural autonomy'—which is most likely to be useful when a group is geographically dispersed. Such divisions of authority, including control over specific subject-matter, may take place at the level of the State or within territorial arrangements. In all cases, respect for the human rights of others must be assured. Moreover, such arrangements should be assured adequate financial resources to enable performance of their public functions and should result from inclusive processes (see Recommendation 5).

18. This is not an exhaustive list of possible functions. Much will depend upon the situation, including especially the needs and expressed desires of the minority. In different situations, different subjects will be of greater or lesser interest to minorities and decisions in these fields will affect them to varying degrees. Some fields may be shared. One area of special concern for minorities is control over their own names, both for representative institutions and individual members, as provided in Article 11.1 of the Framework Convention. With regard to religion, the Recommendation does not advocate governmental interference in religious matters other than in relation to those powers (e.g. concerning personal civil status) delegated to religious authorities.

   This Recommendation also does not intend that minority institutions should control the media— although persons belonging to minorities should have the possibility to create and use their own media, as guaranteed by Article 9.3 of the Framework Convention. Of course, culture has many aspects extending to fields such as welfare, housing and child care; the State should take into account minority interests in governance in these fields.

B. Territorial Arrangements

19. There is a general trend in European States towards devolution of authority and implementation of the principle of subsidiarity, such that decisions are taken as close as possible to, and by, those most directly concerned and affected. Article 4.3 of the European Charter of Local

Self-Government expresses this objective as follows:

'Public responsibilities shall generally be exercised, in preference, by those authorities which are closest to the citizen. Allocation of responsibility to another authority should weigh up the extent and nature of the task and requirements of efficiency and economy'.

Territorial self-government can help preserve the unity of States while increasing the level of participation and involvement of minorities by giving them a greater role in a level of government that reflects their population concentration. Federations may also accomplish this objective, as may particular autonomy arrangements within unitary States or federations. It is also possible to have mixed administrations. As noted in recommendation 15, arrangements need not be uniform across the State, but may vary according to needs and expressed desires.

20. Autonomous authorities must possess real power to make decisions at the legislative, executive or judicial levels. Authority within the State may be divided among central, regional and local authorities and also among functions. Paragraph 35 of the Copenhagen Document notes the alternatives of 'appropriate local or autonomous administrations corresponding to the specific historical and territorial circumstances'.

This makes clear that there need not be uniformity within the State. Experience shows that powers can be divided even with respect to fields of public authority traditionally exercised by central government, including devolved powers of justice (both substantive and procedural) and powers over traditional economies. At a minimum, affected populations should be systematically involved in the exercise of such authority. At the same time, the central government must retain powers to ensure justice and equality of opportunities across the State.

21. Where powers may be devolved on a territorial basis to improve the effective participation of minorities, these powers must be exercised with due account for the minorities within these jurisdictions. Administrative and executive authorities must be accountable to the whole population of the territory. This follows from paragraph 5.2 of the Copenhagen Document which commits OSCE participating States to assure at all levels and for all persons 'a form of government that is representative in character, in which the executive is accountable to the elected legislature or the electorate'.

IV. Guarantees

A. Constitutional and Legal Safeguards

22. This section addresses the issue of 'entrenchment', that is, solidifying arrangements in law. Very detailed legal arrangements may be useful in some cases, while frameworks may be sufficient in other cases. In all cases, as noted in recommendation 5, arrangements should result from open processes. However, once concluded, stability is required in order to assure some security for those affected, especially persons belonging to national minorities. Articles 2 and 4 of the European Charter of Local Self-Government express a preference for constitutional arrangements. To achieve the desired balance between stability and flexibility, it may be useful to specify some reconsideration at fixed intervals, thereby depoliticizing the process of change in advance and making the review process less adversarial.

23. This Recommendation differs from Recommendation 22 insofar as it encourages the testing of new and innovative regimes, rather than specifying terms for alteration of existing arrangements. Responsible authorities may wish to follow different approaches in different situations among central authorities and minority representatives. Without compromising final positions, such an approach may yield good experiences, not least through the processes of innovation

and implementation.

B. Remedies

24. In paragraph 30 of the Copenhagen Document, OSCE participating States 'recognize that the questions relating to national minorities can only be satisfactorily resolved in a democratic political framework based on the rule of law, with a functioning independent judiciary'. The idea of effective remedies is also provided in Article 2.3 of the International Covenant on Civil and Political Rights, while 'a judicial remedy' is specified in Article 11 of the European Charter of Local Self-Government.

Judicial review can be performed by constitutional courts and, in effect, by relevant international human rights bodies. Non-judicial mechanisms and institutions, such as national commissions, ombudspersons, inter-ethnic or 'race' relations boards, etc., may also play critical roles, as envisaged by paragraph 27 of the Copenhagen Document, Article 14.2 of the International Convention on the Elimination of All Forms of Racial Discrimination, and paragraph 36 of the Vienna Declaration and Programme of Action adopted by the World Conference on Human Rights in 1993.

PART TWO

THE PRACTICE:

STRUCTURES, POLICIES AND MULTI-ETHNIC DYNAMICS

Emerging Multi-ethnic Policies in Bulgaria: A Central – Local Perspective

Elena Gyurova

Contents

EMERGING MULTI-ETHNIC POLICIES IN BULGARIA: A CENTRAL – LOCAL PERSPECTIVE

Elena Gyurova

Abstract

This paper presents the diversity of minority ethnic communities in Bulgaria in the context of their cultural identity, problems, political participation and civil mobilisation. The text is concerned with their treatment by the state, in terms of relevant legislation and policy, and with social attitudes toward them in the post-communist period. This analysis also includes a review of the territorial and administrative division of Bulgaria as the backbone of the central-regional-local relationship in policy implementation. Regional development is being explored as the possible political vehicle for solving the socio-economic problems of minorities by reducing the disproportion between and within the various regions, and improving the quality of life and the expansion of human capabilities. Local services are analysed with reference to the democratic and decentralised management strategies applicable for the integration of minorities in the various areas of local social life: preservation of cultural identity and introducing intercultural dialogue in education, learning the mother tongue, media, employment, social assistance and urban amelioration. Minority representation in municipal councils is also analysed. This paper attempts to find an appropriate balance between the positive developments in the building, preservation and development of minority rights in Bulgaria, and the negative aspects of this process, by looking at what has been left out of the public discourse.

1. Introduction

Most public authorities at the national, regional and local levels face a challenge of managing heterogeneous ethnic communities.[1] Such regional and local communities are typical for the entire territory of Bulgaria.

Events of ten years ago signalled a change in the official Bulgarian policy towards ethnic minorities. Even as its economy contracted, Bulgaria made considerable progress.

---

[1] '...there is no mono-ethnic society', as George Schöpflin states, viewing 'ethnicity as the basic (although not the only one) constructive matrix into which people and societies exist'. George Shöpflin (1998) 'Citizenship, Ethnicity and Cultural Reproduction', Sofia: *Etnoreporter,* No. 1, p. 37.

Local legislation and practices were brought in compliance with international standards and with European regulations enforcing respect for human rights. New opportunities during democratisation and the transition to a market economy encouraged minorities to promote their culture and reinforce their identity; this simultaneously created various problems for these groups. In parallel with the lower socio-economic status of some vulnerable minority communities, differences in language, religion and culture act as a divide among ethnic groups in the civil sphere, preconditioning discriminatory stereotypes and cases of intolerance. A climate of neighbourly relations between the various ethnic communities has not yet crystallised into tolerant civil co-existence, regardless of the positive developments in this respect.

In a multi-ethnic democracy, bringing the various issues to the current agenda and solving them is a process conducted in the daily work of the regional and local authorities; decentralisation logically demands that they administer the policies for minority rights. The implementation of an effective regional and local management of multi-ethnic communities is both a challenge and responsibility for public authorities. Ethnic tolerance must be preserved as a component of the democratic processes occurring in Bulgaria, where 'democracy has to have respect for ethnicity and ethnicity has to comply with democracy'.[2]

2. Ethnic Diversity in Bulgaria

Bulgaria is a European, post-communist country situated on the Balkan Peninsula. Its historical past, geo-strategic situation and cultural legacy shape it as 'the border line' between Christian and Muslim civilisations. There is a diverse multitude of ethno-cultural and religious minorities in the country.[3] Each group has its specific demographic features and a type of territorial localisation and habitation. The process of economic restructuring during the last ten years has had an aggravating impact on the gradual drop in the socio-economic status of the largest minority/religious groups: Turks, Roma and Bulgarian Muslims (Pomaks). This economic feature of the post-communist society in Bulgaria is often expressed as ethnic intolerance impeding a coherent ethno-cultural society. This tension is exacerbated by the lack of sufficient public information on the situation of the various minority groups living within Bulgarian territory.

The latest census in the country, dated December 1992, presents statistical data on the ethnic composition of the population: 85.7% of a total of almost 8.5 million identify themselves as ethnic Bulgarians. Of the remaining 14.3%, the largest groups are Pomaks and Roma.[4] The representatives of the smaller ethnic groups represent a total of 1.3% (94,000

[2] Ibid., p. 39.

[3] See the comprehensive Table 1 in the Annex. For more details, see: Anna Krasteva (ed.) (1998) CDMR.

[4] According to unofficial data of the Ministry of Interior and local authorities, the share of the Roma can amount to 6.5%, while other expert assessments point to a figure of 10% of the entire Bulgarian population. See: Ilona Tomova (1995) *The Gypsies in the Transition Period,* Sofia: ICMSIR, p. 27; Martin Emerson (1999) 'Roma Education in Eastern and Central Europe: Some Personal Reflections', *European Journal of Intercultural Studies,* Vol. 10, No. 2, p. 202.

people). These are mainly Russians, Armenians, Jews, Macedonians, Wallachians, Greeks, Karakachans, Gagaus, Tatars, Cherkes and other Slavs.

The demographic and socio-economic features of the ethnic communities in Bulgaria vary.[5] They are mutually dependent on cultural factors, territorial distribution (compact/dispersed), housing (urban/rural) and local socio-economic effects of structural reform, etc.

The majority Christian community (86%) and the minority Muslim group (13%) are ethnically heterogeneous.[6] Notably, the Pomaks are a substantial religious community who adhere to the Muslim religion and speak Bulgarian. According to experts' estimates, they amount to about 200,000. They live mainly in the rural regions of the Rhodope and Pirin mountains in southern Bulgaria, though a small number live in northeastern Bulgaria. During the last several years this religious community has faced multidirectional and complex processes in establishing its identity.[7]

Economic depression, underdevelopment and establishment of competitive conditions has so far doomed the representatives of the largest minority groups to unemployment. This is exacerbated by the poor education and qualifications, especially for the Roma, among which unemployment rates can reach about 80-90%.[8] Bearing that the unemployment problem in Bulgaria is mainly attributed to the so-called 'skills gap', young and poorly educated individuals, especially the ones belonging to ethnic minorities, are exposed to the highest risk of unemployment.[9]

The deterioration of the socio-economic parameters of vulnerable minority groups (the Roma being the most prominent among these) condemns minorities to poverty and sends them to the bottom of the social stratification scheme.[10] All this influences the character

---

[5] See Table 2 in the Appendix.

[6] For a more comprehensive analysis of the relations between the major religious communities in Bulgaria, see: *Interrelations of Compatibility and Incompatibility between the Christians and Muslims in Bulgaria* (1994) and (1997) Sofia: ICMSIR.

[7] B. Panajotova, K. Bozeva (1994) 'The Religious Community of the Bulgarian Muslims', in: *Minority Groups in Bulgaria in a Human Rights Context*, Sofia: CDMR, pp. 27-32; Tsvetana Georgieva (1998) 'The Pomaks: the Bulgarian Muslims', in: Anna Krasteva (ed.) *Societies and Identities in Bulgaria*, Sofia: Petekston, pp. 286-308; Ilona Tomova (2000) 'Social Change and Ethnoreligious Relations', in: Georgi Fotev (ed.) *Neighbour Relations of Religious Communities in Bulgaria*, Sofia: Institute of Sociology at BAS, pp. 184-185.

[8] ECRI (2000) *State Reports, The Second Report from Bulgaria*, Strasbourg: Council of Europe, p. 18. The reasons for the low educational level of the Roma community are complex and comprise cultural, economic, social, discriminatory and other aspects. Poverty, which is the preventive factor for school attendance by Roma children is reinforced by the low value education for parents. The poor proficiency of Roma children in Bulgarian and discrimination in the classrooms demotivate potential students. Early marriages are another reason for dropping out. The lack of any educational policy adequate to the peculiarities of Roma culture also discourages school attendance by the Roma.

[9] The World Bank (1999) *Bulgaria: Poverty during the Transition, Report No. 18411*, Sofia: World Bank Mission in Bulgaria, pp. 4-5; UNDP (1999) *National Report on Human Development in Bulgaria. Part I. Regional Differences: A Burden or a Chance*, Sofia: UNDP, p. 43.

[10] 'There is a distinct "bottom" in Bulgarian society. It is formed mainly by the older social groups, the ethnic minorities, the unemployed and the inhabitants of the villages and small towns, where

and the quality of life of minorities, their opportunities, and their individual and group strategies for dealing with these problems.

Urbanised minority populations include Jewish, Armenian, Russian and Greek communities. Broader opportunities for development and self-fulfillment in Bulgaria's economic, public, cultural and scientific life are available within urban centres. A high level of education and qualification facilitates their equal and full participation in Bulgarian society. As a whole, they can be said to be well integrated.

Bulgarian Turks and Muslims live mainly in villages and this limits their equal access to social benefits and services. Their young representatives often migrate to urban areas, where they have better chances of finding employment. The emigration of Bulgarian Turks to the Republic of Turkey has advanced at varying rates. At present, however, emigrants are primarily motivated by economic concerns (greater employment opportunities elsewhere), unlike the 'Great Trip' of the 1980s, which was forced upon minorities by the government and threatened the ethno-cultural identity of such minority groups.

Generally, the Turkish and Pomak ethnic communities enjoy functional integration in Bulgarian society. They participate in the political, economic, public, cultural and intellectual life of the country. They also maintain good relations with the majority.

The Roma are often beneficiaries of social support, thus engendering a culture of passive assistance. The long-term high unemployment rate among the Roma is a crime-generating factor that contributes to their further marginalisation. Relative to other groups, the Roma are more frequently physically, economically, socially and psychologically ghettoised, and are the object of effective desocialisation and discrimination practices.

The hardships of the structural economic reform process have resulted in the reinforcement of prejudices against ethno-cultural 'others' and the intensification of ethnocentrism. Regardless of this economic tension, regulatory, institutional and civil initiatives have been undertaken in order to facilitate the harmonisation of ethnic relations.

In conclusion, it can be said that:

·   About one-seventh (15%) of the Bulgarian population belongs to minority communities. The largest minority groups are Bulgarian Turks, Roma and the Pomaks (there is debate as to whether this is a religious or ethnic minority). Smaller ethnic groups constitute about 1.3% of the population of the country.

·   The demographic and socio-economic characteristics of the minority communities vary. Housing, territory and employment are traditionally predetermined and heavily influence their way and quality of life, their survival strategies and individual opportunities.

·   The typical feature of the post-communist situation in Bulgaria is that the transition to a market economy has resulted in a drop in the socio-economic status of vulnerable minority groups, which applies mainly to the Roma.

·   In general, all minority groups are well integrated into Bulgarian society, except for the Roma.

---

unemployment is highest. In terms of education, this group encompasses the more poorly educated people, but qualified workers are steadily making their way into it.' A. Raichev, K. Kolev, A. Bundjolov, L. Dimova (2000) *Social Stratification in Bulgaria,* Sofia: Fridrich Ebert Foundation, Social-Democratic Institute, LIK, p. 29.

3. The Legal, Political and Civic Status of Minorities

The democratic 'revolution' of 1989 marked the beginning of processes, which made necessary the search for legislative, political and civil solutions to new and urgent ethnic minority issues. Promoting the issues and implementing measures to improve inter-ethnic relations in the country has been one of the most dynamic areas of democratic development in Bulgaria for the last ten years.

3.1. The political agenda and minority rights discourse

Bulgaria could not afford to seclude itself from human rights discourse as most post-communist countries in Central and Eastern Europe began their transition to democratic rule. Meanwhile, the inflammation of nationalist conflict in the Federal Republic of Yugoslavia, which resulted in armed conflict along Bulgaria's border, forced Bulgaria's politicians and public to explore flexible political solutions and civil strategies in inter-ethnic relations.

The policy of integrating the country into European institutional structures calls for a decisive improvement of Bulgaria's human rights instruments, mechanisms and practices. Negotiations for equal membership are expected to increase the range and effective enforcement of minority integration measures and improvement of the status quo of vulnerable minority groups, especially the Roma.

Ethno-cultural awareness and civil mobilisation among minority representatives is also a catalyst for the political effort for the re-establishment of ethnic and religious rights. The gradual legislative, political and civil empowerment of minorities has pushed minority rights issues higher on the agenda of social discourse. A further positive development in recent years has been the tendency of public authorities to address nongovernmental organisations (NGOs) on minority issues.

3.2. International legal instruments

In the past ten years, distinct processes have been put into place that provide for legislatively enforced respect for human rights, regardless of the ethnic identity of citizens. These processes are in line with Bulgaria's commitments in the field of international human rights protection.

By signing and ratifying a number of international human rights documents, Bulgaria has become a party to nearly all important UN instruments and to 29 legislative documents of the Council of Europe on human rights.[11] This considerable effort made by the

---

[11] Here are some of the instruments ratified by Bulgaria: The International Covenant on Civil and Political Rights and the First Optional Protocol to it; the International Covenant on Economic, Social and Cultural Rights; the International Convention on the Elimination of all Forms of Racial Discrimination; the Convention on the Rights of the Child; the European Convention for the Protection of Human Rights and Fundamental Freedoms, the First Additional Protocol and

state since 1990 has provided a larger scale of international, regional, legislative standards for civil, political, economic, social and cultural minority rights. The opportunity now exists for individuals to appeal to international human rights institutions.[12]

An important step in the settling of multi-ethnic relations was Bulgaria's ratification of the Framework Convention on the Protection of National Minorities. The Convention was signed by the Bulgarian head of state on 9 October 1997. It was not ratified by Parliament until 18 February 1999. In the interim, various political positions on ethnicity converged. The major issue in the political debate was the question of whether to ratify the Convention 'with' or 'without' an accompanying declaration, and (in the former case) what its content should be. The Consultative Council on National Security at the President's Office decided to ratify the Convention with an accompanying Declaration. Policy in the Balkans demands intensive harmonisation of minority rights with the principles of security, territorial integrity, the sovereignty of the state and the prevention of separatist aspirations. Therefore, political forces agreed to draft an accompanying Declaration to Article 21 of the Framework Convention, which was perceived as a protective mechanism.[13]

Bulgaria's ratification of the Convention is an expression of a more civilised attitude toward minorities and their rights and freedoms, and demonstrates efforts to harmonise Bulgarian laws with European ones. The provisions of this document constitute a serious resource for the actual implementation of minority rights in the country by setting forth mechanisms for the harmonisation of the relations between the majority, minorities and the state. Unfortunately, neither the minorities nor the regional and local authorities have made sufficient use of the opportunities presented by the Convention. The reason for this is insufficient information in public sphere: limited dissemination of the texts of the Convention and the accompanying Declaration, inadequate clarification of the actual subject and meaning of the Convention, and the long and veering political debate, which was poorly covered by the media. Public administrators should read this document and should attempt to translate its legal clauses into practical actions in accordance with the specific ethnic, economic and social conditions of the country, region, city, municipality or village in question.

Protocol No. 6 to it, Declarations to Articles 25 and 46 of the Convention; the European Social Charter—Revised, etc.

[12] There are cases of sanctions by the Court of Europe for violations of the human rights of minority representatives. See: Annual Report for 1998 (1998) Sofia: Human Rights Project (NGO); or 'Human Rights—Enforceable or Only Guaranteed' (2000) *Pari*, No. 4, February.

[13] The text of the accompanying declaration says: 'The ratification and the implementation of the Framework Convention for the Protection of National Minorities shall in no way justify any activities aimed against the territorial integrity and the sovereignty of the integral Bulgarian state, its domestic and international security'. The Convention was ratified by the votes of two-thirds of the MPs. The final congratulation words of the prime minister before the Parliament sound emblematic: 'This Parliament said "yes" to patriotism and "no" to nationalism. In this Parliament there is a European majority of two-thirds'. See: 'The Framework Convention: The Way to Consensus' (1999) *Ethonoreporter*, No. 1, pp. 19-27.

3.3. National legal framework

In the past ten years, a number of legislative acts or amendments and revisions to existing laws have been passed, which influence (directly or indirectly) the problems of ethnic communities and inter-ethnic relations, and reinforce the rights guaranteed by the
Bulgarian Constitution.

3.3.1. Constitutional provisions

The Constitution of the Republic of Bulgaria, which was voted on 12 July 1991, guarantees individual human rights, equality and nondiscrimination on the basis of sex, origin, religion, education, convictions, political affiliation, personal or social status or
property standing (Article 6). Specific rights are democratically provided to citizens,
regardless of their ethnic, religious and linguistic belonging: prohibition of organisations inspiring racial hatred; the right to study one's mother tongue and to develop
one's ethnic culture; freedom of religion; etc. The Bulgarian Constitution does not make
any explicit reference to the term 'national minority'. Statutory provisions (Article 11,
paragraph 4) prohibits political parties established on the basis of ethnic, racial or religious affiliation. This regulation is found to be discriminatory because it restricts the
right to association; it is criticised by both Bulgarian and international human rights
monitors.[14]

3.3.2. Other legal texts

Nonpenal regulations and the provisions of civil and administrative law[15] guarantee national and racial equality, nondiscrimination and anti-xenophobia. The tendency of including anti-discriminatory provisions in revising the existing legislation and passing new laws
seems to be a lasting one. Also, progress is being made with respect to the registration
and profession of minority religions. The question remains, however, as to whether the
rights provided for by the legislation are actually being implemented. In this respect, there
is still some inconsistency between the formulated and the implemented rights for minorities, especially for the groups which are in a more disadvantageous position. Negative
stereotypes and discriminatory attitudes are indeed difficult to overcome (especially for
the Roma community).

---

[14] K. Kanev (1998) 'Legislation and Policy to the Ethnic and religious Communities in Bulgaria',
   in: Anna Krasteva (ed.) *Societies and Identities in Bulgaria*, Sofia: Petekston, p. 102.
[15] Penal Code, Art. 162, 163, 164, 416, 417, 418; the Acts on: the Ministry of Interior; Public
   Assemblies and Demonstrations; Bulgarian Radio and Television; Education; Higher Education;
   Vocational Education; Social Benefits; Public Officials, etc.

3.4. Institutions

The elimination of discrimination and the integration of minorities is a process that cannot be conducted only by virtue of decrees, legislative acts and orders. The governmental policy on solving minority problems must be implemented through the establishment of special institutions.

3.4.1. Specialised bodies

In Bulgaria, there are neither anti-discriminatory laws nor specialised state bodies for the prevention of discrimination and the encouragement of equal opportunities for all social groups. Their establishment, however, is essential due to the special character of inter-ethnic relations and the social and economic problems stemming from them. By the adoption of the Framework Programme for the Equal Integration of the Roma in Bulgarian Society in 1999, the government expressed their intention to set up a remedial institution and settle its legislative framework. Roma and non-Roma civil organisations are in the process of drafting an anti-discriminatory legislative act.

During the last two years, the Centre for Social Practices (an NGO), through financing from European programmes, has established a social facilitator, i.e. local ombudsman, in four municipalities. The Centre for the Development of Democracy (another NGO) is drafting a legislative act on the establishment of national and local parliamentary ombudsmen.

The issues concerning specialised institutions and laws to protect human rights are already on the agenda and their political solution is pending.

3.4.2. Consultative bodies

Public institutions at the national level are establishing specialised units and/or hiring minority representatives who correspond between the policy of the state and the interests of the various ethno-religious groups. Such agencies exist in the Parliament, the Office of the President and various ministries. For example, minority experts in the ministries function in the practical implementation of specific sector measures outlined in the Programme for the Integration of the Roma in Bulgarian Society.

During the years of the democratic transition, several consultative bodies have been set up within the Council of Ministers,[16] but their progress in dealing with issues related to issues of minority religious groups has been inadequate.[17] At the end of 1997, a National Council on Ethnic and Demographic Issues (NCEDI) was established at the Council of Ministers. It performs an interdepartmental, consultative and co-ordinating function. Its membership includes representatives of ministries, other governmental institutions and

---

[16] See: Bibliography, Position I.3, Council of Ministers Documents.

[17] These consultative bodies are the result of the efforts of several governments to institutionalise inter-ethnic relations in accordance with their traditional political approaches to the issue. The consultative body, which was established in 1994 did not meet even once. By its philosophy and work, the consultative body which was established in 1995 by the socialist government expresses its perception of minority issues in terms of their social and not their ethnic aspect. None of them has been a force for change.

minority NGOs. The major functions of the NCEDI include: (1) the encouragement of tolerance and understanding among Bulgarian citizens belonging to various ethnic and religious groups; (2) the adoption of specific measures for the implementation of Bulgaria's obligations under relevant international treaties and conventions; (3) the improvement of communication between these groups and similar communities in other countries. This body is responsible for dialogue between the government and the civil sector, and assists the development and implementation of the national policy on ethnic and demographic issues and migration. The NCEDI does not investigate individual claims: it has no powers to appeal before the court and its recommendations are not legally binding.

Within Bulgaria's 28 *regional administrations*, a number of experts on ethnic issues who belong to minority groups themselves have been appointed, many of them from the Roma community. Regional Councils on Ethnic and Demographic Issues are being established— comprised of the deconcentrated authorities of centralised power, regional administration, municipal institutions and the civil sector. Each of the regional councils drafts and adopts its own Working Rules and its own programme for the integration of ethnic minorities in the respective region. It will be necessary to draft a legislative act that regulates the competence of these experts on ethnic issues. At present, their precise role is often not clear.

At the local level, in some municipalities with a mixed population, experts on ethnic issues are being appointed in the municipal administration. In a number of cities where there are compact Roma communities, Roma deputy mayors are being appointed by mayors for the respective quarters. The major function of these officers is to consult with and inform the authorities on the problems of the community in order to co-ordinate the policy of the municipality with the interests of minorities. Most often, however, they have no actual power and cannot make decisions independent of the municipal councils and mayors.

3.5. Programmes

To date, no general government programme has been announced for the integrated development of all minority communities in Bulgaria. The political commitment of the government to the improvement of the situation and the elimination of discrimination against the Roma, who are the most vulnerable and disadvantaged community, was rendered operational by the adoption of the Framework Programme for the Equal Integration of the Roma in Bulgarian Society.

Case Study 1. The Framework Programme for the Equal Integration of the Roma in Bulgarian Society[18]

The issue: Inequality and discriminatory attitudes towards the Roma can be observed, which is a precondition for the problems of the Roma community in terms of the socio-economic and

---

[18] *Sources:* NGO *Human Rights Project* Bulletin (1998) No. 10, Special Issue; 'An interview with R. Rusinov' (1999) *Why not?* Sofia: CEGA, No. 10, pp. 8-14; 'Fifteen months and a half...' (1999) Sofia: *Etnoreporter*, No. 2, pp. 36-38.

cultural-educational plane. The successful integration of the Roma into society calls for the application of an overall strategy of state mechanisms and measures for the attainment of the emancipation of the group.

The actors involved: 1) National, regional and local Roma and non-Roma NGOs; 2) National Council on Ethnic and Demographic Issues at the Council of Ministers (NCEDI); 3) Regional authorities.

The issue proceedings: At the beginning of 1998, the Human Rights Project (a Roma NGO), together with other national Roma organisations in Bulgaria, started to draft the matrix of a programme. The text was vastly debated by both Roma and non-Roma organisations. The government offered their own project. The major issue in the debate between the government and the NGOs was discrimination. Specific measures have been listed to combat this phenomenon. The programme became a compromise between the government project and the document suggested by the Roma.

The strategy addressed: Strategies of advocacy and lobbying have been applied. The initiative of the Roma NGOs was supported by the Roma community, non-Roma civil organisations and representatives of the international community. Two round tables have been organised which have been widely covered and publicised by the media. Deliberately cautious tactics were applied in the advance of the talks on the convergence of positions and the finalising of texts. The programme was composed on the principles of observing the fundamental rights and freedoms of citizens. It was rendered in compliance with the recommendations of the European intergovernmental institutions related to the protection of national minorities.

Result: On 22 April 1999 the Council of Ministers adopted the Framework Programme and placed the solving of the Roma issue on the state agenda. The government document contains the major principles of a general state strategy for the enactment of the actual equal enjoyment of the rights by the Roma in the following ten years. The development of a system of measures (which should be appropriate for their specific ethnic and cultural characteristics) is envisaged for the solving of the problems of the Roma and their sustainable integration. Guarantees are being established for the equal representation of the Roma at all levels of public administration.

Unfortunately, this document is still void of specific content. The concrete commitments of the ministries have not yet been voiced, nor have the envisaged expert councils been formed. 'It is also necessary to allocate the required budget funding for the implementation of this programme'.[19] The society as a whole is not familiar with the Framework Programme. Through this programme, however, the Roma community has made an important step towards its social and political participation in public life.

3.6. Political position

'The basic meaning of the political approach is quite simple: integration will take place on the basis of active participation in political life'.[20] through the implementation of the individual right of suffrage and the group right of association into political parties.

---

[19] Regular Report of the European Commission (1999).

[20] Deian Kyuranov (1998) 'Integration Today: An Attempt at Sysytematic Theses', Sofia: *Etnoreporter*, No. 4, p. 13.

Regardless of the prohibitive constitutional provision, a political minority organisation was established in January 1990: the Movement for Rights and Freedoms (MRF)—consisting mainly of Bulgarian Turks. The party was registered for the very first democratic elections for the Great National Assembly in June 1990. In April 1992 the Constitutional Court did not vote with a majority on the petition for proclaiming the organisation unconstitutional. The MRF managed to survive the obstructions of nationalistic circles and to overcome serious after effects of the 'revival process'.[21] It has been represented in Parliament since 1990. In spite of the decreasing number of Turkish MPs in a succession of Bulgarian parliaments,[22] the MRF has preserved its role as an important parliamentary participant and performs a balancing function in times of political crisis.

The process of political legitimisation has been completely different in the case of the Roma. The emergent Roma civil organisations have been unable to transcend the established two-pole political model and have gravitated toward one pole or the other—the Socialist Party or the Union of Democratic Forces. In the first years of the post-1989 transition, the registration application of the Democratic Roma Union was rejected on the basis of prohibitive provisions of the Constitution. At the end of 1998, about 100 Roma representatives founded a Roma political party named *Svobodna Bulgaria* (Free Bulgaria).[23] In 1999 it took part in local elections.

In February 1999 the Macedonian ethnic minority also registered their political party, OMO Ilinden–PIRIN,[24] which also took part in local elections. A year after its registration the Constitutional Court proclaimed it as unconstitutional, providing arguments related to the threat to national sovereignty and territorial integrity. The members of the party have voiced their intention to file a petition to the European Court for Human Rights in Strasbourg.

The remaining minority communities in the country have no representative political organisations. They adhere to the large national political forces and participate in Parliament through the lists of the political parties represented there.

The ethnic minority communities share a motivation and will to form political parties and participate in power. The majority is reluctant to support the rights of minority communities to political representation and to occupy key government positions at various levels: national, regional and local.[25] This tendency has remained constant throughout

---

[21] The 'revival process', which took place during 1984-1985, was the culmination of the central government's assimilationist policy toward the Turkish minority. The process included the forceful renaming of Turks. Further, Turks were forbidden to speak Turkish in public places and were prevented from performing religious rituals. Turks were branded as 'separatists', and the previously existing trust between the Turkish and Bulgarian communities was replaced by mutual suspicion and alienation.

[22] See Table 5 in the Annex.

[23] P. Kostov (1999) *Drom Dromendar*, No. 6, November.

[24] The complete name of the party is the Ilinden United Macedonian Organisation: A Party for Economic Development and Integration of the Population (PIRIN).

[25] See Table 3 in the Annex. 'Even the rights which have been accepted as a principle and implemented for years are regarded with strong reservation and resistance: such as the right to learn one's mother tongue at school, the right to representation in local authorities and the National Assembly, the right to radio programmes, the right to publish and distribute books and other edi-

_aria's post-communist transition, reflecting the historic negative attitudes of mistrust
d fear that have been generated in a series of social traumas in inter-ethnic relations.[26]
In recent years, civil organisations have worked to assist in breaking through this ethnic
'encapsulation'.

3.7. Civil mobilisation

The right to freedom of association of citizens in NGOs is constitutionally and legally
guaranteed. The social attitudes of the majority do not impede the civil association of
minorities aimed at the preservation and the development of their culture. There is a broad
inter-ethnic consensus on these issues.[27]

The beginning of the democratic transition has marked the registration of numerous
cultural organisations of the Turks, Armenians, Karakachans, Wallachians and
Macedonians that are all aimed at the development and the preservation of their specific
cultures. These organisations are in the process of promoting cultural activities such as:
folklore groups, newspaper publications and mother-tongue education. The Roma community is currently forming a number of national, regional and local organisations for the
protection of their rights and the development of Roma culture.

In addition to those civil organisations founded and staffed by minority representatives, a number of human rights organisations which work toward the attainment of ethnic harmony in Bulgarian society have minority representatives among their staff.

The most recent legislative changes have encouraged the dialogue between public authorities and the civil sector by regulating the right to consultative participation of NGOs in the
work of various public bodies at the three levels of governance—national, regional and local.

NGOs have played an important role in the monitoring and advocacy of human and
minority rights. They have made particular efforts in raising awareness, sensitising and
informing both the wider public and the specialised public administration about the rights
of persons belonging to various minorities. Their activities contribute to the mobilisation
of the civil resources of ethnic communities and their more active representation on the
public scene.

---

tions and other mother-tongue materials, etc. Less than half of the respondents (which were inter-
viewed in 1997 during the second part of the research on the Relations of Compatibility and
Incompatibility between the Christians and Muslims in Bulgaria) state their support for all these
rights, which are already established in post-totalitarian practices'. See: Ilona Tomova (2000)
'Social Change and Ethnoreligious Relations', in: Georgi Fotev (ed.) _Neighbour Relations of Religious
Communities in Bulgaria._ Sofia: Institute of Sociology at BAS, p. 207. See also: _Interrelations of
Compatibility and Incompatibility between the Christians and Muslims in Bulgaria_ (1994) and (1997).
Sofia: ICMSIR; Peter-Emil Mitev (1999) 'From Neighbourhood to Fellow Citizenship', _Etnoreporter_
No. 1, Sofia: IEIHR, pp. 15-17; M. Jecheva (1998) 'Will Integration Be Able to Fight the
Accumulated Effect of the Disadvantaged Position', Sofia: _Etnoreporter_, No. 4, pp. 4-6.

[26] See the above mentioned positions and also: Anna Krasteva (ed.) (1998) _Societies and Identities
in Bulgaria_, Sofia: Petekston; J. Georgiev, I. Tomova, K. Kanev, M. Grekova (1993) _The
Ethnocultural Situation in Bulgaria_, Sofia: ICMSIR.

[27] See Table 3 in the Annex.

In summary, it can be said that:

· The placement and the undertaking of legislative, political, institutional and civil measures towards solving inter-ethnic issues in Bulgaria has been one of the most dynamic aspects of democratic development during the last ten years, which has been stimulated by the democratic changes in Bulgaria of 1989, international events and the process of the accession of Bulgaria to the European Union.

· The question of adopting anti-discriminatory legislation and setting up a specialised administrative body for the prevention of discrimination as well as the establishment of national and local ombudsman is on the agenda.

· The National Council on the Ethnic and Demographic Issues (NCEDI) at the Council of Ministers currently functions as a consultative body. Regional councils on ethnic and demographic issues are being established, and minority-member experts are being appointed. The municipal administration of diversely populated regions also employ such experts to mediate the convergence of local policy and the interests of local communities.

· No comprehensive government programme exists for the integrated development of all minority communities in Bulgaria. Efforts have been made, however, for the integration of the Roma population. The Framework Programme for the Equal Integration of the Roma in Bulgarian Society is a programme unique to Bulgaria, and includes a document indicating the commitment of the cabinet.

4. Regional and Local Dimensions

Democratic Bulgaria is a parliamentary republic with local self-governance. The decentralisation of state power to the local level is constitutionally established. The state acknowledges the right to self-governance of the administrative-territorial units. However, state power preserves its authority and supervising position with respect to the protection of the law and common national interests. A reasonable balance in the proportion between the authorities of the central state and the self-governing territorial administration is a prerequisite for a successful and effective management policy towards the development of multi-cultural communities.[28]

---

[28] On the territorial and administrative structure and local government, see: 'Public Administration and the Democratic Process' (1998) Sofia: *Parliamentary Democracy*, Special Issue; M. Stefanova (1998) 'The Model of Local Government in Bulgaria', Sofia: *Parliamentary Democracy*, No. 8, pp. 22-37; E. Kandeva (1998) 'Reforms in the Public Administration and the Modern State', Sofia: *Parliamentary Democracy*, No. 8, pp. 4-21; E. Kandeva (1997) 'Bureaucracy and the Rights of the Person: the Defence of the Rights of Citizens—a Necessary Element of the Administrative Reform', in: Emil Konstantinov (ed.) (1997) '*The Civil Society and the Rights of the Person*', Sofia: Fridrich Ebert Foundation, The Institute for Political and Legal Research, pp. 109-120.

erritorial-administrative framework

،titution sets forth a two-tier administrative and territorial division of the 111,000
sप्- ،ilometre territory and the 8.5 million inhabitants of Bulgaria. The major territorial structures and the key levels of local government are 28 districts and 262 municipalities.

The administrative district or region (*oblast*) is a governmental level of locally deconcentrated state power. The governance of the district is carried out by the district governor, deputy governors and district administration. The district governor is appointed by the prime minister for an unspecified term. The major functions of the district are related to the conduct of effective regional policy, the local implementation of state governance and the maintenance of accord between national and local interests. The district governor exercises control over the legitimacy of the acts and the actions of local authorities and the locally deconcentrated units of state power within the district. The administrative districts (oblasts) are subdivided into municipalities. An average of 32 municipalities are included in the territory of each district (except for the capital).

The municipality (*obshtina*) is a major unit which enacts local governance. It exists and functions both as an administrative and territorial unit and as a legal entity. The municipality consists of one or more neighbouring settlements whose lands constitute its territory. On average, municipalities are comprised of 21 settlements. As a legal entity, the municipality is entitled to property ownership (both public and private), which it uses in the interest of its territorial community. It has an independent municipal budget, which is funded by permanent sources provided for by law.

The municipality has competencies and exerts public power according to the regulations of the relevant legislation. As a public, legal and juridical entity, the municipality is authorised—by the Constitution (Chapter 7, 'Local Government and Local Administration') and legislation—to perform public services within the established local boundaries, acting, at the same time, as a constituent in the specific relations with the central state power and as a special dependent on the central state power (control over the legitimacy of acts and actions).

The local authorities in Bulgaria are the municipal council and the mayor. They are elected directly by residents of a municipality for a four-year term of office.

The municipal council (*Obshtinski savet*) is the legislative authority of local self-government. It consists of municipal councilors proportionally elected from the election lists of political parties or independent candidates. The membership of the municipal councils varies in number in proportion with the population of the municipality (from 11 to 61 members). The municipal council is a body of general competencies. It determines the development policy for the municipality and the implementation of the public services and activities provided for by the law.

The mayor (*kmet*) is the executive authority of local self-government, which is elected on the majority principle. The mayor functions in a double capacity. As a representative of local executive power he/she manages the administrative activities of the municipality, organises the performance of all the decisions of the municipal council and has representative authorities. As a representative of the authority of the state within the municipality and as a state administrative body, the mayor organises the fulfillment of tasks generated by legislation, acts of the president of the Republic and the Council of Ministers. The mayor may also perform functions assigned to him/her by the central bodies of the state.

The mayoralty (*kmetstvo*) is the smallest unit of local self-government in the Republic of Bulgaria. It is the constituent administrative-territorial unit of the municipality. Any town, village or rural territory belonging to a municipality may be definied as a mayoralty. Under the present legislation a mayoralty of above 500 inhabitants is a valid constituency for the election of a mayor. Mayoralties have no financial independence.

In 1998 the government adopted a Strategy for the Establishment of a Modern Administrative System of the Republic of Bulgaria. The document takes into account the important role of public administration at the national and local level as an instrument for the implementation of state policy, the enhancement of government, the regulation of social processes, the provision of administrative servicing, permanent communication with citizens and their organisations in a civil society environment, and the compliance of Bulgarian legislation with that of the EU.[29]

4.2. Regional policy opportunities

Analysis since 1990 points to a number of problems in regional development. Environmental conditions, inherited socio-economic and territorial structures, past policies and the dynamics of development during the transition period have resulted in significant disparities among Bulgaria's regions in economic development, employment, income and quality of life.[30] Those regions with concentrated minority populations have lagged behind in their development. These regions are characterised by higher unemployment rates, less developed infrastructure, lower investments and incomes, and greater dependence on government subsidies than the national average. For example, unemployment is extremely high in regions with the following compact minority populations: Kurdjali (66%), Razgrad (53%), Turgovishte (40%), Silistra (38%) and Shumen (37%).[31] According to the values of the Human Development Index,[32] the districts most densely populated by Roma communities—Montana, Sliven and Dobritch—are ranked 19TH, 28TH and 22ND respectively.[33]

---

[29] Decision of the Council of Ministers No. 36/9.02.1998 on the Adoption of a Strategy for the Establishment of a Modern Administrative System of the Republic of Bulgaria and the Declaration of the Government on the Strategy.

[30] *National Regional Development Plan for 2000-2006* (1999) *State Gazette,* No. 106, p. 2.

[31] See Table 4 in the Annex.

[32] The Human Development Index (HDI) measures the achievement of three basic dimensions of human development—a long and healthy life, knowledge and a decent standard of living. Since 1990, the UN Development Programme (UNDP) has monitored, compared and ranked HDI values nearly all countries in the world. Bulgaria's HDI ranked 60 out of 147 countries evaluated in 2000.

[33] See Table 4 in the Annex. See also: UNDP (1999) *National Report on Human Development in Bulgaria.* It must be mentioned that the correlation between the values of the Human Development Index at the district level is not straightforward due to the more complex nature of the

ɔnse to these disparities, the central government developed and began to imple-
gional development policy[34] with the objective of achieving sustainable and bal-
ɛvelopment by directing resources and developing infrastructure and economic
᠁s in certain regions. Four types of regions have been targeted for impact: (1) regions
for growth, (2) regions for development, (3) regions for transfrontier co-operation and
development, and (4) regions with particular problems and priorities (including declining industrial regions, underdeveloped rural regions and mountainous regions). The criteria used in defining these categories were established by a team made up of both Bulgarian
and EU development experts. This policy programme is important with respect to minority integration issues, because the last two types of regions are highly populated by minority groups.

In terms of regional development, the major policy objective of the current government is to reduce the number of the municipalities and regions which have reached critical levels of poverty, unemployment, population decline, environmental problems, and
social and ethnic tensions.[35] Favourable conditions for such developments are: the reform
of the territorial and administrative division of the country, the formation of 28 districts,
the adoption of the Regional Development Act[36] and the reform of public administration.[37] Transparency has been introduced into the process of regional and municipality
planning and forecasting, and greater opportunities are being created for civil participation.[38] Additionally, citizens now have wider access to public services.

It is important to stress that the implementation of regional policy in Bulgaria has
been a two-way process: bottom-up as well as top-down mechanisms exist for the drafting of regional development plans. For instance, every year, each of the 262 municipalities develops its own municipal development strategy. On the basis of these strategies,
each of the 28 districts (regions) designs a District Plan for Development. Using these
district plans, the National Plan for Regional Development is put together. Local-level
planning initiatives are thus taken into consideration at higher levels of government. In
light of this process, it is especially important that minority communities be active within their municipalities in order that issues of concern to them are included in these development plans.

---

relation and the averaging of the values of the individual components of the Index.

[34] This policy is laid out in the Regional Development Act—a legislative document that regulates
the planning, management and provision of resources for regional development.

[35] *National Regional Development Plan for 2000-2006* (1999) *State Gazette,* No. 106, p. 2.

[36] *Regional Development Act* (1999) *State Gazette,* No. 26.

[37] During the last two years new legislation and subsidiary acts were adopted, as well as revisions
were made in the existing legislative basis, which shall provide for a modern public administration in Bulgaria: the Public Administration Act, the Public Official Act; the Public Procurement
Act; the Local Finance Act. Revisions: the Act on the Territorial and Administrative Division of
the Country; the Act on the Local Self-Government and Local Administration, etc.

[38] 'It is the administrative reform which, through specific measures, could bring the state and the civil
society closer or make the relations between them less controversial'. E. Kandeva (1997) 'Bureaucracy
and the Rights of the Person: the Defence of the Rights of Citizens—a Necessary Element of the
Administrative Reform', in: Emil Konstantinov (ed.) *The Civil Society and the Rights of the Person,*
Sofia: Fridrich Ebert Foundation, Institute for Political and Legal Research, p. 113.

4.3. Regional differences and municipal budgets

The regional administrative-territorial tier in Bulgaria acts as a kind of intermediary between the central and local government. The sphere of the relations between central and local authority is backed by guarantees for the respect of citizens' right to self-government and for the provision of opportunities for local authorities to exercise their rights and perform their duties. In practice, however, regardless of the process of reforms geared toward increased autonomy and distinct decentralisation in terms of organisation and finance, local government structures in Bulgaria do not yet have the financial independence necessary to perform their functions without the financial support of the state.

Within the structure of the municipal budgets, more than one-third of the incomes column is composed of state transfers in the form of general or specifically allocated subsidies, whereas about half of the funds are procured from taxes shared with the state. Own and raised funds in the municipal budgets have little relative weight. Municipal councils have no powers to levy additional taxes on local citizens except for those provided for by the law. Two-thirds of the municipalities in Bulgaria depend on state budget subsidies above 50%, and 17% of them have a dependency higher than 80%. The 44 municipalities in question are mainly small mountainous ones, economically underdeveloped, with a high rate of migration and with a population of ethnic and religious minorities. The generalised data at the district level confirm the highest dependency of municipal budgets on centralised subsidies for the districts with compact minority populations like Kurdjali, Silistra, Montana, Targovishte, Razgrad, Shumen and Sliven.[39] The reason for this is the limited own revenues generated within the municipal budgets.

People residing in these regions are of unequal standing in terms of their access to opportunities for equal development. Local authorities are restricted in their attempts to launch their own decentralised initiatives due to their drastic dependence on the financial abilities of the state.

About 90% of the municipalities' funds are spent on current expenses: teachers and physicians' salaries, medicines and medicinal products, heating, social services, repairs, etc. Municipalities allocate most of their funds for education, health care and social support. The means for building new facilities are meagre.

Budgets are inadequate for the range of multiple services which municipal authorities are expected to provide to the population. The most frequent practices search for opportunities to raise some of the necessary funding from external sources: international programmes, co-financing of activities by civil organisations and formation of specialised funds.

4.4. Minority representation

Minority representatives have an increasing opportunity to participate in the local government authorities of Bulgaria.

---

[39] See Table 4 in the Annex. See also: UNDP (1999) *National Report on Human Development in Bulgaria*, p. 72..

From the very first democratic elections held in 1991 until the most recent elections in 1999, the Bulgarian Turks, represented by the MRF, have enjoyed significant representation in local government authorities in those municipalities traditionally populated by compact Bulgarian Turk communities. Roma representation at the local level is sporadic. The Roma, like all the other ethnic groups, participate in local authorities as representatives of the dominant political forces in the country.

The results of the latest local elections show the political and the ethnic patchwork of the public vote. In some places voters have supported mayoral candidates and municipal councilors appointed as independent nominees by local and regional coalitions. These 1999 elections were the first in which the Roma and the Macedonian communities had their first participation as politically legitimate forces through their parties, Free Bulgaria and OMO Ilinden–PIRIN, and won mandates as municipal councilors and mayors.[40] The result of the elections was significantly wider multi-ethnic representation in local authorities: municipal councils and mayors.

The latest legislative revisions of local self-government increase the dependency of mayors on municipal council decisions. These decisions, however, will be less and less entrusted to one-party and mono-ethnic majorities, and the groups promoted by civil society will have a greater influence on local policy.

4.5. Local management practices

This wider ethnic representation in local self-government bodies has already begun to yield practical results in the management of multi-ethnic communities.

Case Study 2. Local Government Measures against Discrimination

Case study: Local government measures against minority discrimination and solving minority issues in the municipality of Pazardjik.[41]

The issue: There are overt discriminatory practices against minority groups (which consist of about 20,000 Roma and Turks) in the town of Pazardjik (the municipal centre). Some public posted signs reading, 'We don't serve food to minorities'. In addition to this humiliation, the Roma population has grievous socio-economic problems.

The actors involved: 1) The Municipal Council; 2) The Mayor; 3) Municipal administration; 4) Representatives of the ethnic quarter in the town: municipal councilors from Svobodna (Free) Bulgaria Roma party and other political forces.

The issue proceedings: Between two mayoral polls in October 1999, an agreement was signed for joint government, whereas the Roma party undertook to support the mayoral candidate from the United Democratic Forces (UDF) Coalition, and UDF committed to attending to the problems of minorities. At the third session of the newly elected municipal council where five

---

[40] Central Commission for Local Elections (1999) *Bulletin on the Results of the Local Elections Held on 16 October 1999 and on 23 October 1999, Vol. I, General Results,* Sofia: CCLE.

[41] Sources: I. Bedrov (2000) 'Discrimination in Establishments Is a Disturbance of Social Order', Sofia: *Etnoreporter,* No. 1, p. 14.

minority representatives were sitting, the Ordinance on Observing the Order in Public Food Establishments was revised unanimously. Revisions set forth fines to be imposed on those owners of public food establishments who selected their customers on ethnic grounds. Any attempts to violate the provision for a second time would the invalidation of their license for commercial activity. For the first time ever in the history of the municipality a Human Rights Unit was established which is managed by the head of the Mayor's Office in municipal administration.

The strategy addressed: The political agreement signed for the purpose of winning the local mayor elections has turned into a working strategy for the multi-ethnic government of the municipality. Legislative measures are being taken at the local level to prevent discrimination against minorities, which constitute 80% of the citizens coming to the Mayor's Office to complain about various issues. The recruitment of Roma and Turks as police officers is pending, together with the elimination of segregation in municipal schools and kindergartens. In co-operation with the National Council on Ethnic and Demographic Issues at the Council of Ministers and the Shelter for Everyone Foundation, municipal authorities are developing a programme on building housing facilities for poor minority people. The project is currently raising funds. The construction design plans have been drawn. It is necessary to draw the urban plan for the quarter. The building of the houses will be carried out by the programme, whereas the municipality is committed to building the infrastructure.

The results: Open discriminatory practices against minorities at public places have been restricted. The representation of minorities in the public services is about to grow. Overall work is being done for solving the socio-economic matters, housing and ameliorating the quarter populated mainly by minority groups.

Municipal authorities in Bulgaria have applied various approaches for the expansion of civil participation in domestic legislation and government.

In some municipalities, the drafting of the internal rules of the municipal council is debated together with civil organisations. The exercise of civil control over the work of municipal administration, the mayor and the municipal council is being regulated.

Often, before sessions of the municipal council, public discussions are held on various issues and are covered by local radio and TV stations, thus providing the opportunity for direct participation. Thus public consensus is attained even before any decisions are taken by commissions on the municipal council.

Another approach widely used by the municipalities is the involvement of civil organisations' representatives in the work of municipal commissions.

In many places, public councils for the various areas of municipal administration (mainly unemployment, social care, health care and education) have been established and function successfully. They have consultative functions and their members are volunteers within the council. They consist of representatives of the municipal services, NGOs, other organisations and institutions affected by the relevant issues and representatives of informal communities. Those public councils which have minorities among their members function as intermediaries between the minority population and specialised municipal services.

NGOs participate in the formulation of local development strategies. Thus municipalities with diverse ethnic populations apply a model whereby professionals, regardless of their ethnic belonging or creed, may work together for the sustainable development of the municipality and the region.

The latest local elections have illustrated that a government model is needed that provides for the broader participation of the civil sector in decision-making processes for the development of the country. The development of such a model is already underway.

4.6. Local public services

The Local Government and Local Administration Act[42] (which stipulates the competencies of local authorities) complies with the European Local Government Charter to which Bulgaria is a party. It empowers the local authorities elected by the citizens to solve, within their competencies, issues in all areas of life for the territory of the municipality. Local authorities are obliged to provide services related to: education, health care, culture, amelioration, communal activities, social support, social and housing facilities, environmental protection, rational utilisation of natural resources, and development of sports, recreation and tourism.

4.6.1. Education and intercultural dialogue at school

In Bulgaria, rights to the development of ethnic cultures, education, the study of one's mother tongue and access to the media are all guaranteed by the Constitution. In practice, however, the attitude often persists that the protection of minority rights represents a threat to national interests and national security.

Education is a very sensitive aspect of inter-ethnic relations. Schools are a socialising and cultural institution that do not merely transfer knowledge but also play a crucial role in shaping attitudes about one's 'own' and 'other' ethnic groups. The Bulgarian government does not make use of a clear-cut, well-defined guiding philosophy in developing policies related to multi-cultural and intercultural education.

The education system in Bulgaria is deconcentrated rather than decentralised. The state determines the school curriculum. Between 2% and 10% of the local public school curriculum may be devoted to programmes of their choice, but these programmes must be offered as electives. In 1999 an Act regulating school curricula, minimum-level education and levels of education was adopted. In May 2000 the Ministry of Education and Science issued an Instruction on State Educational Requirements. Together, these two documents determine the content of the public school curriculum and the obligatory skills and knowledge that students must acquire by the end of each level of education. According to these new laws, which will come into force beginning in the 2001-2002 school year, the school curriculum is less tightly controlled by the central government. From that point on, between 12% and 40% of the school curriculum (depending on the level of education) can be determined by the school itself.

This nascent decentralisation process allows for the development of special programmes for intercultural dialogue and leaves open the possibility of greater co-operation between the four major players in the education system: teachers, parents, public authorities (state and local) and students.

---

[42] The Act is published in *State Gazette* (1991) No. 77.

Three types of schools exist in Bulgaria: state, municipal and private schools. State school teachers are paid through the state budget, and municipal school teachers are paid through the municipal budgets. In practice, however, a substantial part of the municipal budget is in reality a state subsidy. As such, a significant part (and often the entirety) of municipal school teachers' salaries come from the state budget. The local government is at present responsible only for building maintenance and not for pedagogical issues. The responsibilities of the local government are merely to ensure that the necessary requirements for the functioning of the school are met, and to ensure that children below the minimum legal drop-out age are enrolled in school.

Appropriate policy decision-making for the schools and the supervision of the results will require the more active participation of parents and civil organisations. The introduction of multi- and inter-ethnic education sensitive to the specific needs of various ethnic groups, the use of adequate pedagogical strategies, flexible teaching programmes and diverse educational forms are all necessary conditions for the improvement of minority education, and represent a challenge which local public authorities must face.

Case Study 3. A Pilot Programme for Tolerance

Case study: A trial for intercultural dialogue in a school in the city of Shumen.[43]

The issue: Children from various ethno-cultural/religious groups experience difficulties in communication due to their mutual unfamiliarity.

The actors involved: 1) Local authorities; 2) The Department of Philosophy at the University of Sofia; 3) The University of Shumen; 4) The Minerva Foundation.

The issue proceedings: Through the financial support of PHARE, a project has been implemented entitled, 'The Enhancement of the Communication Methods between Minority Ethnocultural Communities and Civil Society in Bulgaria'. The project activities are focused in the municipal school of Shumen, which is the centre of a municipality with a large population of Muslim Turks and Roma. Under the supervision of specially trained teachers, students were expected to compare the major moral edicts of the Bible and the Koran and the proverbs of the various ethnic groups: Bulgarians, Turks, Roma and Armenians.

The strategy addressed: Through the use of research, comparative and analytical techniques, proximity is sought between the value systems of the various ethnic and religious groups, as they are reflected by the proverbs and sayings and the major scriptures of Christianity and Islam.

The results: By increasing knowledge of various ethnic cultures and religions and, also, by discovering the similarities and the differences between them, trainees are expected to gain a better mutual acquaintance and understanding.

4.6.2. Mother-tongue education

Mother-tongue education, which was introduced in 1992, was supported neither by a sufficient number of books and classes nor with qualified teachers for bilingual children. These deficiencies serve as major impediments to the effective implementation of permissive provisions on education.

---

[43] D. Boicheva (1999) 'On the Virtues and Vices As They Look from the Perspective of Various Religions', Sofia: *Etnoreporter*. No. 6, p. 26.

The intensified public debate on human rights, closely related to the process of Bulgaria's integration into European institutions, and the conflicts in the former Yugoslavia, have given new status to issues related to mother-tongue education, particularly following the adoption of the Act on the Degree of Education, General Education Minimum Requirements and the Educational Plan in 1999. On the volition of students, mother tongue will be studied at primary and secondary schools within the regular curricular classes allocated electives. The status of the teachers has been changed and there will be no need for their annual re-appointment. This implies that municipal authorities will need to allot the necessary organisational, financial and facility resources in order to provision mother-tongue education at school.

Case Study 4. Hebrew in Sofia

Case study: A successful model of mother-tongue education (Hebrew) implemented in a school in Sofia (Hebrew and English Language Elementary School) which is also attended by Bulgarian children.[44]

The issue: Mother-tongue education in a school with broad Jewish attendance aimed at the preservation of the cultural identity of the ethnic group.

The actors involved: 1) The Ministry of Education and Science, 2) Local authorities; 3) The School Supervisory Board, the School Board and the teaching staff; 4) The Jewish Shalom Organisation in Bulgaria; 5) The Ronald S. Lauder Foundation, New York, USA.

The issue proceedings: The state school is of mixed attendance, with both Jewish and Bulgarian pupils. From the 1998 school year, two curricula are being implemented in the school. In the first one, Hebrew is taught as a mother tongue twice per week as an optional choice. More than one-third of the attendees study Hebrew as their mother tongue. Some Bulgarians also attend this programme. The groups are formed after determining the language proficiency of the children. In the second curriculum, Hebrew is taught as the first foreign language within the regular classes of the school (from the first year onwards). From the third year on the study of the second foreign language (English) is introduced. Books in Hebrew have been approved by the Ministry of Education and Science. The curriculum in Hebrew is uniform for a total of fifteen schools from CEE, that participate in an educational network under the auspices of the Ronald S. Lauder Foundation. The curriculum, the know-how, the preparation of teachers and the various teaching tools such as audio and video recordings, newspapers, magazines, etc., were provided by the Ronald S. Lauder Foundation, New York, USA. Mother-tongue classes are aided by computers where pupils have access to the Internet.

The strategy addressed: The collaboration between the various international, national, local and civil institutions and organisations provide for all necessary means for mother-tongue education. This hones the interest of Bulgarian children who wish to share in the classes of Hebrew groups and thus gain an acquaintance with the language and the culture of the other ethnic group.

The results: The children from the Jewish community in Sofia are able to preserve and develop their ethnic culture through the study of their mother tongue, the Jewish cycle of life and Jewish Festivals. In parallel, the participation of Bulgarian pupils in the Hebrew classes helps to break down social barriers between the different ethnic groups at the school. Steps are being taken for the transformation of the elementary school into a secondary school.

---

[44] *Etnoreporter* (1998) No. 1.

Regardless of the permissive provision, the system still lacks a coherent philosophy of education about and in the mother tongue. But the impediments enumerated above are not fully resolved. Adequate solutions will be sought by the innovative approach of local authority representatives and the teachers in each municipality and each individual school. The partnership of NGOs working in this area is already yielding positive results for the solving of these issues at a local level.

4.6.3. Preventing drop-outs

In combination with various government strategies, the partnership referred to above is useful for solving another serious educational problem: minority children dropping out of school. According to the 1999 National Human Development Report, during the 1998-1999 school year, the official number of school drop-outs was 36,000. Other organisations and NGOs have estimated that the number of school-age children not attending school is closer to 120,000. These are mainly Roma children. Some of them never attend school, while others are unable to pass to a higher grade.

This problem has thus far been addressed by public authorities through various management strategies. Administrative sanctions (such as fines) for the parents refusing to send their children to school are ineffective, especially with poor Roma families.

The attempt to attract Roma children to school by providing humanitarian aid is unsustainable. Once food supplies cease, non-attendance returns to its previous rates. A more successful approach would be to motivate the parents and the children by persuading them that education will give them better opportunities in their lives. This is a slow process, but, in addition to parent-teacher-child work, it is important for the campaign to be reinforced by interesting activities relevant to the everyday life, culture and character of the child.

Municipal decisions in the area of education acknowledge the fact that Bulgarian is not the mother tongue for the majority of Turkish and Roma students. In some schools children attend the 'preparatory classes' provided for by law. In the course of one year during nursery school or their first year of primary school, children are trained in the official Bulgarian language. The attendance rates in such classes for Roma children are still low. In some of the municipalities, ethnic NGO collaborators assist local school authorities by visiting families' homes and trying to convince parents of the benefits of this preliminary education for their children.

Another method is the appointment of assistant Roma teachers as mediators between minority children, their parents and majority teachers. Where this approach has been used the results have been very promising.

The provision of adequate education corresponding to labour market demands, mother-tongue education and the introduction of intercultural dialogue into the curricula of Bulgarian schools are landmarks in the preservation of various cultural identities and the development of the intercultural experience.

4.6.4. Access to the media and intercultural dialogue

In theory, the media should play a crucial role in the development and the encouragement of different ethnic cultures, and of mutual understanding between the majority and minority communities. In practice, however, there is no intercultural dialogue in the media and minority access to the media is limited.

Events are presented and interpreted exclusively from the viewpoint of the ethnic majority. Therefore, the state and local authorities need to implement policies that will ensure the participation of minorities in the media and promote inter-ethnic dialogue rather than the monolithic representation of individual ethnic communities. This participation has to account both for programmes addressing minorities and for the involvement of journalists of diverse ethnic backgrounds.

Examples of programmes by and on minorities exist at a local level. They are supported by local radio stations, cable televisions and NGOs.

Case Study 5. Neighbourhood TV

Case study: Neighbourhood TV programme produced by Trakia Public Television, Plovdiv.[45]

The issue: Plovdiv is the second largest city of Bulgaria and it is typical for its multi-ethnic population. There is a large Roma ghetto in the city. Ethnic groups live in mutual ignorance and mistrust of one another. No media programmes have been launched for or by minorities.

The actors involved: 1) Local authorities, 2) Trakia Public Television, Plovdiv; 3) The Media with A Human Face Association, 4) Local NGOs working for the inter-ethnic relations in the region.

The issue proceedings: Neighbourhood is the first programme in Bulgaria that has made an attempt to address both multi-ethnic needs and the Bulgarian model of inter-ethnic tolerance. The TV programme is financed by the Open Society Foundation (Sofia) and the King Baudoin Foundation (Belgium). The Media with a Human Face Association managed to assemble a good multi-ethnic team of moderators, cameramen and consultants representing Balkan minorities. Very soon, the 20-minute regional programme became so popular that other cable televisions decided to broadcast it as well. It presents the customs and the traditions of the various ethnic communities, their problems and their standpoint on public issues since 1997.

The strategy addressed: Representatives from the different ethnic groups on the team exchange their ideas and views for the TV programme. Thus, through their co-operative work, they present a crystallised formula for mutual acquaintance via electronic media. The programme acted as an impetus for outsiders to speak and show their ways of life, their customs, beliefs and history, thus bridging the differences between minorities and attaining better understanding between the communities.

The results: Minority representatives are provided with an opportunity to access the media. Intercultural dialogue was started on a local TV programme in order to foster the acquaintance and understanding between citizens. The *Neighbourhood* programme in Plovdiv was chosen to represent Bulgaria in a publication of the European Commission Against Racism and Intolerance entitled *Examples of Good Practice Against Racism in the Media,* which was released in April 2000.

Some of the local radio stations have been broadcasting in Turkish since 1990. The National Radio has transmitted such programmes since 1993. There is a programme for minorities on national television. Private TV channels have also allocated time to minority issues. A Turkish-language programme has recently been launched in regions with compact minority populations.

---

[45] E. Tododrov, M. Velikova (1999) 'A TV Programme Standing on its Own (for Now)', Sofia: *Etnoreporter*, No. 5, pp. 51-52.

Nine newspapers have been published in Turkish during the transition period. Some of them have closed down due to funding problems. The Armenian and the Jewish communities each have an independent press. In the case of the Roma, eleven periodicals were designed for publication after 1989. Some of them barely managed to release one or two issues. Nonetheless, for the past six years, the local media space has included the Roma publication, *Drom Dromendar,* released in Sliven (a city with a high Roma population).

Aided by sponsors, NGOs active in some neighbourhoods with compact minority populations have been able to publish information bulletins or newspapers. They publicise the activities of NGOs among the local community and provide information on the initiatives of municipal authorities which address minority problems.

4.6.5. Employment and unemployment

The problems related to the education and qualification of vulnerable minority groups are directly related to the high rates of unemployment among them. There is a definite discriminatory attitude against the Roma in the labour market.

Local unemployment offices are the major vehicles for a number of national programmes aimed at the enhancement of employment opportunities for minority representatives. Among these programmes are: Beautiful Bulgaria; From Social Benefits to Employment; Attaining Literacy, Qualification and Employment; etc. Effective partnership routines are established between local unemployment offices and minority NGOs for the participation of minority representatives in the programmes.[46] Such programmes, however, are not very productive because minority members gain only temporary employment at low salaries that are inadequate to support their families.

A number of municipalities have created and dispatched Public Councils on Unemployment which function on the basis of the 'tripartite' principle (they include representatives of the deconcentrated state and municipal offices, employers' organisations and employees' organisations) and involve minority representatives as their members. According to the varying potential of local economies, the councils have been exploring possibilities for the creation of new jobs. One of the measures that could prove effective is the elaboration of programmes for qualification training and employment that take into account local labour market demand and the specific labour patterns of some Roma groups (especially in regions dominated by seasonal employment).

4.6.6. Social assistance

Vulnerable minority groups (especially the Roma) are the major beneficiaries of social support services. In a large number of municipalities, the meagre budgets and the allocation of funds to other priorities is the main reason for the irregular payment of monthly benefits. As they are the primary source for the survival of the Roma, overdue payments sometimes generate social tension.

---

[46] An example in this respect is the unemployment office servicing the minority neighbourhood of Stolipinovo in Plovdiv. A minority representative from the neighbourhood is employed in the office. Active minority NGOs contributed to the work of the commission responsible to elect this candidate.

Municipal Social Care Offices often rely on the effective assistance of local minority NGOs. In many cases, they participate in Community Councils (which are legislatively provided for by the Rules for Social Assistance). They exercise civil control over the apportioning of the various types of social benefits. Some NGOs have set up their own social offices to mediate in the servicing of the Roma population by the municipality. Legal provisions allow NGOs to be licensed and exercise a specific range of social activities. Holders of such licenses may apply for finances before the National Social Assistance Fund (in order to perform the services).

Case Study 6. A Community Council Improves Social Services for Roma

Case study: Intermediary functions of a Roma community council in social activities in the municipality of Karlovo.

The issue: The municipality of Karlovo (with the town of Karlovo as its centre) is populated by a large Roma community. Its major source of income is social benefits. Municipal social services find it hard to function accordingly due to the poor proficiency of the Roma in Bulgarian.

The actors involved: 1) Local authorities and municipal services; 2) The V. Levski Human Rights Centre, Karlovo (NGO); 3) The Ministry of Labour and Social Policy.

The issue proceedings: In 1999 the V. Levski Human Rights Centre, Karlovo, obtained a license from the Ministry of Labour and Social Policy for carrying out three types of social activities conducted respectively through: The Social Service Office, the Club of the Disabled and the Public Charitable Kitchen. The financing of these activities was supported jointly by the municipal budget and the Social Assistance Fund. In January 2000, by the decision of the Municipal Council, a Roma Community Council was established to exercise civil control over the allotment of social aid and to mediate between the Municipal Social Care Service and the local Roma community. The seven Roma on the council are responsible for a community of 5,000. Such councils are about to be established in the villages near Karlovo where the Roma population is numerous.

The strategy addressed: The national and local authorities and NGOs are joining their efforts to enhance the social services for the population in the municipality.

The results: The Roma community made a step towards its social participation in the public life of the municipality. The services for the minority population are improved.

4.6.7. Housing and public amenities

Housing, public amenities and communal activities constitute a major part of the responsibilities and services provided by local authorities. Multiple investments are necessary in order to improve the technical and social infrastructure, which is in extremely poor condition in the Roma neighbourhoods in a number of towns and villages.

In many towns and villages Roma quarters or parts of them are outside the planning regulations. As such, their status is uncertain and the effective construction and regulation plans for the respective settlement cannot be applied. Public services and public community spaces (parks etc.) are almost nonexistent. These areas are characterised by illegally erected structures, an extreme density of habitation, and appalling sanitary, environmental and technical conditions. Housing facilities are mainly generally ramshackle or make-shift structures.

Local authorities are exploiting an expanding co-operation scheme with NGOs for the improvement of these quarters. Most often, NGOs provide the architectural designs for housing facilities and try to raise funds for their construction. Local authorities have assumed the commitment to improve technical facilities.

In summary:

· Policies implemented in the fields of regional and local development are aimed at decreasing the existing disparities between regions and municipalities. The administrative-territorial units with compact minority populations most frequently experience hardships in their development.

· Regional and local authorities and the NGOs are collaborating to provide a range of services to their communities. The limitations in the financial decentralisation of municipalities are decreasing the opportunities for specific initiatives addressing minority issues.

· Minorities are represented in municipal councils. Municipal authorities apply more flexible solutions and innovative practices for the involvement of citizens' groups in the management and solving of the specific problems of multi-ethnic communities.

5. Conclusion and Recommendations

In the past ten years, the democratic development of Bulgaria and the adoption of measures for the harmonisation of inter-ethnic relations has resulted in the preservation of the Bulgarian pattern of ethnic co-habitation. The issue of inter-ethnic co-operation is more widely voiced in the public sphere than it was ten years ago. Progress has been made in the rendering of national legislation and practices in compliance with international standards for the protection of human and minority rights. There is a growing understanding that targeted measures must be adopted to address the problems of the most vulnerable minority group—the Roma. A government consultative body on ethnic issues has been established which has divisions at the regional level. A persistent tendency is the creation of partnerships between public authorities at all government levels and NGOs. The transition to a market economy affected most unfavourably the socio-economic status of Roma, Turks and Bulgarian Muslims. Uneven development during the transition has resulted in increased ethnocentrism and the manifestation of open discriminatory attitudes, particularly against the Roma community.

The obvious progress that has been made in the field of inter-ethnic relations must be complemented by the adoption of further democratic measures for the preservation of ethnicity and the future integration of minorities:

· The current information on the status quo of the various ethnic groups living in Bulgaria must be made available to the public.

· Criminal accusations made on the basis of race or ethnicity must be explicitly included in the provisions of the Penal Code as an aggravating circumstance.

· It is important to establish an extra-judiciary institution (an ombudsman) to which victims may appeal to resolve problems of discrimination at national and local levels.

· An approach of 'positive action' must be applied to equalise the opportunities of minorities with those for the majority under the conditions of competition and democracy. This is a different approach from 'positive discrimination', which can intensify negative stereotypes and the humiliation of minorities.

· Minorities and their organisations must become active participants in the public sphere by putting forth their problems and decision-making processes for addressing them. This will help in the establishment of programmes for integrated and sustainable development to respond to the specific nature and needs of the local community. The active stand of minorities in the public administrative government at all levels (national, regional, and local) is a prerequisite for the successful implementation of such programmes.

The growing responsibility of public authorities for the democratic and effective management of multi-cultural communities requires more than just a traditional proficiency in the major principles of public administration:

· Political dedication and mutual co-operation between authorities is needed to solve problems at all government levels and to ensure the provision of adequate services to the population.

· It is necessary to know and understand the cultural peculiarities of the various ethnic communities that exist together. Administrative decisions should be made within the broader context of respect for the cultures of all ethnic groups.

· Improvement is needed in the organisational systems, procedures and practices of all levels of public administration in order to ensure that they are as flexible, open, accessible, accountable and democratic as possible in their interactions with minority groups and individuals.

· It is important to establish a clear division of roles, prerogatives, and responsibilities among the various actors involved in community development. This should have a positive impact on efficiency, equity, and economic, political and civil participation at the local level.

· It is of key importance that governors and other public administrators possess the conflict-management and mediation skills necessary to act as 'honest brokers' in the case of inter-ethnic conflicts of interest. These skills should be acquired by students of public administration and by acting public administrators. This requires:

    a) The inclusion of special courses on ethnic conflict management/resolution within the curricula of public administration schools;

    b) The inclusion of specific training courses for acting public administrators that focus on issues of multi-ethnic community management;

    c) The compilation of a database of 'good practices' in managing multi-ethnic communities that should be easily accessible for public administrators;

    d) The encouragement of networking among public administrators in order to facilitate the exchange of ideas and experiences on these issues.

The major requirements of the modern world place a challenge before the public authorities in the management of multi-ethnic communities:

· The world is a multi-cultural place and this calls for the implementation of a managerial policy which combines multi-ethnicity and inter-ethnicity. Therefore, representatives of authority need to be ethnically sensitive in order to be aware of the differences on the intercultural plane. This approach will lead to proactive practices of inter-ethnic collaboration, partnership and co-operation for the joint improvement of each individual local community. The diversity of cultures and languages must not split the community but enrich it.

· The processes of globalisation and localisation are deepening. They can be experienced even at a local level where people act locally even when they think 'globally'. Public authorities must skillfully combine the strategies for global macrodevelopment of the community and individual strategies for human development, which are enacted at a personal level and depend on local conditions for their successful operation.

Further Reading

Aspects of the Ethnocultural Situation (1992) Sofia: Centre for Research on Democracy and Fridfich Nauman Foundation.

Aspects of the Ethnocultural Situation (1995) Sofia: ACCESS Association.

Bell, John D. (ed.) (1998) *Bulgaria in Transition. Politics, Economics, Society and Culture After Communism*, USA: Westview Press.

Danov, Danail (1993) 'Globalization and Ethnic Divides', Prague: *Nationalism Notes*, Institute on Nationalism and Liberty, Central European University, No. 2, March, pp. 4-24.

Herrman, Margaret S. (ed.) (1994) *Resolving Conflict: Strategies for Local Government,* USA: International City/Country ICMA Management Association.

Ivanov, Ivan (1999) *Intercultural Education*, Shumen: Aksios.

Marushiakova, Ö. and V. Popov (1995) *The Roma in Bulgaria*, Sofia: Klub 90 Publishers.

The Minority Press in Bulgaria (1878-1997) (1998) Sofia: Interethnic Initiative for Human Rights Foundation.

Regional Policy in the Republic of Bulgaria. Adaptation to European Experience (1996) Sofia: Ministry of Regional Development and Construction.

Zloch-Christy, Iliana (ed.) (1996) *Bulgaria in a Time of Change*, USA: Ashgate Publishing Company.

Annex

Table A.1. The Largest Ethnic Minorities in Bulgaria and their Main Characteristics:

Ethnic Group	Number in thousands and % of total	Character of distribution (compact/dispersed)	Type of distribution (city/village)	Religion	Region(s)
Turks	800.0 9.43%	Dispersed, but regionally concentrated	Predominantly rural. The ratio: rural to urban population is 68% to 32%	Muslim 98.8%	Southeast: the Rhodope mountain: Kirdzhali, Haskovo; Northeast: (Deliormana): Razgrad, Burgas, Silistra, Targovishte, Varna, Shumen
Roma	313.0 3.69%	Dispersed on the territory of the country but residence in compact homogeneous communities 'Roma areas' or 'Roma neighbourhoods'	Urban 52% and rural 48%	Christians (60.4%) Muslims (39.2%)	Cities: regional centres and towns (Sofia, Plovdiv, Sliven, Pazardzik, Lom, Stara Zagora, Vidin, Montana, Burgas, Varna; Rural population in the regions of Lom, Sliven, Plovdiv, Stara Zagora, etc.)
Russians	17.0 0.20%	Predominantly dispersed	urban	Russian Orthodox	Cities and towns (Sofia, Shumen, Varna, Plovdiv, etc.)
Armenians	13.7 0.16%	dispersed	Urban 99%	Christians	Cities and towns (Plovdiv, Sofia, Varna, Russe, Shumen, etc.)
Macedonians	10.8 0.13%	Predominantly compact, regionally concentrated	Rural and Urban	Christians	Southwest part (the region of Pirin mountain)
Karakachans	5.0 0.06%	Predominantly compact	Rural and urban	Christians	Villages and towns close to the mountain pastures (the region of the Balkan mountain range—Stara Planina—Berkovitza, Montana, Sliven, Tvarditza, Nikolaevo, Peshtera, Samokov, etc.

Ethnic Group	Number in thousands and % of total	Character of distribution (compact/ dispersed)	Type of distribution (city/village)	Religion	Region(s)
Wallachians	5.0 0.06%	Predominantly compact	Rural and urban	Christians	Northwest region near the northern border: the Danube river (the regions of Vidin, Kula, Oriahovo, Lom, Nikopol, Svishtov, etc.) and in the inner parts of the country—in the regions of Peshtera, Dupnitza
Greeks	4.9 0.05%	Dispersed but regionally concentrated	urban	Christians	Black sea coast towns: Varna, Burgas, Tzarevo, Pomorie, Ahtopol, Sozopol, Nesebar, etc.; in towns of central southern part: Assenovgrad, Topo-lovgrad, Plovdiv, etc.
Tatars	4.4 0.05%	compact	Predominantly rural	Muslim	Rural population in Dobrudza region and Ludogorie region
Jews	3.5 0.04%	Dispersed and compact in the capital	Urban—95%	Judaism	Cities and towns: (approximately one-half live in Sofia) Plovdiv. Russe, Shumen, Varna, Burgas, Kyustendil, etc.
Gagaus	1.5 0.02 %	Predominantly compact	Predominantly rural	Christians	Northeast part: the regions of Balchik, Varna, Shumen, etc.

*Table A.2. Some Demographic and Socio-economic Characteristics
of the Major Ethnic Groups in Bulgaria (in %)*

Characteristics	Bulgarians	Bulgarian Turks	Roma	Other
Age group				
0 – 29 years	36.3	51.4	66.0	38.7
30 – 59 years	40.5	37.0	28.9	44.1
60 years and over	22.2	11.6	5.1	17.2
Economically active age				
Under economically active age	18.2	27.5	40.7	14.4
In economically active age	55.4	58.0	53.0	62.4
Above economically active age	26.4	14.5	6.3	23.2
Education				
University/College	20.2	2.0	0.9	
Secondary /11/12 grades/	54.0	24.6	7.8	
Elementary /8 grades/	22.6	55.0	46.2	
Primary /4 grades/	3.0	16.0	36.7	
Illiterate	0.2	2.3	8.5	
Unemployment				
Ethnic group average	14,43	25,04	39.13	20.66
Unemployment men	13,79	24.99	40.73	19.59
Unemployment women	15,08	25.09	37.52	21.72
Poverty level (1996)				
Ethnic group average	10.4	24.5	65.1	
Adults without children	14.7	41.6	76.5	
Adults with children	18.9	30.1	63.3	
Retired	15.0	34.8	71.4	

Sources: National Statistical Institute, Sofia (1994) *Results of the 1992 Population Census, Vol. I Demographic Characteristics*; The World Bank Report (1999) *Bulgaria, Poverty During the Transition.*

Table A.3. Minorities' Rights: Actual Recognition, Real Fulfillment and Public Opinion.
Answers of Christian Bulgarians (in %)

Rights	Actual recognition	Real fulfillment	Positive answers 1994	Positive answers 1997
To establish organisations and associations for preserving and developing their own culture	Yes	Yes	63	67
To publish books and other publications in their native language	Yes	Yes	42	52
To study their mother tongue in state schools	Yes	Yes	21	29
Education in mother tongue at school	No	No	7	9
Representation in Parliament	Yes	Yes	50	50
Representation in local authorities	Yes	Yes	49	47
Public mother-tongue signs (companies, advertisements, road signs, etc.)	Not forbidden	Yes (private)	7	12
To form their own political parties	No	No	23	25
Territorial autonomy	No	No	1.5	3
To have their own TV-channels	Not forbidden	No	–	18
To have broadcasts in their own language on national TV	Not forbidden	No	–	20
To have their own newspapers	Yes	Yes	–	45

Source: Peter-Emil Mitev (1999) 'From Neighbourhood to Fellow Citizenship', *Etnoreporter*, No. 1, Sofia: IEIHR, pp. 15-17. This data comes from the surveys presented in: *Interrelations of Compatibility and Incompatibility between the Christians and the Muslims in Bulgaria* (1994) and (1997) Sofia: IMIR.

Table A.4. Regional (Oblasti) Distribution of the Major Ethnic Groups in Bulgaria and Some Other Characteristics of Regional Scope

District (Oblast)	Total number	Bulgarians	Bulgarian Turks	Roma	Other	No answer	% of minority ethnic groups (1992)	% of Roma population (1992)	Number of school drop-outs (1998/1999)	% of registered unemployed (as of 31 Dec. 1999)	% of nonqualified registered unemployed (as of 31 1998)	% of central subsidy in municipal budgets expenditure 1998	Value of human development index 1999
Country Total	8,487,317	7,271,185	800,052	313,396	94,203	8,481	14.2	4.8	36155	15.97	62.35	38	0.600
Sofia city	1,190,126	1,146,509	4,432	13,902	19,600	5,683	3.2	2.8	2,991	4.20	35.78	24	0.682
Blagoevgrad	351,637	296,636	35,975	8,209	10,769	48	15.6	5.4	1,007	15.29	56.68	49	0.654
Bourgas	440,372	361,159	58,201	16,120	4,308	584	17.9	4.6	1,657	14.34	70.26	28	0.716
Varna	462,970	404,246	33,461	17,077	8,122	64	12.7	5.4	2,132	15.38	59.28	26	0.603
Tarnovo	318,251	286,878	20,824	7,236	3,208	105	9.8	3.3	1,262	18.23	56.82	41	0.638
Vidin	151,636	142,645	295	7,965	731	-	5.9	5.7	716	23.48	57.09	59	0.572
Vratza	270,679	255,763	1,379	11,927	1,548	62	5.5	5.0	1,172	23.29	59.71	30	0.596
Gabrovo	161,967	148,538	9,629	1,585	2,089	146	8.2	2.3	607	9.67	50.21	39	0.700
Kardzali	213,806	72,445	138,249	1,899	851	362	65.9	1.3	1,454	15.07	75.07	65	0.613
Kyustendil	181,347	174,111	358	6,057	786	35	4.0	3.8	918	13.79	59.86	40	0.504
Lovetch	190,262	175,143	7,796	6,384	930	7	7.9	3.8	944	18.41	61.63	45	0.607
Montana	208,198	187,567	322	19,079	1,230	-	9.9	9.8	1,052	24.14	58.82	63	0.536
Pazardzik	326,123	279,284	22,999	21,810	2,014	16	14.3	7.3	1,668	26.01	65.04	43	0.469
Pernik	163,307	160,224	169	2,142	657	115	1.8	1.7	533	12.51	56.33	43	0.648

Pleven	348,614	322,189	14,900	7,111	2,406	8	7.0	2.7	1631	19.52	58.32	39	0.625
Plovdiv	734,495	657,968	46,774	21,239	8,551	63	10.4	4.0	3,357	13.71	63.30	43	0.611
Razgrad	167,410	78,749	79,490	7,464	1,549	158	52.9	5.4	958	26.01	74.90	54	0.514
Rousse	288,702	236,960	35,230	11,934	4,426	152	17.9	5.7	1,350	18.82	59.12	39	0.554
Silistra	161,063	99,702	52,812	6,519	2,030	-	38.1	5.3	829	20.63	64.49	64	0.503
Sliven	234,785	192,740	19,419	18,183	4,262	181	17.8	9.6	1,146	19.69	72.46	51	0.416
Smolian	159,752	147,894	10,708	514	545	91	7.4	0.7	231	25.74	56.00	62	0.599
Sofia	289,962	276,035	1,032	11,664	1,231	-	4.8	4.4	985	13.11	67.42	37	0.511
Stara Zagora	397,339	350,771	18,845	24,143	3,580	-	11.7	7.0	1,977	14.78	69.37	20	0.665
Dobritch	232,780	177,339	33,939	18,449	3,035	18	23.8	9.2	1,663	19.60	64.30	41	0.514
Targovishte	151,339	90,284	50,931	9,474	650	-	40.3	6.7	664	29.69	69.82	59	0.532
Haskovo	295,503	246,658	32,583	14,014	1,687	561	16.3	5.3	1,492	15.79	62.27	44	0.508
Shoumen	220,320	138,633	64,704	14,727	2,234	22	37.1	7.7	1,152	21.83	73.05	53	0.575
Yambol	176,552	164,115	4,594	6,669	1,174	-	7.0	4.4	607	21.52	58.95	46	0.550

Sources: National Statistical Institute, Sofia (1994) *Results of the 1992 Population Census, Vol. I Demographic Characteristics*, Sofia; National Labour Office; National Centre for Territorial Development; Ministry of Education and Science; Ministry of Finance; UNDP Report on Human Development (1999) Bulgaria.

* % of State subsidy in total expenditure in municipality budgets—district level generalised data, 1998

THE FICTION OF ETHNIC HOMOGENEITY: MINORITIES IN THE CZECH REPUBLIC

Laura Laubeová

Contents

THE FICTION OF ETHNIC HOMOGENEITY: MINORITIES IN THE CZECH REPUBLIC

Laura Laubeová

Abstract

This chapter combines descriptive and normative analysis relevant to inter-ethnic relations in the Czech Republic and focuses on their manifestation on local-level governance. While briefly outlining the situation of other minority groups, this chapter will focus largely on the most 'problematic' and marginalised ethnic group—the Roma—and the hostile majority attitudes towards this group. The chapter aims to focus on 'good practices' that have helped foster multi-ethnic co-operation as well as challenges and policy obstacles to Roma integration. The main factors analysed in this chapter are the lack of decentralisation and the politically stymied process of public administration reform, in combination with the so-called 'citizenship principle' (proclaiming equality of all citizens, regardless of ethnicity). Most policies targeted at minorities have been initiated by the central government, largely in response to international criticism (arising when large numbers of the Roma community began to emigrate) and after the establishment of the office of the Government Commissioner for Human Rights in September 1998. Since then, the political discourse on the status of minorities has altered—the citizenship principle has been complemented by specific measures reflecting the need for special recognition and protection measures for national minorities as stipulated in the Constitution and the Charter of Fundamental Rights and Freedoms. Important national documents reviewed in this chapter include the Bratinka Report and the Government Concept on Romany Integration to the Draft Bill on Minorities. The research provides a range of good practices, illustrated by case studies initiated at the local level and by nongovernmental organisations. Conflictual issues and policies are also highlighted.

1. Introduction

Analysis of the situation of ethnic minorities in the Czech Republic clearly identifies several major challenges. The following areas demand critical attention by policy-makers at both the central and the local level of government:
1. Minority rights protection,
2. Perception of ethnic homogeneity,
3. Inter-ethnic tension resulting from increased immigration,
4. The situation of the Roma minority.

In order to deconstruct these pressing issues, however, this chapter operates on the premise that all four of these areas must be understood within the context of the process of decentralisation of authority and power from the central to the local level of government in the Czech Republic. As such, this chapter will devote significant attention to decentralisation, and will argue that one of the major political obstacles to improved minority protection, representation, education and political participation—and improved inter-ethnic relations in general—is the limited degree of authority that has been devolved to local government. Indeed, public administration and policy decision-making remain highly centralised in the Czech Republic. Local administrative bodies make few policy decisions of their own, and instead act largely as deconcentrated state administrative bodies. This chapter will argue that this situation results in irresponsible implementation of state-directed (or 'top-down') policies by local officials, who have little invested in these policies.

Against this conceptual backdrop, this chapter will touch briefly on the first three issues listed above; significant problems exist in each area. But because the integration of the Roma minority constitutes the greatest policy obstacle for the Czech government at all levels, this chapter will focus primarily on the status of this highly marginalised, disenfranchised minority group from a variety of perspectives.

Attention will also be paid to the important role played by nongovernmental actors (NGOs) in developing policy initiatives designed to facilitate minority integration. Because top-down policy-making has produced largely unsatisfactory results in terms of minority issues, and because local administrative actors have such limited authority in policy areas of concern to minorities, the civil sector has played an important role in bridging the gap between policy and practice in the Czech Republic.

1.1. State policies

New policy initiatives relevant to minority rights issues are more apparent at the central level of government than at the local level. Their implementation is often dependent on the capacity and co-operation of numerous agents (public, private and civic) at various levels (central, regional and local) and in all areas of policy-making (education, employment, housing, police, etc.).

Certain programmes do focus on local governments and communities and provide space for multi-ethnic co-operation. For example, the Crime Prevention Comprehensive Programme was initiated by the central government and provides for a number of community centres and Romany advisers at district offices. Another central initiative is the National Employment Plan, which provides space for active employment policies administered at regional and local levels.

Many new policy measures have been introduced and important processes initiated following the establishment of the Office of the Human Rights Commissioner. These are:
·   Work on the new government Concept on the Romany Community, including the proposal of the Commission for Ethnic Equality and a plan for 'equalising action'.[1] (In February 2000 the full Concept on Romany Integration was, however, returned by the Czech government in order to be redrafted.)

- Monitoring the implementation of international commitments of the government, mainly the Framework Convention on the Protection of Ethnic Minorities, and the UN Convention on the Elimination of All Forms of Racism. With the implementation of the Framework Convention, preparation began in 1999 on the Act on National and Ethnic Minorities (the so-called 'Minority Act'). This Act may constitute conditions for minority representation on the local level, though it is still too early to forecast its content and consequences.
- Publishing of the first Annual Report on Human Rights in the Czech Republic in April 1999 addresses issues of ethnic and national minorities and foreign workers and residents.
- Within the Government Council for Human Rights, eight Working Sections were established in April 1999 that provide platforms for communication between central agency representatives and NGOs and aim to assist in finding solutions in the area of human rights protection.
- In April 1999 the government again proposed the Bill on (the establishment of the Office of the) Ombudsman, which was later approved and came into effect in January 2000.
- In May 1999 the government approved the National Plan of Employment with policies targeting Roma.
- In June 1999 'Tolerance'—a campaign against racism—was announced and allocated 10 million CZK. The campaign began in February 2000.
- In July 1999 the government approved measures to clamp down on skinhead organisations.
- In July 1999 the government approved the proposal to amend the Education Act, facilitating Roma access to secondary education. The amendment was later passed by the Parliament.
- In July 1999 the Senate passed a new Citizenship Law; it replaced the discriminatory Citizenship Law of 1993 (that disallowed former emigrants to hold dual citizenship).

Another significant top-down issue not compiled above relates to (the now extremely small) German minority. The historically ambivalent relationship between Czechs and Germans has improved since the signing of the Czech-German Friendship Declaration in May 1997, which brought the two countries closer to resolving the controversial issue of the removal of Germans from Czechoslovakia after the World War II.

---

[1] Otherwise known as 'positive action' or 'affirmative action'.

1.2. Local policies

Although many constructive policy measures have been initiated at the central level of government, these initiatives are not enough to solve the myriad problems facing minority groups in the Czech Republic. Local-level initiatives—or 'bottom up' processes—are crucial to resolving minority issues. A number of locally targeted programmes currently are in progress. The introduction and support of Romany teaching assistants can be regarded as one of the most significant bottom-up policy programmes. The same can be said about other nongovernmental educational projects focusing on tolerance, nonviolence and human rights. Projects facilitating communication and problem-solving at the local level, such as round tables organised by the Czech Centre for Conflict Prevention, have proved quite successful. Without question, policies and practice at the local level should play a more and more significant role in the future.

One of the main problems ethnic minorities face in the Czech Republic is the high level of prejudice and intolerance; this is not sufficiently addressed by the public education system. Other negative factors include the political exploitation of ethnic problems (mainly by local-level political representatives), low levels of professionalism and competence among public administration officials, the lack of relevant training for teachers and administrative staff at all levels, and insufficient communication between municipalities and ethnic minority representatives. For example, poor communication between the local town hall and the Roma community was largely responsible for the widely publicised events in the town of Usti nad Labem, where a wall was built to separate the homes of the majority community from buildings housing Roma (details in Case Study 3). Thus, although the Czech Republic has made important steps in the development of active policies addressing inter-ethnic conflicts, the result has been perceived not as integration but as segregation.

2. Ethnic Homogeneity—Fact or Fiction?

2.1. Ethnic composition

With the division of the former Czechoslovak Republic at the start of 1993, the Czech Republic became a relatively homogenous society in ethnic terms. Almost 94% of the present population is Czech. Slovaks constitute 3% of the population. Other minorities are Roma (2-3%), Poles (0.6%), Germans (0.5%), Hungarians (0.2%), Ukrainians, Bulgarians, Ruthenians, Russians, Jews, Croats and Greeks. More details on ethnic composition, as reflected in the 1991 census, are available in Annex 1.

The Czech Republic has had some traditions of multi-ethnicity as part of the Habsburg monarchy, and later the Austro-Hungarian Empire, for three centuries. The Czechoslovak Republic was established in October 1918. Its composition was multi-ethnic: 51% Czech, 23% German, 14% Slovak and 5.5% Hungarian, according to a census conducted in 1921. Historical development brought about major shifts in the majority-minority ratio. Even after World War II—despite the Nazi genocide directed at Jews and at Czech and Moravian Roma and despite the postwar removal of Germans—Czechoslovakia remained an ethnically heterogeneous state with two distinct nations: Czechs and Slovaks. In 1992, 7% of the Czechoslovak population was composed of ethnic minorities—i.e. more than one million out of a population of 15 million, not including Czechs living in Slovakia and Slovaks in the Czech Republic.

Since the establishment of the Czech Republic in 1993, the percentage of ethnic minorities still represents approximately 6% of the total population—the majority of which are Slovaks who are socio-economically well integrated and generally assimilated in terms of culture and language. The Roma have been largely assimilated in terms of language, as have been the Germans, Poles, Hungarians and other small minorities.[2] Apart from national minorities, whose members—in accordance with the definition of national minority—have Czech citizenship, there are approximately 220,000 foreigners with long-term or permanent residency in the Czech Republic, mainly of Slovak, Ukrainian, Vietnamese and Chinese origin. The number of illegal immigrants has been steadily increasing over the past few years. The issue of illegal Vietnamese traders from Germany residing in the Czech Republic has become a particular source of inter-ethnic tension in Northern Bohemia since 1997. The actual number of foreigners in the country may be much higher than official estimates suggest. Most likely, an additional 200,000 illegal workers and another 100,000 transit migrants[3] are living in the Czech Republic—making the total number of foreigners more than half a million.

Apart from the new phenomenon of illegal foreigners, the most 'problematic' and marginalised ethnic group remains the Roma.[4] This group can also be important as a model case study, as positive experiences of inter-ethnic communication and the elimination of prejudice against them can serve as a springboard for improved relations with other minorities and ethnic groups in the country. For these two reasons, the remainder of this chapter will focus primarily on the situation of the Roma minority.

2.2. Roma in the Czech Republic

The end of communist rule in 1989 brought about the official recognition of the Roma as an ethnic minority group; it also brought with it overt racism and the emergence of extremist, right-wing political parties that have included anti-Roma measures in their political programmes. The number of racially motivated attacks against the Roma has also increased dramatically since 1989. Growing data accumulated by nongovernmental

---

[2] Only Poles who are concentrated in North Moravia have managed to keep their schools in their mother tongue—a system extending from kindergartens and primary schools to several secondary schools. Other minorities are geographically dispersed.

[3] Office of the Human Rights Commissioner (1999) *Zpráva o migraci za rok 1998* (Draft report on migration in 1998), June.

[4] Roma are the largest 'visible' minority. It is very difficult to estimate their number, as there are currently no policies on ethnic monitoring of Roma and the 1991 census figures do not reflect the reality accurately—the method was self-declaration (only 32,903 people declared to be Roma, i.e. approximately one-tenth of the total number). Usual estimates of their number vary, official number has been agreed to be approximately 200-300,000, i.e. 2-3% of the total population. Roma themselves give higher estimates. Recently, however, some estimates say that the number of Roma decreased due to high emigration abroad.

organisations and, more recently, government sources, indicates that Roma in the Czech Republic face discrimination by the state and its public administration, providers of public services, the education system and other institutions. The present despair of the Roma community has been reflected in several recent waves of Roma emigration. Indeed, emigration has become a widespread 'exit strategy' for this vulnerable and marginalised minority group.[5]

The growing tension between the Czech majority and the Roma has become a more significant social problem then ever before. The high number of unemployed Roma, reaching 70% to 90% of the total Roma population,[6] the inappropriateness and ineffectiveness of the education system with respect to the Roma, and limited access to vocational training have all contributed to the violence toward and criminalisation of the Roma community. Roma crime rates cannot be objectively assessed as above-average in comparison with other groups of the same social status, and crime rates also usually include petty crime and minor offenses. The Roma continue to be perceived as the 'most dangerous' group in Czech society.[7] Stereotypes of the Roma as 'inherently criminal' people make it difficult for those Roma individuals who wish to be integrated into the workforce and education system.

The 'social costs' of the current state of affairs have been considerable, and it is apparent that if the situation is not addressed they will continue to grow. The social costs of discrimination, segregation and marginalisation of certain groups in society include increased social expenditures, increased punitive expenditures and greater expenditures on social integration. Though it has become impossible to ignore the need for intervention, it will prove very difficult to introduce structural changes with a long-term impact that would extend to the community level. The difficulties lie mainly in the huge social

---

[5] Followed by Vlach Roma, Hungarian Roma, Moravian Roma, Sinti and other groups.

    Vlach Roma, the only group that had been nomadic until 1958, are the most closed and culturally and linguistically specific group. Their representatives claim to have a status of a separate ethnic minority.

    Within Slovak Roma themselves, there are big differences between those who came to the Czech lands after World War II and those who came in the 1970s and afterwards.

    Although Roma originally came from India around 1000 AD and are known as an itinerant, travelling population, they have long been settled in the Central and Eastern European lands. Slovak Roma, for example, have been settled for 200-300 years. The majority of Czech and Moravian Roma were killed during World War II: very few families survived. Slovak Roma now inhabiting Czech lands were first brought there after 1948 to replace expelled Germans, as well as to provide labour in the industrialised areas of northern Moravia and northern Bohemia. Many others followed in a voluntary migration seeking a better life.

[6] This increased emigration led directly to the reintroduction of visa requirements for Czech citizens entering Canada. The influx to Canada in summer 1997 and to Britain in autumn 1997, as well as later on, brought the issue to the attention of political representatives and the general public, but also increased the expression of negative feelings and attitudes towards Roma in the media.

[7] While the national unemployment rate was 5%. In: Bratinka Report (1997) October, paragragh 7.2. In July 1999 the unemployment in the CR rose to 8.8%. In 2000 it has reached almost 10%. In certain areas the unemployment of Roma exceeds 95% (Czech Helsinki Committee Report 1997, http://www.helcom.cz).

resistance to any changes in the area of social redistribution. In addition, past negative experience with communist indoctrination and social engineering also play an important role in contributing to this resistance.

The communist regime regarded the problems and needs of the Roma population mainly as social and economic concerns. The Roma were viewed as victims of the capitalist class system and a simple solution was designed: by removing poverty and providing employment for the Roma—i.e. by addressing the economic causes of the so-called 'Gypsy problem', and by providing education, health care and social security—their situation would automatically improve. This would enable them to integrate successfully into Czechoslovak society and participate in building a communist future. Thus, policies of assimilation and 'co-ordinated dispersal'[8] were designed and put into practice. The main error in the approach of the communist regime was its refusal to take into account Romany ethnic and cultural distinctiveness, their traditions and their language. The Roma were not recognised as a national minority. As a consequence, they were not entitled to any special legal rights—for example, in education—in contrast to the Hungarian, Polish and Ukrainian minority groups. The Czechoslovak government decided to fully assimilate the Roma into the dominant population.[9] This authoritarian policy was extremely damaging to the social and cultural bonds of the Roma population, particularly because mainstream Czechoslovak society was not welcoming, and often hostile, to them.

Another fatal mistake was the communist government's failure to take into consideration the negative attitudes and deep aversion of the majority population toward the Roma—completely ignoring signs and manifest expressions of racism and prejudice harboured by the majority population, including national and local government officials themselves. Thus, despite officially declared 'equality', the Roma faced all forms of discrimination and were not given equal opportunities in employment.

2.3. Gaps between policy and practice

In analysing the past, it must be noted that before 1989 all relevant political documents declared the integration of Roma as a significant policy goal. In spite of this, no effective legal, institutional or financial means were created to facilitate this integration. Since 1995, a number of positive changes have occurred in this respect. Much progress remains to be made, however, in order to reach the point at which state officials and policy-makers are able to reflect upon the current state of affairs and their own attitudes and prejudice. 'State policy circumvents systems, i.e. it does not change them, but it rather substitutes them with temporary measures (such as special educational programmes only for Roma); however, the basic problem of structural discrimination is not only not being solved, but it is

---

[8] Pamela Jenkins (1999) American Social Problems in a Global Environment, Charles University Prague, a two-week course, summer 1999.

[9] Eva Sotolova (1997) 'Prichod Romu do Evropy', in: Pekarek Pavel et al., Romove–reflexe problemu. Soubor textu k romske problematice, Praha: Pastelka, pp. 71-77.

[10] Resolution of the Central Committee of the Czechoslovak Communist Party, April 1958. See: Eva Davidova (1995) Cesty Romu, Romano Drom 1945-1990, Olomouc: Palacky University.

not even discerned by state policy'.[10] In this respect, positive examples from other countries may be used by Czech policy-makers to accelerate social change.

3. The Legal and Political Position of Minorities

The main legal problem with respect to minority rights thus far seems to be the weak enforcement of relevant provisions of the Czech Constitution and the slow pace at which international conventions signed by the Czech Republic have been integrated into domestic law, norms and regulations. The problem lies not only in insufficient respect for human rights and in insufficient monitoring of their implementation but also in the indolence and ignorance of state and public administration in the area of law enforcement. There are currently no mechanisms with which to monitor and/or limit the racial prejudice of state employees and law enforcement personnel.

The major policy document that influences central policies toward minorities is Government Resolution 63/1994. This document is not legally binding but establishes the basic principles of Czech minority policy, the legal position of minorities and the protection of their rights. The Council for National Minorities of the Government of the Czech Republic, established in 1993, includes representatives of six minority groups. The Council itself has no executive power and serves only as an advisory body to the government. In September 1998 the Council fell within the jurisdiction of the Office of the Government Commissioner for Human Rights.

The rights of national minorities are also protected through international commitments of the Czech Republic that according to the Czech Constitution 'take preference before the law'.[11] An important international instrument is the Framework Convention for the Protection of National Minorities which assigns an obligation to the contracting parties based on the equal social position of people belonging to minority groups in the areas of education, culture, employment and politics. The Framework Convention was ratified in December 1997 and came into effect in April 1998. A year later, the Office of the Government Commissioner for Human Rights published a report on compliance with this convention, stating that 'the absence of more detailed legislation, as presupposed by the Charter, has resulted in a legislative deficit since adoption of the Charter in 1991'.[12]

---

[11] In *Socioklub* (1999) p. 492.

[12] As stipulated in Article 10 of the Constitution of the Czech Republic: 'Ratified and promulgated international treaties on human rights and fundamental freedoms, which are binding on the Czech Republic, are directly binding and take precedence over the law'. They are the following:
 – UN International Convention on the Elimination of All Forms of Racial Discrimination (No. 95/1974 Coll.)
 – UN International Convention on the Suppression and Punishment of the Crime of Apartheid
 – UN International Covenant on Civil and Political Rights (No. 120/1976 Coll.)
 – UN International Covenant on Economic, Social and Cultural Rights (No. 120/1976 Coll.)
 – UN Convention on the Rights of the Child Convention Concerning Discrimination in Respect of Employment and Occupation, ILO No.111
 – European Convention for the Protection of Human Rights and Fundamental Freedoms
 – Framework Convention for the Protection of National Minorities.

The report further states that 'discrimination is commonplace in the Czech Republic, especially against the Roma... The law does not define sanctions for cases of racial (and ethnic) discrimination in the educational system, in the health care system, in prisons and in other areas of society'.[13] According to human rights NGOs, numerous reports of both participants and observers indicate that Roma suffer widespread discrimination in the Czech justice system.[14]

Legal protection of minorities in the Czech Republic is ensured by the Czech Constitution and by the Charter of Fundamental Rights and Freedoms. Further, the Criminal Code and Civic Code explicitly require equality before the law. There is insufficient protection, however, against discrimination in the Criminal Code, under which there is no formulation that makes discrimination a criminal offense. It can be said that Czech law prohibits, but does not penalise, acts of racial discrimination. In other words, in the absence of implementation procedures, the Constitution contains only formal and overly general proclamations that have not been developed into particular laws. The only 'discriminatory' law, the Citizenship Law of 1993, was replaced by a new citizenship law that was approved by the Senate in July 1999. The new Citizenship Law allows former emigrants to hold dual citizenship and facilitates the process of obtaining citizenship for Slovaks living in the Czech Republic since the 1993 secession of its two entities.[15]

3.1. Protection against racism

Many positive changes have occurred since 1995, when a Roma individual was brutally murdered in his house by skinheads in a provincial town.[16] 1995 was a crucial year in terms of the acknowledgement and monitoring of racially motivated crimes. In this respect the Criminal Code was amended, police units focusing on extremism were created and the Chief Prosecutor issued a general directive regulating the procedures in prosecuting racially motivated criminal acts. After the mass emigration of the Roma in 1997, the Ministry of Interior—largely due to significant international pressure—began publicising instances of state action to combat hate crimes and other relevant statistics.

Currently, the Czech Republic is preparing ratification process of the European Charter on Minority and Regional Languages.

[13] *Information about Compliance with Principles Set Forth in the Framework Convention...*, 1 April 1999, Part 1, Section 16.5.

[14] Ibid., Part 2, Article 4, Section 3.

[15] According to the European Roma Rights Centre (ERRC), 'repeated allegations of differential treatment of Roma victims (inadequate investigation of their complaints by law enforcement authorities) and Roma defendants (subjected to more frequent and longer periods of pre-trial detention, and disproportionately severe sentences) suggest that the second class status of Roma in Czech society does not end at the courthouse door'. In ERRC (1998) Submission to the Committee for Elimination of All Forms of Racial Discrimination, Executive Summary.

[16] Such incidents have been frequent and numerous examples have triggered international outrage.

In July 1999 the Czech government approved a plan to fight extremism, drawn up by Deputy Premier Pavel Rychetsky and Human Rights Commissioner Petr Uhl. The plan clamps down on organisations and movements that act against human rights, and provides guidelines to be followed by the Ministries of Education, Interior, Justice, and Labor and Social Affairs.[17] It also lists organisations that can be dissolved by the Interior Minister. The list includes the Patriotic Front and the National Front of Castists, which disseminates propaganda against foreigners, Jews, Roma and homosexuals.[18]

3.2. Central policies targeting the Roma

Pressed by the international implications of the exodus of Roma over the past few years, the Czech government has repeatedly expressed its determination to solve problems faced by the Roma community. In October 1997 the so-called 'Bratinka Report' was adopted by the government and led to the establishment of the Interdepartmental Commission for Romany Affairs and prepared a long-term plan of action.[19] One of the major steps forward was the establishment of Romany social advisers at the district level, as well as the institution of changes in educational policies, such as the introduction of Romany teaching assistants. (See Case Study 1 for details.) However, most changes have been met with resistance from bureaucrats in charge of their implementation,[20] local-level representatives and teachers. In spite of these difficulties, these changes are gradually being introduced with the support of nonstate organisations and initiatives.

In September 1998 the government established the Office of the Government Commissioner for Human Rights and appointed Petr Uhl—a well-known human rights activist—as Commissioner. His role is to initiate and co-ordinate activities in the field of human rights monitoring (with no executive powers or budgetary provisions, however).[21] He also serves as the chairperson of the Interdepartmental Commission for Romany Affairs and of the Council for National Minorities.

---

[17] Upon the pressure from abroad the law was partially amended in 1998 so that citizens of the Slovak Republic who had the place of residence in the Czech Republic as of 31 December 1992 could be forgiven the condition of five-year indemnity. The amendment, however, did not remove the discriminatory effect of the law.

[18] One of the reasons behind this measure is the fact that the number of supporters of extremist movements has risen. In 1997 this community was estimated at 5,500 persons and in 1998 around 10,000 persons. 'Roma who ask for asylum abroad giving arguments that they have been prosecuted by skinheads speak the truth', said the Interior Minister when submitting the Report on Prosecuting Racially Motivated Crimes, approved by the government on 14 July 1999.

[19] 'Stále více lidí sympatizuje s extremisty' (More and more people symphatize with extremists) (1999) *MF Dnes*, 15 July, p. 3.

[20] Radio Free Europe (1999) 29 July.

[21] *Report on the Situation of the Romany Community in the Czech Republic and Government Measures Assisting its Integration in Society* (1997) Office of Minister without Portfolio, The Czech Republic Government Office, 29 October . The so-called 'Bratinka Report', includes Government Resolution No. 686/97.

In December 1998 the government established the Government Council for Human Rights as an 'advisory and co-ordination body in the field of protection of human rights and basic freedoms' and appointed the Government Commissioner as its chairperson.[22] In April 1999 the government adopted the 'Policy of the Czech Government towards the Romany Community Supporting their Integration into Society', which will hopefully serve as a catalyst for long-term systemic change in terms of the rights of the Roma. The draft concept also includes a proposal to establish a Commission for Ethnic Equality, and plans to introduce a widespread policy of 'equalising action' are scheduled to take place between 2001 and 2020. An important component of the new policy is a statement on the value of Romany identity, culture, language and history as positive assets for the majority. The Concept of Romany Integration—elaborated át the end of 1999—was not adopted by the Czech government. According to some Roma, this signalled that the government still preferred a policy of assimilation to one of integration.[23]

The majority of Czech policy-makers and opinion leaders have not yet seriously reflected on the status quo and are usually unwilling to acknowledge past political mistakes.[24] State bodies focus only on open manifestations of racism and too often ignore structural and institutional forms of racial discrimination and segregation (for example, local staff of the Ministry of Education and the Ministry of the Interior, i.e. school administrators and police). Given the level of prejudice in the Czech society on the part of many municipal leaders, political representatives and other influential people, and the high level of resistance to social change, the problems that the Roma face are very difficult to address.

4. The Role of Local Government

4.1. Public administration reform and decentralisation

Democratisation and decentralisation began as dual processes after 1989. National committees that previously had served as state administrative bodies were replaced by district and municipal offices. When the Czech Republic emerged as an independent state in 1993, the new Constitution[25] modified its position on local government by creating two territorial-administrative units—municipalities and regions. Current plans call for the creation of fourteen separate regions beginning in 2001. District offices continue to serve as the decentralised authority of state administration. Municipalities perform self-administrated tasks—independent activity—and perform some previously state-administrated functions—transferred activity. With roughly

---

[22] For example, until March 1998 the Ministry of Education was not willing to start implementing Government Resolution No. 686 and officially recognise Romany teaching assistants.

[23] Resolution of the Czech Government No. 579 on Appointing the Government Commissioner for Human Rights (1998) 9 September.

[24] Resolution of the Czech Government No. 809 on Improving the Protection of Human Rights in the Czech Republic (1999) 9 December.

[25] 'Nemají-li se Romové integrovat, co tedy?' (What else if Roma should not integrate?) (2000) *Romano hangos*, 25 February.

ten million inhabitants and 6,244 municipalities, it seems that, on paper at least, there is a considerable degree of decentralisation.

An important step forward in the process of public administration reform occurred in December 1997 when the Czech Parliament passed a law[26] on the establishment of regions and an amendment to the Constitution. These legal initiatives have laid the fundamental foundations for the implementation of the principles of decentralisation and subsidiarity in the future. The government also approved a timetable for legislative work to allow regional local government to be established by the end of 2000.

In March 1999 the government reviewed the Concept of Public Administration Reform, prepared by the Ministry of the Interior and, in May 1999, set further objectives for its implementation (Resolution No. 511). By September 1999 a package of draft laws, constituting the legislative framework for the reform process were submitted to the government and entered into force in January 2000. The reform concept is characterised by:

· transfer of competence from state administration to self-government of regions and municipalities (decentralisation),
· transfer of competence of central state administration to regional state administration (vertical deconcentration),
· exercise of state administration in the first instance on the level of 'small districts' to be established, numbering some 210,
· exercise of self-government by all municipalities.

The side effect of these reforms is the abolishment of the existing 73 district offices (state administration authorities of general competence, i.e. the district tier) and the establishment of some 210 administrative districts ('small districts').

The actual reform process began in January 2000 with enforcement of this law. In practice, regional administrative and local self-governing bodies should be established by November 2000. All other changes will be connected to the transfer of competencies from the central state administration to deconcentrated regional and local administrations. At the same time, the territorial offices of the ministries and other central state administration agencies will be abolished and their competencies transferred to district or regional administration offices. Regional self-governments will be provided with a host of new responsibilities, including activities related to regional socio-economic development.

This somewhat complicated, and still controversial, system of public administration reform presents certain tensions between the state administration and local governments, mainly with respect to the transfer of competencies and the implementation of state policies at the local level. Political pressures has been exerted, mainly on part of the Civic Democratic Party (CDS), with the aim of hindering the reform process. Compared with other CEE countries in which decentralisation took place shortly after the collapse of communism, the situation in the Czech Republic looks rather grim.

---

[26] As apparent from a discussion with Jiri Pilar and Marta Tepla from the Ministry of Eduaction, 28 June 1999, and an answer by Petr Uhl to a question raised at the conference 'Legal Protection of Roma in the Current Europe', 29 June 1999.

4.2. Romany advisers in district offices

In accordance with the Bratinka Report, Roma social advisers are being placed in district offices throughout the Czech Republic. Since September 1999 there has been a regular training programme for these advisers and their assistants, organised by the Institute for Local Development. In many areas, the advisers' work represents a significant step forward in facilitating communication between the municipalities and the Romany community. They help to initiate projects aimed at improving the situation of the Roma (and majority-Roma relations more generally) and sometimes even perform tasks that fall within the jurisdiction of local self-government personnel.

Almost half of the 72 Romany Social Advisers are not of Roma origin (as of February 2000). According to the Secretary of the Interdepartmental Commission for Romany Affairs, this has occurred as a result of a 'bureaucratic error'—the goal had been to employ Roma. When the formal statute of this position was elaborated by the Ministry of Labour and Social Affairs, however, it included the statement that: 'these positions should *preferably* be filled by Roma'—indirectly offering municipalities a legal basis to hire non-Roma advisers. This corresponds with the current trend of giving preference to the Roma only when no appropriate Roma candidates can be found and then offering positions to non-Roma candidates.[27]

According to some experts, there is only limited space for Romany advisers to develop platforms to unite and mobilise the Roma community in their respective communities. This is largely because these advisers are overwhelmed with the everyday problems of their clients regarding housing, social benefits, citizenship, relations with local authorities and schools.[28]

4.3. Political representation

Regarding the representation of minorities in local governments, members of any minority group may be elected—but only as citizens, not as minority representatives. This is due to the fact that the only principle regulating minority-majority issues has been the 'citizenship principle'—i.e. equal treatment of all citizens irrespective of ethnicity. This formal principle is not always appropriate in practice, due to widespread discrimination and the resulting underrepresentation of minorities in the political sphere. Recently, therefore, the citizenship principle has been complemented by the introduction of specific measures (see in Section 3.2). The shift from the citizenship principle is likely to be a slow one, however, and political participation of minorities remains limited at both the local and central level. The fragmentation of the Roma community, its very low level of self-confidence and its exclusion from the media and other public spaces are among the main problems with respect to Roma political participation.

---

[27] Constitution of the Czech Republic, Law No. 1/1993 Coll., Head 7
[28] Constitutional Act No. 347/1997 Coll.

By April 1999 there were 110 Romany citizens associations in the Czech Republic.[29] The common problem with these associations is that they do not co-operate with each other. The state administration does not support any such co-operation, most likely because of fears that a united and politically mobilised Roma community might (rightly) make a series of political claims.

In spite of their many problems, certain positive changes have occurred recently in terms of Roma political representation. In March 1999 a group of twelve Roma representatives met at the New School Foundation (see Case Study 6) in order to discuss a proposal to create a united Roma political party. Only partial agreement has been reached on this issue, but all parties to the discussion have agreed to continue with further negotiations.

In 1997 the Association of Roma Regional Representatives was established. The primary goal of the Association is to formulate regional solutions to current problems faced by the Roma. One of its most visible political activities was an organised protest against the building of the Maticni wall in October 1999. Association representatives literally dismantled the wall on the same day that it was constructed in October 1999 (see Case Study 3).

State financial support for minority organisations is generally organised on a project-by-project basis. Each year, nongovernmental organisations must submit project proposals for evaluation. Only after these proposals are approved can the funds be appropriated for one year (occasionally for longer periods). The same principle is typically valid for local public and private resource allocation. This process hinders long-term organisational planning and presents problems for hiring new personnel.

4.4. Media, culture and the use of mother tongue

Minority access to media is still insufficient though some progress has been made recently. Only one multi-cultural programme is broadcast on the Czech television every two weeks, though not during prime broadcasting hours. An important precedent was set recently with the employment of one Roma newscaster and one Roma programme announcer by Czech TV. Four Romany periodicals are financially supported by central government. (Apart from the Romany press there are four Slovak, four Polish and three German periodicals, as well as one Hungarian and one Ukrainian periodical financed by the state.) There are also several local-level Roma publications.

Mother-tongue education for minorities is organised only for the Polish minority in North Moravia. Because only a very small number of Roma declared their nationality in the population census in 1991, the Czech government continues to treat the Roma not as a national minority but rather as a 'community'. This is not advantageous for the Roma: it limits their rights. Little has been done in the way of Romany-language education. This is in part because education in the Czech Republic remains highly centralised. As the decentralisation process continues, the possibility remains open that minority education will, in the future, be managed in accordance with local needs.

---

[29] Jaroslav Mitras, interview, Ministry of Interior, 3 May 1999.

4.5. Employment

The ethnic group hardest hit by unemployment has been the Roma. As a result of the declining demand for unskilled labour in the transformed economy and substantial influx of unskilled migrant workers into the Czech Republic, the Roma now have fewer long-term employment opportunities. Industrial areas—containing large Roma populations—are bearing the brunt of the economic restructuring process and their regional unemployment rates are higher than anywhere else in the country.

Apart from these structural causes, other factors have contributed to high Roma unemployment, including low education, virtually no job training, a unmotivating system of social benefits, poor health conditions and discrimination in the labour market. According to numerous sources, there continue to be cases where Roma job applicants are rejected under the pretext that positions have 'already been filled', though they remain open for non-Roma applicants.[30] For many employers, incentives such as the grants offered by regional employment offices for 'effective job creation' are not attractive enough to encourage the hiring of Roma workers. Discrimination in the labour market is one of the primary reasons for the high level of Roma migration to countries with more developed democracies.

4.5.1. Employment policy responses

In May 1999 the Czech government passed the National Plan of Employment,[31] launched by the Ministry of Labour and Social Affairs, which explicitly deals with Active Employment Policies (AEP) targeted at the Roma and equal opportunity policies and practices. It aims to:

- increase employment of long-term unemployed job seekers, with special emphasis on members of the Roma community,
- use public tenders preferentially to ensure the employment of job seekers with 'job placement difficulties',
- reinforce legal and institutional tools and mechanisms in order to eliminate discrimination in the labour market,
- create realistic opportunities to give preferential treatment to those groups whose access to the labour market is markedly limited,
- monitor the level of enforcement of the right to employment of for groups of citizens 'menaced by discrimination'.[32]

In June 1999 the Czech government—after more than two years of pilot verification—implemented a policy document entitled, 'Measures to Address the Employment of Persons with Job Placement Difficulties with Special Regard to the Roma Community'. The doc-

---

[30] According to Mr Mitras, a Rom working at the Ministry of Interior as Administration Councilor (spravni rada) who co-operates with Romany social advisers and with district offices and is in charge of dealing with complaints. Mr Mitras also helps with citizenship issues and he also advises how to establish a citizens association, one of the most common type of nongovernmental organisation.

[31] Jaroslav Mitras, interview, Ministry of Interior, 3 May 1999.

[32] Hilda Pasova, interview; also in Documentation Center for Human Rights.

ument covers four projects: 'Most,' 'Sance,' 'Romstart' and 'Trenink' and lists instruments of Active Employment Policies (AEP). Along with these measures, the government also passed budgetary provisions for these projects' implementation. The largest part of the budget is for the implementation of AEP instruments targeted predominantly at the Roma, including publicly beneficial jobs, youth and adult training, public works jobs and protected workshops.

In order to prevent discrimination the government decided to amend the Law on Employment[33] by inserting an anti-discrimination clause. The amended Law was enforced in January 2000. It made discrimination in the labour market illegal and specified sanctions and fines for such discrimination.[34] Labour offices at the district and local levels are responsible for the implementation of the Law.

4.6. Public education

4.6.1. Top-down policies

Education is one of the sectors that has thus far been least affected by decentralisation. Within the public education system, one of the main problems for the Roma minority is the placement of Roma children in special schools for mentally handicapped children. (See Annex 1 for details.)

Among central-level education policies, there have been some positive changes. In 1993 the government created the framework for an experimental programme of 'preparatory classes' (zero classes) to prepare disadvantaged children for their first year of school. Many districts with large Roma populations participate in this programme, which is funded solely by local governments. In 1998 there were nearly 90 preparatory classes operating throughout the country.

A positive example of democratisation and effective policy-making was the amendment of the Education Act in the fall of 1999 which facilitates access to secondary education for students from special schools. The amendment aims to remove the 'lid' on the special school system which had been kept tightly closed by a provision that only students from elementary schools can sit for secondary school entrance exams. The proposal was submitted by the only Roma MP in the Czech Parliament, Monika Horáková, and was originally initiated through a petition of teachers and other citizens early in 1999.

4.6.2. Bottom-up policies—the role of NGOs

A major step forward was the introduction of Romany teaching assistants in public schools, initiated by the New School Foundation (in co-operation with several schools)—a policy that was formally adopted by the Ministry of Education in March 1998.[35] The position of Romany assistants has not yet been addressed in a fully satisfactory manner, largely due to the continuing lack of communication between the Ministry, NGOs and district school boards. As such, there are still many assistants without official contracts being paid

---

[33] Resolution of the Czech Government No. 418 on the National Plan of Employment (1999) 5 May.
[34] 'Národní plán zaměstnanosti' (National Employment Plan) (1999) *Sociální politika*, No. 6.
[35] No.1/1991 Coll. and No. 9/1991 Coll.

by NGOs. To date, there are about 150 Roma teaching assistants working in mainstream and special schools that have received or plan to receive a two-week intensive training course organised by NGOs and funded by the state.

Case Study 1. Teaching Assistants

The introduction of Roma teaching assistants into the public education system in April 1998 was preceded by similar positive experiences in private schools. The first full-time assistant started to work in 1993 at the Church Primary School of Premysl Pitter in Ostrava. Others followed in Brno in 1995, inspired by Ostrava. At present, the Premysl Pitter school employs nine Roma teaching assistants. Another nineteen assistants are supervised by a Romany NGO—'Romano Jekhetaniben Pre Morava'. This association of Roma in Moravia supervises five educational centres that either employ or assist Romany teaching assistants. The centres are located in: Brno, Bruntál, Ostrava, Olomouc and Stenberk. In Brno, five asisstants are financed by the District School Office (state budget funds) and four are paid by Romano Jekhetaniben Pre Morava (which also sponsors eight assistants in Ostrava). Two assistants in Sternberk are financed by the Church. Another two assistants work in the Khamoro Kindergarten in Olomouc, also funded by the Church. In this kindergarten, Romany assistants were introduced in 1994, initially using Romany mothers as volunteers for a short period of time.

Source: Interviews with Helena Balabanova and Helena Jirincova

---

Other positive examples aimed at increasing the education level of the Roma include the establishment in September 1998 of the Romany Social and Legal High School in Kolín, at the initiative of the Roma community itself. The majority of the school's students live in halls of residence located directly in the school building. After completion of four years of school and passing an exit exam, the graduates will work as professional social workers in the area of minority integration or at district and municipal offices. The school is funded by Roma sponsors in the Czech Republic and abroad. The operational costs of the school are partially covered by the Rajko Djuric Foundation.

Special training programmes for Roma social workers are run by several other institutions, such as the Evangelic Academy in Prague 4 that prepares Romany assistants (through a two-year course) and Romany social advisers (through a five-year course providing full secondary education).

In sum, it can be argued that given the disparity between officially proclaimed government objectives in education policy and the current state of the educational system—in terms of the quality of teacher training, lack of young flexible teachers, system of school management, district-level bureaucracy and inconsistencies between the new Education Concept and the new Education Bill—it will be difficult bring about real change in the short term. Again, one of the primary problems is that real authority over public education has not yet been decentralised. Local authorities still have no say in any education policies. Additionally, co-operation between the Ministry of Education and the non-governmental sector remains very low.[36]

---

[36] Fines up to one million CZK if the law is repeatedly violated.

4.7. Central policies targeting local communities

There are virtually no equal opportunity policies initiated at the local level. Anti-discrimination is widely perceived only in terms of preventing racist attacks on ethnic minorities. Institutional discrimination occurs and is largely ignored (with the exception mentioned above in the new employment measures and legislation). In terms of employment, this means that unemployment is significantly higher among the Roma minority than the rest of the population. In terms of education, the consequence is that Roma children obtain a lower standard of education in special schools and cannot continue on to higher education.

According to municipal representatives and the Roma themselves, there have been some positive efforts made to mitigate inter-ethnic tension at the local level. A short Comprehensive Programme, initiated and funded by the Czech Ministry of Interior, has been well evualuated.

Case Study 2. Comprehensive Programme of the Ministry of the Interior

The Programme aims to support socially deprived Roma communities, to prevent inter-ethnic conflicts and to support 'good neighbour' relations in mixed communities. In 1999 it was implemented in 57 towns in the Czech Republic.

Concrete projects focus on:

· *Education*: preparation of Romany children for school, including special classes at kindergartens, zero classes, social work with families, support of special teaching methods and curricula at schools that respond to Romany children's needs;
· *Employment*: motivating Romany youth to acquire occupational skills and abilities which will allow them to succeed in the labour market;
· *Community work within the Roma community*: improving the quality of nonformal social control, involving larger communities in solving problems of a given community, organising cultural and social activities that directly respond to the community needs;
· *Hobbies and leisure activities*: cultural and art activities, technological clubs, sports clubs and equipment for playgrounds, etc.

In order to receive financial support from the state, the projects must be partially funded by municipalities and Roma have to participate in them. The highest number of projects in the period 1996-1998 were implemented by nongovernmental organisations (35%), schools (34%) and local governments (18%); then by charity organisations (5%), state administration (3%), municipal police (2%), children centres and sports clubs (1%). A total of 110 projects in 32 municipalities were supported in the period 1996-98.[37]

The Comprehensive Programme supports *full integration, not assimilation*, of Roma into majority society. It is expected that integration will be more feasible and acceptable, if the dis-

---

[37] The government resolution 686/97 based on the Bratinka Report stated that at least 20 Romany teaching assistants will be financed out of the state budget for 1998; the Ministry of Education, however, ignored this resolution.

advantages of Roma will be reduced. The remedy of such disadvantages will also contribute to a decrease in crime related to poverty as well as traditional crime.

Source: Ministry of Interior (1999) and data from the conference 'Legal protection of Roma in Europe', 29 June 1999, Prague.

4.8. Local inter-ethnic tensions and the search for solutions

Despite the fact that local governments are often in a better position than central authorities to respond to the needs of ethnic minorities and manage ethnic conflict at the local level, tension permeates the process of decentralisation of power and administrative responsibilities. The protection of human rights and the implementation of human rights legislation has largely depended on political will at both the national and local level. Most policies that have an impact on the everyday lives of minorities can only be implemented at the local level.

There have been numerous cases of racism and ethnic hatred on the part of local-level political representatives that have negatively influenced inter-ethnic relations in the Czech Republic. Since 1997, 'there has been an increase in cases of political abuse of ethnic tension and tolerance towards strong xenophobia. The problem of Czech policy may potentially be not only its incompetence in formulation and enforcement of positive programmes but also a danger of resorting to populism'.[38]

Case Study 3. The Wall in Ústí nad Labem

In May 1998 the municipal leaders in two Czech towns Ústí nad Labem and Plzen introduced 'apartheid-style measures ... reminiscent of the Nazi holocaust when Roma, along with Jews, were separated from the rest of the population'.[39]

In Ústí nad Labem–Nestemice, the municipality considered plans to erect a four-meter high wall, separating houses with Roma tenants from other inhabitants in order to protect the latter from bothersome noise and garbage. In Plzen, the solution of the Roma problem seemed to be even more radical: the municipality planned to construct a compound on the city's outskirts with portable cabins surrounded by a fence and with a police force having 24-hour access to all of the cabins.[40]

Populism proved to be successful when the mayor of Ústí nad Labem was re-elected in the November 1998 local elections.[41]

---

[38] 'Unwillingness and incompetence of the Ministry of Education officers to co-operate with NGOs, that often substitute government's duties (e.g. Romany teaching assistants or multi-cultural education) is inexcusable'. Ludek Novák, Head of the New School Foundation, Debate over the Complaint, G+G Literary Cafe, 15 June 1999.

[39] 'Roma in the Czech Republic after 1989', a presentation of Jiri Zlamal at the conference Legal Protection of Roma in Europe, 29 June 1999, Prague.

[40] *Romove v. Ceske Republice* (1999) Prague: Socioklub, p. 89.

[41] 'Czech Cities Wall off Gypsy Ghetto' (1998) *Independent,* 27 May.

In August 1998 the UN Committee on the Elimination of Racial Discrimination (CERD) demanded an explanation for the proposed plan, and in January 1999 the Czech government adopted a resolution to prevent construction of the wall.

In April 1999 the local municipality of Ústí made an agreement with the local Roma community that a two-meter high ceramic partition would be built and some construction had already started when the Government Commissioner for Human Rights vigorously protested against the partition's construction. In response, the mayor of Ústí demanded the Commissioner resign from his office.

In May 1999 the Czech government asked the head of the Ústí District Office to question the resolution of the Ústí–Nestemice Neighbourhood Council. If the Nestemice council failed to prevent the partition, the Czech Chamber of Deputies would then be asked to block the construction. The local authorities in Ústí nad Labem claimed that nobody can stop them from their decision to build a ceramic partition. In October the wall was constructed; on the same day it was dismantled by Roma residents, and then built again with the assistance of the police.

A month later it was officially removed after the local municipality reached an agreement with the central government that the latter will provide financial assistance (10 million CZK) in order to mitigate the noise and garbage problem by buying out the family houses of non-Roma residents.

On 5 April 2000 the Czech Constitutional Court ruled that the Parliament did not have the right to interfere in local government decision-making, stating that the Act on Municipalities clearly discern executive from legislative powers, only the latter being the domain of the Parliament. This ruling is significant for furthering conflicting views between the central government and local self-governments.[42]

An in-depth analysis of the situation was conducted by a team of experts and financed by the Foundation 'Vize 97'. The conclusions suggest that the main cause of the dispute was an incorrect decision made by the municipality in 1994 to move Roma who do not pay rent into several buildings in one area.[43] Other detrimental factors have been insufficient communication between the municipality and the Roma and a lack of social work in the area. The major findings were:

· Problems exist in terms of co-operation with municipal and town offices—particularly with social departments and their employees.
· There are still many Roma who do not have Czech citizenship.
· There are no Roma represented in the local government.
· Regarding the payments of social benefits, however, there seem to be no problems.

Source: various newspaper articles and documents.[44]

---

[42] 'Ghettos for Czech Gypsies?' (1998) *Economist*, 30 May; 'Czech Town Plans High Wall to Isolate Gypsy "Ghetto"' (1998) *Guardian*, 16 May; Linda Grant (1998) 'In the Ghetto', *Guardian Weekend*, 25 July, pp. 16-22; Stephane Kovacs (1998) 'Republique tcheque: le mur de la honte', *Le Figaro*, 10 August; 'Indésirables chez les Tcheques. Les Roms se heurtent toujours a la xenophobie' (1998) *Liberation*, 27 August; Martin Plichta (1998) 'Des villes tcheques veulent isoler les Tsiganes', *Le Monde*, 05 June.

[43] 'Primatorem Usti nad Labem se stal opet Ladislav Hruska z ODS' (Ladislav Hruska elected again to be the Mayor of Usti) and 'Zastancem 'ustecke zdi' je opet primatorem' (The defender of the Usti wall became again the Mayor) (1998) *Lidove noviny*, 1 December, p. 7.

[44] 'The judges found out that politicians have been violating the Czech constitution for years'. In: 'Ustavni soud: poslanci nemeli branit stavbe v Maticni' (The Constitutional Court: The MPs should not have prevented construction in Maticni) (2000) *Lidové Noviny*, 6 April.

In other municipalities, local governments have to deal with inter-ethnic tensions. In Krnov, for example, the municipality and the Roma representatives came together to settle problems that were reflected in the 'Anti-Roma petition signed by several hundred Krnov inhabitants' that criticises past local governments for confining the Roma to one neighbourhood. The petition makes complaints about 'garbage in the streets, noise and the rude behaviour of young Roma'.[45]

Many Roma have reacted to insufficient policies aimed at improving their situation and inter-ethnic relations by leaving the country. In Rokycany, for example, more than 400 Roma residents have left—more than half of the total number previously living in the town—according to the head of 'Info-Roma', a local Roma association. The mayor of Rokycany claims that this figure is exaggerated and that there are no reasons for Roma to leave. According to the mayor, there is no racism in Rokycany and a number of Roma have 'made a business out of the problem'.[46]

Even in localities where there are no marked tensions and substantial efforts have been made by local governments to improve the situation, Roma emigration rates are high. For example, in Liberec, the municipality helped to establish the Romany Community Centre and has supported several pro-Romany projects with one million CZK. The Roma community in Liberec admits that there are no open inter-ethnic conflicts with the Czech majority but they complain about inadequate job opportunities. Approximately 20 Liberec Roma families left the country already.[47]

But some positive examples of long-term co-operation between the municipality and the Roma community can be found.

[45] *Analyza vzniku, aktuální situace a moznosti resení problému obyvatel Maticní ulice, Záverecná zpráva projektu vypracovaného pro Nadaci Dagmar a Václava Havlovych Vize 97* (1999) Prague–Ustí nad Labem: R Mosty–Socioklub, 30 April, pp. 13-19

[46] 'Ghettos for Czech Gypsies?' (1998) *Economist*, 30 May; 'Czech Town Plans High Wall to Isolate Gypsy "Ghetto"' (1998) *Guardian*, 16 May; Linda Grant (1998) 'In the Ghetto', *Guardian Weekend*, 25 July, pp. 16-22; Stephane Kovacs (1998) 'Republique tcheque: le mur de la honte', *Le Figaro*, 10 August; 'Indésirables chez les Tcheques. Les Roms se heurtent toujours a la xenophobie' (1998) *Liberation*, 27 August; Martin Plichta (1998) 'Des villes tcheques veulent isoler les Tsiganes', *Le Monde*, 05 June; 'Ústí: Plot je v souladu se zákonem' (Usti: The fence is in accordance with law) (1999) *Metro*, 28 May; 'Vláda je proti tomu, aby v Maticní vyrostla zed' (The government is against the wall in Maticni) (1999) *MF Dnes*, 27 May, pp. 1, 3; 'Cabinet Says No to Usti Fence', (1999) *Prague Post*, 28 June; United States Information Service (1999) *Country Reports on Human Rights Practices for 1998—Czech Republic*, p. 16.
Also in : *Analyza vzniku, aktuální situace a moznosti resení problému obyvatel Maticní ulice, Záverecná zpráva projektu vypracovaného pro Nadaci Dagmar a Václava Havlovych Vize 97* (Analysis of beginning, present situation, and possibilities of solving the problems of inhabitants of Maticni street. Final Report) (1999) Praha–Ustí nad Labem: R Mosty–Socioklub, 30 April.

[47] 'Krnovstí celí petici' (Krnov faces a petition) (1999) *Metro*, 4 August, also in the Czech TV News-CT1 (1999) 30 July.

Case Study 4. Co-operating Cities

In 1995, in a project initiated by the Council of Europe, the town of Pardubice became one of the founding members of the 'Network of Czech Republic Cities Co-operating to Solve Romany Issues'. The network aims to achieve optimal communication with Roma communities. The network's founding organisations are the Institute for Romany Studies in Ústí nad Labem in co-operation with 'Movement R', the Town of Brno, the Town of Pardubice and the World Federation of Joint Cities and Municipalities, Paris. The Deputies of the Town of Ústí declined membership and therefore Ústí did not join the network. Other towns in the network are Ceská Kamenice, Vysoké Myto and Trmice.[48] In June 2000 a seminar on 'Roma and Municipality' was organised in Pardubice by the NGO 'Movement–R' with support of the Ministry of Education.

Source: Interview with Mrs Koskova

Sometimes external assistance in analysing existing problems may result in complex strategies and solutions.

Case Study 5. Strategie Planning in Brno

As the result of co-operation with the Council of Europe, the state administration, local self-governments, NGOs and the efforts of many institutions and individuals, in 1997-98 the Town of Brno prepared a strategic plan concerning relations between the Roma minority and the majority community in Brno.

The implementation of the plan is co-ordinated by the Social and Cultural Department of the Brno Municipality. The main actors are: the Brno Employment Office; Brno District School Office; Cultural and Educational Centre for Romany Children and Youth, DROM; Association of Roma in Moravia; Helsinki Citizens Assembly–Roma Section; Museum of Romany Culture; Brno Municipal Directorate of the Police of CR; Municipal Police Brno; and the Secondary Police School in Brno.

The Project focuses on five areas: education, security, social affairs, employment and media.

In the area of education, the School Office aims to create equal conditions for the development of all national minorities, especially the Roma. Emphasis is placed on preschool education, zero classes, transfer of children from special to mainstream schools, Romany teaching assistants at schools, co-operation with families and Romany organisations, and the introduction of multi-cultural curricula. The Brno Municipality Department of Education, Youth and Sports funds projects that focus on leisure time with special attention towards Romany children and youth.

A very important actor in the project is an NGO called DROM—the Cultural and Educational Centre of Romany Children and Youth. It organises after-school activities (20 activity circles for 250 children as well as less organised activities for approximately 70 children) and also serves as an information centre for parents. In January 1999 a Romany adviser started to work at DROM with the goal of removing communication barriers between the majority and the Roma and supportive Roma families.

---

[48] 'Aktivista nabízí informace o azylu' (An activist offers information about asylum) (1999) *Metro*, 4 August.

In other areas the most interesting activities are:
- Co-operation on the 'Crime Prevention Interactive Comprehensive Programme' initiated and funded by the Czech Ministry of Interior;
- Co-operation between the DROM Centre and the police school in teaching the Romany language;
- Efforts to identify and recruit Roma for police training;
- Introduction of 'public benefit jobs' for those unemployed Roma who cannot afford to pay rent. By participating in the project, they can gradually pay their debts and thus solve their housing problems.

In co-operation with the Council of Europe, a new housing project is being prepared where Roma will be involved in the construction of their own houses. This can serve, if successful, as a model for similar activities elsewhere in the Czech Republic.

Source: Community Centre DROM; Council of Europe.

Schools may be used as community centres/community schools—a policy that may become a widespread good practice.

Case Study 6. The Community Centre and School

A Community Centre was established by the Premysl Pitter School in October 1997, in co-operation with and with the support of the Ostrava Municipality and local governments in Moravska, Ostrava and Privoz. The Centre is now administered by 'Together'—a civic association established in February 1999. This association consists of employees of the school and parents of children attending the school. The main aim is to support social programmes as well as educational programmes. Target groups are Roma children, youth and adults. Emphasis is placed on after-school activities of children and youth from several schools in the area that have closed down their after-school clubs because of insufficient attendance. The main problem is that these clubs must be paid for and the Roma cannot afford to keep their children there.

Through preventive activities and by providing positive role models, the Centre has managed to reduce negative social phenomena as well as youth crime.

The Centre also organises regular meetings for mothers and for fathers to play football. On Fridays and Saturdays there are discos for children and adults, and once a month a lecture is organised on various topics, such as drug abuse, sex education, education towards tolerance. Tutoring is available for Roma students any day of the week.

The Centre also organises many other activities, such as cultural and sports events and community work, and co-operates with other NGOs and individuals.

Experience gained at Premysl Pitter School is slowly being used in other communities. Within the framework of the experimental programme 'Romany Children in Czech Schools', recognised by the Ministry of Education, the *curricula model* is being used by several other schools in the Czech Republic. Hopefully, the *community centre* or *community school model* will be used more frequently in the future.

Source: Movement-R Seminar in Brno, 6 May 1999.

Sometimes a school board can initiate good relations and practices.

Case Study 7. Tolerance and Respect

In spite of the problems and the generally negative attitudes of local self-government, the situation in Pribram may be viewed as a positive one thanks to close co-operation among the District School Board, Romany social advisers and assistants, primary and secondary schools, the Centre for Human Rights Education and Bohemia Corps, a Czech volunteer organisation.

The major successful results of this co-operation are:
- The Romany co-ordinator at the district office is in co-operation with the Romany teaching assistant who organises tutorials for Roma children. Students from both Pribram high schools help Roma children with homework on a voluntary basis. Additionally older Romany children systematically help younger Roma children through tutorials.
- The Romany Co-ordinator organises lectures on Roma for students at secondary schools.
- There are in-service training sessions for headmasters in the Pribram district focusing on Roma organised in co-operation with the Government Interdepartmental Commission for Romany Community.
- The Romany Co-ordinator organises in-service teacher training sessions in the Pribram district.
- Romany social workers help families from the local Roma Community in solving their everyday problems.
- A survey was conducted among the students of secondary schools that aimed at raising interest among students in learning more about Roma.
- An after-school programme for Roma and non-Roma children was created.
- A new Romany music group is operating with support from the Municipal Office.
- According to the Romany Co-ordinator, there is very good co-operation between the District Office, District School Office and District Labour Office in Pribram.
- The Romany Co-ordinator is preparing training projects for Roma in co-operation with the Labour Office and the Prince Charles Foundation.

Source: Pribram District School Board, interview with Mrs Hejkrlikova

A very positive role is being played by nongovernmental organisations that design projects to address inter-ethnic problems at the local level. In 1996 the Czech Centre for Conflict Prevention and Resolution and the civic association Movement-R ('R-Mosty') began to conduct an educational project, 'Education towards Tolerance and against Racism in Prague Schools'.[49] The Centre also organised seminars for teachers focusing on interactive methods and practical communication skills.[50] NGO volunteers as well as state and local administration personnel also attended the seminars. The seminars took place in Prague, Brno, Pisek, Most, Pardubice and Beroun.[51]

The Centre also runs programmes directly targeted at local communities. It has established Conciliation Commissions at the local government level and trained staff volunteering in the Commissions.

[49] 'Dalsi rodiny hodlaji opustit svuj domov' (More families are leaving their home) (1999) *Metro*, 11 August.

[50] Alena Koskova, interview.

[51] Until April 1999, a total of 210 discussion seminars in 66 schools were organised for 4,500 students at primary and secondary schools (ages 12-18).

Another important initiative that could serve as role models for other activities at local level is the project 'Strengthening Romany-Czech Relations Through Co-operative Problem-solving'. The project helps to solve problems caused by the existence of barriers between different cultures and lifestyles based on different traditions and values, and problems resulting from insufficient information about other ethnic groups. The project aims to provide basic communication skills to the Roma, public administration, NGOs and other parties at the local level, and to identify and resolve problems that affect both the Roma and non-Roma populations in a given community.

The project was conducted in four municipalities where there are sizeable Roma populations and significant inter-ethnic tensions, but where there is sufficient will to improve the status quo. On the condition that the local government will cover 20% of the project costs, the rest of the costs are covered by grants provided by the EU and the Council of Europe.

The project produced positive results in all four regions where it was conducted.

Case Study 8. Round Tables

Most
As a result of the round-table discussion in Most, the Romany civic association 'Dzivas' was founded in the Chanov neighbourhood, a notorious area which became completely Romany as a result of poor local management under communism.[52] Co-operation started among the town hall, the representatives of Dzivas, the police, the unemployment agency and the Chanov community, with the following results: The unemployment agency started to use a Romany workforce for cleaning jobs in the town in order to keep the Chanov area tidy (some 140 tons of garbage has been moved out from the area). In co-operation with police the issue of security started to be addressed as well as new job opportunities. Sixteen Roma from Chanov were employed, eight for the clean-up work and eight to help the police. In co-operation with the school it was suggested to create a community school in Chanov. For 1999 a second round of the project is being prepared: 'Kvet' (Flower—Community Negotiation and On-the-Job Co-operation) aiming to strengthen and disseminate co-operation in the Most region, especially in Becov, Lom, Obrnice and the town of Litvinov.[53]

Pardubice
The outcome of the round-table discussion called 'Tolerance, nonviolent co-existence and elimination of prejudice' were the following:
· An information youth centre was established which gathers information concerning activities for children and youth, and various prevention programmes.
· The 'Society Club' project gained more support as it provides opportunities for Roma youth to spend their leisure time actively.
· A group of people was trained for further work in the Conciliation Commission, and it was recommended that, after the necessary approval of the town hall, the Commission would start working as a new tool for resolving difficult ethnic problems and issues.

---

[52] In the period October 1997-April 1999 a total of 17 three-day seminars were organised for about 400 teachers.

[53] Tatjana Siskova (1999) *Strucna zprava o projektu Vychova k toleranci a poroti rasismu na prazskych skolach* (A brief report on the project), April.

· An information group was established that should follow activities important for the co-
   existence of the majority and the Roma (so far the plan includes movies about Roma, joint
   summer camps, lectures on xenophobia, training of Roma youth for work in the regional TV and radio as moderators, festivals, etc.).

Pisek

A basic network map of Roma families living in the Pisek region was established. The round-
table discussion, entitled 'The security of citizens in the region and the police', had the following outcomes:

· All Romany applicants who meet the legal requirements (adulthood, clean criminal record,
   additional training) may become members of the Offense Committee.
· Roma representatives may participate in all other committees of the town hall.
· The possibility of establishing a special committee to solve minority issues.
· Surveillance in the streets is used not only for conflict prevention but also as a tool to
   improve the safety of inhabitants. There will be more cameras in the streets in the future.
· The Roma may try to get a job in the local police if they meet the legal requirements.
· The Romany community representatives who would work for the town hall committees,
   the Romany assistants at the district office and the Romany teaching assistants at schools
   will help in investigation of crimes and in crime prevention (with a special focus on drug
   abuse prevention for youth).
· Co-operation among the mayors of Pisek, Milevsko and Protivin, and of police and the
   Roma representatives of these towns will continue.
· Selected representatives of the area (unemployment office, school authority, etc.) will create a joint project for further development of educational level of Romany population, and
   their job opportunities.

Ústí nad Labem

The project focused on support and co-operation with the Roma families living in small flats in Maticni
street, and help in establishing the Roma Rainbow Association, the members of which are active in
solving problems of Maticni street in co-operation with various institutions and NGOs.

Two round-table discussions took place with the outcome of establishing the 'Programme
Group for Ethnic Minorities'. The participants will continue in co-operation in the Ústí region
in the field of ethnic minority issues. The programme group includes six small action groups
with specific features and tasks. These are: housing, jobs and unemployment, education and
leisure time of children, social work, support of Romany initiatives and drug abuse prevention.

Source: Czech Centre for Conflict Prevention and Resolution.

The above project proved that effective communication and problem-solving are two
of the most effective methods of preventing or resolving ethnic conflicts at the local level.
Structural and institutional changes are also important, however, and only an effective
combination of a variety of policy instruments and approaches can lead to long-term solutions.

5. Conclusion

It is very difficult to understand why there is such strong resistance to changes in attitudes, public practices, institutions and structures that are necessary for the peaceful co-existence of multi-cultural communities. Further, it is perplexing why many policy-makers still regard issues of ethnic and cultural diversity, multi-cultural education and racism as irrelevant to their field of work. This chapter has aimed to demonstrate the complexity of the problem in the Czech Republic, focusing on the importance of local-level initiatives within the framework of broader social processes. It has aimed at exploring the manifestations of discrimination and racism, political resistance to accepting minorities, as well as popular attitudes and prejudices. It has examined various policy initiatives and developments in progress in the Czech Republic.

Solutions to the current problems must be found and implemented at all levels of government—emanating upwards from practitioners and local policy-makers and networking at the local level, as well as pushing officials at central level to 'open the gates' to systemic changes. Central government initiatives are undoubtedly essential but can be effective only if complemented by broader social changes and changes at the local level. If the Czech Republic wants to become a truly democratic society and be integrated into European institutions,[54] it must not only improve the political discourse on minorities but take practical steps to improve their opportunities to fully participate in society. It should also implement its constitutional provisions on minorities and the Charter of Fundamental Rights and Freedoms where special concern for recognition and protection of national minorities is stipulated. Preparations of the Minority Act is a positive development, and hopefully enough political will can be garnered to complete and pass this piece of legislation.

6. Policy Recommendations

As mentioned at the beginning of this chapter, one of the major policy obstacles to improved minority integration and participation at all levels of government and stronger minority rights protection is the lack of decentralisation of political power and decision-making authority from the central government to local governing bodies. Significant decentralisation is thus the first and most important step toward increased minority involvement in all areas of Czech society. Within this context, this section devotes attention to three major issue-areas for which policy recommendations are both appropriate and essential:

- Anti-discrimination measures;
- Development and implementation of equal opportunity legislation and policies;
- Promotion and development of multi-cultural education;
- Improving educational provisions for minority students.

---

[54] More details on Chanov are available in 'Chanov se rozpadá, presto je pevností' (Chanov is falling apart, despite that it is a fortress) (1999) *MF Dnes*, 10 June, pp. 1, 9; and 'Bílí utekli, zustalo gheto' (The whites ran away, a ghetto remained) (1999) *MF Dnes*, 10 June, p. 8.

6.1. Anti-discrimination measures

The removal of discriminatory practices presumes a major change in public attitudes. This will undoubtedly be a complicated long-term process. The role of education and media are crucial in this respect, but both must be *complemented by law enforcement mechanisms and concrete anti-discrimination policies* originating at the national as well as the local level of government.

- Czech policy-makers at all levels and in all sectors should review the alleged conflict between the 'citizenship principle' and collective rights for minorities and decide on further steps leading to the elimination of current social and cultural disadvantages which perpetuate discrimination and racism.
- These steps should be based on anti-discrimination legislation and policy initiatives that will allow Roma to compete with non-Roma candidates in employment, education, housing, service provision and other areas.
- Local governments should introduce inclusive policies with respect to minorities and cease to support assimilationist or segregative policies. Such inclusion will depend to a large degree on changes in the attitudes of local majority communities. Nonetheless, the appropriate legal and policy instruments must be in place at the local level to precipitate these changes.
- The central government should continue to review current human rights legislation and work in compliance with international commitments with a focus on improving law-enforcement mechanisms. The government should introduce anti-discrimination legislation in all fields with straightforward enforcement mechanisms.

6.2. Equal opportunity policies

The employment of minority representatives in local governments, police, schools, state bodies and other institutions is a necessary first step on the path to guaranteeing equal opportunities for minority groups (especially the Roma) in the workforce. Only by removing discrimination *through equal opportunity legislation* and other measures, such as intensive training to increase the job qualifications of minorities, can previous injustices can be redressed.

- Employing the Roma in visible public positions (in central and local public administrative positions, for example) would represent an important first step in counterbalancing the dramatic under-representation of the Roma in the public sector. Further, these Roma public employees can serve as positive role models for Roma youth and can contribute to eliminating prejudices and stereotypes in the public sphere.

An important step in this process was introduction of Romany teaching assistants in the official school system and establishment of the position of Romany Adviser at the district level.

There are also initiatives to increase number of Roma in police forces. Again, indirect discriminatory measures are hindering these efforts. Physical height and an ability to swim are discriminating qualifications for police applicants. It is a known fact that Roma are twelve centimetres smaller on average than the Czech population and that they do not swim because of their traditions and values.[55]

---

[55] Milan Sivak, Romany assistant in Most, interview, 24 April 1999.

Efforts to employ Roma often have to cope with mistrust, criticism and negative attitudes on part of majority society. Experiences from other countries, e.g. Britain, show that although there are already many qualified teachers from ethnic minority groups (mainly of Asian background) the important task is to retain them—they often leave their professions because of the strong racism they encounter at their workplace!

6.3. Multi-cultural education

Multi-cultural education can serve as one of the most powerful factors in *enhancing social stability and democratisation* and as a means of long-term ethnic conflict prevention in the Czech Republic and in the Central Europe as a whole. Aside from formal legal instruments against racially motivated crimes, educational programmes that promote inter-ethnic tolerance and provide information about diverse ethnic groups can provide the most effective tool with which to combat widespread racism in Czech society.

- Both the central government and local governments must be involved in designing school curricula at all education levels that deal with multi-ethnic issues and themes related to the value of diversity.
- The improvement of teacher education and teacher training in terms of raising awareness and changing attitudes toward minorities is the most urgent prerequisite to improving the discriminatory 'educational culture' in the Czech Republic.
- The top-down approaches of the Ministry of Education and pedagogical institutions aimed at improving teacher education will succeed only if supported by bottom-up initiatives. Such initiatives include teacher networking at the local level and the work of organisations such as 'Movement R' (teachers and other professionals interested in Romany Education), 'PAU' (Friends of Engaged Learning), 'SVOD' (Association for Citizenship and Democracy Education) and other NGOs committed to education.
- Shifts in awareness and attitudes toward minority issues must also occur at the level of individual school managers—i.e. headmasters, education officers, school boards and local government officials.

6.4. Improving educational provisions for minority students

- Mainstream public schooling should focus on anti-discrimination and multi-cultural educational processes and structures, such as more appropriate teaching methods, better adapted curricula and textbooks, preschool programmes and support classes, availability of support teachers and teacher assistants, increased co-operation with parents and using schools as community centres.
- These changes in education policy cannot simply be 'ordered' from above—local initiatives and programmes are vital players in the process of public education reform.
- A multi-agency approach should be adopted at the local level, co-ordinated by a local office of Romany social advisers in close cooperation with Romany teaching assistants, as well as social workers and other public administration personnel.

Further reading

Alibhai-Brown, Yasmin (1999) *True Colours—Public Attitudes to Multiculturalism and the Role of Government*, London: [ ].

Barsa, Pavel (1999) *Politická teorie multikulturalismu*, Brno: CDK.

Cashmore, Ellis (1996) *Dictionary of Race and Ethnic Relations*, London: Routledge.

Gabal, Ivan (1999) *Etnické mensiny ve strední Evrope*, Prague: G plus G.

Grisham, Vaughn L. Jr. (1999) *TUPELO: The Evolution of a Community*, Dayton: Kettering Foundation.

Mathews, David (1999) *Politics for People. Finding a Responsible Public Voice*, Urbana and Chicago: University of Illinois Press.

Socioklub (1999) *Romové v Ceské Republice (Roma in the Czech Republic)*, Prague.

Thompson, Neil (1993) *Anti-discriminatotry Practice*, New York: MacMillan.

ANNEX 1
SEGREGATION OF ROMA IN THE CZECH SCHOOL SYSTEM

The education level of Roma population is markedly lower than that of the majority. The Czech Schools Law provides for a system of 'special' schools, parallel to the nine-year elementary school system, and catering to 'pupils...who have intellectual deficiencies such that they cannot successfully be educated in elementary schools'.[1] In practice, the law is administered so as to relegate disproportionate numbers of Romany children *to second-class educational facilities* offering inferior curriculum and limited opportunity for skills training or educational preparation. Graduates of such schools have very limited access to higher education. A paradox—whereby children with real intellectual difficulties attend mainstream schools because their parents to not want to place them together with Roma—is not unusual.[2]

The Bratinka Report has acknowledged 'hitherto prevailing practices which led to excessive numbers of Romany children being placed in special schools without any conclusive evidence as to their intellectual and learning capacity'.[3] At present, according to some experts,[4] the majority of Romany children (more than 80%) are placed in special schools. Although this placement is done with the approval of the parents and is based on psychological testing, it is generally deemed to be discriminatory and has been criticised by many NGOs and international organisations as well as Czech practitioner experts.[5] Criticism is targeted at the approval required from parents, often obtained under pressure and without explaining the consequences of such placing. IQ testing is biased against

---

[1] In relation with the Regular Report from 4 November 1998, the European Commission said the Czech Republic and Slovenia performed least well among the six 'fast-track' countries in meeting the conditions that the EU set for each potential members in 1997. Radio Free Europe (1998) 5 November.

[2] Viktor Sekyt (1998) 'Specifics of Romany children Entering Primary School', lecture given on 1 December.

[3] Zákon o soustavě základních skol, středních skol a vyssích odbornych skol (skolsky zákon) (Law on the system of basic schools, middle schools and higher specialised schools—schooling law), in: *Sbírka zákonou Ceské Republiky 1996* (Collected laws of the Czech Republic 1996), C.77 (10 October 1996), Article 31(1).

[4] Interview with Helena Holcova.

[5] Bratinka Report (1997) 29 October, Recommendation 1(e).

[6] Socioklub, p. 350.

Romany children as it requires culturally specific knowledge and a good level of Czech-language knowledge. Some parents also believe that special schools provide a more friendly and less racist environment than regular school. The result of segregating Romany children into special schools has been the denial of equal educational opportunity for most Romany children.

In June 1999 lawyers from the European Roma Rights Centre (ERRC) filed a complaint at the Constitutional Court of the Czech Republic,[6] which was later rejected by the Court as unsubstantiated. According to ERRC, the evidence documented in the legal complaints shows that Romany children outnumber non-Roma in special schools by a proportion of more than twenty-seven to one in the Ostrava region. This racial disparity constitutes what a United Nations committee of experts has condemned as 'de facto racial segregation' in the field of education, which is inconsistent with the government's obligations under international law. The ERRC further states that as a result of their segregation in schools for the 'retarded', Romany children 'have suffered severe educational, psychological and emotional harm'.[7] Although this criticism may been seen as too radical and many may find it unsubstantiated,[8] its acceptance could lead to a much-needed systemic change. Moreover, still more specialists agree that the Czech school is not suitable for Czech children themselves,[9] not to speak of children who are different or handicapped. As proved by many practitioners, good education is good for everybody ('quality in equality').

On 18 April 2000 the ERRC, on behalf of 18 Roma children from Ostrava, filed a complaint against the Czech Republic at the European Human Rights Court in Strasbourg.

---

[7] Helena Balabánova refers to a '30-year-long tradition of segragating Romany children into special schools', ibid., p. 350.

[8] European Roma Rights Center, Press Statement: Lawsuits Filed by Roma Challenge Racial Segregation in Czech Schools, 15 June 1999.
Also in : 'Navzdy do příkopu, Romská zaloba na stát muze přinést zmenu nespravedlivého systému' (Forever to be a digger. Romany complaint may bring a change of unjust educational system) and 'Mentálne retardovany systém. Romové zalují stát, protoze je posílá do zvláštní skoly' (Mentally retarded system. Roma sue the state because it sends them to special schools), *Respekt*, 14-20 June 1999, pp. 25,27; 'Romske deti koncí nekdy ve zvláštních skoláçh zbytecne' (Romany kids end up in special schools without reason), *Slovo*, 27 May 1999; 'Romove se obrátili na soud kvuli skolám' (Roma approached the Court because of schools), *Lidové noviny*, 16 June 1999; 'Romové si stezují k soudu kvuli zvláštní skole'(Roma complain at the Court because of special school) and 'Stížnost mírí na psychologické testy, ty vsak záhy sceká zmena' (The complaint focuses on psychological tests, but they are to be changed soon) and Ztráta sancí, ztráta rovnosti' (Loss of chances, loss of equality), *MF Dnes*, 16 June 1999, pp. 1,4,16; Romové- zvláštnost ceského skolstvi' (Roma- the specialty of the Czech schooling), *MF Dnes* 17 June 1999

[9] The ERRC criticises that Romany children: '... have been subjected to a curriculum far inferior to that in basic schools; have been effectively denied the opportunity of ever returning to basic school; ... they have been prohibited by law and practice from entrance to non-vocational secondary educational institutions, with attendant damage to their opportunities to secure adequate employment; ... they have been stigmatised as 'stupid' or 'retarded' with effects that will brand them for life, including diminished self-esteem and feelings of humiliation, alienation and lack of self-worth; ... they have been forced to study in racially segregated classrooms and hence denied the benefits of a multi-cultural educational environment'. In ERRC Press Statement: Lawsuits Filed by Roma Challenge Racial Segregation in Czech Schools, 15 June 1999.

ANNEX 2
ETHNIC MAKE UP OF THE CZECH REPUBLIC (1991 PUBLIC CENSUS)

Table A.1. Population of the Czech Republic According to National Identity and Mother Tongue

	National identity (absolute number)	%	Mother tongue (absolute number)	%
Czech	9,770,527	94.8	9,871,518	95.8
Slovak	314,877	3.1	239,355	2.3
Polish	59,383	0.6	52,362	0.5
German	48,556	0.5	40,907	0.4
Romany	32,903	0.3	24,294	0.2
Hungarian	19,932	0.2	20,260	0.2
Ukrainian	8,220	0.1	4,882	0.1
Russian	5,062	0.1	–	–
Ruthenian	1,926	0.0	2,307	0.0
Bulgarian	3,487	0.0	–	–
Greek	3,379	0.0	–	–
Romanian	1,043	0.0	–	–
Austrian	413	0.0	–	–
Vietnamese	421	0.0	–	–
Jewish	218	0.0	–	–
Other (of which Czechoslovakian)	9,860 3,464	0.1 0.0	16,664	0.2
Unknown	22,017	0.2	29,666	0.3
Total	10,302,215	100	10,302,215	100

Note:
1. The proportion of the population whose national identity is other than Czech varies in individual districts and regions of the Czech Republic. The Slovak national minority is dispersed throughout the entire Czech Republic; it was de facto the largest national minority in Czech lands in Czechoslovakia and after the dissolving thereof has been recognised as a national minority. The highest concentration of Slovaks is found in the districts of Sokolov (9.9% of population), Cheb (9.3%), Cesky Krumlov (8.3%), Karvina (8.3%), Bruntal (8.1%) and in other cities, including Prague (2.0%). Some citizens who have declared the Slovak (and also Hungarian) national identity are Romany.
2. There is a significant concentration of persons belonging to the Polish minority located in the continuous settlement along the state border with Poland. In two districts, Frydek-Mistek and Karvina, persons belonging to the Polish national minority amount to more than 8% of the local population. The educational system in this region includes Polish minority schools

from preschool establishments to the level of high schools and specialised secondary schools (including the Polish Pedagogical Center seated in Cesky Tesin which was established by the Ministry of Education, Youth and Sports, a special office of the Czech School Inspectorate, and an educational-psychological counseling center) as well as Polish cultural and educational organisations.

3. Persons claiming German national minority live in the eastern, northern and western border regions of the Czech Republic, in an environment of former German-language islands (such as the districts Jihlava and Vyskov). The greatest number of citizens who claim German national identity live in the districts of Sokolov (6.1%), Karlovy Vary (3.1%), Chomutov (2.6%) and Teplice (2.4%). In Moravia, a greater concentration of citizens declaring German national identity is found in the Opava district (0.9%).

4. Despite territorial dispersion of the Romany population throughout the Czech Lands, this national minority can be considered concentrated in industrial cities in Northern Bohemia and Northern Moravia and in Prague.

5. Less numerous minorities—the Bulgarian, Russian, Ruthenian, Ukrainian, Greek, Bulgarian, Romanian and Jewish minorities—are dispersed throughout the country. In the case of Hungarians and Ukrainians there are greater concentrations especially in Prague, the central Bohemian and northern Moravian regions, and in the case of Greeks in the cities of Krnov and Brno.

From Paper to Practice in Hungary: The Protection and Involvement of Minorities in Governance

Jenő Kaltenbach

Contents

From Paper to Practice in Hungary: The Protection and Involvement of Minorities in Governance

Jenő Kaltenbach

Abstract

This chapter will discuss public policy toward minorities in Hungary and the implementation of this policy. The chapter uses a legal approach to analyse the process and impacts of various legal instruments and explain their practical relevance for accommodating multiethnic local communities in Hungary. The main policy issues analysed in this chapter are: (1) the revitalisation of minority groups by a system of minority self-governments (MSGs); (2) protection of minority cultures and languages through a system of minority education; (3) the lack of consistent policy for the socio-economic empowerment of the Roma minority; and (4) the lack of effective protection of the Roma from sundry discrimination. The chapter first outlines the important legal documents that influence the position of minorities in local communities, and then provides a detailed analysis of problems related to the implementation of these legal norms. Finally, the paper provides recommendations to address these problems.

1. Introduction

Minorities in Hungary are in a unique situation, brought about by the country's geographic and historic shifts and its decentralised system of governance. This chapter will discuss the role of government and legal structures in the protection of minorities in Hungary.

The Republic of Hungary is ethnically heterogeneous, but while it includes a number of distinct national and ethnic minorities, in most cases each of these groups is fairly small in number. Collectively, minorities account for less than 8-10%[1] of the total population.

Since Hungary's transition to a market economy, decentralisation through self-governance and the issues of human and minority rights have figured prominently on the political agenda. Decentralisation has resulted in a fragmented public administration system that provides the possibility of autonomy for even the smallest communities. This same

---

[1] According to census data, minorities represent less than 2% of the population. The estimated number of persons belonging to national and ethnic minorities is between 8-10%. (See Annexes 1 and 2.)

system also complicates the implementation and financing of minority policies, because multiple layers and branches of government are often involved in the process.

Hungary has introduced various legal measures to promote individual and collective rights and cultural autonomy for minorities. Minority citizens have rights, privileges and civic responsibilities that are equal in all respects to those of citizens belonging to the majority population. The country adheres to international law and international treaties with regard to the treatment of minorities, and in many ways its standards are quite progressive and provide a useful model for other countries.

The Hungarian Parliament has created a special system of minority self-government (MSG) that functions at both the national and local levels. The law grants minorities the right to choose their own identities, to use their native language, to form organisations (including a self-government), to have a connection with their mother country and to have parliamentary representation. Minority rights in Hungary go beyond those of the European system of individual protection and extend to collective rights.

However, the successful execution of Hungary's minority policies is complicated by the fact that most minorities are widely dispersed throughout the country. Furthermore, gaps remain between policies and their effective implementation. Overlapping responsibilities require co-ordination involving Parliament, government ministries, local governments, MSGs and nongovernmental organisations (NGOs). Local authorities and MSGs, in particular, are undergoing a learning process.

Because MSGs still lack real financial autonomy, the rules of co-operation between local and minority governments require further clarification, and public officials need more extensive training in minority issues. More needs to be done in establishing and maintaining appropriate native-language schooling for minorities. In addition, adequate minority access to the media is also of great importance.

While most minorities are economically and socially well-integrated, the Roma (Gypsies)[2] are not. Roma remain the largest of any minorities in Hungary, and their social and economic situation is consistently worse than that of other minorities or the mainstream population. Widespread prejudice against the Roma further aggravates the issue, and discrimination takes many forms, not all of which can be realistically solved through legislation.

Still, Hungary is continuously working to reform its governmental structures and legal system with regard to the protection of minorities. The country's plans to join the European Union (EU) have encouraged the government to emphasise the minority rights system—and to work toward its improvement.

---

[2] Hungarian Roma use both the term Roma and Gypsy for self-identification, but the term Roma will be used in the text.

2. Ethnic Diversity and Historic Influences

Hungary is situated in a region in which various national, ethnic and religious minorities have intermingled throughout its history. Hungary shares its borders with seven countries: Austria, Croatia, Romania, Slovakia, Slovenia, Ukraine and Yugoslavia. The Medieval Hungarian Kingdom included territories that today belong to neighbouring countries, including: Transylvania (Romania), the Upper-State (Slovakia) and Vojvodina (Yugoslavia). After the Turkish occupation in 1526, western parts of the country were incorporated into the Habsburg Empire, while a small independent Hungarian Principality existed in Transylvania. In 1686, after the recapture of Buda, the Hungarian capital, from the Turks, Hungary became part of the Habsburg Empire, and remained so until the end of World War I. As a consequence of the Treaty of Trianon in 1920, two-thirds of Hungary was appropriated to neighbouring states.[3]

The territory of Hungary has accommodated various national and ethnic groups throughout its history. In the past, most of these groups lived in close contact with other ethnic groups as well as Hungarians. However, in the 19TH century minority populations began to disperse and assimilate. The process of minority assimilation accelerated during the 20TH century, due to policies that discouraged diversity—enforced by the nationalist regime between the two world wars and later by the communist regime.

During World War II, about 600,000 Hungarian Jews and Roma were deported and killed. After World War II, German and Slovak minorities in the country were subjected to population exchange programmes that involved forced resettling. During communism, the state provided education for minorities in separate so-called 'national minority schools'. However, strong political pressure to eliminate national and minority identities under communism meant that the assimilation of minorities continued.

It is difficult to calculate how many people belong to national and ethnic minorities in Hungary at present. The value probably lies between the official census figures and the unofficial estimates, i.e. between 133,936 and 1,085,000 (see Annexes 1 and 2). Because the census does not allow a person to declare double identity, as in cases of mixed race or ethnicity, the data cannot provide a complete picture of the ethnic make-up of the country's inhabitants.

Today, the level of identification with specific minorities varies. Assimilation is quite advanced, and members of many nationalities no longer speak their mother tongues. According to the census, the number of citizens claiming that they are members of a minority is declining for all groups except Germans and Roma.[4]

Most minorities, with the clear exception of the Roma, appear socially and economically well-integrated into Hungarian society. One of the most important indicators of this integration is that the level of education among minorities is equal to the national average. However, the situation varies greatly among individual minorities: Many Germans and Serbs have university degrees, while fewer Slovenians—only half the national average—are as academically accomplished. The Roma population's indicators of equality are

---

[3] *World Directory of Minorities* (1997) London: Minority Rights Group, p. 223.
[4] Most families belonging to minorities stopped passing on their native language to the next generation. Some 40-60% of the adult minority inhabitants are in ethnically mixed marriages.

well below the national average, and below that of other minorities too.[5] Improving the Roma's situation is one of the key challenges in Hungary's current domestic policy, and the challenge is made more difficult by widespread prejudice and discrimination against Roma. Recently, the marginalisation of the Roma population has become an issue relevant to foreign policy concerns as well.

The need to integrate the Roma has been included in Hungary's EU accession agenda, and as a result, the government has shown more willingness to initiate comprehensive policies aimed at their socio-economic empowerment.

3. Minority Legal Policy

European countries have two basic ways of acknowledging minorities: by definition and through taxation. When a legal definition of the term 'minority' is created, all groups fulfilling the criteria can be treated as national minorities. The country can then consider these minority groups as nationally recognised groups, which can receive any tax preferences deemed appropriate.

Hungary legally acknowledges national minorities through established criteria. The 1993 Act on the Rights of National and Ethnic Minorities (Law No. LXXVII, hereafter referred to as the Minority Act), Paragraph 1, Section 2, defines a national minority as follows:

> ... all such nationalities, settled at least one century ago in the territory of the Hungarian Republic, which are in a minority as regards the number of inhabitants of the state, are Hungarian citizens and are different from the rest of the population in their language, culture and traditions, and such a consciousness of banding together can be seen in them which preserves this heritage, protects their historically created societies and represents their interests.

This definition is equally valid for national and ethnic minorities, as the Hungarian legal system does not differentiate between the two. The definition is designed to achieve two aims: first, to ensure that all legitimate minority groups settled in Hungary are able to fulfill these criteria; and second, to ensure that no newly arrived groups or non-minorities would be able to claim national minority status—either for financial preference or any other reasons.

According to Paragraph 61, Section 1 of the Minority Act, the nationalities settled in Hungary are: Armenians, Bulgarians, Croats, Germans, Greeks, Poles, Roma, Romanians, Ruthenians, Serbs, Slovaks, Slovenians and Ukrainians. These minorities fulfilled the necessary criteria at the time the law went into effect, but the list has an open nature, so further minorities can be acknowledged with the according legal status. Paragraph 61, Section 2 of the Minority Act says:

> ... if more minorities than those listed in section (1) wish to prove that they are eligible to fulfill the conditions of the law, then at least 1,000 voters who claim to belong to the minority can submit a nationality initiative in this matter to the Speaker of the Parliament....

---

[5] Report No. J/3670 on the situation of the national and ethnic minorities in the Hungarian Republic, January 1997, Dr Pál Vastagh, Minister of Justice

While earlier laws and regulations contained provisions for minority protection, the legal system lacked sufficient statutory regulation. Now the minority rights system is coherent—its basic principles are stated in the Constitution and the details for implementation are contained in the Minority Act. Protections for minorities are also contained within several basic laws, especially: the fourth Law on the Penal Code, passed in 1978; Law LXXIX, passed in 1993, on Public Education; and the first Law on Radio and Television, passed in 1996. Additional legal guarantees of minority rights are contained in international treaties and other documents.

This section analyses the various legal instruments that form public policy for minorities in Hungary.

3.1. Hungarian law and international norms for minority protection

Since the early 1990s, Hungary has played an active role in codifying international minority laws. According to the Constitution, international treaties take precedence and internal law must be harmonised with international treaties.

3.1.1. European Charter for Regional and Minority Languages

Although it deals only with specific rights involving languages, the European Charter for Regional or Minority Languages is a significant international treaty that defines the direction of minority rights development. Hungary was one of the eleven states that signed the Charter on 5 September 1992. The country submitted its ratification document in 1999.

The Charter leaves the state to decide which languages to protect. According to Paragraph 42 of the Hungarian Minority Act, the following languages are used by minorities in the country: Armenian, Bulgarian, Croatian, German, Greek, Polish, Roma languages (Romany and Beás), Romanian, Ruthenian, Serbian, Slovak, Slovenian and Ukrainian. But Hungary did not include all of these languages in its documentation ratifying the Charter—the Roma language being the most significant omission.

The official argument for not giving all of Hungary's official minority tongues the full protection of the Charter on Regional or Minority Languages had to do with territorial concentration. As most minority groups are widely dispersed throughout the country, Hungary only chose to take responsibility for establishing institutional types of instruction for Croatian, German, Romanian, Serbian, Slovak and Slovenian. The lack of protection for any of the Roma dialects under the Charter may contribute to the further erosion of the Romany and Beás languages and thus promote the linguistic assimilation of the Roma minority.

3.1.2. Framework Convention for the Protection of National Minorities

The Council of Europe accepted the Framework Convention for the Protection of National Minorities (FCNM) on 10 November 1994. Unlike the Hungarian law, the FCNM does not contain the definition of a minority because it was difficult to obtain international agreement on the best way to describe the term. Omitting the definition allows more states outside of the Council of Europe to join the Convention.

The other significant difference between Hungary's laws and the Convention is the
nature of the rights that are ensured. Hungarian law acknowledges the existence of collective minority rights, while the FCNM is based on individual rights. The Convention's
first article states:

'The protection of national minorities and of the rights and freedoms of persons belonging to those minorities forms an integral part of the international protection of human
rights, and as such falls within the scope of international co-operation'.

The Framework Convention does not include the right for autonomy and positive discrimination, or the right to participate in cultural, economic and social life as a collective
legal entity, which the Council of Europe's Recommendation 1201 does. With these omis-
sions, the number of clauses that could be categorised as 'shy minority protection'[6] increased.

The Framework Convention's control mechanism rests on the nations' periodic obligation to make progress reports to the Council of Europe's Ministry Committee. Government
decision number J/1397 of June 1999 is the first report on the implementation of the
FCNM in Hungary.[7]

3.1.3. Bilateral treaties

A bilateral system of agreements in Central Europe has proven to be an effective means
for securing the protection of specific minorities. The first document of this type was the
Hungarian-Ukrainian basic agreement in 1991.[8] Since 1991, Hungary has signed bilateral treaties with Slovenia, Croatia, Germany, Slovakia and Romania.

The process of signing and ratifying these treaties brought about the interpretation of
minority rights in the form of several freedoms, including: freedom to choose identity, freedom from discrimination, freedom from forced assimilation, freedom of assembly, freedom
to use minority languages, freedom to preserve culture, freedom in education and media
and freedom to use the native language on settlements, street signs and in public notices.

---

[6] Dr Péter Kovács (1996) *International Law and Minority Protection*, Budapest: Osiris, p. 114.

[7] The report has been published by the Office for National and Ethnic Minorities in the publication 'Minorities in Hungary' in 1999.

[8] After intensive talks, the following minority bilateral agreements were signed:
  · 1991 Declaration of the Principles of Co-operation between the Hungarian Republic and the
     Ukrainian Soviet Socialist Republic in the Area of National Minority Rights.
  · 1991 Agreement for Good Neighbour Policy and the Basis of Co-operation between the Hungarian
     Republic and Ukraine.
  · 1992 Agreement for Ensuring Special Rights for the Slovenian National Minority in the Territory
     of the Hungarian Republic and for the Hungarian National Community in the Slovenian Republic.
  · 1992 Treaty of Friendship and Co-operation between the Hungarian Republic and the Slovenian
     Republic.
  · 1992 Treaty between the Hungarian Republic and the Croatian Republic on Friendly Ties and Co-
     operation.
  · 1992 Treaty between the Hungarian Republic and the German Federal Republic on Friendly Co-
     operation and European Partnership.
  · 1992 A Joint Declaration between the Hungarian Republic and the German Federal Republic on
     the German Minority in Hungary and Support for German to be Taught as a Foreign Language.

3.2. Minorities' status as constituents of the state

The Hungarian legal system acknowledges the rights of both minority individuals and minority communities. These rights are enforced through general legal institutions and through specialised institutions established expressly for this purpose. The Constitution's minority prescriptions can be categorised into two groups: those that define the constitutional rights of minorities, and those that seek to ban prejudicial discrimination.

According to the Constitution, minorities are regarded as 'constituent factors of the state',[9] and therefore have rights and duties equal to those of the Hungarian nation. Minorities share in the benefits accruing to the rest of the country, but they also share in the responsibility to handle statutory, social and economic tasks—and therefore must have adequate representation. This constitutional description of minorities can be regarded as granting equal rights for minorities, but minority consultants have different opinions on the matter.

A more accurate definition of minority status is contained in the Minority Act of 1993, which says that national minorities have the same rights as other citizens. Parliament has also created the MSG system of special institutions to protect minority rights and elected a Parliamentary Commissioner for Minority Rights. The Minority Act acknowledges the right to choose an identity, the right to use a native language, the right to form organisations, the right to have a connection with the mother country, the right to self-government and the right to parliamentary representation.

3.3. Collective rights

The Preamble of the Minority Act establishes that the individual and collective rights of national minorities are fundamental human rights, which the Republic of Hungary respects and ensures. The passage of the Minority Act was a major milestone in the process of establishing collective rights. At the Venice Session of the Human Rights Committee it was noted that the Hungarian legal system had recognised and codified the need to protect minorities' community rights at a time when international law had not even acknowledged the existence of such rights.

In the Hungarian legal system, minority communities may exercise the following rights:
·   the right to exist as a minority group;

· 1995 Treaty between the Hungarian Republic and the Slovak Republic on Good Neighbour Policy and Friendly Co-operation.
· 1996 Treaty between the Hungarian Republic and Romania on Understanding, Co-operation and Good Neighbour Policy.
[9] Paragraph 68, Section (1) of the Constitution: The national and ethnic minorities living in the Hungarian Republic shall share in people's power, being constituent factors of the State.
(2) The Hungarian Republic shall accord protection to national and ethnic minorities, ensuring their *collective participation in public life*, the cultivation of their own culture, the use of their mother tongue, education in their mother tongue and the right to use names in their own language.
(3) The Hungarian Republic's laws ensure the *representation* of the national and ethnic minorities living in the country.
(4) National and ethnic minorities are allowed *to create local and national self-governments*.

- the right to protect and develop their own culture and language;
- the right to political representation;
- the right to form local self-governments;
- the right to exist without discrimination;
- the right of access to electronic media.

The Minority Act ensures rights which may, by their nature, be exercised by entities other than individuals—such as minority communities. These rights include:
- the right to identity;
- protection against discrimination;
- the right to education, culture and traditions.

The provision of collective rights is an important development that will surely have an impact on future public policy regarding minorities in Hungary.

3.4. Statutory guarantees

The guarantee of minority rights appears in the laws regarding self-government, but the enforcement of those rights is the task of the state government. This enforcement is accomplished through the following special minority rights organisations and general government institutions.

3.4.1. Parliament's Human Rights, Minority and Religious Committee
The Human Rights, Minority and Religious Committee deals with minority issues at the top level of state power. The role of the Committee is to prepare legislation for the protection of human rights, including the rights of national and ethnic minorities.

3.4.2. Parliamentary Commissioner for the Protection of National and Ethnic Minority Rights
Article 32/B of the Constitution provides for the institution of a Commissioner for the Protection of National and Ethnic Minority Rights. The Commissioner provides a constitutional check on public administration and has the right to investigate any abuse of minority rights that come to his attention. Moreover, the Commissioner can initiate measures to redress abuses, and he can initiate procedures to investigate the enforcement of minority rights.

Since the creation of the office, the Commissioner has investigated a number of cases. Most of these cases involved discrimination on the grounds of national and ethnic origin, and the majority of the cases involved the Roma community. More than half of the cases investigated by the Commissioner related to local governments.

3.4.3. Office for National and Ethnic Minorities
Since 1990, the Office for National and Ethnic Minorities has carried out state tasks related to the accommodation of minorities in Hungary. This Office is part of the central public administration and operates under the auspices of the Ministry of Justice, which is responsible for preparing and enforcing statutory decisions about minorities.

3.4.4. Action Plan for the Roma

In 1997, the government introduced a medium-term action plan to improve the situation of the Roma minority. This plan touched on a broad range of policy issues, including education, socio-economic empowerment, prevention of discrimination, protection of culture and access to the mass media. In spite of its ambitious goals, the action plan has achieved almost no tangible results to date. Although the new government in 1998 continued planning a major policy initiative under the medium-term action plan, the package is still in the development phase. Thus far, it has generated virtually no efforts to design or implement concrete policies.

3.4.5. Central public administration

The Ministry of Education and the Ministry of Internal Affairs are two general government bodies that deal with cultural autonomy. The Ministry of Education is involved in educational issues in connection with MSGs. The Ministry of Internal Affairs is the central supervisory authority for local governments, which means that it is ultimately responsible for legal supervision of MSGs.

3.4.6. Local public administration

The local governments' duties include minority protection and enforcement of minority rights in their respective settlements and at the county level. As most public services are delivered at the local level, local public administrations play a major role in distributing resources and providing equal access to public services. Furthermore, local governments are responsible for co-operating with MSGs. The rules for this co-operation are clearly spelled out in the Law on Local Government and the Minority Act. However, due to the unequal distribution of power and financial dependence of MSGs, the level of participation of minorities in local policy-making really depends on the good-will of the local governments (see Section 4).

According to the Act on Local Governments, candidates can run as minority representatives for seats in the local governments. A total of 1,055 minority deputies were elected in 1998. Most of them belong to the two largest minority groups, the Roma and the German minority.

3.5. Territorial autonomy

The Hungarian system of minority protection is often praised in the international community as one of the most generous systems. The Minority Act of 1993 guarantees national and ethnic minorities a special community right to establish their own local governments.

The main reason behind this generous provision of cultural autonomy for minorities in Hungary was to provide Hungary's neighbours, who accommodate large Hungarian minorities, with a powerful model of minority protection.

The Hungarian legal system ensures cultural autonomy through a two-tier local government system: Minorities are allowed to form their own self-governments (MSGs)—either in connection with local government elections or in independently organised elections.

According to the Minority Act, MSGs regulate or administer jurisdiction over cultural autonomy of their community. However, by their legal nature, MSGs can only affect a public law through another public legal entity, mainly the local and central governmental bodies. This means that MSGs can have an impact on laws through participation in the decision-making process.

The Minority Act allows for another special form of territorial autonomy—it is possible to declare a MSG after local government elections if more than half of the elected board belongs to the same minority group. This right is very rarely applied in practice, however, because of the dispersed geographical nature of most minority groups.

3.6. Cultural autonomy of minorities:
The system of minority self-governments

Because Hungary's minorities live scattered throughout the country, it was sensible to create a system connected to the local government system. Hungary's minorities established their first self-governments in 1994-95.

According to the Minority Act, each individual can claim to belong to any national or ethnic group, but they are not required to do so, and there is no minority registration in Hungary. This free choice of identity is the basis of the MSG model. Minority citizens vote locally for their MSG candidates according to the idea of free choice of identity.[10] The MSG representatives have created—through electors—the national MSG.

The local MSGs can make certain key decisions within their jurisdictions, including: their own organisational regulations; signs and names; and the establishment of institutions, especially in the area of local public education and local media.

The MSG system is set up to work closely with the local government system, and the Minority Act outlines the local governments' responsibilities to the MSG system. For example, according to Paragraph 29, Section 1, in questions that have an impact on the minority population—such as local public education, local media, the patronising of local traditions and culture and collective language use—the local government's board can only decide in accordance with the local MSG. According to Section 2, the relevant MSG's agreement is required when appointing leaders of minority institutions or making local government decisions that have an impact on minority education.

The situation is similar with the national MSGs. They must be allowed to declare an opinion about proposed laws affecting their minorities, and they have the right of approval in the creation of the basic material for minority education. They also have the right of approval in the creation of rules pertaining to the preservation and maintenance of historic settlements and architectural monuments.

The local government is also required to consider the interest of the minorities living in the settlement, to create rules for communal living and to maintain the regulations of the Minority Act. For their part, MSGs must learn the technique and rules for representing and enforcing their own interests. These are the new tasks for both types of governments, and fulfilling them sometimes causes difficulty.

---

[10] There are 3,200 settlements in Hungary. Some 679 minority self-governments were created in the 1994 local government elections and 138 were created in 1995. On 18 October 1998, 1,375 minority self-governments were elected.

3.6.1 Practical problems

The law requires that municipalities and MSGs conclude co-operative agreements, which prescribe the extent and utilisation of assets separated for use by the MSGs. Budgeting is often a bone of contention, because there is frequent disagreement about the utilisation of funds.

Paragraph 102/C of the Act on Local Governments makes it possible for a local government to transfer—if it so wishes—a number of its functions to the local MSG. In practical terms, such a transfer runs into two major hurdles: First, there is sure to be debate over how much funding is sufficient to handle the duties being transferred. The second problem is that the law *does not* allow the local government to transfer powers connected to its scope of authority or to public utilities.

4. The Role of Local Government

During the past ten years, the local level of government has become a major actor in public policy formulation and service delivery. Local governments also play a key role in implementation of minority policy. This section discusses major issues of local management of multi-ethnic communities.

4.1. Decentralisation and public services

The former system of local public administration followed the Soviet scheme of councils, undemocratic due to their centralised character and the absolute domination of the Communist Party. After the adoption of Act No. LXIV of 1990 on Local Elections, a new system of local democracy was established, based upon the principles of Hungarian tradition and the European Charter of Local Self-Governments of the Council of Europe.

The Constitution and the Act on Local Governments recognised the rights of local communities, including the smallest of settlements, to manage their own local affairs. The number of local units has increased to 3,149. All of these elect their own representatives and executive bodies.

Local government in Hungary exists at two levels: the municipality and the county. Municipalities are settlements, which in Hungary includes villages, cities and cities with county rights. The middle-tier of local government, also referred to as 'regional' government, consists of 19 counties. The capital city, Budapest, has special legal status. There are no hierarchical relations between the two levels of local government. Municipalities provide local public services to their settlements while counties provide public services that settlements are not capable of performing, as well as services that have a regional character.

Municipal governments have broad responsibilities in providing local services. While some local services are optional, the Parliament determines mandatory functions and powers of local governments. Parliament must simultaneously ensure the financial means necessary for the fulfillment of these tasks. The Act on Local Governments further requires that municipalities provide: healthy drinking water, kindergarten education, primary school education, basic health and welfare services, public lighting, local public roads and public cemeteries, and the protection of the rights of ethnic and national minorities.

Despite the fact that the scope of duties to be performed by MSGs differs from that of local governments, legislation has provided MSGs with a similar legal status. Local and minority elections are based on the same principles of voting rights and the same regulatory framework.

As minority rights apply to a specific group of people within society, a constitutional question worth considering is whether the MSG system is best served by an election system based on equality and universal voting rights, like the one used for local governments. It could be a cause of concern that non-minority members can participate in MSG elections. But, because the descriptive value of the term 'minority community' is not absolute, and because every citizen is granted the right to vote in MSG elections, the foundations of the current system cannot be questioned on formal, constitutional grounds.

Nonetheless, under the current system it is constitutionally crucial that all minority members be ensured their rights to vote, as well as easy access to MSG elections, so that voters identifying with a particular minority can vote for candidates of the MSG. For example, MSG elections should perhaps be held separately from regular local elections, to make sure that voters have a clear understanding of the issues in the minority election. And voters should be granted the chance of getting to know minority candidates and their programmes, thus making a real choice between individual candidates possible.

4.2. Local governments and minority self-governments

The MSG system—due to its nature—works in close connection with the local government system, which is why the Minority Act gives local governments certain commitments to the MSGs and attempts to establish co-operative decision-making. The MSGs' strongest power is their 'right of veto' in questions impacting on minorities, such as local public education, local media, collective language use, etc. Another, weaker power grants local and/or national MSGs the opportunity to express an opinion in cases where either the law on minorities or another statute of law provides this right.

Unfortunately, in many cases, these rights only exist on paper. Practical experience indicates that disregarding the rights of agreement and of expressing opinions entails no real legal consequence. As we have indicated above, the Act on Local Governments allows the body of representatives of a municipality to transfer some of its duties and tasks to the local MSG. But there are some special regulations included in this act that prevent minority governments from exercising the powers of an authority.

Although the Act on Local Governments excludes any means for an MSG to allocate support for the needy under social welfare legislation, there have been efforts to transfer some of this responsibility as a means of helping underprivileged Roma populations. In recent years local governments have tried to give MSGs representing the interests of Roma communities certain social functions—and appropriate funds—without formal transfer of the responsibility or direct access to the budget.

The attitude of local governments is crucial to the successful implementation of minority rights and the operation of the MSG system for several reasons:

· The overwhelming majority of public affairs affecting citizens are local affairs, and hence in the domain of and the responsibility of local governments. The average person's perception of public affairs is mostly determined by his/her opinion of local government.

· Local governments operate the most important public service systems, the largest two being education and health care, both of which are entwined with the issue of minority rights.

· Minority communities may be defined locally, and local tensions are typically the main concern in minority affairs.

· Approximately one-third of the central budget is channelled through local governments.

According to the statistics prepared by the Office of the Parliamentary Commissioner for Minorities, every prominent case of minority rights violation in 1999 concerned municipal governments. It would be a simplification to claim that officials in municipalities are more inclined to commit legal offences. It is more likely that their frequent involvement in minority issues, and heavy caseloads, make municipal governments more prone to committing rights violations.

The current MSG system grants large discretion to local governments, which means MSGs are often at the mercy of the local 'big brother' financially, professionally and in terms of local policy. A great deal depends on the attitude of the mayor as well as the local council. While a good relationship with the local government is always important to the MSG, the reverse is not necessarily true. Local mayors or councils may prefer not to share power, and there has been a definite trend towards the significant politicisation of minority problems. This is also true of minority affairs in general. Irregularities in benefits, housing and education are at once charged with political content if the clients are minorities, especially Roma.

A genuinely dangerous occurrence that gives reason for real concern is that some mayors and municipal boards, aware of the backing of local public opinion, consciously ignore laws protecting minorities, or construe and apply them in their own particular way.

4.3. MSG checks on local government

Despite initial difficulties, including local hostility and inconsistencies in legal regulation, the system of MSG is on the way to consolidating its status and role in Hungary. Nevertheless, the Hungarian system, which gives wide responsibility and autonomy to local authorities, lacks adequate controls on the local level. A small, or insufficiently organised, community is vulnerable to rigid oligarchies, due to the lack of division and distribution of local power. The risk of a local 'one-party regime' becomes more likely if the local government does not receive sufficient financial and professional support from the national government.

MSGs do have some checks on local governments, including participatory rights in minority matters at the local level. In addition, the chairman of the MSG, or other minority representatives, are allowed to take part in meetings of the municipal council. The MSGs can also address any requests to local government organisations and the organisations are obliged to reply to the request. And, as mentioned above, MSGs have co-operative decision-making rights and definite regulative and administration rights on the local level.

4.4. Financial guarantees for cultural autonomy

Serious concerns have been raised, however, about the autonomy of MSGs when it comes to financing. MSGs are often dependent on relations with local authorities and must compete with them at the local level for allocation of scarce funds. This competition has been known to create hostility between majority and minority members.

Roma MSGs frequently have the greatest difficulties due to their communities' socio-economic position. At the local level in particular, Roma representatives feel squeezed by the reluctance of municipalities to help, compounded by increased responsibility to address problems that their MSG is incapable of handling—such as distributing social aid, fighting discrimination and racism and organising measures against unemployment.

Co-ordinating the financing of MSGs and minority organisations is difficult because minorities are administered by many bodies, including Parliament, the Ministry of Internal Affairs and the Prime Minister's Office, as well as local governments. Parliament has jurisdiction over an amount defined in the annual central budget (HUF 87.8 million in 1999), which is provided to the NGOs of national and ethnic minorities, based on the tenders received.

MSGs receive subsidies, distributed through local governments, from the Ministry of Internal Affairs. The maintenance of minority and majority school facilities is covered by the local governments, and they receive national government grants for this purpose, equal to about 65-70% of the total costs. In addition, minority education institutes receive further subsidies because the government has acknowledged that minority education involves additional costs.

The present financing system is wasteful, for as long as MSGs receive money in equal proportions, irrespective of the kind of activities they perform, MSG officials will have less impetus to do more locally. It would be more efficient to subsidise MSGs based on the services they provide that directly reduce the burden of the local and national government. An MSG that assumes more governmental tasks that are beneficial to minorities should receive a correspondingly larger subsidy.

Hungary's principle of free choice of minority identity makes it impossible to give MSGs financing on the basis of the local minority population. But there are ways to measure the number of people an MSG serves. For instance, it is possible to count the number of students enrolled in a minority education programme, or the number of people visiting a minority library. It is also possible to measure the exact cost of other services, such as upkeep of a minority museum. Unfortunately, the Ministry of Finance seems to find it simpler to distribute funding evenly, and simply claim that it is too hard to estimate the exact costs of MSG work.

4.5. Parliamentary representation

Although the Constitution requires that minorities be represented in Parliament, the legislation necessary to implement this requirement has not yet been passed. The Constitutional Court has ruled that Parliament's failure to create this law is in violation of the Constitution, but still no progress has been made.

The issue of minority representation was raised in 1990, when Article 68 of the Constitution was supplemented with Paragraph (c): 'Representation of national and language minorities living in the Republic of Hungary shall be ensured. Irrespective of the elections for Parliament as per Article 71(1) the Parliament shall elect members of Parliament for the representation of minorities—of a number and in a way to be specified by a separate law'.

Parliament never passed the separate law necessary to define the system for minority representation, however. In 1991 the Constitutional Court was petitioned to rule on the legislature's inaction on the matter. Because a law on the rights of minorities was expected soon, the court suspended the case until 1 January 1992. But the Parliament still did not act by that date, so the Court ruled in the case.

In its resolution No. 35/1992 (VI.10.) AB, the Constitutional Court declared that: 'The statement by the Constitution that it recognises national and ethnic minorities as part of the state of Hungary renders the statutory regulation of the rights of national and ethnic minorities extremely important ... Representation is a necessary prerequisite for national and ethnic minorities to fulfil their roles as constituents of the state'. The resolution also stated that 'the Parliament failed to carry out its task as per Article 68 of the Constitution whereby it created an unconstitutional situation'. Consequently, the Constitutional Court called on the Parliament to fulfill its legislative task, but the Court noted that it is up to the legislators to decide whether they will carry out the task by adopting one or several acts of law.

On 7 July 1993, the Parliament adopted the Minority Act, which says in Article 20 (1) that: 'minorities have a right to parliamentary representation—to be specified in a separate act of law'. Thus, instead of resolving the question of representation, the Minority Act transferred the issue to the scope of another law. It did not specify, however, whether it was necessary to create a separate law specifically on elections by minorities or whether the task can be performed by an appropriate modification of the act on general elections.

After the Minority Act's passage, another petition to the Constitutional Court sought to declare the Elections Act unconstitutional because it did not have an appropriate provision to treat minorities as a 'constituent of the state'.

The Constitutional Court rejected this motion without substantive discussion, arguing that it sought to terminate an unconstitutional status in the form of failure to carry out an action and is therefore a judged fact. But in resolution No. 24/1994 (V.6.) AB, the Court ruled that: 'The No. 35/1992 (VI.10.) resolution by the Constitutional Court had already established the fact of the violation of the Constitution in respect of the parliamentary representation of national and ethnic minorities'.

The 1994 resolution by the Constitutional Court clarified the fact that the Parliament remained in violation of the Constitution. Furthermore, by failing to create the necessary provisions for minority representation outlined in Article 20 (1) of the Minority Act, the Parliament failed to carry out its own promise.

Even though adequate representation is a necessary precondition for minorities to fulfill their role as constituents of the state, the law to provide this representation has yet to be passed, and Parliament has been in breach of the Constitution by failing to act for almost a decade. This failure deprives minority communities living in Hungary from exercising their constitutional rights and weakens trust in the Parliament.

4.6. Education

For individuals in minority groups, familiarity with the group's language and culture can be a great help in freely choosing and preserving minority identity. Generations of minorities have lost their language due to assimilation, but kindergartens and schools can help children—and their parents—preserve their identities and stop the assimilation process. The education of ethnic nationalities is therefore a high-priority area of minority rights.

Hungary provides for native-tongue education for members of national and ethnic minorities in Article 68, Paragraph 2 of the Constitution. Paragraph 43 of the Minority Act leaves the decision of whether the child is to be educated in Hungarian or in the language of a different nationality up to the child's parent or ward.

There is no separate minority education system in Hungary. Minority education is conducted as an integral part of the Hungarian public education system. The education of national minorities has a well-established structure of schools, education programmes and qualified teachers belonging to the specific national minorities. There are two major types of minority education systems—larger minorities have their own educational network within the framework of the public education system, while smaller groups have no autonomous network but have separate classes to host their children. The Roma are poorly served and do not enjoy an adequate version of either of these two minority education systems.

Case Study 1. Changes in Minority Education

In 1996 the amendment of Law No. 1993/LXXIX on Public Education brought significant changes to legislative regulations concerning minority education. The rules of the previous public education law did not take the regulations of the Minority Act into account. The old law was ambiguous about which institutions might be considered minority institutions, and as a result the MSGs have not always been able to practice their rights to consent and opinion on the subject. The financing system for public education did not provide for small schools for nationalities, and the regulations ignored the fact that the per capita costs of small nationality schools are higher than those of schools with more students. In seeking a solution to the problem, the Parliamentary Commissioner on the Rights of Ethnic and National Minorities has had meetings with the president of the Human Rights, Minorities and Religious Affairs Committee and leaders of the National and Ethnic Minorities Office.

In striving to create cultural autonomy, the Minority Act gives great importance to autonomy over minority education. The current form of ensuring educational autonomy is the right to consent and opinion—exercised through the MSGs—in local decisions that concern the education of minorities.

Small national minority schools often face serious financial constraints. Financial shortfalls have been temporarily averted thanks to co-ordinated government intervention, but a permanent solution is still required.

The Minority Act makes minority education possible, even for classes of lower-than-average size, by transferring the additional expense to the national and local governments. Since these regulations ensure the upholding of constitutional rights, executing them inadequately can lead to legal and constitutional controversies.

The Law on Public Education strives to reform the education system as a whole. A new national basic curricula was passed, leaving room for locally maintained public schools to make a range of choices in setting their curricula. This reform, which has increased the independence of schools, also affects minority education. But it is too early to tell what impact the law will have on minority institutions.

There are *three types of settings* for providing minority education:

- minority language taught as a foreign language;
- so-called 'bilingual schools', where some subjects are taught in the mother tongue;
- schools where all subjects are taught in the mother tongue.

Special programmes/schools for Roma children are also considered as part of the system of minority education. However, due to the lack of trained teachers specialised in Roma language and culture, these institutions often address the disadvantages of the Roma children rather than building their identity.

The creation and operation of a minority class or student group is mandatory if requested by eight parents belonging to the same minority, or by their legal representative. Paragraphs 86 and 87 of the Law on Public Education regulate the tasks the local government has to perform in providing education. For example, the local government must ensure compulsory attendance by all children, regardless of ethnicity, at kindergarten, elementary school and junior high school.

The amendment to the Public Education Law has made it clear that the official languages of education are Hungarian as well as the language of the national minority in question. Examinations may be in the language of the national minority, while the grade certificate must be written in both Hungarian and the minority language.

Local and national MSGs may maintain educational institutes, and often also have the right to consent and opinion on a range of educational matters. For example, local governments must obtain the consent of the local and national MSG in order to establish public education institutions, to extend the scope of an existing institution's responsibilities or to discontinue the operation of an institution or certain services.

This version of educational autonomy is probably well suited to most MSGs, because most minority schools are so-called mother-tongue schools in settlements with a population of less than 5,000. In these communities, MSGs do not have the professional and financial capacity for maintaining schools by themselves.

The amended Public Education Law provides for a gradual transfer of minority institutions from local governments to MSGs. Paragraph 88, Section 7 regulates the conditions under which the local government may transfer the ownership or operating rights of educational institutions. Because transferring an institution to MSG control only involves a change in maintenance, such a transfer does not have a dramatic impact on public education.

4.6.1. Financing minority education

The Minority Act acknowledges that minority education involves higher costs than standard education. To offset these costs, the government has established the Earmarked State Grant to Support Minority Education. The amendment to the Public Education Law states that the grant cannot be used for other purposes,[11] but the legislation does not spell out exactly what counts as a 'minority education' cost. It is not clear, for example, whether the grant can be used to pay operating costs at a school building where both minority and regular classes take place. The Parliamentary Commissioner has ordered a nationwide investigation to examine this controversial situation.

It is understandable that it may cause a conflict in smaller settlements if the minority institute receives more grants than a majority school or kindergarten, but nationality education clearly involves higher costs, and the failure to cover these costs can constitute a breach of national and ethnic minority rights. It falls to Parliament to find a solution for financing minority education.

Financial constraints have lead to problems, such as the poor supply of textbooks for nationality education. Nationality education can only become an integral part of the public education system if appropriate teaching materials are published in accordance with the basic national curricula.

More funding and facilities are also needed for nationality teacher training. Minority education can only live up to the new challenges and growing demand if an appropriate number of properly trained teachers are available to train each nationality. Since the amendment to the public education law applies higher standards when employing faculty for these nationalities, the government must elaborate appropriate measures to assist in their professional development.

4.6.2. Provisions for Roma education

The education of the Roma is clearly insufficient in Hungary. Roma students perform statistically poorer than the countrywide average, and they lack appropriate minority classes and special educational programmes. In many cases, educational policy aimed at improving the

---

Facts and Figures. Provisions for National Minority Education

· *According to the Ministry for Education and Culture, the present network of national minority institutions contains 298 kindergartens and 370 regular schools.[12] Some 56% of kindergartens teach German, 23% Slovak and 11% Croatian. Other minority languages are each taught in under 5% of the kindergartens. Similar figures apply to schools for older children.*
· *More than 60% of the institutions are in settlements of less than 5,000, and all Serbian, Romanian and Slovenian educational institutes are in small townships and towns.*
· *German schools and kindergartens are represented in all types of settlements.*
· *60% of the nationality schools have less than 200 students, and 25% have less than 100 students.*
· *Bulgarians have one educational institution, which contains grades K-12 and was previously financed by the Bulgarian government. It is now supported by both Hungary and Bulgaria. The institution has 100-120 students per year.*
· *Greeks have only elementary and junior high schools, and it is provided in approximately six settlements.*

---

[11] Normative Grant For Minority Education: See Annex 3, Budgetary Support for the Education of National and Ethnic Minorities.

[12] These figures do not include those institutions that provide education for Roma students, but do include institutions training two nationalities at once.

> - Croatian-language education is carried out in 40 kindergartens and 41 elementary and junior high schools, seven of which are bilingual. There are two high schools that have Croatian-language education. There is no Croatian university education, but there are undergraduate four-year teacher training courses in Pécs and Szombathely.
> - Poles have one educational institute, which incorporates elementary, junior high and high school classes and uses the current Polish curricula.
> - There are 198 German-language kindergartens and 198 German schools. Nine of the latter are high schools that are either independent or have nationality branches. German teaching degrees may be acquired in eight institutions of higher education in Hungary. University-level training in German is carried out at the University of Sciences in Pécs, and there is a four-year teacher training course in Szeged.
> - During the 1995-96 academic year, Romanian-language education was carried out in twelve kindergartens, eleven elementary and junior high schools—five of which are independent Romanian nationality schools—and one high school. Romanian-language kindergarten teacher training is carried out in Szarvas, grade school teacher training in Békéscsaba and general Romanian teacher training is available in Szeged and Budapest.
> - Also during the 1995-96 academic year, an experimental Ruthenian-language education programme commenced in a Ruthenian settlement with eighteen elementary and junior high school students.
> - There are currently four Serbian kindergartens and eleven Serbian schools, one of which is a Serbian-language high school in Budapest. Teachers are trained at the University of Sciences in Szeged, and in Budapest.
> - There are 74 Slovakian kindergartens, 67 elementary and junior high schools and two high schools. Kindergarten teachers are trained in Szarvas and Esztergom. Slovak-speakers may acquire grade school teaching degrees in Esztergom and Békéscsaba and general teaching degrees in Szeged and Budapest.
> - Slovenian-language education is present in five kindergartens and four schools; teachers are trained in Szombathely.

situation of Roma schooling can only be successful if conducted as part of co-ordinated government efforts to mitigate the economic and social disadvantages of Roma communities.

Even though 7.12% of students in Hungary are of Roma origin, there is only one Roma educational institute, the Gandhi High School in Pécs. Although the number of Roma who have finished junior high school has increased since 1990, the ratio of those continuing through secondary education is still very low. While more than half of non-Roma students continue their studies in high school, only 3% of Roma students are admitted to high schools and only 0.1% of these students continue on to higher-level education.

Roma students' lack of success is not only due to their very poor social and economic situation. There are clear patterns of discrimination in the public education system, and the government has not made any real effort to remedy the current situation or to prevent discriminatory practices.

The Hungarian public education system has no tolerance for the Roma's different cultural background, and the emphasis on uniformity characteristic of governmental education systems is so strong that Roma students either drop out or are forced into so-called auxiliary schools. Some new programmes have focused on helping Roma students to catch up. The pedagogical methods of these programmes, however, are not yet clear. Research has proven that auxiliary and special education can actually constitute a form of institutionalised segregation.

Case Study 2. Discrimination in School

Perhaps Hungary's most notable case concerning discrimination in education was the separate graduation ceremony for Roma pupils in Tiszavasvári.*

The leaders of three Roma community organisations appealed to the President of the Republic to take measures concerning the case of a primary school in Tiszavasvári that decided to organise a separate graduation ceremony for Roma pupils. According to information published in the local press, Roma pupils were not allowed to use either the school gymnasium or the school shop. The Parliamentary Commissioner for Human Rights (Ombudsman) ordered the case to be investigated ex officio, and the President of the Republic also began an inquiry.

One of the housing estates in Tiszavasvári is significantly populated by Vlach (Romanian) Roma, whose children have always studied at Ferenc Pethe Primary School. The school has a tradition stretching back 40 years.

On 23 April 1997, on the basis of a resolution adopted by the majority of the faculty, the school decided to organise a separate graduation ceremony for Roma students. The reason given for the decision, was that, at that time, a high percentage of children were infected with various contagious conditions ranging from lice to skin conditions, and the faculty meant to protect parents and guests attending the ceremony from the risk of infection. The use of the gym was denied to Roma pupils for the same reason, although no formal decision was made on the issue. Parents were informed about the separate ceremonies at a parents' meeting and during individual discussions.

The teachers' reason for a separate ceremony—a high rate of infection among Roma students —is placed under question by the fact that there was never any such measure taken earlier, though there was a similar rate of infection. Due to the collective nature of the decision, the result affected the infected and the uninfected alike. Although discriminatory intent as a motive for the faculty's decision cannot be proven, the incidents, including the lack of preparation and the method of administering the ceremony, clearly appear to have led to discrimination.

The separate graduation ceremony for Roma students prevented others at the ceremony from becoming infected, but the fundamental problem, i.e. the infection of most Roma children, remained unresolved.

In one sense, the events described above could be regarded as the consequence of grave social and sanitary conditions that cannot be dealt with in isolation, without also addressing the root causes of the problem. As long as there is no change in the living conditions at the housing estate, sanitary risk may be used as an excuse for discriminatory educational measures.

The problem can only be solved through co-operation among Roma and non-Roma residents of the estate, the mayor, representatives of the local government, teachers, community organisations, and various institutions and authorities. There is apparently a desire for such co-operation in Tiszavasvári. The local board of representatives has urged constant co-operation and mutual assistance between the institutions and organisations concerned.

Teachers agreed to take part in a training course in which they sought to widen their knowledge of Roma culture. At a reconciliation meeting, town administrators presented a package of measures to be used to improve the living conditions of the estate's Roma population, as far as the municipality's resources allow. It is to be hoped that as a result of these measures and continued co-operation the issue of the segregation of the Roma minority in the community life of the estate can be resolved over time.

The Parliamentary Commissioner for Minority Rights significantly contributed to the final outcome and solution of the issue by making recommendations to the municipality and to senior officials respon-

---

* Primary and secondary schools in Hungary traditionally organise a ceremonial farewell for graduating students, who walk along the school corridors singing graduation songs.

sible for solving constitutional anomalies. The local board of representatives accepted provisions from these recommendations, and used them to elaborate a detailed package of measures put together in the form of a resolution Both the Minister of Culture and Education and the Minister of Welfare welcomed the Ombudsman's proposals and specifically pledged to implement them in practice.

Thus, auxiliary schools fail to promote equal opportunities for the Roma.[13] At the same time, any kind of special programmes for Roma face difficulties in the increasingly competitive environment of Hungarian public education, because they require further budget resources.

These specialised programmes can only be successful if the economic and social disadvantages of regions inhabited by Roma are addressed through co-ordinated, overall government efforts.

The key to the Roma population's ability to integrate, without forced assimilation, is a breakthrough in the field of education. Hungary's pending accession to the European Union means that language, computer skills and overall education are more important than ever. If the Roma are excluded from the opportunity to acquire these skills, then the huge gap between Roma and the majority could widen further—creating tensions that are difficult or impossible to resolve.

4.7. Regulations to promote minorities in the media

The right to choose an identity is a key principle of Hungarian minority legislation. But this choice can only be considered voluntary if it is based on conscious decisions by autonomous individuals. In order to increase individuals' understanding of what it means to belong to a minority, it is essential that the minority's distinctive language, culture and traditions are made clear to a wider audience.

Paragraph 18 of the Minority Act says, 'public radio and television—according to the regulations of a separate law—has to provide for the creation and broadcast of national or ethnic programmes'. The Constitution and the Minority Act both promote equal rights to participation in public life and access to the media. Financial, procedural and organisational regulations of the 1996/I Law on Radio and Television—referred to as the RTV law—should help in creating a balanced and realistic picture of minorities.

The RTV Law implements a wide range of guarantees for minority rights by putting most minority programming in the special category of a public service broadcast. Information conveying the culture, life and viewpoints of minorities is classified as public service broadcasting, and can be subsidised within the framework of the system.

One of the RTV Law's basic principles is that public or private broadcasters may not breach human rights or serve to incite hatred against minorities. Public broadcasters are expected to be particularly vigilant in portraying minorities with respect and fairness. Violations of these regulations can be sanctioned by the National Radio and Television Public Board, with the most severe punishment being revocation of a broadcaster's license.

---

[13] See the works of Ladányi and Csanádi and Havas and Kertesi.

It is the duty of public broadcast providers to help maintain the cultures and languages of minorities and to offer regular information in their native tongues. Regulations enforce this duty by insisting that the ratios of air time allotted to different minorities cannot be less than they were before the law came into effect, and may not be changed arbitrarily.

National MSGs have significant rights in the public service media, such as determining how the broadcast time allotted to minorities is used. Their decision must be respected by the public service broadcaster. National self-governments may jointly delegate one person to the advisory boards of Hungarian Radio, Hungarian Television and the Hungarian Television Public Foundation.

The RTV Law's regulations are appropriate for shaping the depiction of minorities in electronic media. The Law's greatest merit is that it does not declare the rights of minorities, but rather provides an appropriate order of procedures and sanctions against those who breach those rights. It may also pave the way to for practical enforcement of previously established minority laws.

5. Forms of Minority Rights Protection

The Hungarian Constitution makes the protection of minority rights a fundamental element of the entire legal system. Every governmental organisation is bound to protect minority rights, and every citizen is bound to respect minority rights in the Republic of Hungary. The breach of these rights may be remedied in court.

MSGs are the cornerstones of the system of institutions upholding minority rights. The Parliamentary Commissioner for Minority Rights plays a key role in applying the Constitutional protection of those rights to administrative issues.

NGOs and legal consulting offices dealing with minority rights protection help enforce the practical implementation of those rights. These organisations are relatively well trusted by citizens belonging to minorities and consequently have the opportunity to perform certain forms of minority rights protection that governmental organisations cannot practice. Unfortunately, these institutions do not have sufficient government funding. They maintain themselves through funds from domestic and international organisations, and professionals working for them often volunteer for these tasks, receiving no financial compensation.

The attitude toward international human rights watchdogs and other monitoring organisations in Hungary has changed in recent years. Government organisations are now helping these agencies, largely thanks to the Euro-Atlantic integration process, as reports from these NGOs and international agencies can strongly influence how Hungary is viewed abroad.

The Hungarian Constitution prohibits discrimination in general, and specific legal regulations take concrete steps against it. The 1996 amendment of the Penal Code has special significance, because it provides an opportunity for authorities to use increased rigour when dealing with violent actions committed against a group or an individual for reasons of nationality, ethnicity, race or religion.

5.1. Protection against discrimination

Ethnic conflicts appear to be growing in frequency and seriousness in Hungary, and discrimination against the Roma population is particularly evident. Legislation to remedy this discrimination can follow two courses: either 'positive discrimination' (affirmative action) to reform the social circumstances that form the basis of discrimination; or 'anti-discrimination' legislation, which effectively prohibits discrimination and punishes those responsible for breaches of rights. A Draft Anti-Discrimination Law was submitted to the Human Rights Committee of the Hungarian Parliament in October 2000.

Although Hungary has not had a specific anti-discrimination law, anti-discrimination regulations are contained within the paragraphs of laws dealing with other scopes of interest. The highest level of law, Paragraph 70/A, Section 1 of the Constitution states that: 'The Hungarian Republic ensures human and citizen rights for all individuals within its borders without distinguishing between any race, colour, gender, language, creed, political or other opinion, national or social origin, wealth, birth or other position'.

According to Judicial Decree 61/1992 (XI.20) AB, this section of the Constitution covers more than human rights and basic citizens' rights. The prohibition of discrimination covers the whole legal system. Hungary has accepted the obligation to prohibit and eliminate all racial discrimination against any person, group or organisation using all available tools—even legislation if necessary—in accordance with the international treaty on the elimination of all forms of racial discrimination published in the Eighth Executive Order of 1969. According to the 1993 Law on the Rights of National and Ethnic Minorities, all kinds of discrimination against minorities are prohibited.

These laws, and the existing Constitutional protections, represent sufficient guarantees for the elimination of direct legal discrimination against minorities. However, the administrative aspect of the legal system can only be enforced in practice if it contains other guarantees. There must be an appropriate system of regulations created for:
- exposure of discriminatory legislation;
- the control of potentially discriminatory legal relations;
- the resolution of existing breaches of rights;
- a system of compensation.

Minority protection and anti-discrimination legal regulations passed during recent years have created the basis for this system, but this does not mean that the process of administrative legislation can be considered complete.

5.2. Employment

Employment discrimination is especially significant, because unemployment poses a serious social problem in Hungary. Examples of discrimination in the field of employment include the illegal, discriminatory refusal to establish an employment relationship and discrimination in the rights and obligations of the employment relationship based on the employee's national or ethnic background.

Paragraph 5, Section 1 of the 1992/XII Law on the Labour Code states:

It is forbidden to implement discrimination concerning the employment relationship between the employees based on their gender, age, nationality, race, origin, creed, political views, membership of employee's federation or activities related, as well as all other circumstances not related to the employment relationship.

Case Study 3. Remedy for Discrimination in a Pub

A Roma MSG complained that Roma individuals were not admitted into a pub in the centre of their town.

The county-level consumer protection authority, together with the Roma MSG, organised a test purchase involving Roma customers in order to prove the act of discrimination. Subsequently, the authority made a precedent-setting decision:
- · it obliged the business to serve every customer regardless of ethnicity;
- · it demanded the business to report on the relevant actions within 15 days; and
- · it warned the business that failure to meet these obligations would result in the initiation of temporary closure by the district administrator.

In legal terms, the decision was important because it was not only based on the Act on Protection of Consumers but also on the discrimination prohibition contained in the Law on the Rights of National and Ethnic Minorities.

The procedure of the consumer protection authority creates a precedent as well, because it used an effective method—test purchase by Roma customers—to reveal a case of discrimination for the first time in Hungary.

The law transfers insurance obligations and burdens to the employer in the event of an argument concerning discrimination. The trial date has to be set within fifteen days of the labour court receiving the petition if no other measures are necessary. If the discrimination takes the form of an illegal termination of the employment relationship, the employee has to be employed in his/her previous position upon request, and the arrears of pay as well as other damages must be compensated. According to the 1996/LXXV Law on the Control of Work Affairs, a fine of HUF 50,000-1,000,000 may be imposed on the employer.

Paragraph 75, Section 1 of the 17/1968 (IV.14.) Governmental Decree on Transgressions also regulates discrimination against the employee:

The employer, who
(a) illegally refuses employment based on gender, age, nationality, race, origin, creed, political views, membership of employee's federation or activities related as well as all other circumstances not related to the employment relationship;
(b) implements discrimination of employees according to section (a) may be punished with a fine of up to fifty thousand forints.

Pursuant to the provisions of Act III of 1952 on Civil Practice, effective 1 January 1999, claims against unlawful discrimination by an employer may now be filed not only as a civil case; legal remedy can also be sought under the Labour Law. An amendment to the Act extended the meaning of a 'case under labour law' to include cases arising during negotiations preceding the actual conclusion of the labour contract. As a result, legislation that defends prospective employees—such as the reversal of their obligation to provide evidence, and the rule on the relevant court procedure to start within 15 days—now also applies to labour cases initiated during employment.

This amendment is intended to provide job-seekers with a more effective means of defence against potentially discriminative employers, though it is clear such negative discrimination will not be eradicated by legal means alone. It is crucial that legislators gather ever-more-accurate information on the extent of this important—though elusive and subtle—social problem. A more profound knowledge of the situation can facilitate the preparation of structural-organisational measures to fight job discrimination—and even further amendments to the law, if necessary.

5.3. Police violence against Roma

The most serious forms of discrimination in practice are violent acts committed against minorities. Among such acts, crimes committed against Roma by members of the police force bear separate mention. Acts perpetrated against Roma by individual members of the police force may not lead to the conclusion that the police as such are prejudiced against minorities, but they do draw attention to the fact that training with respect to ethnic minority issues and the screening of prejudiced candidates during police training.

Since it is legally possible to limit basic rights during police procedures, the use of police powers in a prejudicial and abusive way may cause significant grievances. Measures have to be taken to ensure a lawful state of affairs and to have those responsible answer for their actions when any kind of discrimination is perpetrated by police.

Violent crimes committed by members of the police force are severely punished by law. The penalty for assault during an official procedure is imprisonment for up to two years, and this may be as much as five years in the case of forced interrogation. An officer found guilty of detaining someone illegally may be subject to five years imprisonment, or up to eight years in an aggravated case. A fiduciary relationship between the police and minorities, especially the Roma minority, can not be created solely by remedying breaches of rights—it requires a deeper change in attitudes.

6. Conclusions

The policy of protecting minority rights is new to the Hungarian legal system, so it may seem surprising that that it already needs improvement. It should be understood, however, that the 'experimental' nature of the current legal system was apparent the minute it was formed.

The unique Hungarian system that offers 'half-municipal autonomy' is a legislative response to the question of whether minority communities that are in a state of advanced assimilation are capable of independent, autonomous action.

It has become evident after a few years of observation that it is not only possible to revitalise minority communities, but the process has started spontaneously—especially among groups with relatively large numbers, like Roma, Germans, Slovaks, Croats and Romanians. The creation of the system of minority rights protection has merely helped in this process.

The legal framework must be further expanded, in part through the creation of institutions that were 'promised' earlier and, in part, by making the existing system more coherent. The best example of the former is the creation of the minorities' representatives in Parliament. An example of the latter is the need to make the theoretical aspects of autonomy real.

The minority right to parliamentary representation was first regulated through a 1990 amendment of the Constitution and later reaffirmed by the Constitutional Court. Yet, no formula has been found that is acceptable both to political parties and minorities. The common feature in the plans elaborated so far—including a proposal that was turned down by Parliament in 1993—is that they make it easier for minority organisations to nominate candidates, and minority candidates would not need the 5% of the vote required for a typical Parliamentary mandate. According to the current plan, the least preferential mandates would require 10,000 votes. This would offer a real chance of representation to the 'bigger' minorities, like the Roma, Germans, Slovaks and Croats, but, unsurprisingly, the smaller minorities object to the plan.

The creation of cultural autonomy for minority groups has already begun to some degree. The Parliamentary Commissioner for Minority Rights suggested directions for development in his 1996 annual report, which says that mechanisms for functional and financial autonomy for MSGs should be gradually developed. Thus far, however, these mechanisms have not been created. The local, and in some cases national, aspects of public education and cultural services that relate to minorities should be delegated to the MSGs, along with sufficient budgetary resources.

The true test of the viability of the MSG system will be whether Hungary is ready to take this next step forward toward MSG autonomy.

7. Recommendations

1. The regulation of the competencies of MSGs must be as precise as possible, to avoid unnecessary conflicts with local councils.
2. Special training programmes on minority law and conflict prevention should be provided for local policy-makers and representatives of minority groups.
3. There should be well-organised, regular contact among the different actors in local communities.
4. Two of the key issues in managing multi-ethnic communities are, on the one hand, delegating power to the minority community in issues where it can decide autonomously and, on the other, (re)integrating the community by allowing minorities to participate in decisions on 'common' issues.

5. The fundamental fields of local policy-making in multi-ethnic communities are education and cultural issues. The education system and cultural services must reflect the multi-cultural nature of the relevant community.

6. Although the issue of social welfare payments should not be devolved entirely to MSGs, self-governments of the Roma minority should be allowed to comment on the allocation of social aid for Roma.

7. Due to its broad social impacts, a nationwide investigation into the issue of education for Roma is needed. The goal of this investigation should be to shed light on controversial practices and arrangements in public education, and to devise regulations to remedy them.

Only a properly functioning control system can efficiently diminish the vulnerability of citizens, especially weaker groups in society that are less capable of defending their own interests. The creation of such a control system is the constitutional duty of the state.

Further Reading

Dr. Kovács, Péter (1996) *Nemzetközi jog és kisebbségvédelem* (International law and minority protection), Budapest: Osiris

Csefkó, Ferenc and Ilona Kovács Pálné (1999) *Kisebbségi Önkormányzatok Magyarországon* (Minority Self-Governments in Hungary) Budapest: Osiris Kiadó.

Kemény, I., G. Havas, and G Kertesi (1994) *The Education and Employment Situation of the Gypsy Community: Report of the 1993/4 National Sample Survey,* ILO/Japan Project, Working Paper 17., Budapest, Hungary.

Kertesi G. (1994) *The Labour Market Situation of the Gypsy Minority in Hungary,* ILO/Japan Project, Working Paper 14., Budapest, Hungary.

Ladányi, J. (1993) *Patterns of Residential Segregation and the Gypsy Minority in Budapest,* International Journal of Urban and Regional Research, Vol. 17., No. 1., pp. 30–41.

J/2259 Beszámoló a nemzeti és etnikai kisebbségi jogok országgyülési biztosáról 1999 (Annual Report of the Parliamentary Commissioner for the Rights of National and Ethnic Minorities, 1 January-31 December 1999, Budapest.

Project on Ethnic Reations (1998) *Self-Government in Hungary: The Gypsy/Romani Experience and Prospects for the Future,* Princetown, New Jersey.

Puporka, L. and Zádori, Z. (1999) *The Health Status of Romas in Hungary,* World Bank Regional Office Hungary, NGO Studies, No. 2.

Riba, I. (1999) *Minority Self-Government in Hungary,* The Hungarina Quarterly, Volume 40.

ANNEX 1
1980 AND 1990 CENSUS DATA ON MINORITY GROUPS

Table A.1. Census Data According to Native Language

Minority groups	Number of people		Per cent of the total population in
	1980	1990	1990
Slovaks	16,054	12,745	0.1228
Romanians	10,141	8,730	0.0841
Croats	20,484	17,577	0.1694
Serbs	3,426	2,953	0.0285
Slovenians	3,142	2,627	0.0253
Germans	31,231	37,511	0.3616
Roma	27,915	48,072	0.4634
Armenians	-	37	0.0004
Bulgarians	-	1,640	0.0158
Poles	-	1,370	0.0132
Ukrainians, Ruthenians	-	674	0.0065
Total	112,393	133,936	1.291

Note: National population:
    in 1980   10,709,463 inhabitants
    in 1990   10,374,823 inhabitants

Source: MAPSTAT Central Statistics Office (1992) Budapest.

ANNEX 2
ESTIMATED MINORITIES IN HUNGARY

Table A.2. Estimated Population of Minorities in Hungary

Minorities	Number of inhabitants
Roma	400,000 - 600,000
Germans	200,000 - 220,000
Slovaks	100,000 - 110,000
Croats	80,000 - 90,000
Romanians	25,000
Poles	10,000
Serbs	5,000
Slovenians	5,000
Bulgarians	3,000 - 3,500
Greeks	4,000 - 4,500
Armenians	3,500 - 10,000
Ukrainians	1,000
Ruthenians	1,000
Total	790,500 - 1,085,000

Source: Ombudman's Office.

ANNEX 3
MINORITY EDUCATION IN HUNGARY

Table A.3. Budgetary Support for the Education of National and Ethnic Minorities

Minority Education	1980-81. School year	1990-91. School year	1997-98. School year	1997-1998. institution	teachers
	Pupils number				
Kindergartens	11,082	14,009	20,470	386	993
Elementary Schools	35,482	44,545	53021	390	1,357
Secondary Schools	790	1,301	2310	27	179
Total:	47,354	59,855	75801	803	2,529
				1998	1999
Earmarked state grant for one pupil:				75,000	86,000
Earmarked state grant allocated on the basis of quotas					
	1998.	1999.	Number	Grant	
	HUF/pers.		person	HUF (in millions)	
Kindergarten	23,000	25,000	33,000	825	
School	24,500	26,000	48,000	1,568	
National minority school	27,000	32,000	10,000	320	
Total:			91,000	2,713	= 30,000 HUF/pers.
Earmarked state grant for Education of Roma:					
'Closing Up' Roma education	24,000	27,000	53,000	1,431	
Grant for Roma students, living in student-hostels	10,000	20,000	1,710	34	
				1,465	= 27,600 HUF/pers.

Source: Hungarian Ministry of Education.

ANNEX 4

HUNGARY'S COMMITMENTS IN THE THIRD PART OF THE REGULATIONS IN THE EUROPEAN CHARTER ON REGIONAL AND MINORITY LANGUAGES

Article 8
1.	a)	(iv)	
	b)	(iv)	
	c)	(iv)	
	d)	(iv)	
	e)	(iii)	
	f)	(iii)	
	g)		
	h)		
	i)		
2			

Article 9
1	a)	(ii)	(iii)	(iv)
	b)	(ii)	(iii)	
	c)	(ii)	(iii)	
2	a),	b)	c)	

Article 10
1	a)	(v)			
	c)				
2	b)	e)	f)	g)	
3	c)				
4	a)	c)			
5					

Article 11
1	a)	(iii)
	b)	(ii)
	c)	(ii)
	e)	(i)
	f)	(i)
	g)	
3		

Article 12
1	a)	b)	c)	f)	g)
2					
3					

Article 13
1	a)

Article 14
1	a)	b)

EQUALITY IN LAW, PROTECTION IN FACT: MINORITY LAW AND PRACTICE IN POLAND

Piotr Bajda,
Magdalena Syposz and
Dariusz Wojakowski

Contents

EQUALITY IN LAW, PROTECTION IN FACT:
MINORITY LAW AND PRACTICE IN POLAND

Piotr Bajda,
Magdalena Syposz and
Dariusz Wojakowski

Abstract

Systemic transformation in Poland has brought important changes for all parts of the population, including minorities. In the past ten years, most minority communities, with the exception of the German minority, have been further disenfranchised in economic terms. While some considerable improvements in minority protection have been made in Poland, the process towards achieving equality in law, as well as in fact, is nowhere near complete. For instance, there is no comprehensive anti-discrimination law in Poland. This chapter focuses on local management of multi-ethnic communities in Poland both in law and practice. It analyses the legal position of minorities after 1989, including Poland's obligations under international law, and then focuses on implementation of laws and policies at the local level and the management of multi-ethnicity and minority protection in practice. The chapter includes case studies as examples of good practices, and concludes with policy recommendations.

I. Introduction

1.1. Ethnic diversity in Poland

Today, national minorities in Poland make up between 2-3% (official estimate)[1] and 3.5-4.5% (unofficial estimates) of the population of 38,654,561. According to the Minority Rights Group's *World Directory of Minorities*, there are 750,000-1,100,000 Germans (1.9-2.8% of the population); 350,000-500,000 (0.9-1.3%) Ukrainians; 200,000-300,000 Belarussians (0.51-0.8%); Roma, whose estimated numbers vary from official estimate of

---

[1] The official estimates are according to Ministry of Interior and Administration, with the exception of Roma (see footnote 2). Post-WWII censuses have not included questions pertaining to ethnic identity.

[2] *World Directory of Minorities* estimates the number of Roma in Poland at 15,000. This is low, considering that Polish Ministry of Education estimates it at 30,000 (*Information Concerning the Education of Children and Youths of Roma Origin in Poland*, OSCE Human Dimension Implementation

30,000 to unofficial estimate of 50,000-60,000;[2] and smaller communities of Lithuanians, Slovaks, Czechs, Greeks, Macedonians, Kashubs, Lemko Ruthenians, Tatars and Jews.[3]

Until World War II, Poland had, for centuries, a high proportion of ethnic and religious minorities. In the 17TH and 18TH centuries, religious minorities—particularly Jews—fled to Poland to escape persecution. In 1795 Poland was partitioned between Austro-Hungary, Russia and Prussia, and it regained independence only in 1918. Still, in 1918, more than one-third of Polish citizens belonged to national minorities. In the 1931 census, 68.9% Polish citizens declared Polish nationality (22,000,000 inhabitants), 13.9% Ukrainian nationality (4,450,000), 8.6% Jewish (2,800,000), 5.3% Belarussian (1,700,000), 2.3% German (750,000), 1% others (350,000) among them Russians, Lithuanians, Slovaks, Czechs, Gypsies/Roma, Armenians, Tatars and Karaims.[4] This diversity and high proportion of minorities posed a serious political problem in Poland and in relations with its neighbours. Minority protection was used as a pretext for justifying German and Soviet aggression against Poland in 1939.

The ethnic structure of Poland was changed considerably during and in the aftermath of World War II. During World War II, approximately 3,500,000 Polish Jews and hundreds of thousands of Roma, together with approximately 3,000,000 ethnic Poles, were murdered by the Nazis. Following WWII, the new Polish borders were moved about 500 kilometres westward to what had been German territory. As a result of the loss of territories in the east and on the basis of a bilateral repatriation agreement between Poland and the Soviet Union 490,000 of the 600,000 ethnic Ukrainian and 36,000 ethnic Belarussian Polish citizens were—often forcibly—moved to the Soviet Union in 1945-46. The remaining 160,000 ethnic Ukrainians who had been concentrated in southeast Poland were forcibly dispersed across northwestern Poland. 'Operation Wisla' was part of repression against what was perceived by the authorities to be a Ukrainian independence movement. There is no agreement about how many ethnic Germans were expelled from the new western territories during 1945-1949, but it is estimated that before WWII, 10,000,000 people lived on the lands which Poland acquired after the war. Minority Rights Group estimates that 3,200,000 ethnic Germans were expelled.[5] Between 1944-1950 millions of ethnic Poles were repatriated; this included 2,100,000 Poles from the USSR; 2,100,000 from Germany; and 200,000 from other western countries.[6] They settled main-

Meeting, October 2000, document 267; P. Liegois and N. Gheorghe put the figure at 50,000-60,000. See: Liegois and Gheorghe (1997) Roma/Gypsies: A European Minority, London: Minority Rights Group.

[3] Minority Rights Group (ed.) (1997) World Directory of Minorities.

[4] P. Eberhard (1996) Między Rosją a Ńiemćami. Prźemiańy ńarodowośćiowe w Europie Środkowo-Wśćhodńiej w XX w (Between Russia and Germany. Nationalities Changes in Central East Europe in 20TH century), Warsaw, pp. 102-107.

[5] World Directory of Minorities.

[6] S. Lodzinski (1989) 'Repatriacja osób narodowosci lub pochodzenia polskiego w latach 1989-1997. Problemy prawne i instytucjonalne' (Repatriation of persons with Polish orgins or Polish nationality between 1989-1997. Institutional and legal issues), in: Repatriaćja osób ńarodowośći polskiej lub pochodźeńia polskiego w lataćh 1989-1997, Biuro Studiów i Ekspertyz Kancelarii Sejmu, Informacje i opinie, pakiet IP – 76S, Warsaw, p. 9.

ly in the newly acquired western territories. As a result of war extermination, forced and voluntary emigration, and assimilation policies, Poland has become one of the most ethnically homogeneous countries in Europe.

The communist government considered national homogeneity as one of the fundamental goals and achievements of the new state. Throughout the communist period, the Polish government did not have a uniform policy towards national minorities. The policies varied at different times and towards particular minorities, and hung on political movements. However, in general, from 1945 to 1989 minorities were excluded from public life on the basis of their ethnicity, had limited possibilities to maintain their own cultures and were subject to the assimilationist policies of the state. From 1945 to the early 1950s, the policies were overall the most repressive and extended to curtailing freedom of association as well as curtailing freedom to preserve minority cultures and speak minority languages. In the late 1950s and 1960s, the official attitude towards minorities was more open. Minorities were allowed to establish their own socio-cultural organisations and had limited opportunities to teach and learn their native languages, with the notable exception of the German minority who could not enjoy these rights. In practice, each minority could establish only one socio-cultural organisation. The Ministry of Internal Affairs strictly controlled minorities' activities. In 1968 most of the remaining Jews were expelled, and thus the authorities continued to fully realise the idea of a nationally uniform Poland. Throughout the communist period, the Polish government treated Roma appallingly; it tried to forcibly assimilate Roma, continued expelling Roma Polish citizens until the 1980s, and considered Roma to be a social problem and not part of society.

In the 1960s and 1970s, Poland underwent modernisation and industrialisation. This included an intensive migration movement from the countryside to cities and the promotion of mass culture in Polish (radio and television broadcasts). Migration into the cities meant that more members of minority communities became dispersed; this contributed to a reduction of opportunities for minority members to learn their mother tongues and to participate in indigenous, local cultural activities.

1.2. The fall of the communist system in 1989

The protection of minority rights became a key issue in Poland after the democratic changes of 1989. The most characteristic moment of this new attitude was the printing—in May 1989—of Lech Walesa's letters addressed to the public on national minority issues, where he declared that minorities should have rights not only to preserve but also to develop their own culture and language.[7]

The first non-communist government was established as a result of June 1989 elections. The government made some effort to change the situation of national minorities. A Department for National Minorities' Culture was established in the Ministry of Culture and National Heritage. The new department took over responsibility to support minority cultures from the Ministry for Internal Affairs. Still in 1989, the Polish Parliament adopt-

---

[7] Lech Walesa (1989) 'Lech Walésa do wyborców w sprawie mniejszosci' (Lech Walesa's letter to electors on minorities), *Gazeta Wyborcza*, No. 6, May 15, p. 1.

ed a new law on associations, which gave freedom to associate without any ethnic limitations. In 1997 more than 130 national and ethnic minorities associations were registered in Poland; this included 9 Belarussian organisations, 8 Roma, 4 Lithuanian, 5 Lemko/Ruthenian, 76 German, 9 Ukrainian, 6 Jewish and others.[8]

The new political space created more positive conditions for the public activity of minorities. Minority candidates took part in parliamentary elections in 1991, 1993 and 1997. In 1991-1993 parliamentary election laws were adopted which includes special measures for effective participation of minorities: namely, election committees of registered minority organisations are not bound by thresholds based on the nationwide number of votes cast. As a result, the German minority has been represented in the Parliament since 1991. Other minorities, such as Ukrainians and Roma, have not been able to benefit from this law because they do not live in compact settlements.

Although it is rarely acknowledged, prejudice, racism, discrimination and xenophobia are not uncommon within Polish society. Roma are, by far, the most marginalised group in Poland. There have been several recent violent attacks and demonstrations against Roma; in Mlawa in 1991, Sandomierz (1995), Kielce (1996) and Bielsko Biala (1998). These are not isolated 'disputes' but manifestations of persistent discrimination and racism. Furthermore, the incidents provoked little reaction from the general public. The Council of Europe's European Commission against Racism and Intolerance, in December 1999, expressed concern about violence against the Roma, including allegations of police violence, lack of appropriate response by the authorities to cases of violence, and the fact that prejudice in Polish society leads to discrimination in everyday life, including access to education and employment.[9] While Roma are most often the victims, discrimination and prejudice extends to other ethnic groups. For example, in 1994 the Center for Research of Public Opinion (Centrum Badania Opini Spolecznej—CBOS) conducted research asking ethnic Poles about their feelings for members of particular minorities. The most negative feelings were towards Roma and Ukrainians: 54% of those polled said that they disliked them, 37% disliked Jews, 8% disliked Belarussians while 46% were indifferent, 28% liked Germans while 30% disliked them. A similar poll was conducted by CBOS in 1999, and more than one-third of those polled disliked Roma, Jews and Ukrainians.[10] While this proportion is still high, it is lower than in 1994 and might indicate a trend towards greater tolerance.

Currently, two important trends related to the protection of minorities are emerging in Poland. For the first time in recent history, Poland is becoming a country of immigration. There are also many small religious movements emerging in this predominately Catholic country. It will be important to see what provisions are made for the protection of new minorities and small religious groups.

---

[8] L. Adamczuk (1997) *Wyznania religijne. Stowarzyszenie narodowosciowe i etniczne w Polsce 1993-1996* (Religion and National and Ethnic Associations in Poland 1993-1996), Warsaw, pp. 169-184.

[9] European Commission Against Racism and Intolerance (2000) Second Report on Poland, June.

[10] Slawomir Lodzinski (2000) The Policy of Multiculturalism in Poland in the 1990s. National Minorities and Immigrants). Legal Solutions and Social Perceptions. Paper presented at World Conference Against Racism Regional Seminar, Warsaw, July 2000.

2. The Legal Position of Ethnic and National Minorities After the Democratic Transition in Poland

2.1. The legal and institutional framework for minority protection in Poland

Protection of minority rights is based on constitutional principles and relevant international legal and political instruments.[11]

2.1.1. Constitutional provisions

The 1952 Constitution did not include minority rights provisions but solely general principles of equality and nondiscrimination (Articles 67 and 81). Such weak protection was due to lack of importance of the Constitution in the communist state, and to government policies which considered ethnic homogeneity as an asset.

The new Polish Constitution was adopted in 1997. Article 32 guarantees everyone equality before the law and includes a general anti-discrimination clause, stating that 'no one shall be discriminated against in political, social or economic life for any reason whatsoever'. National minorities are officially recognised by the Polish Constitution, as is the 'multi-cultural character' of the Polish state. The Polish Constitution takes an individual approach to minority protection, and restricts protection to Polish citizens. Specifically, Article 35 reads:

1. The Republic of Poland shall ensure Polish citizens belonging to national or ethnic minorities the freedom to maintain and develop their own language, to maintain customs and traditions, and to develop their own culture;
2. National and ethnic minorities have the right to establish educational and cultural institutions, institutions designed to protect their religious identity, as well as to participate in the resolution of matters connected with their cultural identity.

Article 60 ensures all citizens the right to equal access to public services. Significantly, Article 79 guarantees citizens the right to complain to the Constitutional Tribunal against the legal basis of administrative decisions that violate any human rights and freedoms written in the Constitution. It is too soon to assess the effectiveness of Article 79, but potentially it could prove a useful instrument for minority rights protection. Undoubtedly, the 1997 Constitution improved the position of national and ethnic minorities. But, while these steps are positive, the current level of legal protection is not sufficient (see draft law issue below).

Poland also has an Ombudsman for Human Rights. He has dealt with cases of minority protection on the basis of individual petitions.

---

[11] For a comprehensive overview of international minority rights instruments, see: Patrick Thornberry (1997) 'Contemporary Legal Standards on Minority Rights', in: Minority Rights Group (ed.) World Directory of Minorities. See also: Gudmundur Alfredsson and Goran Melander (1997) A Compilation of Minority Rights Standards, Raoul Wallenberg Institute of Human Rights and Humanitarian Law.

2.1.2. International obligations

Poland has ratified a range of international human rights instruments that provide minimum standards for minority protection. This was primarily for two reasons: (1) a desire to join European institutions, such as the Council of Europe and the European Union, and (2) a desire for good relations with its neighbours. According to the Constitution, a ratified international treaty constitutes part of the domestic legal order to be applied directly, unless its application depends on enactment of a statute (Article 91). International law takes precedence over domestic legislation. International instruments ratified by Poland include the European Convention for the Protection of Human Rights and Fundamental Freedoms (ratified in 1993); the International Covenant for the Elimination of All Forms of Racial Discrimination (1968); and the Council of Europe's Framework Convention for the Protection of National Minorities, or FCNM (2001).[12] Poland has also adhered to the UN Declaration on the Rights of Persons Belonging to National or Ethnic, Religious and Linguistic Minorities (1992), and the OSCE Document of the Copenhagen Meeting of the Conference on the Human Dimension (1990). Poland has not signed the European Charter of Regional or Minority Languages.

Bilateral treaties are also an important element of minority protection in Poland. Poland has entered into bilateral treaties with all its neighbours, notably Germany and Ukraine, as well as other countries.[13] All treaties confirm the main principle of international law: that it is a matter of choice of persons belonging to minorities whether to identify as such and exercise minority rights and no disadvantage may arise from the exercise or nonexercise of such choice. These treaties are important because they codify principles enshrined in OSCE documents and they address the use of minority languages in private and public, learning of the mother tongue, freedom of religion, freedom of association and rights to maintain peaceful contacts across frontiers.[14] Weaknesses of such bilateral treaties are the fact that each treaty refers only to specific minorities and that different treaties offer different levels of protection. There is also the danger that minority protection might be provided on the basis of reciprocity and not as a matter of right.

In 1993 Poland signed a Concordat with the Holy Sea. As a result, religious celebration and teaching in minority languages can be organised in the Catholic Church.

2.1.3. Draft Law on National and Ethnic Minorities

There is no effective institutional framework for the protection of national minorities in Poland. Minority rights have been built into general legal provisions and this results in lack of consistency of provision in certain legal acts and a lack of co-ordination among

---

[12] Poland has entered a declaration that FCNM only applies to Polish citizens.

[13] Poland has signed and ratified treaties on good relations with the following countries: Federal Republic of Germany (1991), Czech and Slovak Federal Republic (1991), Hungary (1991), Ukraine (1992), Russian Federation (1992), Belarus (1992), Latvia (1992), Estonia (1992), Spain (1992), Romania (1993), Bulgaria (1993), Lithuania (1994). Recently Poland signed treaties with Kazakhstan, Tajikistan and Turkmenistan.

[14] For a detailed discussion see, A. Bloed and P. van Dijk (eds.) *Protection of Minorities through Bilateral Treaties: The Case of Central and Eastern Europe*, The Hague: Kluwer Law International.

different organs of state administration responsible for their implementation.[15] This is why most minority organisations and other human rights NGOs advocate for the adoption of a comprehensive Law on National and Ethnic Minorities. Unfortunately, the Constitution does not refer to the adoption of a special statute. However, such a law is seen by minority representatives as a necessary condition for effective protection. It was also initiated in an attempt to improve the human rights protection system in Poland.

A Parliamentary Commission for National and Ethnic Minorities was established in 1989 and has drafted a Law on National and Ethnic Minorities, with the aim of providing effective protection for national minorities, which has been debated in the Parliament since 1993 (the newest Draft was submitted to the Sejm, or lower house, in 1998). The Draft defines an ethnic or national minority as a group of Polish citizens who wishes to preserve its language, culture, tradition and national (or ethnic) consciousness and who remains in minority in relation to the rest of society (Article 2).[16]

The Draft focuses on the protection of cultural identity, and it does not contain provisions on political representation or administrative autonomy, beyond recognising the right of persons belonging to national minorities to participate effectively in public life. It proposes the creation of a governmental Office for National Minorities, which would support minority cultures, propose and execute national policy towards minorities, liaise with minority organisations and co-ordinate the work of other governmental bodies in this respect. The government has proposed to create an Ombudsman for National Minorities instead. Both proposals may not effectively address issues of participation and institutional discrimination. The Draft also proposes the recognition of minority languages as auxiliary languages, specifically to be used in public, courts, names of cities and streets. It contains positive obligations of the state to support minorities' education and culture. The Draft Law also contains a provision guaranteeing access to information in minorities' mother tongues, and provides that one of the tasks of public broadcasting is promoting knowledge about life, history and culture of national minorities as well as producing and transmitting programmes in minorities' mother tongues. Since 1993, there has not been political will to adopt the Draft. Passing the Law on National and Ethnic Minorities is currently the most debated minority issue in the Parliament; the delay in preparation of this law is seen by many minority representatives as one of the most important legal barriers to the protection of their rights.

2.2. Affirmative action or positive discrimination

Poland has recognised the well-established principle of international law that the prohibition of discrimination is not sufficient for the effective protection of minorities. Where discrimination is entrenched, special measures are needed to ensure equality in law as

---

[15] Jerzy Kranz (ed.) (1998) Law and Practice of Central European Countries in the Field of National Minorities Protection after 1989, Center for International Relations.

[16] S. Lodzinski and P. Bajda (1995) Ochrona praw osób nalezacych do mniejszosci narodowych (Protection of persons belonging to national minorities groups), Warsaw, p. 164.

well as in fact. So far, Poland has only adopted special measures in three areas: (1) minority participation in public life, limited to minority representation in Parliament, (2) education, and (3) protection and promotion of minority cultures.

2.2.1. Electoral law and representation of minorities in the Parliament

The Parliament is the highest legislative body in Poland. It is bicameral. The Sejm (lower house) is made up of 460 members who are elected through a mixed system of proportional representation system and direct majority. The Senate (upper house) is made up of 100 members who are elected by direct majority. In 1991-1993 parliamentary election laws were passed which contained special measures to try to enable minority participation. Thresholds needed to eligible for election, based on the nationwide number of votes cast, are set at 5% for all political parties and 8% for coalitions. Electoral committees of registered national minority organisations are exempt from the thresholds. As a result of 1993 and 1997 elections, only the German minority has held seats in Parliament (4 in the Sejm and 1 in the Senate from 1993 to 1997, and 2 in the Sejm since 1997). The consistent success of the German minority is possible mainly because ethnic Germans live in compact communities. Therefore, while the special measures enable some minority representation, they do not adequately address the needs of all minorities.

2.2.2. Access to education and the right to learn in mother tongue

Education in Poland is regulated by 1991 Act on the System of Education. Education is within the scope of activities of local governments. However, special legal measures to ensure equality between minority and majority children are detailed below.

The Education Act specifies that schools cannot make admission and teaching conditional upon a child's race, religion or nationality. There is a lack of data on whether minority children are discriminated in access to and quality of education in practice; indeed, in 1999 the European Commission Against Racism and Intolerance has recommended that the government develops a reliable monitoring system.[17] It is, however, clear that Roma children face particular disadvantages and many do not complete primary education. This is likely due to a combination of factors, including exclusion and discrimination in the classroom, family poverty, teachers' lack of respect for Roma culture, children's poor health, children's poor knowledge of Polish and parents' lack of value for formal education.[18] Thus, the nondiscrimination provision in the Education Act—even if it is effectively implemented, and of which we cannot be certain of given the absence of monitoring—is not sufficient to ensure equality in access and provision, at least for the Roma minority.

It must be iterated that education is one of the most important ways in which minority groups preserve and develop their identity, including the preservation of mother tongue.

---

[17] European Commission Against Racism and Intolerance (1999) Second Report on Poland, December.

[18] For a comprehensive analysis of why many Roma children perform poorly in schools or drop out in a number of European countries, see: N. Gheorghe and P. Liegois (1997) Roma/Gypsies: A European Minority.

Education in and of minority languages is regulated by the 1991 Education Act and by Minister of Education's Resolution on the Organisation of Educational Programmes Enabling Minority Pupils to Retain their Sense of National, Ethnic and Linguistic Identity (1992). The Resolution specifies that classes with minority language as medium of instruction may be organised when parents of at least seven children express interest at the primary level, and when at least fourteen students are interested at the secondary level. When there are not enough students establish a 'minority class', teaching of a minority language may be provided when at least three pupils in one locality express interest. If this is the case an 'interschool' group is established to teach the appropriate language. The Guidelines also provide for issuing bilingual certificates. Minority classes, minority schools and interschool groups were financed by the central government's budget until 1999. Between 1996-1999, responsibility for and financing of education, including minority education, was devolved to local governments. Currently, comprehensive education reform is under way in Poland.

In the 1996-1997 school year, minority languages were offered in 440 institutions, either in schools or interschool groups.[19] In some of these institutions, instruction in minority languages was offered. This compared to 121 institutions offering minority language education in 1989.[20]

With the notable exception of the Roma, the recent changes in minority language education can be seen as positive from the point of view of minority rights to preserve their identity. But there remain a glut of problems, which vary from region to region. These include finances, typical of the entire education sector in Poland. In addition, there is a lack of textbooks and qualified teachers for minority classes. Textbooks are imported from minorities' kin states and distributed among pupils for free; this is particularly the case in German, Lithuanian and Slovak minority primary schools. Teachers and writers from minority communities have also prepared textbooks and educational curricula for approval by the Ministry for Education. Within the Ministry, a Special Office for Minority Education and Bilateral Textbooks Committees was established to verify the contents of textbooks, particularly geography and history, and appoint experts to prepare books and curricula.

2.2.3. Supporting minority culture and language

The Department for National Minorities' Culture operates within the Ministry for Culture and Art. The Department provides support for cultural activities of minority communities, including newspapers and books. Until 1994, the Department was involved in a broader range of activities than those within its formal mandate, especially the political participation of minorities. However, over time, and partly as a result of the establishment of the Commission on National and Ethnic Minorities, the role of the Department has diminished. Now, the Department supports activities of minorities in

---

[19] S. Lodzinski (1998) 'The Protection of National Minorities in Poland', p. 151.

[20] Ministerstwo Edukacji Narodowej, Informacja o sytuacji edukacyjnej mniejszosci narodowych w Rzeczpospolitej Polskiej (Ministry of Education, Information paper on the education situation of national minorities in the Republic of Poland), Warsaw, 1994, table 1.

a narrow cultural sphere. Some claim that this leads to the ghettoisation of minority cultures.[21] Furthermore, according to new finance regulations, governmental bodies are not allowed to support the permanent costs connected with functioning of non-governmental organisations (such as salaries for full-time workers, equipment, rents, telephone costs, etc.). Therefore, the Department support is limited to concrete activities and events. Minority NGOs are forced to look for additional financial sources to survive.

2.3. Political and public debate on minorities issues

Public debate on minority issues is relatively infrequent in Poland. But this is not because there is no discrimination and no problems; rather it is because national minorities make up a relatively small proportion of the population. The most important debates are on discrimination against the Roma, anti-semitism, immigrants and newly emerging religious minorities. At times, minorities are portrayed in a very negative light. For example, if a politician is Jewish, or is perceived to be Jewish, other politicians and some media frequently use their ethnicity to discredit them. An important political debate on rights took place during the drafting of the 1997 Constitution, and more recently in relation to the Draft Law on National and Ethnic Minorities. In addition, two cases are detailed below.

2.3.1. Different interpretations of history: The Polish-Ukrainian case

In southeast Poland, some members of the Ukrainian minority erected monuments which were perceived by some ethnic Poles as commemorating a guerrilla movement responsible for killing Poles in eastern Poland during WWII. The monuments, built without permission in 1994, met with strong opposition, mainly from WWII veterans' organisations. To resolve this conflict, voivodship (regional) authorities established a negotiation team made up of minority and majority representatives. The difficulties resulted from the conflict between the Ukrainian community's need to commemorate dead soldiers and the feelings of Poles about experiences during WWII. This disagreement, called by the mass media 'the battle for monuments', highlighted the different interpretations of history by the Polish and Ukrainian communities. The 'battle for monuments' showed that one main source of minority-majority conflicts in Poland is connected to cultivating the collective memory regarding modern history and its symbolic meaning.[22]

2.3.2. Dual citizenship and loyalty

According to the German Constitution (Article 116), every displaced person that had German citizenship before WWI has the right to have their German citizenship recog-

---

[21] Beata Klimkiewicz (1999) *Participation of National and Ethnic Minorities in the Public Sphere: Recommendations for Poland*, Open Society Institute, p. 6.

[22] T. Kamusella (1996) 'Asserting Minority Rights in Poland', *Transition*, Vol. 2, No. 3, p. 17.

nised. This right is inherited by children of displaced persons.[23] At the same time the Law on Polish Citizenship (1962) neither recognises nor forbids dual citizenship. Dual citizens are treated as if they were Polish citizens only.[24] Approximately 170,000 persons have both German and Polish citizenship.[25] Some dual citizens stayed for an extended period of time in Germany, allegedly to evade military service in Poland. Some persons belonging to the majority have used the dual citizenship issue to question the loyalty of the German minority.

2.3.3. Positive Developments

Positive trends in the debate on minority issues should also be noted. As a result of democratic changes in 1989, minority questions are no longer a taboo subject. Many people in Poland agree that the protection of minorities is connected to everyone's rights, and should not be on the basis of reciprocity. One positive signal in political life is the fact that, in a few cases, members of minority groups are invited by mainstream political parties to represent the parties at the national and local levels. For example, a Ukrainian MP in the Sejm represents the Union of Freedom; another, a Belarussian, represents the Alliance of Social Democrats.

3. Local Authorities and the Managing of Ethnicity

3.1. The local government system in Poland

The aim of this section is to present an overview of the local government system and to focus on the competencies of local authorities that are important from the perspective of managing multi-ethnicity.

Poland's Constitution provides the legal basis for the local government system. It specifies that Poland is a unitary state and that public authority is decentralised through the local government (Articles 15 and 16). The Constitution also regulates relations between state administration and local government. The prime minister, voivodes (heads of regions) and regional accounting chambers supervise local government. Local government units are legal entities and have the right to own property. Importantly from the perspective of managing multi-ethnicity, the Constitution also stipulates that local governments have the right to form associations, participate in international associations of local and regional communities and work with other countries' local governments. The process of decentralisation and the reform of local government system in Poland began in the early 1990s and it is still under way.

---

[23] B. Johannes (1996) 'Podwójne obywatelstwo: szansa czy bariera we współpracy polsko-niemieckiej?' (Dual citizenship: a chance or obstacle on the road to a Polish-German co-operation?), in: P. Bajda (ed.) *Obywatelstwo w Europie Srodkowo-Wschodniej* (Citizenship in central-east Europe), Warsaw, p. 72.

[24] J. Jagielski (1998) *Obywatelstwo polskie. Zagadnienia podstawowe* (Polish citizenship. Basic issues), Warsaw, p. 34.

[25] T. Kamusella, ibid.

Table 1. The Local Government System in Poland[29]

Levels of self-government	Self-government bodies	Legislative executive	Competencies and tasks of the self-government connected with managing multi-ethnicity
Region / Voivodship (wojewodztwo)	Voivodship Assembly (sejmik wojewodzki)	Voivodship Board (zarzad wojewodztwa) headed by chair/speaker (marszalek)	· formulation and realisation of a strategy for regional development, in that a strategy of cultural and educational development
County (powiat)	County Council (rada powiatu)	County Board (zarzad powiatu) headed by chair (starosta)	· co-ordination of the popularisation of culture; · allocation of funds for cultural development of powiat; · protect some cultural institutions (museums, theatres); · running and controlling secondary schools;
Municipality (gmina)	Municipal Council (rada gminy)	Municipal Board (zarzad gminy) headed by the mayor (wojt/burmistrz/ prezydent)	· including in the commune plans the tasks directed towards popularisation of culture; · allocation of commune funds for cultural development; · co-ordination of culture popularisation; · making investments of cultural character; · running elementary schools and gymnasiums, ensuring teachers and methodology do not discriminate; · preservation of monuments; · supervision over historic architecture; · assigning names to streets, localities and others

A three-tier local government system has been established by the 1990 Act on Local Self-Government,[26] the 1998 Act on County Self-Government and the 1998 Act on Voivodship Self-Government. The three tiers are municipality (*gmina*), county (*powiat*) and region/voivodship (*wojewodztwo*). The municipality (*gmina*) is the primary and the smallest unit of local government. There is no formal rural urban division of municipalities; there are approximately 2,500 municipalities in Poland which range in size from a few villages to the largest cities, with the exception of Warsaw.[27] The second tier is the county (*powiat*). There are more than 300 counties in Poland; each consists of several

---

[26] There have been several minor amendments to this Act throughout 1990s.
[27] Warsaw is governed by the Act on Local Self-Government of Warsaw (1994), which establishes a multi-layer system and is in need of reform.

municipalities. The third level of local government is the region or voivodship (*wojew-odztwo*); there are 16 voivodships in Poland. Each level is governed by legislative councils and executive boards, with one person at the head of each board. Legislative authorities at all three levels are elected directly. An official appointed by the prime minister, the voivode (*wojewoda*) is the chief of state administration at the voivodship level.[28] A decentralised system of self-government also offers more opportunities for minorities to participate in decision-making processes. Minority representation in elected bodies and participation in decision-making processes is discussed later in this chapter and presented in Table 1.

The strength of local government in Poland is determined not only by administrative decentralisation but also by decentralisation of the budget and devolution of power. Approximately 40% of revenues collected locally are allocated to local authority budgets at different levels of local government.[30] A very important source of income for the local government is its share of personal and corporate income tax. These revenues are transferred to each local budget according to the budgetary power of the municipality via a central redistribution system. The implication for municipalities in the poorer eastern part of Poland—where Belarussian and Lithuanian minorities are concentrated and where many ethnic Ukrainians also live—is that they get less tax revenue than their counterparts in the richer western part of Poland, including the regions where the German minority is concentrated. While cross-regional subsidies may not be the way forward for political reasons, something has to be done to develop these lagging, underdeveloped regions. Other important sources of income include earnings from council rents, sale of communal property and property tax. In addition, local governments receive state grants, which in 1997 amounted to 38.7% of the total municipal revenue structure.[31]

According to the Constitution and the 1990 Local Self-Government Act, local governmental structures have *inter alia* the following tasks within their jurisdiction: health care, social services, housing and infrastructure (roads, water supply). Importantly from the perspective of managing multi-ethnicity, the self-government—particularly municipal authorities—has large competencies in the field of development of education, and protection and development of culture.

The most important tools which can be used by municipal authorities to create their own policy of managing multi-ethnicity are:

1. Protection of minority language rights by assigning names to streets and localities;
2. Protection of minority cultural rights by including in the commune plans the tasks directed towards maintaining and making accessible minority cultures; allocation

---

[28] For a detailed description of the local government system and analysis of its effectiveness, see: A. Kowalczyk (2000) 'Local Government in Poland', in: Tamás Horváth, *Decentralisation: Experiments and Reforms*, Budapest: LGI.

[29] *Sources:* Regional Self Government Act (1998) *Dziennik Ustaw*, No. 91, position 578, 5 June; Powiat's Self Government Act (1998) *Dziennik Ustaw*, No. 91, position 576, 5 June; Self-Government Act (1990) *Dziennik Ustaw*, No. 34, position 198, 17 May.

[30] *Ogólne zalozenia reformy ustrojowej panstwa* (General guidelines on the reform political system in Poland) (1998) Warsaw, p. 19 and appendix 2.

[31] A. Kowalczyk, op. cit.

of commune funds for cultural development; co-ordination of directions of culture popularisation to reflect the multi-cultural character of the municipality; investment in cultural activities. Municipalities are also responsible for graves and war cemeteries, preservation of monuments, register of monuments and supervision of historic architecture.

3. Protection of minorities' economic and social rights by ensuring equal access to employment and health services.

4. Protection of education rights—including the right to learn the mother tongue—by means of running elementary schools and gymnasiums and control of teachers and methodologies used in schools run by a commune do not discriminate or exclude pupils.[32]

The competencies of county authorities are parallel to competencies of municipal authorities. The county co-ordinates the promotion of local culture, allocates funds for cultural development and protects some cultural institutions (museums, theatres). The county also plays an important role education because it is responsible for secondary secondary schools.[33]

The main task of the regional/voivodship self-governmental authorities is to formulate and execute a strategy of regional development. One of the goals of the regional development strategy is 'to cultivate the Polishness and development of national, civic and cultural consciousness'.[34] Therefore, the voivodship authorities have an important role in determining whether 'Polishness' reflects the multi-cultural character of a region. This strategy also contains the development of education. The regional authorities cannot directly influence schools or cultural organisations. But if these authorities formulate their own regional policy of managing multi-ethnicity (in the framework of the regional strategy of development) they will affect the functioning of the lower levels of local self-government as well as allocate some funds for realising minorities' needs.

As detailed above, the scope of activities of municipalities somewhat overlaps with the scope of activities of the county and voivodship. Furthermore, the central government still has many territorial offices (biura rejonowe) which remain from the former centralised system and carry out some similar tasks. The territorial offices, however, are being phased out. Some changes in the local, county and voivodship acts are needed to clarify the competencies.

This presentation shows the significant role local government has (or rather will have) in improving inter-ethnic relations. Local government in Poland has not only decision-making powers but also owns resources to support minority education and culture. From 1990 to 1999, the local self-government functioned only at the level of municipality. Thus municipalities already have some experience managing multi-ethnicity. In contrast, we cannot say anything about such policies at the regional/voivodship level, because regional policies and plans are still being developed. Some municipalities have drawn up worse or better strategies for multi-cultural management. Therefore, if we want to examine the

---

[32] See: Self-Government Act (1990) *Dziennik Ustaw*, No. 34, position 198, 17 May.

[33] See: Powiat's Self-Government Act (1998) *Dziennik Ustaw*, No. 91, position 576, 5 June.

[34] See: Regional Self-Government Act (1998) *Dziennik Ustaw*, No 91, position 578. 5 June.

management of multi-ethnicity in Poland, we must base it on the actions taken up on the level of municipality. The reform of public administration gives an opportunity to use these experiences by authorities on other levels.

Although there were no self-governments on the county and regional/voivodship level, the process of democratisation of the state offered possibilities for multi-ethnic management (in academia, journalism, some public institutions) as well as building inter-ethnic bonds in regional communities.

3.2. Tensions between central and local authorities

Using the examples below, we will attempt to illustrate the tensions between central and local government policies and their relevance to managing multi-ethnicity. These examples also show that both local and central authorities can have a positive or negative impact on intercommunal co-operation.

A crucial dispute between central and local authorities took place in Opole region in 1998. Central government experts—who prepared the reform of administrative structure which would cut the number of voivodships from 49 to 16—proposed that the Opole voivodship be dissolved. Opole is in western Poland, and it is one of the main regions where the German minority live; approximately 30% of the region's population are ethnic Germans. The proposal was to attach Opole Silesia to neighbouring Katowice Silesia. The reasons given were mainly economic (Opole is comparatively better-off than Katowice), but regardless of the motivation, the consequence of the restructuring would alter the ethnic proportions of the population. The percentage of ethnic Germans in the new larger voivodship would have been lower. Warsaw governmental officials and experts did not expect the response of people who lived in the Opole region. Poles and Germans together started a huge campaign against removing the Opole voivodship from the administrative map of Poland. The action was supported by Polish and German minority NGOs, representatives of local governments and even the central government's delegate to the Opole region. Identification with the Polish majority or the German minority within the region was replaced by identification with 'we'—the inhabitants of Opole region—and 'others'—representatives of central government and members of Parliament interested in dissolving the Opole voivodship. The inhabitants of the voivodship won their battle with the central government and preserved the voivodship in the new administrative system. Interestingly, co-operation between Poles and Germans did not finish with this lobbying campaign and the subsequent positive decision of the Polish Parliament. It has continued during local elections when a new multi-ethnic local majority was formed. In Opole, local identity combines with and complements ethnic identity.

The case of Przemysl, however, shows that local authorities are, at times, unwilling or unable to promote co-operation between ethnic groups. Central government has occasionally played a positive role in this respect. Przemysl is a city in southeast Poland where representatives of local government did not stop a campaign by residents against the Ukrainian minority. The conflict was concentrated on the case of an illegally erected monuments dedicated to the UPA (Ukrainian Uprising Army), which was active during WWII. Polish veterans' associations criticised the monuments and organised a media assault against the Ukrainian minority. Complaints were mainly directed against the inscriptions on the monuments.

Animosity from this conflict finally immersed the local Ukrainian Cultural Festival, organised since 1995. The veterans' organisations saw the Festival of Ukrainian Culture as an attempt at re-Ukrainisation of the region. The local government did not react and allegedly secretly supported the veterans' demands. This caused Ukrainian minority-Polish majority relations to suffer.[35] The reluctant attitude of local authorities also was evident in 1997, when the next Ukrainian Cultural Festival was organised. The authorities of Przemysl opposed and obstructed the organisation of the festival. It led to the direct intervention of the central government in support of the festival. In fact, there was an open conflict between central and local authorities.[36]

While there are important similarities between Opole and Przemysl, such as a relatively high proportion of minority residents and recent antagonism between the different communities, there are also important differences. One is that Opole is a wealthier region than Przemysl. But the crucial difference in the way that these two disputes were handled has to do with minority participation in local goverment structures. The German minority is well represented at all levels of local goverment in Opole, while the Ukrainian minority is underrepresented in local government structures in Przemysl. An important factor which enabled intergroup dialogue and co-operation in Opole was effective minority participation in local government.

3.3. Participation of national minorities in local governments

3.3.1. 1990-1998

There is no special provision for national minorities in the Local, County and Regional Election Laws (1990, 1998 and 1998 respectively). Nevertheless, candidates nominated by national minority NGOs were successful in the 1990 local elections and many won seats in local councils. The German minority in the Opole region was the most successful mainly because the Gerrmans live in compact communities. They collected about 30% of valid votes in Opole voivodship (which corresponds with the proportion of ethnic German population) and gained 380 seats (out of 1440) which gave them majority in 26

---

[35] See M. Malikowski (1997) 'Polish-Ukrainian Relationship in the Province of Przemysl in the Period of Political Transformation', in: M. S. Szczepanski (ed.), *Ethnic Minorities and Ethnic Majority. Sociological Studies of Ethnic Relations in Poland*, Katowice, pp. 203-223. See also K. Bachmann (1999) *Polska kaczka—europejski staw. Szanse i pulapki polskiej polityki europejskiej* (Polish duck—European pond. Chances and traps of Polish European policy), Warsaw, pp. 99-111.

[36] About relations between Poles and Ukrainians in that region see: G. Babinski (1997) *Pogranicze polsko-ukrainskie,* Kraków. The attitude of authorities of Przemysl is illustrated by the comment of president of Przemysl, who said that he would rather organise an Eskimo Culture Festival in the city than the Ukrainian one.

[37] S. Lodzinski (1992) *Aktywnosc spoleczno-polityczna i dzialanosc kulturalno-oswiatowa mniejszosci narodowych w Polsce w okresie 1989-1992* (Social, political, cultural and education activity of national minorities in Poland between 1989-1992), Biuro Studiów i Ekspertyz Kancelarii Sejmu, Pakiet IP-19M, Warsaw, p. 27.

of 61 local councils.[37] In the next local election in 1994, German minority representatives received fewer votes and seats in local councils, but they have proven that they are a strong political power in the region.[38]

The Belarussian minority was also able to achieve good results in local elections. In a few local councils, members of the Belarussian minority composed the ruling coalition (for example, Bielsk Podlaski, Hajnówka, Gródek and Narewka).[39] They had more than 70 seats in local councils. The Lithuanian minority had a dominant position in Punsk (northeast Poland). They had also members of councils in the nearest ethnically mixed territory. Like Germans, Belarussians and Lithuanians live in compact settlements.

The Ukrainian minority was in a much more difficult situation because they are dispersed across Poland. Ukrainians had minority representation in local councils (more than 70 seats) but nowhere were they part of the ruling coalition.

In the case of the Roma, virtually no political participation has been possible.

3.3.2. Current situation as a result of 1998 local elections

The ongoing reform of administrative structure and formation of new levels of local administration in 1998 brought a challenge for national minorities living in Poland to participate in decision-making bodies at any level higher than the municipality (*gmina*). National minorities met with two primary difficulties during elections. First, the 1998 campaign was dominated by national political parties and political fighting between the ruling coalition (Solidarity Election Action and the Union of Freedom) and opposition post-communist parties (the Alliance of Left Democrats and the Peasant Party). National minority committees operating in local circumstances as well as other local committees were not able to compete with strong nationwide political parties. Secondly, the Law on Local Elections (1990) does not include any special provision to enable minority participation. Furthermore, it is necessary to receive more than a 5% total of votes cast to be eligible for seats in the county and voivodship councils. All these conditions decreased the chances for minorities to gain seats in higher levels of local government. And although representatives of national minorities held their positions in the lowest level of local government (municipality), they found it very hard to gain seats in county and voivodship councils. The exception was the German minority who performed unexpectedly well.

In the 1998 local election, the German minority received approximately 600 seats in the Opole voivodship in all three levels of local government structure (out of a total number of 1,980 seats). Now representatives of the German minority hold 13 seats (of 45) on the voivodship council. This was the second best result in the whole voivodship.[40] Members of German minority are part of ruling coalition in the Opole voivodship together with Solidarity Election Action (11 seats) and the Union of Freedom (4 seats). Such a decent result was possible because of the concentration of German minority in the Opole voivodship and, to a lesser extent, their

---

[38] *Mniejszosci narodowe w Polsce Informator 1994* (National minorities in Poland in 1994), Warsaw, 1995, pp. 93-94.

[39] Ibid., p. 92.

[40] 'Gminy lokalne, sejmiki partyjne' (Gminas in local committees hands when powiats and voivodship councils in hands of political parties), *Rzeczpospolita* (daily newspaper), No. 250, 24-25 October 1998, p. 3.

campaign tactics and composition of candidate lists. Local leaders based their campaign on local solidarity rather than basing it only on ethnic self-identification. Candidates focused on issues important for all inhabitants of Opole regardless of nationality. Often the German minority candidate lists also included ethnic Poles, sometimes in first place.[41]

The leaders of the Ukrainian minority had to use other tactics. Because Ukrainians are dispersed, their representatives tried to build partnerships with majority local or party committees. The Ukrainian minority has now one representative in the voivodship council of Warmia and Mazury (northeast Poland) and more than 10 seats in different county councils. This is very low, considering that the Ukrainians are the second largest minority in Poland, at 250,000-350,000 (official statistics) or 350,000-500,000 people (unofficial estimates).[42]

The Belarussian and Lithuanian minorities were able to gain seats only in municipal councils and very rarely in county councils. To this day, there is virtually no Roma representation in local government structures.

The size of a minority and its territorial distribution are important factors for minority participation in political life at the local level; other factors are likely to be traditions of self-rule, political elite, intercommunal relations, populations ties to the region and economic factors.

3.4. Financial support for minority culture

There are three potential sources for financing minority cultural activities. The most stable source is the Department for National Minorities' Culture within the Ministry for Culture and Art (see Section 2.2.3. for details).

The second source of money for minority culture is local governmental budgets. The scale and the kind of support for minority cultural activities differ by region. They often depend on relations between the minority community and the majority in local councils and boards. The most favourable conditions are in places where a minority rules or is part of the ruling coalition at the local level (e.g. Lithuanians in Punsk, Germans in Opole Silesia). In these cases, the minority can decide on the local budget and the plan of expenditure.

Generally, minority cultural organisations function as NGOs. One of the tasks of local authorities is co-operation with NGOs. Local authorities support NGOs through direct or indirect financing of cultural activities. Some local authorities also organise multi-cultural events and lend municipal equipment and premises for minorities' cultural activities. The range of help of local authorities is limited by their financial abilities. Most of the areas inhabited by Belarussians, Lithuanians and many Ukrainians are in the poorest part of Poland (called the 'Eastern Wall'). Local self-governments have problems with financial support of cultural institutions. But they can help. In Zagorz in southeastern Poland, a Ukrainian 'Festival on the Oslawa River' is organised by the local branch of Association of

---

[41] *Nasze Slowo* (1998) (Ukrainian minority weekly magazine), No. 45, 8 November, p. 6.
[42] *World Directory of Minorities.*

Ukrainians in Poland. The local authorities have lent musical equipment to Oslawiany, a Ukrainian folk group, and Oslawiany have used an artistic adviser, who is employed by local self-government. Co-operation between local authorities and minority organisations has provided support for minority cultural activities. The problem is that this co-operation is often limited to the cultural sphere and, as such, stays at a symbolic level.

More and more minority organisations rely on private donors. Many important events organised by minority communities are supported by private businesses or foundations.

3.5. Minority access to the media

Minority access to public mass media is guaranteed by the Act on Public Radio and Television Broadcasting. Article 21 states that 'duties of the public radio and television shall include in particular ... the consideration of the needs of national minorities and ethnic groups'.[43] Minority access to mainstream and minorities' own media has improved considerably in the 1990s, with increased access both to electronic and print media. However, there are problems. For example, in addition to national TV and radio, Poland is divided into seventeen regions for the purposes of electronic media. Each region has a Council for Radio and Television Programming. The councils are responsible *inter alia* for the content of the programmes. There is no provision for minority participation in these Councils and only two (Bialystok and Silesia) include some minority representation. Minority access to mainstream TV varies from region to region. Management in a number of TV regions states that they are co-operating with minority communities; however, most organisations representing national minorities claim that they are, in reality, very often ignored by public TV staff.[44] The volume of radio programming in minority languages varies from 1 hour per week for each minority language (in Bialystok in Belarussian, Ukrainian and Lithuanian), to 25 minutes a week in German in Opole, to no programming in minority languages in several regions. TV broadcasting varies from no provision to 10 minutes a month in Ukrainian in most TV regions to 20 minutes a month in Belarussian in Bialystok. The leaders of Belarussian, Ukrainian and other minority communities would like more broadcast time in minority languages, and broadcasting at more viewer-friendly times according to a set schedule. It is common practice that the times of minority-language programmes change from month to month, information about the changes is not widely available in advance, and the programmes are broadcast at unfriendly hours, such as early on Sunday mornings.[45] Minority journalists are usually involved in the production of minority-language programmes, but with important exceptions, such as TV programmes in Belarussian in Bialystok. However, often minority journalists are employed on short-term contracts and thus have no job security, less access to equipment and no access to training.

---

[43] *Dziennik Ustaw* (1993) No. 7, item 34.

[44] Piotr Tyma (1998) *1998 Raport: Dostep Mniejszosci Narodowych do Mediow Publicznych w Polsce* (Report on access of national minorities to public media in Poland), prepared as background paper for discussion in the Polish Parliament.

[45] Minority Rights Group (1999) *Minorities and the Media in Central and Eastern Europe Workshop Report.*

Case Study 1. Media and Prejudice

The issue: Media have a strong influence on any society's attitudes. Media can create positive or negative attitudes towards minorities. It can play an important role in the integration of a multi-ethnic community.

Actors involved: 1) regional and local journalists; 2) Ukrainian minority representatives.

Good practice: Local weekly newspaper *Zycie Przemyskie* (Life of Przemysl) works to overcome prejudices in Przemysl. Przemysl is a town in southeastern Poland. Ethnic Ukrainians were concentrated in the Przemysl County before they were expelled and forcibly dispersed in 1947 as part of 'Operation Wisla'. Przemysl County was also the center of the Ukrainian underground movement during WWII. Today, Polish-Ukrainian relations are very tense in Przemysl. In 1997, on the 50TH anniversary of Operation Wisla, *Zycie Przemyskie* publishers organized a round table to begin to discuss different perceptions of history. Publishers also organised a discussion in the weekly about the co-operation between Polish and Ukrainian underground movements after WWII. Ethnic Poles and Ukrainians participated in both initiatives, and excerpts of the discussions were published in *Zycie Przemyskie*. These initiatives enabled readers to encounter an unknown history of Polish-Ukrainian relations which is far from the stereotypical vision of permanent conflicts. *Zycie Przemyskie* aims to create a good atmosphere for Polish-Ukrainian contacts in Przemysl and to show other leaders, including local authorities, that Polish-Ukrainian dialogue is possible, even on issues which have been a main source of conflict since WWII.

Sources: Zycie Przemyskie (1997) 23 and 30 April; *Zycie Przemyskie* (1998) 7, 21 and 28 January

---

Channel 5 of Polish Public Radio broadcasts programmes in the official languages of neighbouring countries. The programmes contain information about Poland and are aimed at audiences in neighbouring countries. Because the programmes are in minority languages, persons belonging to national minorities are part of the listenership. However, because of technical difficulties (Channel 5 uses different frequencies than other radio programmes in Poland), these programmes cannot be received in some regions where minorities live.

Showing the problems of minorities, bringing cultures closer together and striving against negative attitudes toward minorities are all important goals for media in the context of managing multi-ethnicity.

3.6. Use of minority languages in public administration

Article 27 of the Constitution states that 'Polish shall be the official language in the Republic of Poland. This provision shall not infringe upon national minority rights resulting from ratified international instruments.' But there is no law on the use of minority languages in public administration. Consequently, there is almost no provision. The Draft Law on National and Ethnic Minorities includes considerable provisions, including the recognition of minority languages as auxiliary languages, and use of minority languages in public, in courts, and to name cities and streets.

3.7. Education in mother tongue

Minority-language education, together with cultural activities, were the only two areas of minority rights tolerated by the communist regime. With the exception of the German minority, minority children could learn their mother tongue in some form in public schools since 1952. The new post-1989 political context, combined with a tradition of mother-tongue education, offered possibilities for improved regulation and provision. As detailed in Section 2.2.2., education in Poland is governed by 1991 Act on Education. Education in and of minority languages is regulated by the 1992 Education Minister's Resolution on the Organisation of Educational Programmes Enabling Minority Pupils to Retain their Sense of National, Ethnic and Linguistic Identity.

The education system is decentralised. Preschools and primary education are the responsibility of municipal governments; secondary and vocational education are the responsibility of county governments; and higher education is the responsibility of regional/voivodship governments. In practice, educational provision in and of minority languages varies from region to region.

Case Study 2. German Minority Education

The issue: German minority children in Opole Silesia could not learn or study in their mother tongue until 1990. This caused serious problems with preservation of mother tongue among the 250,000 ethnic Germans.

Actors involved: 1) Polish government; 2) German government; 3) German minority NGOs.

Good practice: Between 1945-1989, learning and using the German language was forbidden in the Silesia region and western territories acquired by Poland after WWII. This is the region where the German minority lives. Using German in public was heavily fined. The government banned learning German as a foreign language in primary and secondary schools in Silesia and western Poland (while German as a foreign language was taught in other parts of Poland). As a result, in 1990 there were neither German-language teachers nor textbooks. Furthermore, research conducted in the early 1990s showed that only 30% of the native population in Silesia declared German as their first language. This group was made up mainly of people over 65. It was obvious that any action taken by German minority NGOs together with the Ministry for Education would not be enough to make up for lost time. On the basis of a bilateral agreement between Poland and Germany, a group of German teachers were sent to Silesia and western Poland to teach German language in primary and secondary schools. Two teacher training colleges were established to prepare Polish teachers to teach German. This brought positive results as early as the 1990-91 academic year when German as a native language was taught in 184 primary schools, and by 1993-94, in 268 schools in the Opole voivodship alone. In the 1994-95 academic year, German was taught to more than 6,100 students; the number of schools which offer German increases every year. These schools are also open to Polish students, as any public school. Graduates of these schools may continue their education in any universities in Poland. As the result of Polish-German bilateral agreement and co-operation between German minority organisations and the two governments, an effective system of minority-language education has been developed in Opole Silesia. This gives the German minority an opportunity to maintain their own language.

Sources: T. Urban (1994) *Germans in Poland. History of the minority in the 20ᵀᴴ century*, Opole, pp. 150-151; D. Berlinska (1993) 'Realisation of decisions of the Treaty between Poland and Germany on good neighbourly relation and friendly co-operation in the context of human rights', in: *Poles and Germans on Common Ground and Normal Relations. Priesthood and Education*, Opole, p. 88; *Information Paper on Education Situation of National Minorities in Republic of Poland* (1995) Ministry of Education; *National Minorities in Poland in 1994*, Warsaw: Wydawnictwo Sejmowe, p. 224.

In addition to educational provision, schools in multi-ethnic communities can perform important functions to enhance inter-ethnic co-operation. Schools can help to integrate minority groups into wider communities, while offering minority students possibilities to maintain their own language and culture (see Case Study 3 below). Furthermore, schools can help to overcome prejudices and offer opportunities for majority pupils to learn about minority culture and history. Textbooks, curricula, training methodoligies and teachers play a key role in determining whether a school fulfills these additional functions.

Case Study 3. Public Schools for Minority Groups

The issue: The Polish state organises the system of ethnic minority education, a potentially good opportunity for local communities to maintain their own language and culture.

Actors involved: 1) the management and teachers of minority schools—Lithuanian and Ukrainian; 2) local communities.

The strategy: The integration of a local minority community and maintaining its culture and language are some of the most important functions of public schools for ethnic minorities. The model realising these functions is found in a Lithuanian-language secondary school in Punsk. Research shows that the pupils have a strong awareness of ethnic identity and the school gives them competence in their native culture. Lithuanian language is used in the school at all times. All interaction between teachers and pupils is in Lithuanian.

The school also influences the local community: 'The teachers' subjects important for preservation of identity (e.g. Lithuanian literature, music education) are the animators of the cultural life in the community. They use traditional elements of the Lithuanian culture and folklore in their work with the pupils. For example, around All Saints' Day teachers and pupils together organise evenings devoted to the memory of community members—open to everyone in town.

The school balances an unprejudiced philosophy while instilling youth with cultural competence (fluent knowledge of Polish language). This is a deliberate technique to avoid 'the syndrome of the ethnic ghetto'.

A public minority school may also positively influence a larger, regional community, as in the case of a Ukrainian school in Przemysl. In Podkarpacie, the Ukrainian minority is small and dispersed in a large territory. The school in Przemysl plays an important role in the local Ukrainian community and, at the same time, it animates the educational activity of other Ukrainian communities in the region.

The role of ethnic minority school is not only to teach the minority culture and language. Such a school is also a local cultural centre which may play an important role in enhancing co-operation between communities

Sources: Miroslaw Sobecki (1997) *Ethnic-Cultural Function of Ethnic Minority's Schools*. Bialystok: TransHumana, p. 168-175; Dariusz Wojakowski (1996) 'The Teaching of the Ukrainian Language in the Southeastern Poland', in: T. Lewowicki, B. Grabowska (ed.) *Borderland Communities. Multiculturalism. Education*, Cieszyn: Uniwersytet Slaski, p. 184-193.

While there is no accurate monitoring of whether minority children face discrimination in education, it is certain that Roma children have less access to and poorer quality of education than majority children. In approximately twenty places in the south of Poland experimental classes have opened for Roma children. It is difficult to present the exact number: many of these initiatives were organised by NGOs or individuals in co-operation with local authorities and local representatives of the education administration. The main idea of the programme is to give a chance for Roma children to finish primary school and to prepare them for admission exams for secondary schools. In the past, Roma children very often dropped out of school at the beginning of their primary education for a variety of reasons, among them language barriers and a lack of teachers' skills or will to help them integrate into the classroom. Authors of the project, which was accepted by the local education authority in 1993, organised a special compensatory course in the Polish language for Roma children at the beginning of primary school. It is not always a success; sometimes there are not enough qualified teachers (the schools are often in small villages or towns) or some parents do not send their children to those classes. Some Roma leaders now criticise the idea because of the danger of furthering segregation between Roma and Poles at schools. Undoubtedly, these initiatives raise the question of how to organise a system of education which is inclusive of and effective for all children. In the near future, we can expect the Ministry for Education to present an official programme for the integration of Roma children into schools.

3.8. Searching for a new self-government policy

Five of sixteen regions/voivodships in Poland have a relatively high proportion of minorities. These regions are: (1) Katowice Silesia—where ethnic Germans are concentrated, (2) Opole Silesia—Germans, (3) Podkarpacie—Ukrainians, (4) Podlasie—Belarussians and Ukrainians, and (5) Warmia and Mazury—Ukrainians, Germans, Lithuanians. It is too early to present a comprehensive assessment of policies of regional management in the new (post-1998) administrative system as yet. Some local and regional authorities have yet to present their development strategies. However, in the five multi-ethnic regions during the past ten years, local leaders have been implementing more or less explicit policies towards minorities. We will use selected examples to show ideas and possible methods which can be used to develop effective regional policies for managing multi-ethnicity.

In Podlasie and Opole Silesia, the largest minorities live in compact settlements (approximately 250,000-300,000 ethnic Belarussians in Podlasie or 30% of population, and at least 250,000 ethnic Germans in Opole Silesia, or 30% of the population).[46] In the other regions minorities are smaller and territorially dispersed. The composition of the population in the regions makes a real difference in how multi-ethnicity is managed. This is at least partly because, in Poland, more effective minority participation in local government

---

[46] See: Andrzej Sadowski (1991) *Great and Little Nations. Belarussians in Poland*, Krakow: Nomos, p. 121-122; Maria Szmeja (1998) 'Historical and Social Underpinnings of Development of German Minority and Silesian Nation in Poland', Warsaw: Studia Socjologiczne, No. 4 (151), p. 55.

structures has been possible for large and compact minorities. Participation in decision-making processes is an important factor for effective management of multi-ethnicity and good relations between groups.

Uniquely Opole Silesia has a multi-ethnic leadership at all levels of local government. In addition to special measures for the protection of minority rights (e.g. in education), regional policies have been addressing issues important to both ethnic Germans and ethnic Poles (e.g. economic development). Working together towards common goals has brought people from different ethnicities closer together. Other factors in Opole which seem to be important include: the local population's strong ties to the region (in contrast with neighbouring Katowice Silesia where a large proportion of the current population came to Katowice during industrialisation in the 1960s and 1970s), a strong economy (in comparison to Podlasie, for example) to which the German minority contributes disproportionately because of its ties with Germany, and a tradition of self-management (albeit as part of both Germany and Poland).

Local leadership makes a difference. While minority participation in government structures at all levels is the most effective, an engaged community leadership—elected or informal—can make an important contribution to, or hinder, effective management of multi-ethnicity. This is illustrated through the cases of Katowice Silesia and Podlasie.

In Katowice Silesia, the German minority is smaller than in Opole and dispersed within big cities. After 1989 community leaders have made efforts to know and understand the minority's problems and needs and to build social agreements to overcome ethnic divisions. Sociologists from the Silesian University in Katowice have been engaged in systematic research of the native inhabitants in this region. Their research has provided important (also from the perspective of a political practice) information about attitudes, needs and the social situation of the German minority.[47] In 1995 most significant Silesian decision-makers—including government and informal community leaders—have signed a political agreement—the Regional Contract for the Voivodship of Katowice Silesia—which is perceived as an important success in determining the future of the region. One party to the agreement is the central government; the second party is composed of regional trade unions, economic organisations, local self-governments and regional political and social associations, including German minority associations. The Regional Contract includes *inter alia* plans for economic development of Silesia, formation of a new regional self-government and development of education. Local leaders and decision-makers initiated the idea of the Regional Contract and this idea brought them closer together.[48]

---

[47] Here the most important works should be mentioned: Jacek Wodz (ed.) (1990) *Upper Silesia from the Upper-Silesians' Point of View*, Katowice: Uniwersytet Slaski; Kazimiera Wodz (ed.) (1993) *'Ours' and 'Aliens' in Upper Silesia*, Katowice: Uniwersytet Slaski; Kazimiera Wodz (ed.) (1995) *Regional Identity—Regional Consciousness. The Upper Silesian Experience*, Katowice: Uniwersytet Slaski; Krzysztof Lecki, Kazimiera Wodz and Piotr Wroblewski (1997) *Social World of Silesians. Reconstruction of the Common Consciousness*, Katowice: Uniwersytet Slaski.

[48] Marek S. Szczepanski (1996) 'People without Local Homeland and the Regional Education', in: T. Lewowicki, B. Grabowska (ed.) *Borderland Communities. Multiculturalism. Education*, Cieszyn: Uniwersytet Slaski, pp. 167-170.

As a result of the Regional Contract, a Postgraduate School of Knowledge of the Region was established within the framework of the Silesian University in 1996. The goal of this institution is training of teachers to teach a new school subject entitled Knowledge of the Local Homeland. The aim of the introduction of this subject in schools is the study of regional history and traditions and to emphasise the values which are common for most inhabitants of the region. This initiative can be perceived as an interesting example of building inter-ethnic (or 'over-ethnic') bonds in the region. The Postgraduate School of Knowledge of the Region was founded by teachers from Silesian University. The classes are in Polish but the students are taught the regional dialect. The curriculum contains: sociology (local communities, social integration in Silesia, Silesian identity), economic transformation, ecology, culture (regional dialects, regional literature, music and art) and history (history of nation-building processes in the region, issues of autonomy). The School is financed by the Polish government and partially by students.[49]

Community leaders and decision-makers in Podlasie (where the Belarussian minority is concentrated and many ethnic Ukrainians live) are less engaged in the protection of minority rights and promoting diversity. Similarly to Katowice Silesia, in Bialystok (Podlasie) academics also research issues related to the Belarussian minority and try to publicise problems.[50] But decision-makers and community leaders, including the media, regional authorities and church authorities, are not responsive to the research findings.[51] Lasting stereotypes persist in Podlasie—a nationality is identified with a religious denomination and a political orientation. These stereotypes give a false picture of a community's real situation. The stereotypes reinforce isolation among both ethnic Belarussian and ethnic Polish leaders.

Podkarpacie is a voivodship in southeastern Poland where Ukrainians have traditionally lived. Now, the ethnic Ukrainian population is relatively small and dispersed. The question of Ukrainian minority has always been a local question—in Przemysl, Jaroslaw or Sanok. Local leaders are engaged in building good inter-ethnic relations at the local level in these municipalities. But regional leaders have not been active in trying to effectively manage multi-ethnicity. One recent initiative is that the governor of Podkarpacie has set up an Office of the Governor's Plenipotentiary for the Ukrainian Minority. While, this Office should work to resolve the Ukrainian minority's problems in the region, its competencies are unclear. Furthermore, the governor has no competencies to create regional cultural and educational policy; this is a role of the regional self-government, namely the Voivodship Board.[52]

---

[49] Ibid., pp. 162-167,170, 173-175.
[50] Since 1991 the University in Bialystok has edited the social studies journal Borderland devoted the ethnic problems in the region. Until 1997, six volumes of this journal have been edited. See also: Andrzej Sadowski (1995) Polish-Belarussian Borderland: Identity of its Inhabitants, Bialystok: TransHumana.
[51] See: Maciej Tefelski (1995) Press on the Borderland, in: A. Sadowski (ed.) Eastern Borderland from the Perspective of Sociology, Bialystok: TransHumana, p. 217-228; W. Maziarski (1998) 'Sleepily, silently, threatenly', Gazeta Wyborcza, 5-6 September, p. 16-19.
[52] Such office also existed in the former Przemysl Voivodship, but it was not influential in moderating ethnic conflicts in Przemysl.

4. Conclusion

Systemic transformation in Poland has meant the process of building a democratic state based on the rule of law and protection of human rights, and building a market economy. This transformation has also brought the process of decentralisation to government. Important changes have taken place for all parts of the population, including minorities. Most minority communities, with the exception of the German minority, have been further marginalised in economic terms. On the positive side, since 1989, the protection of minority rights and issues connected with managing diversity have been discussed in public for the first time since World War II. The 1997 Polish Constitution offers a higher level of protection of minority rights than under the previous system. Poland has also ratified and is bound by relevant international instruments.

While some considerable improvements in minority protection have been made in Poland in the last ten years, the process towards achieving equality in law as well as in fact is nowhere near complete. Ten years on, there is no comprehensive anti-discrimination legislation in place. There is also no effective institutional framework for minority protection. Problems with implementation of international minority rights standards and constitutional provisions do exist, particularly in the sense that minority protection varies from region to region and often depends on local conditions. As regards local management of multi-ethnic communities, there are examples of good practices, including minority participation in decision-making processes, and co-operation between majority and minority communities. This is particularly the case in Opole Silesia. At the same time, the conflict continues to simmer at the local level in Przemysl and Bialystok.

Several factors important for the future of minority protection in Poland should be highlighted. One is the process of decentralisation; this process has offered opportunities for some minorities to participate in local government structures. Finding ways to manage multi-ethnicity at the local level will be key. A second factor will be the adoption of a comprehensive law to protect national minorities; most minority representatives advocate for the adoption of the Law on National and Ethnic Minorities, which has existed as a draft since 1993. Finally, international pressure can play an important role in ensuring a minimum level of minority protection. Here, the European Union can have particular leverage in the context of accession negotiations, and treaty-monitoring bodies can also play an important role.

5. Recommendations

1. The Parliament should immediately pass the comprehensive Law on National and Ethnic Minorities. Representatives of minority communities and other human rights activists stress that this Law is a necessary step towards effective protection. This Law should include articles which would specifically oblige regional and local authorities to support minority cultures and education. The Polish government should then take steps to ensure the effective implementation and monitoring of the Law.

2. Poland should be reminded of its obligations under international law to effectively implement international instruments it ratified, including the Framework Convention for the Protection of National Minorities, which provides minimum standards of protection.

3. Local governments should—on the basis of Poland's as well as other European states' experiences—build new policies for the protection of minorities and build the policies and institutional framework necessary for managing multi-ethnicity.

4. Local governments, in consultation with minority leaders, should work towards ensuring effective participation of minorities in decision-making processes at the local level in areas where participation needs to be improved.

5. Local governments should adopt programmes for multi-cultural education in primary and secondary schools where history and culture of minorities should be taught. Minority issues, as well as migrant and refugee issues, should be discussed. They should also set up initiatives to raise the awareness of minority rights among the adult population, including government employees, police and judges.

6. As recommended by the European Commission against Racism and Intolerance, Poland's government should set up procedures to monitor whether there is discrimination, for example, in access to education.[53]

7. Central and local authorities—together with Roma community leaders—should develop a programme of integration of Roma into society at large. A key to any such programme will be active participation of Roma leaders from programme inception through implementation.

8. The government should set up an institution at the central level to co-ordinate and promote good practices in management of multi-ethnic communities at the local level.

Further reading

Alfredsson, Gudmundur (1998) *Minority Rights: International Standards and Monitoring Procedures* in: Minority Rights Handbook, *Latvian Human Rights Quarterly*, No 5/6.

Kowalczyk, Andrzej (2000) 'Local Government in Poland' in: Tamás Horváth (ed.) *Decentralisation: Experiments and Reforms*, Budapest: OSI/LGI, pp. 297-342.

Liegois, P. and N. Gheorghe (1997) *Roma/Gypsies: A European Minority*, Minority Rights Group.

Lodzinski, Slawomir (2000) The Policy of Multiculturalism in Poland in 1990s (National Minorities and Immigrants), Legal Solutions and Social Perceptions, Paper presented at World Conference Against Racism Regional Seminar, Warsaw, July 2000.

---

[53] European Commission Against Racism and Intolerance.

ANNEX 1
MINORITY POPULATION IN POLAND

Table A.1. Minority Population in Poland
1920-1990

National minority group	Census data on minority population of 1931[1]	Estimate census on minority population by Parliamentary Research Office (1993)[2]	Estimate census by the Minority Rights Group (1997)[3]
Germans	748,300 (2.2%)	350,000 – 400,000	750,000 – 1,100,000 (1.9–2.8%)
Ukrainians	5,042,500 (15.7%)	250,000 – 350,000	350,000 – 500,000 (0.9-1.3%)
Belarussians	1,956,600 (6.1%)	250,000 – 300,000	200,000 – 300,000 (0.5-0.8%)
Jews	3,050,000 (9.5%)	8,000 – 10,000	
Slovaks		10,000 – 15,000	10,000 – 20,000 (less than 0.1%)
Czechs		5,000 – 10,000	5,000 (less than 0.1%)
Lithuanians		15,000 – 20,000	10,000 – 30,000 (less than 0.1%)
Roma/Gypsies		20,000 – 25,000	15,000 (less than 0.1%)
Others*		309,700 (1%)	2,000

* Others: Tatars, Armenians, Greeks, Macedonians, Russians

[1] P. Eberhard (1996) *Miedzy Rosja a Niemcami. Przemiany narodowosciowe w Europie Srodkowo-Wschodniej w XX w* (Between Russia and Germany. Nationalities Changes in Central East Europe in 20th century), Warsaw, p. 106.

[2] S. Lodzinski (1994) Poland's Policy towards National Minorities 1989-1993, Warsaw, p. 1.

[3] *World Directory of Minorities* (1997) London: Minority Rights Group, p. 237.

Annex 2
Selection of Legal Regulations Relating to Minorities in Poland

(unofficial translation)

Protection of National Minorities

Law of 2 April 1997; Constitution of the Republic of Poland
Dziennik Ustaw (Journal of Law) of 1997, No. 78, item 483

Article 27

Polish shall be the official language in the Republic of Poland. This provision shall not infringe on national minority rights resulting from ratified international agreement.

Article 32

1. All persons shall be equal before the law. All persons shall have the right to equal treatment by public authorities.
2. No one shall be discriminated against in political, social or economic life for any reason whatsoever.

Article 35

1. The Republic of Poland shall ensure to Polish citizens belonging to national or ethnic minorities the freedom to maintain and develop their own language, to maintain customs and traditions, and develop their own culture.

2. National and ethnic minorities shall have the right to establish educational and cultural institutions, institutions designed to protect religious identity, as well as to participate in the resolution of measures connected with their own cultural identity.

Article 60

Polish citizens enjoying full public rights shall have a right of access to public services based on the principle of equality.

Article 79

1. In accordance with principles specified by statute, everyone whose constitutional freedoms or rights have been infringed, shall have the right to appeal to the Constitutional Tribunal for its judgment on the conformity to the Constitution of a statute or another normative act upon which basis a court or organ of public administration has made a final decision on his freedoms or rights or on his obligations specified in the Constitution.
2. The provisions of paragraph 1 above shall not relate to the rights specified in Article 56.

Law of 22 July 1952; Constitution of the Republic of Poland
Dziennik Ustaw (Journal of Law) No. 7, item 36, with subsequent amendments

Article 67

2. Citizens of the Republic of Poland shall have equal rights irrespective of sex, birth, education, profession, nationality, race, religion, social status and origin.

Article 81

1. Citizens of the Republic of Poland, irrespective of nationality, race or religion, shall enjoy equal rights in all fields of public, political, economic, social and cultural life. Infringement of this principle by any direct or indirect privileges or restrictions of rights by reference to nationality, race or religion shall be punishable.
2. The spreading of hatred or contempt, the provocation of discord, or humiliation of man on account of national, racial or religious differences, shall be prohibited.

Law of 20 June 1997; Penal Code
Dziennik Ustaw (Journal of Law) No. 88, item 553

Article 256

Whoever in public propagates a fascistic political system or other totalitarian systems or exhorts to hatred on the basis of national, ethnic, racial or religious differences or on the basis of not having a religious affiliation shall be subject to the penalty of fine or deprivation of liberty for up to 2 years.

Article 257

Whoever in public insults a group of people or an individual person by reason of their national, ethnic, racial or religious differences or their not having a religious affiliation, or for those reasons violates personal immunity of other people shall be subject to the penalty of deprivation of liberty for up to 2 years.

Protection of Language Rights of National Minorities

Decree of 30 November 1945 on the Official Language of Government and Self-Government Administrative Authorities
Dziennik Ustaw (Journal of Law) No. 57, item 324

Article 1

The official language of the Republic of Poland is Polish. The official language is to be used by all government authorities and administrative offices.

Law of June 14,1960; Code of Administrative Procedure
Uniform text in *Dziennik Ustaw* (Journal of Law) No. 9, item 26 with subsequent amendments

Article 69

§2 Transcripts of testimony, which was offered in a foreign language, must include the identity and address of the interpreter who rendered the translation; the interpreter must also sign the court transcript.

Law of 17 November 1964; Code of Civil Procedure
Dziennik Ustaw (Journal of Law) No. 43, item 296 with subsequent amendments

Article 265

§1 The court may appoint an interpreter in order to examine a witness who does not possess a sufficient command of the Polish language.

Law of 19 April 1969; Code of Criminal Procedure
Dziennik Ustaw (Journal of Law) No. 13, item 96 with subsequent amendments

Article 62

If the defendant does not know Polish, decisions regarding pending criminal charges, the criminal complaint and final verdicts as well as those subject to further appeal will be communicated to the accused together with a translation.

Article 159

§1 An interpreter will be summoned if the need arises to examine:
   1) (...),
   2) a person who does not possess a sufficient command of the Polish language.
§2 An interpreter will also be summoned if the need arises to translate a document written in Polish into a foreign language.

Article 354

If the court communicated with the accused through an interpreter, before the accused makes his/her final statement, the accused shall receive a translation of at least the concluding remarks of the prosecutor and the defence attorney.

Law of 29 September 1986; Law of Civil Registry
Dziennik Ustaw (Journal of Law) No. 36, item 180

Article 20

If a person who is obliged to register a birth or death cannot communicate either orally or in writing with the chief clerk of the civil registry by reason of physical disability or inability to speak Polish, the chief clerk shall summon an expert or an interpreter.

Article 50

1. The chief clerk of the civil registry shall refuse to register a child if the name chosen by the child's parents is ridiculous, indecent, in diminutive form or does not indicate the sex of the child.

Resolution of the Minister of Internal Affairs of 14 February 1987 on Civil Registry Records, Administration and Control of Civil Registry Records, their Preservation and Security
Dziennik Ustaw (Journal of Law) No. 7, item 43

§2 The civil registry should be organised carefully and legibly; each individual entry should be clear and in conformance with obligatory orthographic norms, except for names, which can be recorded using the traditional spelling used by the person so named.

Education Rights of National Minorities

Law of 7 September 1991 on the Educational System
Dziennik Ustaw (Journal of Law) No. 95, item 425

Article 13

1. Public schools shall enable pupils to retain their sense of national, ethnic and religious identity, and in particular shall make it possible for them to learn their own language, history and culture.
2. At the request of the parents, the educational instruction in paragraph 1 may be conducted in:
   1) separate groups, section or schools,
   2) groups, sections or schools—with additional language lessons and conducted on history and culture.
3. The Minister of Education emphasises, in executing this resolution that the Minister shall determine the way in which the schools organise the classes outlined in paragraphs 1 and 2, and in particular shall establish the minimum number of children needed to organise such classes.
4. In carrying out their educational function, public schools shall ensure retention of regional culture and tradition.

Resolution of the Minister of Education of 24 March 1992 on the Organisation of Educational Programs Enabling Minority Pupils to Retain their Sense of National, Ethnic and Linguistic Identity (1992)
Dziennik Ustaw (Journal of Law) No.34, item 150

§1

1. Public preschools and schools shall provide for pupils conditions under they retain their sense of national, ethnic and linguistic identity, as well as their own history and culture.2. The conditions from paragraph 1 shall be created in the course of generally accessible curricular in extracurricular instruction.

§3

1. Native language instruction for minority pupils as well as other classes outlined in paragraph 2 will be organised on a volunteer basis. The school (preschool) principal at the request of the parents or legal guardians shall organise these classes. If students above the elementary level express a desire to participate in such classes, the students themselves may submit this request.

§6

A minority native language class (section) may be organised if at least 7 elementary school pupils from one class or 14 upper-level pupils declare an interest in forming such a class.

§7

1. If the number of children declaring an interest is less than the number in paragraph 6, native language classes can be organised with students from different grades or class sections, subject to the following:

1) a class composed of pupils from different sections, (for example third-grades from sections A and B) must have at least 7 pupils,

2) a class composed of pupils from different grades (for example second and third grade) will function as a combination class and should have at least 3 but no more than 14 pupils.

3) if a single pupil from one class declares an interest in participating in native language instruction, he or she may attend class together with a bilingual class or a combination class.

2. If it is impossible to organise a native language class because of an insufficient number of children or lack of teachers, the school principal shall draw up a list of children who have declared an interest in native language education and present it to the appropriate educational authorities. They in turn will organise inter-school groups for native language education, taking into consideration transportation possibilities. The number of pupils in such a group cannot be smaller than 3 nor bigger than

§14

In schools with native language instruction, report cards shall be written in Polish and in the native language.

§15

Graduates of native language schools shall have access to upper-level Polish schools.

FROM THE UNITARY TO THE PLURALISTIC: FINE-TUNING MINORITY POLICY IN ROMANIA

István Horváth and Alexandra Scacco

Contents

FROM THE UNITARY TO THE PLURALISTIC: FINE-TUNING MINORITY POLICY IN ROMANIA

István Horváth and Alexandra Scacco

Abstract

This chapter constructs a typology of the principal minority groups in Romania, incorporating three types—the Hungarian minority, the Roma minority and the 'smaller' minority groups (comprised of fewer than 100,000 members). The purpose of this typology is to highlight the fact that the various minority groups in Romania should not simply be 'lumped together' in one monolithic category. These three types of minority groups in Romania are highly distinct and are characterised by varying degrees of social, political and economic integration. Furthermore, these three groups have diverse needs and enjoy disparate levels of political mobilisation. The chapter puts forth the argument that Romanian policy-makers and administrators must take into account the plurality of the country's minority groups when addressing challenges and issues relevant to these three diverse types. This kind of typology can be useful to policy-makers at both the local and central level of government, and can inform those responsible for the management of multi-ethnic communities in Romania. The chapter analyses and assesses both centrally directed and locally initiated minority policies in Romania since 1989, emphasising particular problem areas and policy challenges in the fields of legislation relevant to minority communities, minority rights, the institutional framework for minority protection, minority issues in post-1989 public administration reform and minority education. The study concludes by offering a number of policy recommendations for each of these issue areas.

1. Introduction

Romania presents a fascinating case for the study of the management of multi-ethnic communities. Ethnic minorities comprise more than 10% of Romania's total population. At least sixteen different minority groups can be identified, exhibiting a great variety of cultural, political and demographic profiles. Minority groups in Romania enjoy varying degrees of social, political and economic integration. These distinct groups have also employed different political strategies and have pursued widely divergent policy goals in the post-communist period. An analysis of this diversity can access the particular problems faced by Romania's minorities as they attempt to reproduce their cultural and ethnic identities.

This chapter advances the argument that, in dealing with minority issues, Romanian policy-makers must recognise the important cultural, political and demographic differences that exist among the various minority groups. In policy and in practice, the central government has thus far failed to do this to a significant degree, and instead has tended to lump together the questions and problems posed by these diverse groups. As this paper will demonstrate, this kind of unitary policy-approach is inappropriate given Romania's ethno-cultural complexity. A more sensitive approach is necessary—one which takes into account the plurality of the needs and demands of Romania's minorities.

We suggest that it can be useful to distinguish at least three separate types of minority groups in Romania based on the following attributes: size, territorial concentration, degree of political mobilisation, political objectives, historical status and socio-economic status. The three types we discern in our analysis are: (1) the Hungarian minority, (2) the 'smaller' minority groups, (comprised of fewer than 100,000 members), including Germans, Ukrainians, Lipovans and others, and (3) the Roma. The construction of this kind of typology, we will argue, can be useful to policy-makers at both the local and central levels of government in dealing with issues related to the multi-ethnic community management in Romania.

1.1. Demographic characteristics

According to the 1992 census, minorities make up more than 10% of Romania's total population (Tables 1 and 2). The largest minority group is the Hungarian (7.1% of Romania's total population), followed by the Roma (1.8%) and the German (0.5%) communities.[1] The minority population in Romania has gradually decreased over the past few decades (Table 2). This decrease is largely due to significant emigration on the part of Hungarians, Germans and Jews—a process that has accelerated since 1989.[2]

It should be noted at the outset that the term 'nationality' rather than 'ethnic minority' is used in the 1992 census to refer to the various ethno-cultural identities of Romanian citizens. In Romanian political discourse, the terms 'ethnicity' and 'nationality' are used interchangeably. Although this paper is not primarily concerned with semantic issues, it

---

[1] During the census in 1992, many Roma individuals hesitated to officially declare themselves as Roma due to widespread negative prejudice against them. Their actual number is therefore significantly higher than the number calculated in the census. A number of nongovernmental organisations estimate that between 1-1.5 million Roma live in Romania—a figure comprising more than 5% of the country's total population.

[2] In 1992 they represented only one-fifth of the number of Germans registered in 1930. During the period between 1977 and 1992, 228,252 emigrants of German origin were registered. The number of Hungarian emigrants in the period between 1977 and 1992 was greater than 68,000—more than half of them leaving the country between 1988 and 1990. See: A. Radocea (1995) 'Structura etnică a populaţiei României şi evoluţia ei în ultimele decenii' in *Recensământul populaţiei şi locuinţelor din 7 Ianuaria 1992. Structura etnică şi confesională a populaţiei,* Comisia Naţională pentru Statistică, pp. VII – LXXI.

Table 1. Ethnic Structure of Romania's Population
Censuses of 1930, 1956, 1966, 1977 and 1992

	Population				
Census year	1930	1956	1966	1977	1992
Total	14,280,729	17,489,450	19,103,163	21,559,910	22,810,035
Romanian	11,118,170	14,996,114	16746,510	18,999,565	20408,542
Hungarian	1,423,459	1,587,675	1619,592	1,713,928	1624,959
German	633,488	384,708	382,595	359,109	119,462
Roma	242,656	104,216	64,197	227,398	401,087
Ukrainian	45,875	60,479	54,705	55,510	65,764
Serb, Croat*	50,310	46,517	44,236	43,180	33,493
Lipovan	50,725	38,731	39,483	32,696	38,606
Jew	451,892	146,264	42,888	24,667	8,955,
Tatar	15,580	20,469	22,151	23369	24,596
Slovak	50,772	1,930	4,165	4,681	2,342
Turk	26,080	23,331	1,956	2309	4,028
Bulgarian	66,348	14,329	22,221	1,966	452
Czech**	0	12,040	18,040	21,286	1,977
Greek	23,161	11,821	11,193	23,422	19,594
Polish	15,804	11,166	9,978	10,372	29,832
Armenian	12,175	7,627	9,088	7,683	9,851
Other	49,182	6,441	5,860	6,262	5,797
Undeclared	5,052	13,357	3,436	4,641	3,940

* Until the 1992 census, Slovenes were also included in this group; in 1992 they were included in 'Other nationalities'.

** In the 1930 census, Czechs were included among Slovaks.

is important to distinguish between ethnicity and nationality if we are to avoid plunging into the terminological chaos that plagues so much social science literature. For our purposes, we will make a simplified distinction between the two terms: nationality involves a higher degree of political mobilisation and coherence than ethnicity and often (though not necessarily) implies a more confrontational relationship between the given group and the state. Throughout this paper, however, we will make a concerted effort to use the more neutral term 'minority group', whenever possible, for no clear set of criteria has been instituted in Romania to determine which communities are national groups and which are merely ethnic groups.

According to the census, the degree of native-language use varies significantly among the different minority groups (Table 5). The Hungarian population has the highest percentage of members who speak Hungarian as their mother tongue (97.8%). In marked contrast, more than half of the Roma surveyed declared Romanian as their first language. Among the other minority groups, fewer than 70% of Armenians, Jews, Greeks and Poles declared a mother-tongue language correspondent with their minority group.

Table 2. *Ethnic Structure of Romania's Population*
Censuses of 1930, 1956, 1977 and 1992 (in per cent)

	Population percentages			
Census year	1930	1956	1977	1992
Total	100.00	100.00	100.00	100.00
Romanian	77.85	85.74	88.12	89.47
Hungarian	9.97	9.08	7.95	7.12
German	4.44	2.20	1.67	.52
Roma	1.70	.60	1.05	1.76
Ukrainian	.32	.35	.26	.29
Serb/Croat*	.35	.27	.20	.15
Lipovan	.36	.22	.15	.17
Jew	3.16	.84	.11	.04
Tatar	.11	.12	.11	.11
Slovak	.36	.01	.02	.01
Turk	.18	.13	.01	.02
Bulgarian	.46	.08	.01	.00
Czech**	.00	.07	.10	.01
Greek	.16	.07	.11	.09
Polish	.11	.06	.05	.13
Armenian	.09	.04	.04	.04
Other	.34	.04	.03	.03
Undeclared	.04	.08	.02	.02

* Until the 1992 census, Slovenes were also included in this group; in 1992 they were included in 'Other nationalities'.

** In the 1930 census, Czechs were included among Slovaks.

With respect to religion, significant differences can be observed along ethnic lines (Table 3). The vast majority of Romanians (94.7%) are Orthodox Christians, while most Hungarians and Germans belong to the Roman Catholic Church or to various Protestant denominations. With respect to the other smaller minorities, approximately 68% belong to the Orthodox Church. Religious differences between the majority and the minorities have been a source of tension and conflict, within both social and institutional contexts. Over the past ten years Protestant and Catholic churches have received significantly less financial support from the Romanian state than have Orthodox churches. This discrepancy is in part the result of the ambiguous relationship between church and state in Romania.

The regional distribution and the degree of urbanisation of the various minority groups are also important to consider because each helps to determine the degree to which the groups are able to maintain their specific cultural identities. The more concentrated a

Table 3. Ethnic and Religious Structure of Romania's Population
Census from 1992 (in %)

Religion	Total	Romanian	Hungarian	Roma	German	Ukrainian
Total	100.00	100.00	100.00	100.00	100.00	100.00
Orthodox	86.81	94.68	1.71	85.30	6.80	80.35
Roman Catholic	5.09	1.77	41.20	4.81	59.42	0.94
Reformed	3.52	0.08	47.10	4.39	2.34	0.10
Greek Catholic	0.98	0.94	1.44	0.89	1.59	2.57
Pentecostal	0.97	0.99	0.27	1.97	0.42	7.66
Baptist	0.48	0.46	0.79	0.23	0.37	0.33
Adventist	0.34	0.32	0.51	0.42	0.29	1.57
Unitarian	0.34	0.01	4.56	0.23	0.14	0.14
Muslim	0.25	0.00	0.00	0.15	0.01	0.01
Christian Evangelic	0.22	0.22	0.15	0.23	1.86	0.29
Evangelic Augustan	0.17	0.02	0.44	0.06	22.86	0.01
Christian Old Style	0.12	0.02	0.01	0.02	0.01	0.18
Orthodox Old Style	0.14	0.13	0.00	0.03	0.01	3.53
Evangelic Presbyterian	0.09	0.01	0.79	0.01	2.39	0.01
Mosaic	0.04	0.01	0.01	0.00	0.05	0.06
Other	0.25	0.19	0.73	0.22	1.12	1.96
Atheists	0.05	0.04	0.04	0.06	0.07	0.05
No religion	0.11	0.08	0.20	0.80	0.17	0.16
Undeclared	0.04	0.03	0.05	0.18	0.08	0.07

minority group is in a given area, the higher is its chance to use its mother tongue in every-day communication and in the public sphere. Further, urbanisation is important—in as much as urban settings make the concentration of financial and administrative resources necessary for the maintenance of cultural and educational institutions easier—and facilitates political mobilisation.

The bulk of Romania's minority population is concentrated in Transylvania, where Hungarians represent 21% of the region's population and constitute a majority in two counties (see Table 4).[3] Most of the smaller minorities, with the partial exception of the Germans and a number of small urban Jewish and Armenian communities, live in rural areas. The Roma generally live in rural rather than urban settings.

---

[3] See Figure 1.

Table 4. Ethnic Structure of Romania's Population by Districts. (Percentages)

District	Romanian	Hungarian	Roma/Gypsy	German	Other	P*
Alba	90.10	5.98	3.06	.78	.07	T
Arad	80.51	12.51	2.73	1.93	2.32	T
Argeş	98.91	.06	.95	.03	.06	
Bacău	98.03	.63	1.11	.03	.20	
Bihor	66.54	28.44	3.41	.25	1.36	T
Bistriţa Năsăud	90.43	6.45	2.76	.29	.07	T
Botoşani	99.14	.03	.44	.02	.37	
Braşov	85.98	9.38	2.43	1.56	.64	T
Brăila	98.06	.05	1.08	.02	.79	
Buzău	97.78	.03	2.15	.01	.02	
Caraş-Severin	86.56	2.09	2.07	3.17	6.11	T
Călăraşi	96.37	.04	3.40	.01	.18	
Cluj	77.59	19.85	2.22	.19	.15	T
Constanţa	91.66	.18	.62	.07	7.47	
Covasna	23.40	75.24	1.13	.11	.12	T
Dâmboviţa	97.69	.07	2.01	.02	.21	
Dolj	97.48	.05	2.37	.04	.07	
Galaţi	98.72	.07	.99	.03	.19	
Giurgiu	96.48	.04	3.42	.01	.06	
Gorj	98.75	.13	1.07	.02	.03	
Harghita	14.05	84.72	1.10	.06	.07	T
Hunedoara	91.84	6.09	1.02	.66	.39	T
Ialomiţa	96.53	.03	3.22	.01	.20	
Iaşi	98.73	.06	.73	.03	.45	
Maramureş	81.10	10.17	1.24	.63	6.87	T
Mehedinţi	97.50	.13	1.50	.12	.75	
Mureş	52.05	41.41	5.70	.75	.08	T
Neamţ	99.06	.07	.67	.02	.17	
Olt	98.87	.04	1.06	.01	.02	
Prahova	98.64	.11	1.13	.05	.07	
Satu Mare	58.52	35.03	2.45	3.58	.42	T
Sălaj	72.17	23.67	3.46	.05	.65	T
Sibiu	87.71	4.24	4.14	3.78	.13	T
Suceava	96.68	.06	.73	.34	2.19	
Teleorman	97.78	.02	2.18	.01	.01	
Timiş	80.17	8.98	2.12	3.82	4.92	T
Tulcea	88.68	.04	.48	.05	10.75	
Vaslui	99.37	.01	.56	.01	.05	
Vâlcea	99.03	.10	.78	.05	.03	
Vrancea	99.03	.04	.88	.01	.04	
Bucureşti	97.53	.36	1.40	.19	.51	

*Counties marked with a 'T' are in Transylvania.

Figure 1. The Historical Regions of Romania

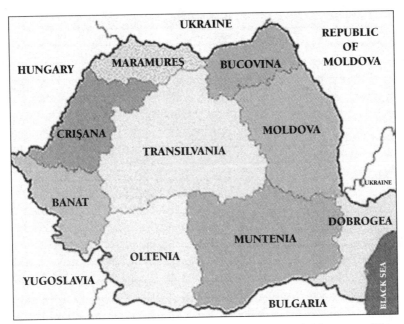

Note: What is conventionally understood as Transylvania includes the provinces of Banat,
      Crisana and Maramures.

1.2. Historical background

Without question, the diverse historical experiences of the various minority groups in
Romania must be taken into consideration when looking at the degree to which they have
been integrated into the domestic social and political systems. Rather than offering a
detailed analysis of the history of each minority group—a task that would be well beyond
the scope of this paper—a brief overview of the Romanian state-building process and its
impact on minority communities will be presented.

The first year of the modern Romanian state is generally considered to be 1859, the
year in which the provinces of Moldavia and Wallachia (including Oltenia and Muntenia)
were united. In 1878 Romania was officially recognised as a sovereign principality (later
kingdom). Transylvania, which had previously been part of the Habsburg Empire, was
ceded to Romania after World War I. Bessarabia, formerly part of Russia, was also award-
ed to Romania after 1918, but was taken by the Soviet Union in 1940 and has, since 1991,
been a part of the Republic of Moldova.[4]

With the acquisition of the Transylvanian lands in 1918, Romania—up to that point
largely ethnically homogeneous—inherited a substantial minority population, comprised

---

[4] *World Directory of Minorities* (1997) London: Minority Rights Group, pp. 240-244.

Table 5. Romania's Population According to Mother Tongue

Minority Group	Mother Tongue		
	Minority Group Language	Romanian	Other
Romanian	99.87	–	0.13
Hungarian	97.87	2.03	0.10
German	78.91	11.16	9.93
Roma	40.86	54.31	4.83
Ukrainian	91.97	7.11	0.92
Serbian	89.63	9.40	0.97
Lipovan	78.79	20.97	0.24
Jewish	9.46	72.09	18.45
Tatar	93.20	7.19	0.61
Slovak	91.46	6.18	2.36
Turk	90.63	9.08	0.29
Bulgarian	85.47	13	1.53
Czech	83.47	11.39	5.14
Greek	61.17	37.59	1.24
Polish	69.07	26.51	4.42
Armenian	44.86	49.72	5.42

Source: A. Radocea, idem., p. XLIV.

of Hungarians, Germans and others. Crucially, though self-government was promised for the region's minorities in 1918, no such concession was made.

The regions incorporated in 1918 brought with them significantly different historical and administrative traditions than those of the core regions of Moldavia and Wallachia. In the western provinces, due to the influence of several centuries of Habsburg rule, the development of a modern administration was far more advanced than in the rest of the country. These different administrative and legislative histories continue to resonate today, even after nine decades of Romanian governance. For example, land property registers (*cadastru funciar*) were institutionalised in Transylvania at the beginning of the 20ᵗʰ century, but this type of administrative and juridical system was introduced in the rest of the country only very recently.

When the western territories were incorporated into Romania, the rulers of the Old Kingdom, 'long acclimatised to using the administrative machine for paying for services rendered, were not anxious to forgo the large opportunities for patronage and influence that the new territories offered'.[5] Thus, the relationship between the newly incorporated territories and the Old Kingdom could be described as a form of internal colonisation, through which the central administrative structure was used to exploit the newly integrated periphery.[6]

---

[5]   R. J. Crampton (1994) *Eastern Europe in the Twentieth Century,* London: Routledge, p. 108.

[6]   On the concept of 'internal colonialism', see: M. Hetcher ([ ]) *Internal Colonialism: The Celtic Fringe in British National Development, 1536-1966,* London: Routledge.

Historically, the Old Kingdom's administrators did little to protect the cultural diversity of their subjects. Before 1918, only 8% of the total population of Romania belonged to ethnic minority groups (the two main groups being the Jews and the Roma), and their treatment was poor in comparison with Romanian citizens. For instance, the state refused to grant citizenship to Jews living in Romania. Given this legacy of insensitivity to minority issues, the political and administrative elite faced a significant challenge in 1918. With the acquisition of the Transylvanian lands, ethnic minorities—largely Hungarians and Germans—constituted 30% of the Romanian population.

Although self-government was promised for the region's minorities in 1918, no such concession was made. Instead, the Romanian government opted for overly assertive educational and cultural policies that generated discontent among the minorities.[7] Rather than integrating minority communities through efficient judicial and administrative processes, the central government pursued assimilationist policies and made extensive use of nationalist rhetoric that emphasised the spiritual unity of all Romanians.[8]

This assimilationist legacy continued, despite a brief period of limited accommodation, during the communist period. Beginning in 1945, relations between the Hungarian minority and the majority actually improved. Hungarians were allowed to maintain an extensive network of Hungarian-language schools, including a Hungarian university. Furthermore, a measure of formal administrative autonomy was granted to Hungarians in regions in which they represented a majority of the population. Smaller minorities were also granted a limited degree of cultural autonomy. The German minority, however, was treated severely, for Germans were blamed for Romanian collaboration with the Nazis during World War II. Large number of Germans were forced to emigrate, many deported to labour camps in the Soviet Union. The third group in our typology, the Roma, remained politically and socially marginalised and economically disadvantaged throughout the communist period.

Beginning in the 1970s, conditions worsened for all minority groups as Ceausescu increasingly began to rely on the use of pugilistic, nationalistic rhetoric in order to bolster his declining legitimacy.[9] Throughout the 1970s and 1980s the Ceausescu regime gradually deprived Hungarians of the limited degree of autonomy they had been granted in the previous few decades, dramatically reducing the amount of Hungarian-language education available and closing the Hungarian university in Cluj. Education in other minority languages was also curtailed. Ethnic Romanians were promoted to key political and bureaucratic positions at the expense of minorities, and the issue of minority rights was raised only to serve as evidence of 'secessionist plots' and promote xenophobia among the majority.

The collapse of communism in December 1989 has provided new opportunities for the management of inter-ethnic relations and the reform of public administration. Many significant challenges remain, however, and policy-makers and administrators at both the central and local levels of government must confront the difficult burden of recent histo-

---

[7]   I. Livezeanu (1995) *Cultural Politics in Greater Romania: Regionalism, Nation Building and Ethnic Struggle, 1918–1930*, Ithica: Cornell University Press.

[8]   See C. Durandin (1995) *Historire des Roumains*, Librarie Artheme Fayard.

[9]   K. Verdery (1991) *National Ideology under Socialism: Identity and Cultural Politics in Ceausescu's Romania*, Berkeley: University of California Press.

ry. Romanian politicians and policy-makers have inherited an unenviable combination of elements: dissatisfied minorities, no real tradition of protecting cultural diversity and accommodating minority demands, and a surfeit of nationalistic ideology and rhetoric at all levels of public discourse. What is beyond doubt is that established patterns of governance and long-standing attitudes about cultural and ethnic diversity must change if conditions for Romania's minority communities are to improve in any meaningful way.

1.3. Political mobilisation of minority groups

As we have seen, Romania's ethno-cultural map is too complex to view all minority groups as part of a single category. In terms of political mobilisation, clear differences can be observed between the three types we have identified:[10]

- *The Hungarian minority* is currently attempting to its renegotiate its political status with the Romanian State. The major political goal of the Hungarian minority community, expressed repeatedly in the public sphere since 1989, is the achievement of greater cultural and political autonomy. The Hungarian minority also desires to be considered a 'co-nation' along with the Romanian nation. In other words, the Hungarian minority desires to be considered an equal but distinct and autonomous constituent of the Romanian political community. Hungarians hope to acquire 'official' status for the Hungarian language, and to establish a coherent political and institutional framework that will guarantee greater administrative autonomy and more favourable cultural and educational policies for the their community. Finally, and most radically, they hope to gain some form of territorial autonomy for the regions in which large communities of Hungarians are concentrated.

- *The 'smaller' minority communities* (comprised of fewer than 100,000 people) face unique problems in attempting to preserve their cultural identities largely because of their size. They are integrated into the political system through specific mechanisms of representation (see the section below on the political participation of minorities). In clear contrast to the Hungarian minority, their needs and demands can, in general, be satisfied within the political and administrative systems currently in place in Romania. They have not demanded official language status or a separate university. When expressed, their grievances do not usually generate major political and public debates.

- *The Roma minority*, residing throughout Romania, is socially and culturally marginalised, faces discrimination and, occasionally, violent aggression from the local majority communities. Having only a very limited stratum of political and intellectual elites, the Roma minority is characterised by a strikingly low level of political mobilisation. Crucially, their concerns are not articulated to a sufficient degree in the political sphere.

---

[10] For a different typology, see: Ted Gurr (1993) *Minorities at Risk: A Global View of Ethnopolitical Conflicts,* United States Institute of Peace Research. This can be found through the Minorities at Risk Project Web site at: http://www.bsos.umd.edu/cidcm/mar/trgpvs.html.

The Hungarian and Roma minorities clearly present the greatest challenges in political terms to the Romanian state. The fundamental political objectives expressed by the Hungarian minority conflict with the underlying ideologies in the Romanian political ethos and the vision of the 'unitary state' upheld by the Romanian political and administrative elite. With respect to the Roma, the state lacks the necessary know-how, institutional and material resources to lessen tensions between the Roma and other citizens at the local level. The Roma remain socially and politically marginalised and their integration into mainstream Romanian society will be a difficult task.

2. The Legal Framework for the Protection of National Minorities

Several key legal documents comprise the nascent legal framework for minority protection in Romania. This section will analyse this framework on two different levels: the domestic and the international. As regards the former, we will analyse two dimensions: (1) constitutional provisions referring to the status and protection of minority groups, and (2) the discourse surrounding the proposed draft Law on Minorities.[11] At the international level, we will look principally at European legislation on human and minority rights.

2.1. Constitutional provisions

The Romanian Constitution,[12] adopted in 1991, is both generous and limiting in its provisions on minority protection and has contributed to a great deal of confusion in public and political discourse on minority issues. It should be noted at the outset that the framers of the Constitution made the explicit *decision to consider minority rights on an individual and not on a community basis.* The treatment of individuals rather than groups as the subject of minority rights legislation has been fairly consistent over the past decade, much to the chagrin of the Hungarian minority.

A number of constitutional contradictions have hindered the political process of establishing and implementing the legal framework necessary to ensure consistent and reliable protection of national minorities.[13] For example, according to the Constitution, minorities are granted the right to 'preserve, develop and express their ethnic, cultural, linguistic, and religious identities' (Article 6.1).[14] In marked contrast to this provision, however, the Constitution clearly defines Romania as an indivisible, unitary state with

---

[11] In the second half of the paper, we will take a closer look at sectorial legislation that is relevant to the protection of the rights of minorities in Romania.

[12] For an online version of the Constitution in English, see:
http://www.uni-wuerzburg.de/law/ro00000_.html.

[13] For a detailed analysis see R. Weber (1998) 'The Protection of National Minorities in Romania: A Matter of Political Will and Wisdom', in: Kranz and Küpper (eds.) *Law and Practice of Central European Countries in the Field of National Minorities Protection After 1989,* Warsaw: Center for International Relations, pp. 199-268.

[14] Romanian Consitution, Article 6.1. See Table 6 for relevant articles of the Romanian Constitution.

only one official language—Romanian.

The Constitution declares that Romania is a 'nation-state', implying that the relationship between individuals and the state is based first and foremost on ethnic and cultural criteria. This ethno-cultural definition of citizenship is apparent in a number of the Constitution's articles, particularly those which address the fundamental rights and freedoms of Romanian citizens and describe the nature of the Romanian state. However, in contradiction to this unitary definition of the state and exclusive concept of citizenship, the Constitution stipulates that all citizens of Romania are to be treated equally, 'regardless of their nationality'.[15]

The Constitution contains a number of important provisions that, directly or indirectly, affect the situation of national minorities. These provisions and their impact upon minority groups are described in the table below.

Table 6. Romanian Constitutional Provisions Relevant to Minorities

Relevant Themes	Constitutional Provisions (Articles)
Fundamental character of state/ political community	Romanian state defined as a unitary national state (1.1.).
Constitutional status of national minorities	Explicit provision of equality of citizens, and non-discrimination on the basis of nationality. (4.2.and 16.1).
Right to national/ethno-cultural identity	Recognizes and provides the right to preserve, express and develop specific national identities (6.1.) of citizens, but the measures of protection are limited, stating that the measures to promote this identity could not discriminate against the majority (6.2 and 16.1).
Linguistic status of minority languages	The only language having official status is Romanian (13) No explicit provisions regarding the status of minority languages.
Use of minority languages in education	Minorities have the right to acquire their mother tongue through public instruction and the right to be instructed in their mother tongue(32.3)
Political representation of minorities	Special facilities are accorded to the representative organisations of minorities failing to obtain the necessary votes to appoint a representative to the parliament (59.2.)
Legal procedures	Only conducted in Romanian (127.1). Upon request, translators are provided for those who do not speak Romanian (127.2.).
Individual/collective rights	The notion of collective rights is not accepted. The terminology used with respect to minority rights is rights of "persons belonging to national minorities" (see, for example, Article 6.)
Status of international legislation	International legislation on human rights, signed and ratified by the Romanian Parliament take priority over the internal legislation if the former and the latter conflict (20.)
Limitations regarding possible amendments to the Constitution	Explicit provision stipulating that articles concerning the national and unitary character of the state, and those regarding the official language may not be changed (148)

---

[15] Romanian Constitution, Article 4.1.

By including both the principle of nondiscrimination on the basis of ethnicity, national affiliation or language *and* a unitary, monolingual definition of the Romanian state, the Constitution is highly ambiguous as to the precise nature of the legal relationship between citizenship, ethno-cultural identity and the state. Contrary to the spirit of multi-culturalism that underlies several constitutional provisions, the use of the term *nation-state* evokes an image of the state as the expression of a historically constituted human community, bounded together by common ethnic origin, language, culture and religion.[16] This sends an important symbolic message to Romania's minority population and raises crucial questions about the inclusiveness or exclusiveness of Romanian citizenship so defined. National identity is thus presented as an ethno-cultural given rather than a civic construct. The 'nation' is rooted in ethnic and cultural ties, and not in the 'every day praxis of citizens who actively exercise their civil rights'.[17]

In addition to their symbolic dimensions, the aforementioned constitutional provisions have worked to hinder the overall political process of negotiations between ethnic minorities and the majority. For example, in a heated debate on education legislation in 1998 the 'nation-state' concept was evoked in political rhetoric in order to disallow the use of minority languages in Romanian history classes.

2.2. Draft laws on minorities

At the moment there does not exist a single corpus of law regulating the rights of minorities in Romania that includes provisions on political participation, language use, education and other relevant issue-areas. Although most of these issues are addressed to some degree in other legislation, the creation of a separate law on minorities could serve as an important political precedent and confidence-building measure between minorities and the majority.

In the immediate aftermath of Ceausescu's overthrow and execution in December 1989, the provisional government of the National Salvation Front (NSF)[18] promised to draft a law on national minorities. Soon after this promise, however, the NSF began to make extensive use of nationalist rhetoric in order to bolster its political support base (in light of its waning legitimacy in the months following the December Revolution).[19]

Under these circumstances, and under the continuing leadership of ex-communist official Ion Iliescu, no law on minorities was seriously debated. Moreover, progress on minority issues was stifled by the Iliescu government's continuous use of reactive nation-

---

[16] M. Constantinescu (1992) *Constituţia României—comentată şi adnotată*, Regia autonomă 'Monitorul Oficial', Bucurest, p. 7.

[17] J. Habermas (1994) 'Citizenship and National Identity', in: B. van Steenbergen (ed.) *The Condition of Citizenship*, London: Sage Publications, 1994, pp. 20-35.

[18] The ad hoc political force constituted after the power shift from December 1989. The political grouping (under other names) was the dominant party until 1996.

[19] T. Gallagher (1999) *Democracy and Nationalism in Romania: 1989-1998*, Bucharest: All Educational, p. 1.

alism, particularly when dealing with the increasing demands of the Hungarian minority for cultural and administrative autonomy. Thus, instead of negotiating with the minority groups (especially the Hungarians), discussing the sources of their expressed dissatisfaction over a range of issues and looking for workable solutions, the government adopted a highly defensive line, accusing minority groups of disloyalty, and secessionist or irredentist motives.

Following the 1992 presidential and parliamentary elections, and particularly beginning in 1993, the integration of Romania into Euro-Atlantic institutions was declared as a foreign-policy priority for Iliescu and his party (now the Party of Social Democracy in Romania—PSDR), and the central government began to pay more attention to minority rights issues.[20] As a result of this shift in policy, the Iliescu government's response to minority group demands and proposals became somewhat more sensitive. A new institution for the representation of minorities was created—the Council of National Minorities (CNM)—and a commitment to adhere to European standards of minority protection was expressed.

In light of the seemingly more favourable climate for negotiations on minority issues, two key minority organisations—the German Democratic Forum (GDF) and the Democratic Alliance of Hungarians in Romania (DAHR)—and several NGOs focusing on human rights issues produced drafts for a Law on National Minorities. Although seven draft laws were ultimately produced, not a single draft has been debated in Parliament. This neglect of minority issues has sent a powerful message to minority groups that their persistent efforts have been in vain, and has prompted many members of minority groups to accuse the central government's expressed interest in minority issues as mere 'window dressing' for external (i.e. European and American) observation.

Although some problems raised by minorities have been addressed by other laws, which we will discuss in our analysis of the institutional framework for minority protection and minority-language use in education, a number of formidable legal challenges remain to be tackled. For example, the official legal status of minorities has yet to be clearly defined, and a clear procedure has not been established through which an ethno-cultural group can establish itself as a 'national minority', and thus benefit from a different set of legal and institutional mechanisms.

But perhaps the most pressing issue in need of a proper legal and regulatory framework is the continued social exclusion of and widespread discrimination in numerous areas against the Roma population. Although a draft law on the prohibition and elimination of all forms of discrimination has been debated in public, it is still waiting to be included in the agenda of the Parliament. Clearly, serious legal measures will be necessary to combat the pervasive discrimination against the Roma and to facilitate their integration into Romanian society.

---

[20] Regarding Romania's foreign policy orientation see, Pal Dunay (1997) 'Hungarian-Romanian Relations: A Changed Paradigm', in: Monika Wohlfeld (ed.) *The Effects of Enlargement on Bilateral Relations Between Central and Eastern Europe*, Paris: Institute for Security Studies, Western European Union.

2.3. International legislation

As discussed in the previous section, international legislation on Human Rights adopted by Romania (signed and ratified), in theory, takes priority over domestic legislation where the two conflict. In practice, however, the Romanian political elite has been reluctant to accept international recommendations on minority rights issues.

Table 7. International Documents (Multi-lateral and Bilateral Treaties) Signed by Romania

Document	Note
The Universal Declaration of Human Rights	
The International Covenant on Civil and Political Rights	
The Convention on the Elimination of All Forms of Racial Discrimination	
The Framework Convention for the Protection of National Minorities	
Declaration of 18 December 1992, of the General Assembly of the United Nations on the Rights of Persons Belonging to National or Ethnic, Religious and Linguistic Minorities	
The Copenhagen Document of the CSCE Conference on the Human Dimension	
The Recommendation 1201/11993 of the Parliamentary Assembly of the Council of Europe	
The European Charter for Regional or Minority Languages	signed/not ratified
The European Charter of Local Self-Government	signed/not ratified
Treaty between Romania and the Federal Republic of Germany on Friendly Co-operation and Partnership in Europe	
Treaty on Friendship, Good Neighbourhood and Co-operation between Romania and the Federal Republic of Yugoslavia (1996)	
Treaty on Understanding, Co-operation and Good Neighbourhood between Romania and the Republic of Hungary (1996)	
Treaty on Good Neighbourhood and Co-operation between Romania and Ukraine (1997)	

The debate that surrounded the adoption of the Council of Europe's Recommendation 1201 (1993) is illustrative. Although all political parties represented in Parliament consented to ratify the Recommendation in 1993, and thereby incorporate its provisions into domestic legislation, no action was taken in this direction until 1996. Two of the Recommendation's articles in particular—Articles 11 and 12—began to raise difficulties for Romanian politicians as they entered into negotiations on a bilateral treaty with Hungary. These two provisions, concerning the delegation of administrative autonomy and special political status to ethnic minorities and the granting of collective rights to minority groups, were viewed by a number of parties in Parliament as stepping-stones on the path to the territorial dissolution of Romania. Although Recommendation 1201 was ultimately signed, it was only accepted with the reservation that the document should not be interpreted in such a way that minorities can be granted territorial autonomy.

The Framework Convention for the Protection of National Minorities (FCNM) was signed and adopted by Romania in 1995 but this initiative was largely motivated by a desire to take advantage of those provisions of the Framework Convention which offered a lower degree of minority protection than the Romanian Constitution.[21] Two other European documents have not yet been ratified by Romania: the European Charter for Regional or Minority Languages and the European Charter of Local Self Government.

3. The Institutional Framework for Minority Protection

At the level of government institutions, we will look closely at two dimensions of minority protection: (1) minority representation in the legislature, and (2) the means by which minority groups are able to influence decision-making in the executive. It is important to note at the outset, however, that the effectiveness of either of these institutional mechanisms is highly dependent upon the political configuration of the ruling coalition at any given time.

3.1. Representation in the legislature

The Constitution guarantees political representation for minorities in the legislature through Article 59.2, which stipulates that, regardless of the number of votes they obtain, minority organisations have the right to one deputy seat each. This provision is qualified by the Electoral Law for the Chamber of Deputies and the Senate—Law No. 68/1992—which states (Article 4) that minority citizens must obtain at least 5% of the average number of votes at the national level in order to enter the Chamber of Deputies.[22] According to this provision, those officially recognised minority organisations[23] are registered as 'associations' rather than political parties and can participate in general and local elections. In general elections, those minority organisations which obtain the highest number of votes (but just one for each minority) benefit from the aforementioned constitutional provision. This provision applies only to the lower house (Chamber of Deputies) of Parliament. There is no equivalent provision for the Senate.[24] The requirement that only one organisation can represent a given minority in Parliament creates a highly undesirable 'winner takes all' dynamic and inhibits co-operation by the various organisations that claim to speak for a given minority group. In the case of the Roma, for example, a number of different organisations and personalities, often with contrasting policy proposals and ideological

---

[21] Weber, p. 205-206.

[22] Article 4, Law No. 68/1992.

[23] These organisations have the status of nongovernmental organisations.

[24] In real terms, this means a relatively small number of votes. In the 1992 general elections, the Bulgarian Union from Banat-Romania managed to obtain parliamentary representation with 1,906 votes (0.02% of the total vote).

standpoints, claim to represent the Roma community. The fact that only one Roma organisation can have access to political power is exclusionary and can be politically counterproductive.

Since the general elections in 1996, 13 deputies in total have represented the smaller minorities (one for each registered smaller minority group) in the Lower House of Parliament. None of these deputies received enough votes to be directly elected, but were allocated seats according to Article 59.2. These deputies account for 4.3% of the total parliamentary vote. No non-Hungarian minorities are represented in the Senate. The Democratic Alliance of Hungarians in Romania, supported by the overwhelming majority of ethnic Hungarians, hold 25 seats in the lower house and eleven in the Senate, all of which were directly elected.

3.2. The Council of National Minorities

In the spring of 1993, against the backdrop of Romania's application for membership in the Council of Europe, the central government announced its decision to establish a 'consultative body' on minority issues. This body—the Council of National Minorities (CNM)—was intended to facilitate consultations between minority representatives and both local and central government, and enable minority groups to offer recommendations to the government on issues of direct concern to them. Among the Council's other prerogatives was the administration of financial support to minority organisations and the initiation of draft legislation on minority issues.[25]

The Council operates on the basis of equality among minorities. Thus, regardless of the size of a given minority, a similar number of representatives from each of the minorities' organisations is appointed. This procedure clearly reflects the mentality of the PSDR-led ruling coalition in 1993, which stressed that minority issues should be approached from a human rights perspective (i.e. on an individual rather than a group basis). From this perspective, it was argued that political or administrative measures that benefited one minority group in particular were not justified. This rhetoric, though, only thinly masked the primary goal of the pre-1996 ruling coalition: to use the presence of the smaller minorities on the Council as a counter-balance against the political agenda of the Hungarian minority.[26]

The pursuit of this strategy by the PSDR was made possible by the extensive control exercised by the ruling coalition over the various smaller minority organisations. This control was based primarily on the lack of clear-cut regulations on the allocation of budgetary resources for these minority organisations. In practice, therefore, the allotment of funds to minority groups was highly politicised and rarely impartial.[27]

---

[25] For detailed information on the legislative basis and structure of the Council, see: *The Legislative and Institutional Framework for the National Minorities of Romania*, Bucharest: Romanian Institute for Human Rights, 1994.

[26] Weber, p. 245.

[27] D. Oprescu (1999) 'Politici publice pentru minorităţile naţionale din România', in: *Sfera Politicii*, No. 66, January, pp. 13-18.

The Council's lack of political independence and authority soon became clear to the Democratic Alliance of Hungarians, which quickly withdrew from the body in September 1993, only six months after it had joined. Soon after, the Council's Roma representative decided to withdraw from the organisation when the central government failed to act decisively following a serious of violent attacks against a Roma settlement in Transylvania. The ruling coalition's thinly veiled attempts to manipulate the Council and the withdrawal of the representatives of the two largest minority groups greatly undermined the institution's credibility and effectiveness.

Following the change in government in 1996, the Council was renamed the Council *for* National Minorities, and three major changes were instituted that directly affected its modus operandi.

First and foremost, the new government established the Department for the Protection of National Minorities (DPNM) that operated within normal government channels (i.e. the DPNM is not simply a 'consultative body' but a functioning government department headed by a Minister for National Minorities). Since its establishment, the DPNM has promoted recommendations made by the Council, thereby giving the body more opportunities to shape government minority policies.

Another government initiative which served to empower the Council was the establishment of a special Inter-Ministerial Committee on National Minorities, whereby representatives of different government ministries can participate in Council meetings.[28]

A third important institutional change relates to resource allocation. The Council receives annual funding from the central government, and the Council's members decide how these funds should be allocated. As of 1996, no government minister is allowed to intervene in this process where content is concerned. The only supervisory role given to the Minister of the DPNM is to ensure that no Council decisions on financial matters contravene Romanian law. While this shift in procedure may appear subtle, its implications are important. As a result of this change, the financial means of political control exercised by the ruling coalition before 1996 have been eliminated.

3.3. The Department for the Protection of National Minorities

As mentioned above, the Department for Protection of National Minorities (DPNM) was established in 1996 with the mandate of facilitating co-operation between the Council of National Minorities and various government agencies. The Department also plays a significant role in the implementation of relevant legislation and programs in the field of minority protection. Five DPNM territorial offices (located in Arad, Cluj-Napoca, Constanta, Suceava and Turnu Severin) have the power to monitor local authorities regarding the uniform implementation of legal provisions on the protection of national minorities.[29] This deconcentration was aimed at increasing the Department's impact at the local level, and to facilitate communication between regional minority organisations and both local and central authorities.

---

[28] Government Decision No. 460/1998

[29] LGI *Decentralisaton Volume 3*, 'Local Governments in the CEE and CIS—An Anthology of Descriptive Papers: Romania', p. 18. Work in Progress.

Although the DPNM is an officially recognised department, it does not enjoy the same status as most departments in the Romanian government, as it is subordinated under the Office of the Prime Minister. Despite this never happening in practice, the prime minister therefore has the authority to intervene and block decisions reached by the DPNM, and the capacity to seriously hamper its effectiveness as an institution. Additionally, this institutional arrangement means that the Department has no financial autonomy. Nonetheless, the Department has its own minister and is, therefore, represented in the Cabinet. Through this representation, the DPNM is involved in the executive policy-making process and can exert a great deal of influence on issues relating to minority interests and the protection of minority rights. Indeed, since its inception, the DPNM has become one the most influential actors in shaping policy on minority issues.

In 1997 the Department created a separate National Office for Roma in order to develop better communication with Roma organisations and other governmental agencies whose mandates directly or indirectly affect the social integration of the Roma minority. The Office's mandate is to handle all issues related to the situation of the Roma. It maintains contacts with all organisations dealing with Roma issues, prepares and co-ordinates central government strategy toward Roma issues, and co-ordinates inter-ministerial Roma subcommittees. The Office does not have a separate budget, but is financed by the DPNM.[30] Although the body is extremely small (only two full-time employees), its establishment reflects a positive policy-approach in that it is a specialised body designed to deal with the particular problems of a unique minority group.

3.4. Specific issues

In accepting a lower threshold of votes for the minority organisations in parliamentary elections, a form of positive discrimination on behalf of minority groups has been promoted through which the smaller minority communities can promote their specific interests in the legislature. While this provision is undoubtedly to the advantage of the smaller minority groups, it presents several problems in terms of their representation, as it encourages competition rather than co-operation between the various groups that claim to represent different minority communities.

Because in general elections only one organisation can represent a given minority, a 'zero-sum' or 'winner takes all' situation has arisen, excluding potential minority actors and organisations. This is particularly damaging in the case of the Roma community, for which a number of organisations, often with highly different policy programs and objectives, claim to represent the Roma population in Romania. By recognising only one organisation as the 'legitimate' representative of the Roma, many issues of concern to this minority may be overlooked. Further, although any minority organisation is entitled to funding from the Council of National Minorities, only officially recognised minority 'associations' can make decisions regarding the allocation of funds for minority organisations.

---

[30] Zsuzsa Bereschi, Adviser on International Relations to the President of the DAHR, interview, October 2000.

This system of minority representation is based on *the false presumption that minority groups are unitary political actors*. This assumption must be abandoned and the system should be reformed to allow for more participation of various minority organisations. (A number of policy recommendations will be discussed at the end of this paper that address the issue of political representation for minorities.)

Another fundamental problem related to the institutional framework of minority protection is its centralised character, which directly contributes to the lack of local empowerment of minority groups. In particular, when minority communities are very small, they are not in a position to participate in the political processes and decisions that often directly affect them (for example, decisions on the maintenance of cultural and educational institutions). The process of administrative decentralisation is crucial in this respect. As more powers are ceded from central to local authorities, minority interests are likely to be better represented and minority groups are less likely to be left out of political decision-making on issues that concern them. It should be noted, however, that decentralisation on its own is not necessarily sufficient to guarantee greater participation for smaller minority groups at the local government level. Larger minority groups now living in compact settlements will benefit more from decentralisation than small or dispersed groups. Thus, in addition to decentralisation, complementary forms of political participation, such as consultative bodies, could alleviate this problem.

In as much as the regional offices of the Department for the Protection of National Minorities reflect a systematic attempt by the Department to increase contact between representatives of minority organisations and local authorities, it is progress towards the institutionalisation of minority protection.

4. Local Public Administration in Romania

The process of restructuring Romania's public administration system was initiated immediately following the December 1989 Revolution. The Adoption in 1991 of Law No. 69/1991 on local public administration, Law No. 70/1991 concerning local elections, and Articles 119-120 of the new Romanian Constitution established the necessary framework within which serious administrative reform could begin. These laws and constitutional provisions made possible a degree of power devolution from the central to the local administrative level. On paper, at least, a considerable degree of local administrative autonomy has been sanctioned. At present, a number of public services are administered locally, including: social services, heating, water, electricity and the maintenance of public buildings. In addition, some taxes are collected at the local level. In general, however, public administration in Romania remains very centralised. The central administration still controls the police, personnel from the Ministry of Education, agricultural directorates, forestry staff and even cultural policy and subsequent posts.

Broadly speaking, in Romania, the *central public administration* develops activities of national interest throughout the country to be carried out by the executive, the ministries, those central authorities subordinated to the executive and the ministries, and deconcentrated territorial bodies. *Local public administration* develops activities of local importance within local administrative-territorial units. Local administration is comprised of a two-

tiered system: the *local level* and the *county level*. The local authorities are the local council, the county council and the mayor. Central and local administrative authorities co-operate and maintain communication through government representatives called *prefects*.
Appointed by the cabinet, prefects are government representatives present in each county who supervise the public services of ministries and other deconcentrated administrative
functions (police, agriculture, health, education, environment and social protection).[31]
Another key mandate of the prefect is to ensure that all decisions made in the local administrative bodies are in accordance with Romanian law. During the period between 1992
and 1996, instead of acting as public functionaries with clearly delimited competencies (as
defined by the Constitution), prefects tended to promote the political agendas of the parties that backed their appointment. In practice, prefects spent much of their time competing with local political actors for effective authority over a range of activities.[32]

Prior to 1996, the law on public administration seriously limited the effective exercise
of local autonomy. Since 1996, the process of revising and expanding Law No. 69/1991
on local administration and the relevant system of public finances has been underway,
but the results have been highly ambiguous. Emergency Act 22/1997 introduced several
key changes in minority-language use in public administration. This Act and its relevance
for minority communities will be discussed in the following section. Regarding public
finance reform, a new Law on Local Public Finances was adopted in November 1998 and
became effective in January 1999.[33] Two positive steps in the direction of fiscal decentralisation were initiated through this new law:

· A certain percentage of personal income tax is now allocated to local and county-
  level administrative bodies, representing a new source of local revenue.[34]
· Local administrative bodies now can exercise full autonomy in the management of
  local public funds, including tax collecting (in 1999 local governments established
  their own tax revenue offices).

Another important dimension of public administration reform relates to the presence
of minorities in public administration—a sensitive issue in Romania due to the ethnically selective personnel recruitment policies carried out during the communist period. The
communist regime did not simply use nationalistic rhetoric for self-legitimisation,[35] but
also promoted a policy of ethnically preferential recruitment, unequally distributing administrative positions to ethnic Romanians even in regions where Hungarians represented a
majority of the population. According to the 1992 census, ethnic Hungarians comprise
only 3.73% of people working in the fields of public administration and social security—

---

[31] LGI *Decentralisation Volume 3*, Romania Chapter, p. 5.
[32] Due to the intensive protest of the political opposition and the international community, the
    powers of the prefects were reduced in 1996.
[33] Zsuzsa Bereschi, interview, October 2000.
[34] The percentage of personal income tax allocated to the local level according to the new law was
    40% and to the district level was 10%, though these figures are subject to annual changes accord-
    ing to budget legislation.
[35] Katherine Verdery (1991) *National Ideology under Socialism: Identity and Cultural Politics in
    Ceausescu's Romania*, Berkeley and Los Angeles: University of California Press.

a figure well below their percentage of the total Romanian population (7.1%).[36] This serves as a clear example of the underrepresentation of minorities in public administration. Problems arise when minority groups account for a very small percentage of the local population. In those cases, minorities often fail to obtain adequate political representation, and no special institutionalised mechanisms exist through which their particular interests can be promoted.

The situation is particularly difficult for the Roma community, in spite of its large numbers. This group, often representing a substantial percentage of the population in different localities, typically enjoys no representation in the local or county councils. Thus, far from being able to promote their specific interests, they are not even in a position to put their issues on the local political agenda.

Two attempts to place the Roma problem on the agenda of the local administration and in the public eye should be mentioned:

1. In Odorheiu Secuiesc, two foundations (CIVITAŞ from Romania and 'Fekete doboz' from Hungary) initiated, in co-operation with the local cable company. a training program for the Roma with the intention of promoting TV journalists originating from the local Roma community. The goal is to place the special problems of this community in the public eye, and to highlight the projects and solutions proposed by local policy-makers.

2. The Roma Office of the Department for the Protection of National Minorities administrates a fund intended to help those local administrations willing to make investments to help improve the social conditions of the Roma communities. This financial incentive has prompted many local administrations to redesign their investments in order to serve the interests of Roma inhabitants.

These efforts, though symbolically important, only scratch the surface of the problem of Roma exclusion from mainstream social and political life. In summary, it can be argued that, following the fall of the Ceausescu regime in December 1989, minority communities in Romania viewed the possibility of redesigning Romania's system of local administration as providing an opportunity for minorities to improve their political standing and to renegotiate power-sharing at the local level. This has not happened to the degree that minority groups anticipated a decade ago. Undoubtedly, minority and majority perceptions have differed and continue to differ as to what exactly 'minority representation' or 'minority presence' in public administration entails.

4.1. Minority language use in local administration

As seen in the introductory chapters to this volume, minority groups consider language to be one of the most important aspects of their culture: the general tendency of the various minority communities is to maintain their specific languages. The existence of an

---

[36] E. Á. Varga (1998) 'A romániai magyarság főbb demográfiai jellemzői az az 1992 évi népszámlálás eredményei alapján', in: Varga, *Fejezetek a jelenkor Erdély népesedéstörténetébol*, Budapest: Pùski, pp. 260-276.

'official language' and minority language use in public administration have long been, and continue to be, two of the most controversial topics related to minority protection. In more general terms, designating a particular language as 'official' has always had a major social and political impact when a number of cultures co-exist within a single state, region or local community. Whenever the state promotes a given language as the means of official communication they undermine the actual and symbolic importance and legitimacy of other languages used.[37] Without question, the various language policies that have been pursued in the past decade in Romania have served nationalistic purposes. Against this cultural backdrop, government policies on language-use have resulted in intense public and political debates in the past decade.

The concept of minority language use in public administration was rejected outright in Law No. 69/1991 on Local Public Administration. This law was adopted when the National Salvation Front (Ion Iliescu's original post-1989 party) held a 75% majority in Parliament. The law did not facilitate the use of minority languages in public adminstration through the employment of bilingual or multi-lingual public administration functionaries. In addition, written communication in native languages was only possible if an offical Romanian translation was attached. This thus entailed the use of Romanian even in localities where the vast majority—or even the entire population—belonged to a minority community.[38]

A relevant example of a problematic aspect of the 1991 Law as far as minorities are concerned is that, although it allows minorities to submit documents to local authorities in their mother tongue, the law requires that they attach official Romanian translations of the documents.[39] According to the Law, translation fees had to be paid by those individuals submitting the documents. In the case of verbal communication, if an administrator did not speak the given minority language, a translator was required, also at the minority citizen's expense. Thus, the imposition on minorities of the financial burden of obtaining 'official translations' offers a clear example of preventing equal access for minorities to services provided by public authorities.

In spite of the demands of minority parties for a more precise and extensive law on minority-language use, and the pressure exerted by different international institutions,[40] no real progress was made until 1997, when the 1991 Law on Local Public Administration was modified by emergency decree.[41] Emergency Act No. 22/1997 provided solutions to four issues concerning the use of minority languages in local administration. The Act was applied to those territorial-administrative units in which at least 20% of the population belonged to a minority community. The Act provides for:

---

[37] One of the major theorists of multi-culturalism provides a stimulating analysis on the lack of the ethno-cultural neutrality of the state and the alternative of multi-culturalism. See W. Kymlicka (1995) *Multi-cultural Citizenship: A Liberal Theory of Minority Rights*, Oxford University Press.

[38] Zsuzsa Bereschi, interview, October 2000

[39] Law No. 69/1991, Art. 54

[40] See the recommendations made by the High Commissioner on National Minorities on 9 September 93, or the *Report on the Application of Romania for Membership of the Council of Europe*, 19 July 1993, Doc. 6901, especially paragraphs 44 and 59.

[41] Emergency Ordinance, No. 22/1997.

- Bilingual notices (signs and inscriptions);
- Use of minority languages in communications with local authorities, both written and oral;[42]
- Publication in minority languages of information of general interest by local authorities;
- Use of minority languages during local or district council meetings if at least one-third of the members of the council belong to a minority group (Romanian translation must be provided).

The debate over this Emergency Act has been stormy. The Senate did not approve its adoption with the necessary majority, and the Constitutional Court declared the entire Act unconstitutional. To make matters more complicated, Romanian jurisprudence is deeply divided as to whether the Act is now effective, or whether the original 1991 law remains effective. The Constantinescu government (elected in 1996) has since elaborated a Draft Law on the General Provisions of Local Autonomy and the Organisation and Functioning of Local Public Administration, that contains the four above measures. The Draft Law was adopted by the Senate in May 1999 and approved by the Commission of Local Public Administration in the Chamber of Deputies in March 2000, but it has still not made it through Parliament as a whole. It remains unlikely that the law will be adopted before the 2000 general elections.

5. Minority-language Education

Minority-language education in public schools in Romania is another important component of public administration and of multi-ethnic community management. The debate over Hungarian-language public education in particular has been highly charged over the past decade. The question of whether the government should allow for the establishment of separate Hungarian-language public schools and universities remains unresolved and politically loaded. The creation of a separate Hungarian public university remains closely tied to Hungarian demands for greater 'cultural autonomy'—i.e. greater decision-making and administrative power on issues related to the preservation and promotion of minority cultures.

In response to increased minority demands in the realm of public education after 1989, a significant part of the Romanian political elite quickly began to question the institutional separation of schools based on the language of instruction, and the extent to which mother-tongue education for minorities was necessary. In 1990 the Romanian government initiated a far-reaching process of minority public educational reform. Minority groups, particularly Hungarians, immediately began to call for the separation of higher education institutions based on the language of instruction, and, in the case of the Hungarians, the re-establishment of a separate Hungarian-language public university. As a result of this

---

[42] According to the 1997 Act, the responsibility of hiring bilingual personnel and paying for written translations was transferred from minority citizens to the local administration itself.

pressure, a number of schools previously merged with Romanian ones were re-established as separate institutions with Hungarian as the language of instruction.

Beginning in 1990, a number of public universities that had previously offered Hungarian-language instruction began to re-establish Hungarian faculties and programmes. However, in the absence of clear legal and institutional norms regarding the administrative organisation of Hungarian-language education within these universities, the atmosphere in these faculties became highly politicised. Furthermore, minority groups argued that a more clear and uniform legislative framework was necessary in order to protect minority rights to education in their mother tongues. In 1994 the DAHR initiated a Draft Law on Native Language Education of Minorities. The Draft Law guaranteed minorities the *freedom to organise autonomous, public educational institutions at all levels*. Although the Romanian Constitutional Court ruled that the DAHR's legislative initiative was constitutional, it was never debated in Parliament. This neglect sent a clear message to the Hungarian community that efforts to promote their interests through legal and democratic means would simply be ignored. This lack of consideration prompted widespread Hungarian demonstrations and civil disobedience campaigns. This ultimate result of this publicly expressed outrage was the passage of a new Law on Education in 1995.[43]

The 1995 Law allowed for the establishment of separate minority-language educational units through the secondary level. With respect to university-level public education, however, no form of institutional autonomy (not even at the level of departments and faculties) was permitted. Another limiting provision of the new Law was the stipulation that, beginning at the secondary level, both Romanian history and Romanian geography must be taught only in Romanian. Further, and most controversially, the new Law required that all university entrance examinations be issued and taken in Romanian, regardless of the native language of the students seeking admission. The limitations of this can be examined on two basic levels:

· The maintenance of 'double-standards' between the organisation of Romanian and minority-language education;
· The limited extent to which the teaching of minority languages is permitted at all levels of education.

These explicit limitations of the Law produced intense opposition by the Hungarian community and, in combination with external pressure (from the European Union and other European institutions to which Romania had begun to apply for membership), the government suspended the entrance exam provision.

One of the first initiatives of the newly elected government in 1996, due to significant pressure by the DAHR,[44] was to amend the 1995 Law. Several provisions considered unacceptable by minority groups were altered or eliminated and the Law was adopted. According to the amended Law (effective in 1999), education in the Romanian language must be organised according to regional needs and demands. University entrance exams can now be held in the language in which students obtained their secondary degrees. Most impor-

---

[43] Law No. 84/1995.
[44] In 1996 the DAHR became part of the ruling coalition—an unprecedented political event in Romania.

tantly for the Hungarian community in particular, *Article 123 of the law specified that separate private minority-language universities could be established*. Although the Law did not prohibit the establishment of public minority-language universities, it stipulated that 'complementary legislation' was needed to address the issue. This ambiguous wording angered many Hungarians, who argued that Hungarian (or other minority) universities should be established and maintained by public funds like any other university in Romania.[45] This claim has been rejected outright by majority politicians and public opinion.

The only alternative solution that arose out of the heated political debates on the issue has been a proposal, made in 1998, to establish 'multi-cultural universities', though no political consensus was reached on a definition of the term 'multi-cultural'. [46] Mainstream Romanian opinion considers the status quo (i.e. tolerance of Hungarian-language instruction within Romanian university structures) to be multi-cultural, whereas the Hungarians viewed a multi-cultural solution as implying greater institutional separation within mixed universities.[47] No mutually acceptable solution to this disagreement has yet been found.

While the Hungarian minority remains dissatisfied with the current situation, the smaller minorities have made less noise about educational issues and have not demanded separate public universities. Although the issue of mother-tongue education at lower levels remains important to these minority groups, their small size has made it easier for the government to accommodate them. The Roma community presents a particularly difficult challenge in terms of education and, as such, we will take a closer look at Roma education in the next section.

5.1. Special educational measures for the Roma population

As we make clear in our typology, the Roma community, in spite of its large size, is the most culturally and socio-economically marginalised minority group in Romania. In terms of public education policies, the institutional and legal measures that have benefited the other minority groups in the past decade (extension of the rights to learn in mother tongue) have not been sensitive to Roma needs. One of the most pressing problems is their low level of integration into the education system. The rate of illiteracy among the Roma is extremely high. According to research conducted in 1993, 44% of Roma males and 59% of females are unable to read.[48] According to the Ministry of Education, approximately 80% of school-age children not attending school are of Roma origin.[49]

---

[45] It should be noted that a private Hungarian university does in fact exist in Oradea. Hungarians support the maintenance of this institution but, in general, argue that public as well as private universities should be established for minorities if desired by minority tax-payers.

[46] I. Horváth (1999) 'Multiculturalism in Romania: Alternative or Evasion?', in: Culic, Horváth and Stan (eds.) *Reflections on Differences, Focus on Romania,* Brussels: IPIS, pp. 1-12.

[47] The Hungarian equation of multi-cultural schools as separate schools for their minority group derives from this community's memories of 'mixed schools' being used to advance assimilationist policies in the past.

[48] E. Zamfir and C. Zamfir (1993) *Tiganii. Între ignorare si îngrijorare,* Editura Alternative. See also: A. Miroiu (ed.) (1998) *Invatamântul românesc azi. Studiu de diagnoza,* Polirom, pp. 141-144.

[49] See http://www.edu.ro/strarrom.htm.

Various circumstances have contributed to this bleak situation. Most crucially, the fact that many Roma families are not registered in a given administrative territory makes it very difficult for their children to attend local schools. More than 7% of Roma children do not have birth certificates, and many adults do not possess ID cards giving proof of residence in a particular town. Further, much of the Roma population in Romania has a semi-nomadic way of life, making the enrollment of children in local schools difficult if not impossible in the medium to long term.

In light of these difficulties, the Ministry of Education initiated several programs aimed at increasing the sensitivity of local administrators and to facilitate the integration of Roma children into the public school system. Serious efforts have been made to appoint Roma school inspectors at the level of each county school, who are responsible for Roma issues. At present, there are 38 Roma inspectors—only four school districts do not have one.[50] Efforts have also been made (separate entrance quotas, curriculum development designed to reflect the particularities of the Roma culture) to include Roma in special training schools for elementary school teachers. Additionally, special entrance quotas for Roma students have been established at a number of universities in departments specialising in social work and pedagogy.

In order that Roma students can benefit from the right to receive instruction in their mother tongue, a special Department for Romany Language has been established at Bucharest University, and several Romany textbooks and other teaching materials have been compiled. Although a number of positive policy developments have been initiated to help address the challenges presented by Roma education, many obstacles remain to the integration of this community into Romania's education system, and persistent discrimination continues to hinder efforts in this direction.

6. Conclusion

Although the management of ethnic and cultural diversity in Romania is often viewed as a success, particularly when compared with the policies pursued over the past decade in the former Yugoslavia, a number of serious challenges remain with respect to minority representation, protection and integration in the political, social, commercial and educational spheres. This paper has argued that, although conditions in Romania have improved since 1989 for minority groups, significant political and administrative reforms have been hampered by the tendency of the central government to lump all minority groups together, ignoring their significant political, demographic and socio-economic differences. Through the creation of our (imperfect) typology, we have demonstrated that monolithic minority policies fail to meet the diverse needs and objectives of the Hungarian minority, the smaller minority groups and the Roma. Additionally, this paper has argued that minority rights protection in Romania has a long way to go in terms of minority-language use in public administration, minority-language instruction in public schools and minority political participation. Minority representation in local politics and administration remains minimal in many parts of the country. In sum, although significant progress on minority issues has been achieved since Romania's transition in 1989, serious work remains to be done, par-

---

[50] Zsuzsa Bereschi, interview, October 2000.

ticularly with respect to the highly marginalised Roma population. Both legislative and institutional reforms are needed to improve minority rights and ease tensions among minority groups (namely, the Hungarians and the Roma) and the majority population. These challenges are not insurmountable and we therefore propose a number of policy recommendations that might help to improve the situation of ethnic minorities in Romania.

7. Recommendations

With respect to the *legislative framework* for the protection of minorities and minority groups the following changes should be made:
· Exclusionary constitutional provisions including the definition of Romania as a 'nation-state' and the designation of Romanian as the only 'official language' should be replaced by less exclusive wording, as they exacerbate the ambiguity in the relationship between the state, citizenship and ethnicity in Romania and make peaceful negotiations for legitimate power-sharing impossible.
· The amendments to Law No. 69/1991 on Local Public Administration (as manifest in Emergency Act No. 22/1997 and the subsequent Draft Law) should be passed by Parliament as quickly as possible, in order to begin the process of standardising the use of minority languages in local public administration.

The following recommendations pertain to the *institutional framework* for the protection of minorities:
· Forms of institutional collaboration between organisations representing a given minority should be initiated.
· Institutional mechanisms must enable the implementation of relevant legislation on minority issues. To that end, training of public administration officials on inter-ethnic issues must be conducted.

With respect to *public administration reform*, the following measures are recommended:
· The language barrier that exists in the relationship between local administrators and minorities must be overcome by shifting the financial responsibility for translation of documents and conversations from minority individuals to the local administration.
· Serious measures must be taken to end the legacy of 'ethnically preferential hiring' in public administration and to ensure the 'de-ethnicisation' of certain sectors of public administration. To that effect, bilingualism and multi-lingualism among public administration officials should be considered as an important resource, and should be taken into consideration when hiring public employees.
· State-sponsored training programs for local public administrators should be initiated that focus on minority issues and multi-ethnic community management in order to sensitise local administrators to minority concerns and better equip them to mediate in the case of ethnic conflicts.

In terms of *minority-language education*, the following recommendations are offered:
· Legislation establishing the right of minorities to establish separate public schools

at the primary and secondary levels must be consistently implemented.
- Clearer legislation should be drafted and passed that establishes what level of Romanian-language education is necessary for minorities to be integrated into Romanian society.
- Greater legislative clarity is also required with respect to the rights of minorities in mixed schools to receive instruction in their mother tongue.
- Consensus should be reached regarding a working definition of 'multi-cultural universities' as a first step towards resolving the controversial issue of the establishment of a separate public Hungarian-language university.

The following recommendations relate to *special educational measures for the Roma*:
- Ministry of Education policies should enable greater administrative flexibility in the registration of Roma children at public schools. The absence of identification cards should not be used as a pretext to exclude Roma children from the public school system. In spite of the circulation of a Ministerial Letter prohibiting this practice, its enforcement is limited. Further steps allocating resources, training officials and implementing policies aimed at the integration of the Roma into the public school system must be taken.
- The nascent system of 'positive action' for Roma students seeking to enter universities should be expanded and developed.
- A greater amount of public funding for Roma education initiatives is necessary to encourage the development of new strategies aimed at integrating the Roma community into the school system, increased publication of Romany textbooks, the creation of Romany-language departments at universities and training Roma teachers.
- Innovative solutions to the challenge of Roma education—such as the establishment of mobile 'caravan schools' compatible to the semi-nomadic lifestyle of some of the Roma population should be further explored. This kind of educational experiment should be researched (by NGOs and think tanks, as well as by the Ministry of Education) and subsidised in order to open the door to new policy initiatives on this critical issue.

Further Reading

Linz, Juan and Alfred Stephan (1996) *Problems of Democratic Transition and Consolidation,* Baltimore: Johns Hopkins University Press.

Gallagher, Tom (1995) *Romania After Ceausescu: The Politics of Intolerance,* Edinburgh: Edinburgh University Press.

Rady, Martyn (1992) *Romania in Turmoil: A Contemporary History,* London: I. B. Tauris.

Schöpflin, George (2000) *Nations, Identity, Power,* London: Hurst.

Verdery, Katherine (1991) *National Ideology under Socialism: Identity and Cultural Politics in Ceasusescu's Romania,* Berkeley and Los Angeles: University of California Press.

Weber, Renate (1998) 'The Protection of National Minorities in Romania: A Matter of Political Will and Wisdom' in Kranz and Küpper (eds.) *Law and Practice of Central European Countries in the Field of National Minorities Protection After 1989,* Warsaw, Center for International Relations.

Responding to Diversity: Solutions at the Local Level in Slovakia

Ján Buček

Contents

274

Responding to Diversity:
Solutions at the Local Level in Slovakia

Ján Buček

Abstract

The present study summarises various approaches towards minorities in the dynamics of central/local relations in Slovakia since 1989. It documents the growing role of the local level in addressing the needs of the different ethnic groups living in Slovakia. In this context, the national government and the international environment are powerful actors capable of shaping change. Therefore, attention is given to central decisions trying to misuse the local electoral legislature and to redraw the existing territorial-administrative division. This leads to the underrepresentation of local minority populations in regional governments and undermines mother-tongue education. It will be shown that the local public administration can improve the situation of minorities and help foster ethnic co-existence in localities where minorities directly participate in the local management of their community. From this perspective, the stable political representation of the Hungarian minority and insufficient representation of the Roma minority is reviewed. In addition, a growing search for more flexible means and ways of inter-ethnic communication outside mainstream local institutions, such as informal self-governments, traditional leaders and minority political parties will be presented. It will be concluded that, in general, despite a wide range of possibilities for local initiatives responding to the needs of minority communities, the scarcity of financial resources—linked with the lack of meaningful local powers and competencies—limit their success. Effectiveness in addressing minority issues at the local level is documented by some relevant cases in the fields of education, culture, housing and living environment, employment and social security. Future changes should include meaningful decentralisation, the establishment of more responsive and more professional local governments with the extensive participation of the various local ethnic communities coupled with a series of reforms in sectoral policies, i.e. in employment policies, housing and the social security system.

1. Introduction

In Slovakia, a significant part of the population belongs to various non-Slovak ethnic groups. Institutional instruments and policies need major restructuring if they are to successfully solve problems concerning ethnic co-existence, participation and representation for Slovakia's minority communities. Pressure to prepare for candidacy for the European Union has been instrumental in starting a process of reform on the part of local and national officials to address the interests and needs of minority communities. This process was stifled in the mid-1990s due to the presence of a neo-totalitarian/nationalist regime in Bratislava headed by Prime Minister Mečiar that actively resisted any form of pressure to improve the status of minority groups. Measures taken by the Mečiar government met with strong international disapproval and domestic opposition, especially on the part of minorities. However, neither of these sources of pressure could significantly alter the implementation of the planned political changes. Only with the election of a reform-oriented coalition government in 1998 did this situation begin to transform into an acceptable scenario for minorities.

Multi-ethnic relations in Slovakia are dominated by the Slovak ethnic group. Dispersed among this majority are minority groups that make up 15% of the population. A sample of current minority groups includes: Hungarians, Roma, Ruthenians, Ukrainians, Germans, Poles, Jews, Czechs, Silesians and Moravians.

The situation of minorities—including their own policies, their influence on both local and national levels as well as the central policies directed towards them—greatly depends on a series of factors. These factors include: (1) the deeply embedded historic memories of the various communities in the field of majority/minority relations, which influence current attitudes and policies on all sides; (2) the size and demographic development of various minority communities; (3) territorial distribution, i.e. concentration or dispersion, of a particular minority population; and (4) socio-economic differences based on ethnic grounds. All the above mentioned factors can help in understanding some basic dimensions in the complexity of majority-minority relations. At the same time, it has to be understood that these factors can be easily politicised and misused in furthering misinterpretations, prejudices and stereotypes which deepen and manipulate divisions among the various ethnic communities.

In the 1990s the major inter-ethnic disputes in Slovakia coalesced around heated political debates on the use of minority languages in public, education of minorities in their mother tongue and public administration reforms involving new territorial divisions that have had an impact on the ethnic composition of regions where minorities live. These disputes were in fact bipolar as they mainly involved representatives of the Slovak majority and those of the Hungarian minority. However, due to growing international pressure in the second half of the 1990s, more and more attention has been paid to the situation and treatment of the Roma. Against the background of the increased commitment of the new government to look at minority needs, public understanding of the political participation of minorities at all levels and of the role of the local level in the effective management of Slovakia's multi-ethnic society has grown significantly. It can be said that the majority of society has needed time to understand and acknowledge that effective democracy can only be established by and through the often tiresome process of gaining the consent of Slovakia's minority population.

1.1. A brief history of inter-ethnic co-existence

Most minority groups living in present-day Slovakia are deeply rooted in Slovakia's national history (see Table 1). From the perspective of inter-ethnic relations, it is important to note that Slovakia was an integral part of the Hungarian Kingdom for more than nine centuries. The Slovak population, along with other ethnic communities, was the subject of intense 'Magyarisation' beginning in the second half of the 19TH century. In the 20TH century, following more than seven decades of co-existence between Czechs and Slovaks, Slovakia declared its independence on 1 January 1993. In this section, however, attention will be paid to processes related to three historical periods including: (1) the establishment of Czechoslovakia as a multinational state, (2) events related to World War II and (3) the treatment of minorities under the communist regime. These processes and events help to explain the various dynamics of inter-ethnic relations in contemporary Slovakia.

During the interwar years, the Czechoslovak Republic respected some basic minority rights, especially in the field of the use of minority languages in public. Minority languages were allowed for official use in courts, public administration and cultural institutions. They were the languages of instruction in settlements where the minority population constituted more than 20% of the population. In cases when an ethnic group made up more than 50% of the local population, its language became an official language.[1] At the same time, numerous restrictions were introduced against the Roma, including mandatory police registration, legislation prohibiting their nomadic way of life, as well as forced internal population transfers and the dissolution of many of their settlements.[2] During this period, Slovaks consolidated their national identity in reaction to the Magyarisation policies of the Austro-Hungarian Empire.

As a consequence of the Munich Treaty of 1938, which lead to the disintegration of Czechoslovakia and the 1939 annexation of southern Slovakia to Hungary upon her request, an independent Slovak state was declared. Slovakia entered World War II as an Axis Power. The annexation brought about the closure of Slovak schools, forced expulsion of Slovaks and confiscation of Slovak and Czech property on this territory. All of these events are among the main sources of historic grievances on the Slovak side.[3] But the most catastrophic events of this period included the deportation of 70,000 Slovak Jews to extermination camps by the Slovak state in 1941. Much of the Roma population was concentrated into working camps which, after the occupation of the Slovakia by German troops in 1944, became the sites of numerous massacres. The majority of the Slovak Roma survived, however, though in an extremely poor socio-economic state.[4]

Postwar developments in Czechoslovakia are remembered with bitterness, especially by the Hungarian minority. Among the most dramatic events were the population exchange

---

[1] Based on The Languages Act 122/1920. J. Plichtová (1993).

[2] Various cases are documented, e.g. from Gemer region by Gecelovský, 1992.

[3] This part of history is often misused by nationalists for rising tension among Slovaks and Hungarians. We can find brief comments on this historical period, e.g. in Čierna-Lantayova (1992); Janics (1994).

[4] For more details, see: e.g. Říčan (1998); Kollárová (1991); or UNDP National Report on Human Development Slovakia (1998). There are no reliable data on all Roma victims in Slovakia during

between Hungary and Czechoslovakia and the forced resettlement of the Hungarian population from its traditional habitat in southern Slovakia to Czech lands. The anti-Hungarian
measures included re-Slovakisation policies[5] and the confiscation of agricultural land.
Hungarian institutions and a network of Hungarian schools were liquidated, and the use
of Hungarian language in public was curtailed in the period of 1945-1949.[6]

During the communist period, some opportunities were created for education in
Hungarian and Ukrainian, but not at the university level (with the notable exception of
teacher training). A few Hungarian and Ukrainian institutions, newspapers and journals
were supported by the state. The Ruthenian minority was not officially recognised and
they were formally considered Ukrainians. As a result of this forced 'Ukrainisation',
Ruthenian schools were closed, along with the Greek Catholic churches to which they
belonged. Ruthenians were forced to attend the Eastern Orthodox Church.[7]

The communist regime adopted a strictly assimilationist policy with respect to the
Roma, turning this group into a faceless socio-economic 'problem'. As a consequence of
anti-Roma legislation and policies, the traditional nomadic way of life of the Roma was
prohibited and their settlements liquidated. They were forcibly moved to high-rise housing complexes and dispersed among the rest of the population. The ethnic identity and
culture of the Roma were suppressed. As such, the results of this paternalistic 'social engineering from above' were highly negative.

In conclusion, it can be said that Slovakia's present ethno-cultural map reflects communist ideological engineering, forced migration and expulsion that occurred during the
re-establishment of Czechoslovakia after World War II. This traumatic history, common
throughout Central and Eastern Europe, helps to explain much of the underlying tensions
based on mistrust and fear that dominate inter-ethnic relations in Slovakia today.

1.2. Demography

The most recent representative data on minorities in Slovakia is found in the results of
the Statistical Census held in 1991. According to this census, minorities compose 14.3%
of the population. From the perspective of their size, minority communities in Slovakia
can be divided into *three major groups*. Hungarians and Roma are the most numerous
minority communities and, as such, much of this analysis focuses on the situation of these
two groups. Other smaller minority groups include Czechs, Moravians, Silesians,[8]
Ukrainians, Germans, Jews[9] and Poles. The smallest minority groups, such as Croatians
and Bulgarians, compose the final tier.

World War II. Unfortunately, it has long been a forgotten issue for Slovak historians, only investigated now.

[5] The aim of re-Slovakisation was to 'restore' the Slovak nationality of ethnic Hungarians who were
supposedly victims of previous 'Magyarisation'. See Olejník and Šutaj (1998).

[6] For more details concerning the situation of the Hungarian minority after World War II, see: e.g.
Bačová (1996); Janics (1994); Hunčík (1999).

[7] For selected details about the situation of the Ruthenian minority see, e.g. Jurová (1992); Zeľová
Bačová (1993); Plichtová (1993); Sisak (1997); Zubriczký (1998).

The Hungarian minority has 570,00 members and comprised 10.8% of the total Slovak population in 1991. Comparing this with data from the same year on native languages, more than 600,000 Slovak citizens declared the Hungarian language as their mother tongue. This number corresponds to almost 12% of Slovakia's total population (Bakker 1997). These figures illustrate the strength of the Hungarian identity and its resistance to assimilation.

It is difficult to compile reliable data about the *Roma*. Only in the 1991 Statistical Census were the Roma given the chance to freely identify their ethnic affiliation. Unsurprisingly, only 1.44% of Slovak citizens identified themselves as Roma. Most of the Roma chose to declare themselves as Slovaks or Hungarians. Due to historical experiences, such as anti-Roma legislation and widespread discrimination, they feared the consequences of openly declaring their ethnic identity.

Census officials collected data on the Roma unofficially during statistical censuses under the communist regime. According to data from 1980, Roma composed 4% of the population. More precise data is available from the registry of state administration from 1989 (Bačová 1993), when it was estimated that the Roma made up 4.8% of the total population. Present estimates (from 1998) suggest figures between 300,000 and 400,000 (about 7% of the total population).[10]

As of 1995, almost 40% of the Roma population was below reproductive age. The high birth rate of the Roma minority is generally considered to be the most serious obstacle to its peaceful co-existence with the majority and other ethnic groups. As the Roma generally suffer from severe poverty, illiteracy and unemployment, they are simply considered as a burden by much of the Slovak population (UNDP National Report on Human Development Slovakia 1998).

---

[8] The size of the Ruthenian and the Ukrainian minorities is frequently discussed. According to estimations there are somewhere between 100,000 and 130,000 Ruthenians living in Slovakia. These estimates are based on mother tongue and historical interpolations, and they present nearly the entire population with Ruthenian roots. Ruthenian was declared as the mother tongue of 50,000 citizens. Russian Orthodox religious affiliation was declared by almost 40,000 and Greek-Catholic affiliation by almost 190,000 citizens (both with very close ties to the Ukrainian or the Ruthenian population) in the Statistical Census of 1991. See: Duleba (1997).

[9] The size of the Jewish community is estimated at 3,000 people, living mostly in cities (Salner 1998), although the 1991 Census recorded only 134 persons who considered themselves Jewish. See: Olejník and Šutaj (1998).

[10] The highest estimation for the size of the Roma population in Slovakia was mentioned at 480-520,000 by D. Ondrušek (1999) Centre for Conflict Prevention and Resolution, *Pravda*, 24 April; and at 480-500,000 by the Chairman of the Slovak Parliament's Commission for Solving the Roma Issue, I. Tóth (1999) *SME*, 24 June.

Table 1. Population Development by Nationality

		Slovak	Hungarian	Roma	Czech Moravian Silesian	Ruthenian Ukrainian	German	Polish	Other and un-declared
1930	Abs.	2,337,816	571,952	Na	121,696	90,824	148,214	7,023	44,509
	%	70.4	17.2	Na	3.7	2.7	4.5	0.2	1.3
1961	Abs.	3,560,241	518,776	Na	45,700	35,411	6,266	1012	6,640
	%	85.3	12.4	Na	1.1	0.8	0.2	0.0	0.2
1991	Abs.	4,519,328	567,296	75,802	59,326	30,478	5,414	2,659	14,032
	%	85.7	10.8	1.44	1.1	0.6	0.1	0.0	0.27
1997	Abs.	4,614,547	568,291	87,779	59,005	32,496	5,365	3,186	16,981
	%	85.56	10.55	1.63	1.1	0.6	0.1	0.06	0.31

Na – Data not available

Note: Data for 1930, 1961 and 1991 are the results from statistical censuses. Data for 1997 is the result of the population movement register.

Sources: Statistical Yearbook of the Slovak Republic 1992,1998; Podolák, 1998.

1.3. Territorial distribution

The territorial dispersal of a minority population strongly influences its political partici-pation at different levels. The Hungarian minority is concentrated in the southwestern, southern and southeastern part of Slovakia, in districts near the Hungarian border. In sev-eral towns (Dunajská Streda, Komárno, Galanta and Štúrovo), Hungarians constitute the majority, making up more than 50% of the local population. Their spatial concentration and large proportion in the local population support the Hungarian minority's demands for various types of autonomy, including territorial and administrative forms.

The Roma are scattered throughout the country but are concentrated to some degree in south-central and eastern Slovakia where there are some 300 Roma settlements. Roma quarters can also be found in larger cities where their compact settlement (in ghettos) and poor living conditions often lead to ethnic segregation. In practice, these settlements have become ghettos sequestered on the edges of various towns.

Overall, it can be concluded that regional concentration is significant only in the case of the Hungarian minority, which is comprised of compact settlements in several coun-ties of southern Slovakia, such as Dunajská Streda and Komárno, where approximately 87% and 73% of the respective populations are Hungarian. Nevertheless, at the level of communes, local concentration of other minority populations can also be identified. Tables 2 and 3 illustrate in greater detail the presence of minorities in communes. As the total number of municipalities in Slovakia exceeds 2,800, it can be said that between one-third and one-half of the total number of localities have minority populations that constitute more than 10% of their total populations.

Currently, minority status at the national level is often juxtaposed with a local majority. This discrepancy concerning minority representation has yet to be addressed in legislation.

Table 2. Hungarian Minority Population in Municipalities (Statistical Census 1991)

Share of Hungarian population in municipalities (%)	Number of municipalities
0.01-0.9	792
1.0-4.9	125
5.0-9.9	23
10.0-24.9	31
25.0-49.9	60
50.0-74.9	118
75.0-89.9	244
90.0-100	76
Total municipalities with Hungarian population	1,469
Share of Hungarian population in the total population (%)	10.8

Source: Podolák (1998).

Table 3. Minority Population in Municipalities (Statistical Census 1991)

Share of national minorities in municipalities (in %)	Number of municipalities with minority population					
	Roma	Czechs Silesians Moravians	Ruthenians	Ukrainians	Germans	Poles
0.01-0.9	442	1,672	274	528	337	580
1.0-4.9	349	376	56	90	13	6
5.0-9.9	137	6	28	36	7	0
10.0-24.9	102	1	66	44	5	0
25.0-49.9	33	0	45	11	1	0
50.0 and more	9	0	11	1	0	0
Total municipalities	1,072	2,055	480	710	363	586
Share of total population (in %)	1.44	1.1	0.32	0.25	0.1	0.05

Source: Elaborated from Podolák (1998).

1.4. Socio-economic indicators

It is difficult to directly evaluate the social and economic situation of minority groups. In general, the main socio-economic indicators are not aggregated from the perspective of minority populations and relevant research is rare. One possible method of research is to identify situations that combine poor economic and social conditions with a large minority population.[11]

High unemployment rates are typical for the Hungarian minority in south-central and southeast Slovakia and for the Ruthenian and Ukrainian minorities in east and north-east Slovakia. In general, however, it is the Roma who are by far in the worst situation measured by any indicators (unemployment, education, health).

A large number of districts with a higher share of minority population combine inherited underdevelopment with problems related to the transition period, including untapped human potential, inadequate technical infrastructure, the closure of old industrial plants and changes in agriculture. The age structure and/or lower education level, characteristic of almost all minority populations in comparison with the Slovak majority, have diminished opportunities for external support of development (new private investments) and possibilities for local initiatives from below.

2. The Legal Position and Political Participation of Minorities at the Central Level

While the importance of the national level cannot be underestimated in the protection of minorities, the role of the international environment has had an increasing impact in this field over the last decade. Of course, it is the domestic legal environment and political arena that are responsible for the formulation of a general framework of multi-ethnic co-existence both at the centre and locally. But processes related to globalisation and Slovakia's commitment to integrate into Euro-Atlantic structures, including the European Union and NATO, have greatly influenced domestic minority policies, not in the least for security reasons. The role of bilateral treaties concluded by Slovakia with her neighbours is very important from this perspective, since most minorities, with the notable exception of Ruthenians and the Roma, have kin-states in the region which act as advocates on behalf of their interests.

2.1. Constitutional guarantees

The Slovak Constitution guarantees the principal rights of minorities living in the Slovak Republic. The Slovak Constitution made great progress in granting rights unprecedented in Slovak history (Bakker 1997). A series of rights are mentioned explicitly: the use of minority languages is granted under Article 6 and shall be determined by law. Article 12 guarantees basic rights and liberties regardless of nationality or ethnic adherence and Articles 33 and 34 guarantee full development for minorities. These articles define the rights of minorities on the individual level, or as rights realised in groups.[12] While some

---

[11] Rare attempts to characterise the social and economic situation of the Hungarian minority in Slovakia is presented in: Bakker (1997) or Hunčík (1999).

[12] Šutaj and Olejník (1998) explain: 'The legal norms of the Slovak Republic aim at the protection of national minorities; however, they do not create a special mechanism for the protection of minorities. All rights of national minorities are guaranteed as individual rights'.

authors (Čič et al., 1997) interpret these articles as preferential approaches to minorities (regarding culture, access to information, associations, education and language), it must be noted that 'affirmative action' or 'positive discrimination' is not explicitly mentioned in the Slovak Constitution. Article 34 also protects the state's interests: minority rights guaranteed by the Constitution may not threaten the sovereignty and territorial integrity of the Slovak Republic or discriminate against other citizens. This wording is extremely problematic and can be easily used to restrict minority rights.

The main obstacle concerning constitutional provisions for minorities is the lack of subsequent legislation developing important rights declared in the Constitution. Article 34 is compromised by the phrase 'and shall be fixed by law'. While the Constitution can only be amended by a two-third majority of the Slovak Parliament, the indicated acts proscribed in its articles are susceptible to the whims of a simple majority. Although at first glance it appears to be a highly flexible mechanism, it also allows for a new round of political wrangling for minority rights protection in Parliament, systematic political fights over ethnic issues and disputes with the state administration. From 1994 to 1998, minority rights were actively undermined in Slovakia. Many constitutional principles were not implemented. There is a some chance that the new constitution being drafted in 1999-2000 will also redress the mentioned deficiencies concerning minority rights.[13]

2.2. Participation at the central level

The size of a minority and its ability to mobilise its resources during parliamentary elections is strongly related to its political influence at the national level. The ability to exercise political influence depends largely on surpassing the 5% threshold for any political party to gain representation in the Slovak Parliament since the Slovak Electoral Law does not contain any special provisions for the representation of minorities in the Slovak Parliament. Under this Electoral Law, only Hungarians (given their size and degree of political mobilisation) have been represented in the Parliament. The Roma minority is active but fragmented and, in spite of its large size, cannot actively participate in and influence decision-making at the central level. For other minorities, the political participation of their members is not based solely on ethnicity. Many minority citizens are members of nonminority parties. These minorities' interests are negotiated with political parties through cultural associations and organisations, a phenomenon more applicable locally than nationally.

2.2.1. Hungarians

Since the beginning of the post-communist transition, several parties have emerged to represent Hungarians. They include the national-liberal party, Co-existence (Spolužitie), the liberal Hungarian Civic Party (Maďarská občianska strana or MOS) and the conservative Hungarian Christian Democrat Movement (Maďarské kresťansko-demokratické hnutie or MKDH). Their position was originally strengthened by the dissident credentials of

---

[13] The approval of a new constitution of the Slovak Republic is one of the main aims of the coalition government ruling since 1998.

many of their leaders. The permanent presence of their members in the Slovak Parliament since 1990 documents the solid popular support of these parties. To increase their influence in the Slovak political arena, these three parties formed a coalition before the 1994 general elections. This coalition was then turned into a single political party—the Hungarian Coalition Party (Strana Madarskej Koalicie—SMK). They receive about 10% of the total national votes in each parliamentary election, consolidating their position as legitimate political representatives of the Hungarian minority. Following the 1998 elections, the SMK entered into a coalition with its rivals, thus gaining the central government posts of Vice Prime Minister, Minister of Environment and Minister of Construction and Public Works. The Hungarian Coalition defined co-operation as its priority. Its success is due to the precise definition of minority interests and responsive leaders. This pragmatic strategy needs to be replicated among other minority communities. Owing to the importance of the coalition-building process in Slovak political life, Hungarian political representation is influential and the Hungarian party is attractive as a coalition partner. The presence and lobbying of Hungarian politicians in the central government provides opportunities for the establishment of an improved local-level co-existence framework that benefits all minorities. However, it is important to note that, despite being part of the governing coalition, Hungarian politicians face difficulties in fulfilling their primary policy goals related to the use of the mother tongue in public, the establishment of higher level education in the mother tongue and the granting of special status to regions where Hungarians live in a majority (including the ratification of the European Charter for Regional or Minority Languages, changes in the Constitution, territorial-administrative division, etc.).

2.2.2. Roma

The Roma minority has not had representatives in the Slovak Parliament or in any central government since 1989. Its political representation is poorly organised, fragmented and burdened by unco-operative political leaders and numerous political ideologies. The Roma Civic Initiative (Rómska Občianska Iniciatíva or ROI) was created immediately after 1989. Though the most influential Roma political party, ROI achieved only very marginal political results. It also sought support from the Mečiar administration (Drozd 1998) and therefore has been somewhat discredited. A more critical voice was founded in 1996— the Roma Intelligentsia for Co-existence (Rómska inteligencia za spolunažívanie), or RIS. The RIS has preferred democratic political elements and has gained more influence since the 1998 elections. Until the Roma build a coalition, or one party succeeds in garnering votes from other ethnic groups (unlikely given the negative stereotypes of the Roma that pervade the Slovak population at large), they will not be able to capitalise on opportunities for minority participation under current rules for entering Parliament. Even a small parliamentary presence would give the Roma important negotiating and coalition-building power on a national scope.

Until now, Roma parties have lacked the ability to mobilise support among their own constituencies, have failed to clearly formulate or articulate their interests to their own communities and have not built the trust necessary for real political leadership. Despite the poor performance of Roma parties, they remain *the* representatives of the Roma minority. The consequence of this situation has been that various Roma political groups have attempted to affiliate themselves with the main political parties. The Hungarian Coalition has been the most receptive to Roma interests. They fielded four Roma candidates for the 1998 parliamentary elections, though none were elected. Representatives of the Roma community have made inroads into the state administration (Office of the Prime Minister, Ministry of Culture, Ministry of Education). A Roma representative was nominated to the Office of the Plenipotentiary of the Government for Solving the Problems of Roma Minority in 1999 (V. Danihel). Roma parties must address their ability to co-operate, organise, formulate problems and strategies, negotiate and communicate. The last attempt to form a large Roma political block was the signing of an agreement on joint electoral program by 14 Roma political parties and 29 Roma nongovernmental organisations, with the aim to gain seats in the next parliamentary elections for Roma political representation. This initiative has yet to be tested by political praxis.[14]

2.3. The international environment and bilateral treaties

Article 11 of the Slovak Constitution emphasises that 'international treaties in regard to human rights and liberties, ratified by the Slovak Republic, have precedence over its laws if they secure a greater range of basic rights and liberties'. This measure gives an appropriate role to any international document. The most important binding international document is the Framework Convention for the Protection of National Minorities, signed and ratified by Slovakia in 1995. A positive shift influencing the role of local governments was the ratification of the European Charter of Local Authorities in 1999. It is also expected that the European Charter for Regional or Minority Languages will be ratified during this electoral period. Nevertheless, various deficiencies mentioned in this chapter prove that the integration of international documents into domestic Slovak law has yet to be completed.

A crucial positive step in Slovakia's bilateral relations was the signing of the bilateral treaty with Hungary in 1995.[15] The treaty has some problematic aspects, however (despite the above mentioned constitutional commitment). For example, Article 15 says that the Contracting Parties should respect Recommendation 1201 of the Council of Europe. Critical Article 11 of the Recommendation has never been fully respected by Slovak legislation.[16] It was considered as an expression of the Hungarian minority's aspirations for territorial autonomy and evoked memories of the revision of Slovak boundaries in 1938.

International organisations have played a significant role in the accommodation and resolution of ethnic conflicts, especially during the Mečiar government, and they sys-

---

[14] Kotian (2000).

[15] The Treaty of Good Neighbourliness and Friendly Co-operation between the Slovak Republic and the Republic of Hungary.

[16] Article 11 of Recommendation 1201: 'In the regions where they are in a majority the persons belonging to a national minority shall have the right to have at their disposal appropriate local or autonomous authorities or to have a special status, matching the specific historical and territorial situation and in accordance with the domestic legislation of the state'. For more details in Slovak-Hungarian context, see: e.g. Sándor (1996), Olejník and Šutaj (1998).

tematically monitored the situation, identified key problems, evaluated relevant legislation and mitigated inter-ethnic conflicts by raising public awareness. The most active participant has been the OSCE High Commissioner for National Minorities. Thus far, the international pressure has been only partially successful (for example, in leading to the modification of the administrative reform process and more systematic approaches toward improving the position of Roma). By increasing activities related to European integration, the role of various EU institutions is rapidly growing.

3. Central – Local Relations and Local Initiatives Addressing Minorities

The role of local public administration in addressing minority issues depends on the overall structure of state government and the dynamics of central-local relations. This section addresses a series of important political issues concerning the position of minorities in Slovakia that has come to the forefront of debates about local government. Among the many issues relevant to minority interests, the most highly debated have been:
· the Local Electoral Act and its amendments,
· territorial-administrative division and the reform of state administration,
· the Act on the Use of Minority Languages, combined with its effect on the official state language,
· alternative schooling and requirements to study the official state language.

These debates have reflected the attempts of the 1994-1998 governing coalition to intervene into the lives of minorities at the local level, to change principles of local government and to dissolve local government functions serving minority communities. These attempts brought about the strong criticism of the domestic political opposition—particularly the Hungarian parties—and were partially responsible for the political disqualification of Slovakia as a European Union accession country in the first round. At the December 1997 EU summit meeting in Luxembourg, the Slovak Republic was moved from the first to the second wave of applicant countries.

3.1. The dual model of local public administration

The Slovak Republic adopted a dual model of public administration after 1989. This consists of two separate entities: (1) the local government and (2) the state administration. Local governments operate in each village and city. District and regional state administration consists of district and regional offices for general state administration, as well as several offices directly under the control of various ministries (for example, tax and custom offices). Selected sections of administration with specific functions were transferred to public self-governing bodies and/or underwent a process of 'de-etatisation' during the last decade. Bearing in mind problems of post-communist transition, the most important institution has been the National Labour Office (NUP), with nationwide networks of district labour offices (see Figure 1). Responsibility for the majority of Slovakia's technical infrastructure is still under the control of state monopolies (electricity, gas, water and sewage).

Figure 1. *Basic Model of Local Public Administration in Slovakia (since 1996)*

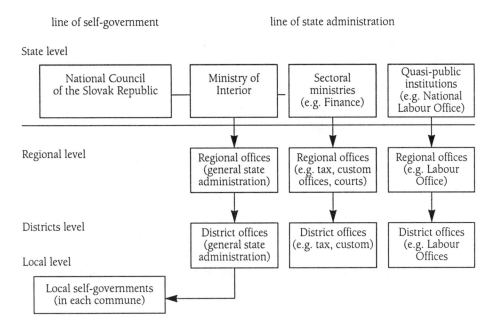

line of self-government   line of state administration

3.2. Local public administration: structure and competencies

The scope of decentralisation and the territorial distribution of minorities are two major factors that influence the efficiency of local government in addressing minority needs. During the first phase of public administration reform—from 1990 to 1993—the tendency of decentralisation of power and competencies to the local level prevailed. The following phase (from 1994 to 1998) was characterised by the strengthening of the state administration, deconcentration and the marginalisation of minority issues.[17] Their limited degree of power has prevented local self-governments from playing a more influential role in satisfying minority needs. Local governments are the main actor in the administration of certain local matters, but usually play a role in all areas of local life. District and regional state administration offices are responsible for many important competencies relevant to minorities (including nearly all aspects of educational administration and planning at the primary and secondary levels,[18] health care and social security), as well as financing from the state budget (See Table 6). Local state administration can only act

---

[17] The most visible proof of the predominance of deconcentration is the introduction of the new regional state administration and the postponement of the introduction of regional self-governmental institutions.

[18] The state administration has nearly complete legal authority over the school curriculum, the payment of teachers and building maintenance of public schools. There is some space, however, for

strictly within the law, and it is too dependent on central level guidelines. Furthermore, it suffers from a lack of opportunities to initiate specific or innovative approaches toward minority issues.

The most important asset of local governments is the degree of autonomy they are granted.[19] Local governments are legal entities that, according to the law, administer their own property and their own financial resources.[20] Local autonomy is therefore protected by law, and municipalities can only be given duties and set limits by acts approved by the Parliament. The right to approve local by-laws confirms the right for initiatives. The best case documenting the potential strength of local autonomy was the local referendum in Štúrovo, realised in spite of strong opposition from the central government.[21] Local autonomy is only restricted in the sense that, if local by-laws are in disagreement with the Slovak Constitution or valid legislature, they are overturned by the Constitutional Court.

The main failure of this arrangement is the limited degree of local financial autonomy. Its advantage has been confirmed in cases when local governments have adjusted previous local by-laws that limited minority rights. Attempts were made, for example, to refuse incoming Roma the right to settle down in the city of Jelšava, and local by-laws in Ňagov and Rokytovce (communes in eastern Slovakia) banned Roma from entering their municipalities.[22] The importance of constitutional and legal guarantees for local public administration that aim to meet minority needs is well documented in the 'Komárno Document'.[23] This document stresses the need for more extensive decentralisation, including: the transfer of powers that are important for minorities (in the fields of education, culture, public safety, health and environment) to the local level, the transfer of financial and material resources, and the right to use Hungarian in oral and written communication with public administration officials wherever Hungarians make up at least 10% of the population. Special status for the regions where Hungarians make up the majority is advocated.

---

activity on the part of local governments through local school boards on smaller issues such as small maintenance issues and personnel issues.

[19] The mentioned approach to local autonomy is inspired by Clark (1984), who emphasises two values: initiative and immunity.

[20] Although Slovak local self-governmental municipalities are defined as economically independent entities, in practice they depend on transfers from the annually approved state budget.

[21] The referendum in Štúrovo became a symbol of resistance against central government. The local self-government organised a local referendum that replaced the national referendum cancelled by V. Mečiar (on the direct election of the president, and on joining NATO). For details, see: Hrabko (1999).

[22] Bančanský (1999); SME (1998) 28 November.

[23] For more details on this very important document for the Hungarian minority in Slovakia in English, see: Bakker (1997). While part of this document was modified later, many of the declared conditions have remained among the main political goals of the parties representing the Hungarian minority.

Table 4. Distribution of Key Powers among Main Lines of Local Public Administration

Local self-government*	District and Regional State Administration** in:
General administration, Municipal enterprises and budgetary organisations	General internal administration, management of state property, public tendering and trade licensing, international co-operation, control
Administration of local taxes and fees, administration of own property	Fire protection, state defence, civil protection
Regulation of economic activities, local economic development	Small entrepreneurs, consumer protection
Planning documentation preparation and approval	Regional development and regional planning, strategy of regional development
Administration and maintenance of local roads and parking sites, public spaces, public green spaces, public lighting, market places, cemeteries	Education Primary schools, primary art schools (district) Secondary schools, secondary vocational schools, special schools, youth and sport
Waste collection and disposal, water supply, sewage and water cleaning stations, street cleaning, central heating	Environmental administration and protection, water management, territorial planning, construction order, waste management, landscape protection, air protection
Kindergartens, health ambulances, elementary day-care social services, personal services for elderly	Social affairs, social care, state social payments distribution, state social facilities network, co-operation with humanitarian institutions
Administration and operation of local cultural and social facilities, sport and leisure facilities	Culture—museums and galleries, regional and district libraries, cultural heritage protection
Support in the fields of education, historical heritage protection, cultural and art activities, sport	Health care administration, health centres, hospitals, clinics state veterinary care
Support of humanitarian activities	Transport and road management
Support of housing	Cadastral register and land ownership changes
Local police and fire brigades	Agriculture, forestry and hunting

* the scope of involvement of local self-government depends mostly on the size of the commune.

** competencies of general state administration without separated lines of state administration and quasi-public institutions with nationwide network (the most important is the National Labour Office).

Sources: Act No. 369/1990 the Communities Act; Act No. 222/1996 Coll. on Organisation of Local State Administration, Nemec et al. (2000).

3.3. The Local Election Act

Among the most important issues concerning minority groups has been the heated debate surrounding the drafting of a new Local Election Act. The Mečiar coalition government attempted to usurp civic principles with nationalist and ethnic principles in order to strengthen the role of its political affiliates in local elections and local policy-making. The

government often cited the insufficient representation of the Slovak minority in local councils in southern Slovakia in order to bolster and justify its efforts to guarantee better positions at the local level for its coalition member parties (Mečiar's Movement for Democratic
Slovakia, the Slovak National Party and the Association of Slovak Workers).

The new Local Election Act contained special measures for municipalities with ethnically heterogeneous populations. According to this Act, the number of local councilors
must be obligatorily distributed according to the ethnic composition of the population.
Minorities must be represented proportionally in localities where their share of the population exceeds 5% (and by at least one councilor). This system of proportional representation based on ethnic composition was highly criticised by municipal associations,
opposition parties and the OSCE High Commissioner for National Minorities, Max van
der Stoel. In their opinion, the new Act would prevent candidates for local councils from
having equal access to local seats. Under the Act, ethnic groups would have predetermined shares of seats on local councils, contributing to highly polarised elections and
removing opportunities for moderate party candidates. Further, this forced 'ethnicisation'
of local councils would reduce space for political compromise.

Another problem resulted from the fact that 'ethnic composition' was determined
according to the results of the 1991 Statistical Census, which were highly inaccurate.
Notably, a fair representation of the Roma minority could not have been achieved by this
mechanism as many Roma declared themselves as other nationalities during the census.

The Local Election Act (No. 302/1998) was approved by the Mečiar coalition before
parliamentary elections in 1998, in spite of strong protests by opposition parties and
organisations representing Slovakia's communes and cities. This act was never applied,
however, thanks to the decision of the Constitutional Court, which declared several of
the Act's articles unconstitutional, and because of the change of government after the 1998
elections.[24] The consequence of this development has been that all local elections since
1990 have been conducted according to almost identical legal regulations. Their most
typical features have been the majority principle, the direct election of mayors, the use of
'multimember constituencies'[25] in the election of local councilors and greater opportunities for independent candidates to compete.

3.4. Representation of minorities in local public administration

The representation of minorities in local public administration opens opportunities for
more effective participation and a stronger influence in decision-making. Local governments also offer a useful platform for the solution of minority problems: the local level is
generally more sensitive to minority needs and is more likely to understand the dynamics of local inter-ethnic relations better than central government officials.

---

[24] The new parliamentary majority of the former opposition amended this Act immediately following the elections.

[25] Larger communes are divided into several multi-member constituencies, for which a certain number of council seats are allocated.

Despite the absence of precise information on minority representation in state administration, it seems that the participation of the Hungarian Coalition in the central government has led to wider participation of Hungarians in both regional and district state administration. Members of the Hungarian minority had limited access to higher positions in local state administration under the previous government, but this is changing.

The position of minorities in local self-governments can be examined through the local participation of their political parties. While the Hungarian minority has a long tradition of participation in local power, the Roma are only now strengthening their position step-by-step after a long history of disenfranchisement.

The 1990 elections offered a long-anticipated opportunity for parties representing minorities to gain political office. Three active Hungarian parties were successful and achieved good results. The total number of mayors representing the Hungarian minority during the first period of free local self-government was 164 (6% of a total of 2,727 mayors elected in Slovakia). The number of local Hungarian councilors elected was 4,052 (10.5% of a total number of elected councilors). Hungarian parties and their candidates also supported other candidates in many localities, notably those of VPN (Public Against Violence Movement), and independent forces that had pushed for democratic change. Roma parties were not nearly so successful and only gained two mayoral posts (0.07% of total mayors) and 88 local councilors (0.2% of total councilors).

Table 5 documents the results of two main minority communities in two consecutive local elections (1994 and 1998). The representation of the Hungarian minority is quite stable. The Roma minority remains strongly underrepresented, although its results have improved. Six candidates of the Roma Civic Initiative were elected mayors in 1998. A further two mayorships were also gained in coalition. The local elections of 1998 have provided several excellent examples of inter-ethnic co-existence. In Nové Zámky, the mayor is Hungarian even though Hungarians are in the minority in this town, while in Štúrovo, a town with a Hungarian population of over 70%, a Slovak mayor was elected. These candidates ran for office independently.

Table 5. Position of the Two Largest Minorities' Political Parties in Local Self-Government

Election	Minority	Mayors	Mayors** (in %)	Councillors	Councillors** (in %)
1990	Hungarian	164	6	4,052	10.5
	Roma	2	0.07	88	0.2
1994	Hungarian	249	8.9	4,404	12.5
	Roma	2	0.07	72	0.2
1998	Hungarian	227+25*	8.7	3,841+324*	11.8
	Roma	6+2*	0.3	100	0.3

* elected candidates of minority parties plus candidates of coalitions with minority parties.

** percentages in comparison to the total number of mayors/councilors elected in Slovakia.

Source: Statistical Office of the Slovak Republic (1990, 1994, 1998). Local self-government election results.

3.5. Territorial division and public administration reform

The Slovak Parliament accepted new territorial divisions in 1996. Act No. 221/1996 on the Territorial and Administrative Division of the Slovak Republic introduced eight new regions and 79 districts. This reform only concerned state administration. Discussion of self-governance issues was postponed. The divisions were presented as a rational technocratic solution justified according to the standard of 'economic viability', leaving plenty of room for gerrymandering against minorities and political opponents.

Pressure came from opposition parties, most notably the Hungarians, and international bodies to change or repeal the divisions.[26] Without question, the aim of this territorial-administrative re-division—that also intended to establish electoral districts within the new boundaries—was the fragmentation of the Hungarian ethnic minority. Hungarian regions have been divided in such a way that the number of primary and secondary administrative regions with a Hungarian majority or a Hungarian population share of more than 20% has diminished drastically.[27]

Carrying forward the process of public administration reform—including new regional divisions—has continued to be a major aim of the new government. In the present stage of political development, power-sharing is generally accepted at the local level, but there is a reluctance to apply full-scale power-sharing at the regional level (in regions with more than 50% Hungarian inhabitants). One of the potential outcomes of the debates on territorial division is the acceptance of more regions with greater than 20% minority populations, combined with an extended minority rights framework at the regional level. This could improve the position of the minority population and its representation, preserve the rationale of the regional division (its multi-criterion principle) and prevent the instinctive majority fear of potential minority secessionist movements.[28]

3.6. Communication and co-operation

Communication and co-operation with minorities in local life are needed even in the case of their absence in locally elected bodies. They can be improved by using minority self-governing institutions, local minority political party organisations and activists, and traditional leaders.

In some localities, these links were developed with Roma communities, their main goal being improved communication between the minority and the local authorities (e.g. in the

---

[26] Under the original proposal, e.g. Nové Zámky district, having a Hungarian numerical majority, should have been split into three new districts (Krivý 1997). Finally, the administrative boundaries of the districts with the highest share of Hungarian minority were not changed (e.g. Dunajská Streda, Komárno, Nové Zámky).

[27] For details of the 1996 administrative territorial division, see: e.g. Bakker, 1997.

[28] Nevertheless, Slovak representatives should respect Recommendation 1201 of the Parliamentary Assembly of the Council of Europe and the Framework Convention for the Protection of National Minorities and avoid territorial changes that change share of ethnic minorities in administrative units. For details on international aspects of territorial administrative changes, see: Kusý (2000).

towns of Prievidza, Michalovce, Žarnovica).[29] The formation of local Roma minority self-governments depends on local conditions and is not always successful. The main obstacle to their establishment is the internally divided local Roma community and the undifferentiated, untapped human potential that makes the creation of a political class very difficult.[30] Local minority organisations are usually informal, depending on the presence of local activists and natural leaders. Their legitimacy can easily be challenged—by the minority community itself and by other local actors. Attempts to use traditional Roma leaders (vajda) for this purpose face similar difficulties. The traditional organisation of the Roma community has often dissolved and the size of many local Roma communities is often too big for monocratic control by one leader. Some representatives of the Roma minority at the local level are self-elected (political party activists, natural leaders), with respected positions as part of the local minority community. They serve as consultants in the articulation of local minority community needs to local institutions. They become regular members of various special committees in local public administration and organise the participation of the minority communities in local life. A similar initiative is the establishment of the District Roma Council in Kežmarok district (eastern Slovakia).[31] Functioning communication links and co-operation with local administration prevents conflicts and the worsening of Roma living conditions (but is still missing in many localities).

Case Study 1. Participation, co-operation and communication

The issue: What are effective tools leading to effective co-operation and communication with the local Roma community.

The actors involved: Mayor of Zbudské Dlhé, traditional Roma leaders (vajda), local councilors

The issue proceeding and strategy: This is the case of Zbudské Dlhé, a small village in eastern Slovakia (Humenné district), with a majority of the Roma population (57%) living in their own settlement. There are five Roma local councilors out of a total of twelve. This official line of co-operation is multiplied by the activity of the vadja (a nonmember of the local council). He is in regular direct contact with the mayor, informing her of the Roma community's needs and problems. The most pressing of these problems is that the entire Roma settlement is served by a single well, and therefore receives poor quality water.

The results: The participation of Roma in local self-government and the regular communication with the vajda has improved their participation in all spheres of local life. Roma co-operate in local voluntary work projects, as well as in local cultural festivities (having their own music group). But the most important achievement is that one of the local self-governments' priorities is to finish the construction of a water-pipe system and an access road leading to the Roma settlement.

---

[29] *SME* (1996) 7 December; Piecka (1999).

[30] As it is confirmed in the Project Svinia's case. This project is supported by the Canadian government and other western organisations. Despite of its successes in other fields, the attempts to form a well-functioning Roma self-government have faced difficulties. See: Borszék (1998); *Hospodárske noviny* (1999) 8 June.

[31] *Pravda* (2000) 24 January.

Lesson: A series of links can be used for effective co-operation with minorities, for their full integration in all spheres of local life. Official structures of local self-government together with
effective traditional leaders can create efficient ways to address Roma problems.
Source: J. Hrubovčák (2000) 'S Rómami nemáme ziadne problémy' (We have no problems with
the Roma), *Obecné Noviny*, No. 3, p. 20.

Table 6. Main Sources of Income of Local Self-Government in 1996

Item	SKK (Millions)	Per cent of Local Budget
Tax incomes	10,163.1	39.9
Shared taxes	5,857.3	23.0
Local taxes (real estate tax)	2,878.9	11.3
Other (local fees, road tax)	1,426.9	5.6
Non-tax incomes	8,992.6	35.4
Own property, entrepreneurial activities	633.8	2.5
Administrative fees	1,370.1	5.4
Capital incomes	2,265.9	8.9
Other non-tax	4,722.8	18.6
Central grants	3,608.7	14.2
General grants	1,377.4	5.4
Capital grants	2,231.3	8.8
Incomes from credits and borrowing payments, sold shares	93.8	0.4
Credits received	2,565.7	10.1
Total Incomes	25,423.9	100

Source: According to Berčík (1998).

3.7. Local finances

Finances hinder local governments' attempts to play an active role with respect to minority issues. Two aspects of local finances are important to consider: (1) financial autonomy, and (2) resources available for activities aimed at and fulfilling minority rights and
needs. Limited local tax revenue (real estate tax) and local fees collection (maximum limits defined by law) have hampered local attempts to generate revenue. Municipalities are
strongly dependent on shared taxes and specific grant transfers from the state budget.
Resources from suitable municipal property management are available only for larger
localities. This serves as a substantial barrier against more active local self-government in
the area of minority relations.

The worst financial situation is found in small communes. A large percentage of their
expenditures go to operational costs rather than to programs and initiatives that address
community issues. Minority groups are especially concentrated in such small communes.

Financial scarcity at the local level quite simply limits good intentions with respect to minority needs. More sophisticated co-operation between state and local administrations could help to solve this problem. Local state administration also suffers from a long-term lack of financial resources in the most sensitive areas for minorities: education, culture and health. These strained resources inhibit chances for experiments and new approaches to local government.

3.8. Education and use of minority languages

Issues of education and mother-tongue instruction are the two primary concerns of minority groups. They directly influence the protection and survival of minority languages and cultures, and serve as a basis for group identity formation. Major issues related to minority schooling are available levels of mother-tongue education (kindergarten, elementary, secondary, university level), the number of subjects offered in minority languages (all subjects, selected subjects), minority teacher training and the existence and accessibility of school facilities. On the other hand, good teaching in the Slovak language, suitable for minority school students, is also a crucial factor contributing to the social and economic advancement of minorities.

3.8.1. The school system serving minorities

The Hungarian and Ukrainian minorities have well-developed and stable networks of kindergartens and elementary schools.[32] The Hungarian minority also has a network of secondary schools with various vocational trainings. In addition, Slovakia has a strong tradition of mixed schools, hosting classes 'under one roof' with both Slovak- and minority-language instruction. The network of Ukrainian schools also constitutes a 'good practice': in addition to the schools presented in Table 8, there were 26 schools hosting 74 classes in which Ukrainian was the language of instruction in 1996-97.[33] The teaching of the Ruthenian language as a mother tongue was accepted as of the 1997-98 school year (the written form of the Ruthenian language was constituted in 1995), but was instituted only in seven schools (eight classes with 66 pupils), reflecting the lower interest of parents in Ruthenian-language education.[34] The future expansion of schooling in this language will be supported by the Ruthenian Department established at Prešov University in 1999.[35]

The miserable level of education among the Roma minority group is one of the major factors contributing to the group's gritty social and economic position. Roma children are educated in Slovak, despite the fact that they live within their own linguistic community (or combine the Romany language with other local languages). Their basic right to be educated in their mother tongue is not fulfilled. Roma children are generally unsuccessful in

---

[32] The number of kindergartens decreased as a consequence of the economic transformation after 1989. The number of schools serving minorities have increased, with the exception of the schools with Ukrainian-language instruction. See: Gabzilová (1994).

[33] According to information of UIP MS SR (1998).

[34] According to UIP MŠ SR (1997).

[35] SME (1999) 20 April.

school and are considered 'backward'.[36] There is no network of education facilities in the Romany language and there are insufficient capacities and resources (prepared teachers, full collection of teaching materials) to establish such a network at the present time.

Two successful policy initiatives aimed at the improvement of Roma education are currently being expanded: (1) the preparation of Roma children in so-called 'zero' classes or in kindergartens, and (2) the introduction of teacher assistants for Roma children in some classes with a higher proportion of Roma pupils. These initiatives have been combined with afternoon centres for children (and their mothers). In the past few years, many local councils have decided to support local kindergartens in their effort to prepare Roma children for Slovak schools. Both mixed and entirely Roma kindergartens function in various municipalities. Schools serve as centres for the delivery of public goods (e.g. hygiene, health, school lunches) and as training centres for future employment.

Table 7. Structure of Local Self-Government Expenditures (1996)

Expenditure	SKK (Millions)	Per cent
Economy	3,547.7	15.3
from this: transport	2,346.1	10.1
Banking operations and technical services	2,518.6	10.9
Education	131.5	0.6
Sport	397.0	1.7
Culture	1,076.4	4.6
Housing	5,232.4	22.6
Health	200.3	0.9
Local services	2,227.0	9.6
Social security	392.3	1.7
Environment	1,385.7	6.0
Other social services	103.0	0.4
Security	487.9	2.1
Administration	5,014.7	21.7
Other	439.2	1.9
Total	23153.7	100

Source: According to Berčík (1998).

The main centres for university-level, minority-language studies and teacher training are Comenius University, the University of Constantine the Philosopher in Nitra (including a Department of Roma Culture and an affiliate in the Spiš region) and Prešov University. The Hungarian minority's attempts to establish university-level education in the Hungarian language have not yet been realised. In Komárno and Kráľovský Chlmec, 'city universities' were established at the initiative of the local governments, with the participation of universities based in Hungary. Their legal status is not fully recognised and the Ministry

---

[36] Magdolenová (1998).

of Education vigorously opposed their establishment during the 1994-1998 period. In 1998 Comenius University offered talented Roma minority students the opportunity to apply for places reserved exclusively for them. This type of 'positive action' was more or less a gesture of goodwill without success. There is an outstanding need for more elaborated and complex initiatives to increase the number of Roma university applicants. In 1998, only two Roma students attended the biggest Slovak higher education institution—Comenius University—according to the Foundation 'InfoRoma'.[37]

Table 8. School Network According to Minority Language of Teaching in 1997

	Hungarian	Ukrainian	Slovak and Hungarian	Slovak and Ukrainian	German
Kindergartens	283	35	104	3	1
Elementary	274	8	30	1	0
Grammar	14	1	8	0	0
Secondary vocational	5	0	20	1	0
Secodary vocational apprentice training	6	0	26	0	0

Source: Statistical Yearbook of the Slovak Republic (1998).

3.8.2. Disputes over education in minority-languages

The most sensitive issues in the field of education have been attempts to introduce the so-called 'alternative schooling' model and to cancel bilingual certificates in schools with Hungarian-language instruction. According to the alternative schooling model, some of the subjects (e.g. history, geography) had to be taught exclusively in Slovak. The main argument for this provision was the need for the improvement of minorities' proficiency in Slovak. The Hungarian political parties and other Hungarian institutions, such as the Association of Hungarian Teachers, with the broad support of parents, opposed this initiative as a blatantly assimilationist policy. Alternative schooling was applied only in a very small number of schools and it was not successful. An initiative requiring that only Slovak teachers can teach Slovak-language classes in Hungarian-language schools was similarly unsuccessful.

The decision to replace bilingual study certificates with certificates only in Slovak (as a result of the 1995 Act on State Language) also caused great commotion. Bilingual certificates had been issued since 1921 and have important symbolic value. In spite of the state administration's decision, some schools did not stop delivering bilingual study certificates, and in other schools students refused to accept study certificates in Slovak. Teachers and parents organised protests and submitted petitions and, as a result, some teachers and school directors were fired and others received reduced salaries. The conflict was fully resolved in 1999 by returning to official bilingual certificates.

---

[37] *SME* (1998) 15 April.

It should be noted that these initiatives were combined with legislation that strengthened the role of state administration in managing schools. School directors were granted only very limited powers, depending in most matters on the approval of the state administration. Parents' associations and local self-governments served only in consultative positions. The state administration used its new rights to remove school directors from office if they opposed these policies or refused to implement them. The situation was reversed in November 1999, when a new Act[38] balanced the position of the state administration and self-governing institutions in education. Reconstructed school councils now act as powerful self-governing institutions working at each school and in district and in regional offices. The councils have advisory status and the right to initiate new programmes. These councils represent the interests of parents, local self-governments and teachers in the fields of the quality of education, personnel issues, facility-use and future development. School activities can therefore be modified according to local needs and serve as important local community centres.

Case Study 2. Slovak as a Second Language

The problem: Improvement of Slovak teaching in schools with Hungarian language of instruction
The actors involved: Two Hungarian teachers (Rózsa Skabela, Irén Bóna), 'Foundation Forum' (later the 'Forum Institute'—a Hungarian organisation)
The issue proceeding: One of the best examples of initiatives in the field of minority schooling is the introduction of the innovative Skabela-Bóna method for the teaching of Slovak in Hungarian-language schools. This was the best response to the Mečiar government's assimilationist tendencies and the Ministry of Education's attempts to introduce alternative schooling that would have meant teaching of selected subjects in Slovak instead of Hungarian. One of the most often cited reasons for these measures was Hungarian students' poor knowledge of the Slovak language limited their chances for success in public life. Two Hungarian teachers developed a new, more efficient and modern method of teaching Slovak in Hungarian schools. This initiative attracted the attention of the Foundation Forum (later Forum Institute) and received basic support from it. After the method's final elaboration, due to its good references, Forum Institute took over also the management of its dissemination.
The result: In the first, experimental stage the method was introduced in 20 schools, and in four years this number raised at 260. This meant teacher training and delivery of four years' complete teaching materials for 20,000 pupils. This initiative grew into a massive movement for substantial modernisation, and was instituted in the majority of Hungarian schools. This program was elaborated without the support of the 1994-1998 Ministry of Education, although it was fully in agreement with the Ministry'original aims for more communicative teaching of Slovak in minority schools. Enormous work was conducted without state support—largely on a volunteer basis. Only in November 1998, after the change of government, did the Ministry of Education offer its official support for this initiative. This program will continue with state support and a full range of applications in schools. The highly constructive and responsive approach of the Hungarian teachers' representatives, combined with third sector support, documents one of the best cases of dealing with existing problems and interest for good co-existence.

---

[38] Act on State Administration in Education and School Self-Government

Source: Based on a speech of Károly Tóth, director of Forum Institute, Dunajská Streda, delivered at a seminar in the presence of Milan Ftáčnik, Minister of Education of the Slovak Republic and László Szigeti, State Secretary of Ministry of Education of the Slovak Republic, Komárno, 28 Nov. 1998.

3.8.3. Use of minority languages

The Act on the Use of Minority Languages was not adopted until 1999, in spite of repeated requests by minority groups, international pressure and the promises of the central government. To the contrary, Mečiar's government approved a new Act on State Language of the Slovak Republic (valid since 1996) under the pressure of its nationalist, right-wing coalition partners. This Act replaced the earlier Act on Official Languages, which allowed the use of minority languages in official matters. The new Act limited the use of minority languages in many fields (in public administration, minority media and education). After intense international protests, the governing coalition was urged to prepare legislation on the use of minority languages. At the end of 1997, however, the government proclaimed openly that the existing legal framework was sufficient for the regulation of the use of minority languages. Many local self-governments in southern Slovakia responded to the restriction in the use of Hungarian by applying Article 34 (see Section 2.1) of the Slovak Constitution. They adopted their own by-laws allowing the use of Hungarian in official conduct. One example is the city of Samorin, where the city council adopted measures according to which citizens have the right to use either Hungarian or Slovak in public.[39] A similar approach was adopted by approximately 40 other local governments.

3.9. Central – local co-operation in public works

The organisation of local public works is an example of good co-operation in the field of employment between the state administration and local governments. This co-operation was a reaction to high levels of local unemployment and was especially suitable for the Roma minority. Unemployment among the Roma has been estimated at 90%, and in many local communities it is 100%. Attempts to improve this situation have been limited by informal discrimination in the labour market.[40]

Many local governments formed working groups with unemployed people. In some cases these groups were composed entirely of Roma and their leaders were also Roma. Public works were largely financed by the National Labour Office and organised by local self-governments. The town of Trnava created eleven jobs for Roma residents in street cleaning and road maintenance. A similar approach was applied in the town of Kolárovo.[41] Unemployed people were frequently channelled into projects aimed at improving the local environment and infrastructure, including improvement works in Roma settlements.

---

[39] Sutaj and Olejnik (1998).

[40] *SME* (1998) 7 January; *Hospodárske Noviny* (1998) 17 December.

[41] Krajčovič (1997); Tóth (1998); see also case study on Kolárovo later in this section.

In spite of the limited number of jobs created in this way, public works provided selective support for the local Roma population. The project also helped improved relations between local governments and local Roma communities.

3.10. The social security system according to local needs

The state plays a major role in the social security sphere. Its competencies include direct state social support, such as family allowances; nationwide institutions, such as Social Insurance (pensions, sickness allowances); and the National Labour Office (support for unemployed). Social allowances constitute a substantial portion of the income of many Roma families. Approximately two-thirds of Slovak Roma live well below the national standard of living.[42] The general rules of the distribution of social allowances by the state administration cause some problems in targeting the specificity of particular minority communities. Social security allowances are easily accessible and allow the distribution of resources without actively motivating anyone to improve his or her personal situation.[43] Despite the existence of many types of social benefits, they are still not elaborated enough in addressing specific minority problems (e.g. housing).

Many local governments operate their own social support schemes. Due to the limited local resources, they are delivered occasionally, they cannot be obligatorily demanded and often they are distributed on a case-by-case approach. Local offices can be more flexible and successful when addressing families in trouble. As local self-governments can freely decide about the forms of delivering social benefits from the local budget, they often combine financial support with other forms of distribution (food, clothing). The main impediments to local self-governments playing a more active role are the scarcity of resources, narrow personnel capacities at local offices and the very large size of some minority communities needing support.[44]

A promising form of state social benefit delivery is the 'special recipient', developed in attempt to avoid misuse of social payments distributed by direct financial transfers (on alcohol, gambling).[45] This form allows the distribution of allowances through local self-governments (for covering selected basic expenditures, e.g. meals in schools, housing). The beneficiaries receive vouchers for buying specific goods and services (food, pharmaceuticals, etc.) in local shops. They receive the rest of the payments in cash. This co-operation between the local state administration, local self-governments and local businesses helps to stabilise the situation of many families. The deficiencies of these alternative forms of distribution are dependency on local services and the local price level. In some rele-

---

[42] In his interview. Čerňanská (1999).

[43] Some discrepancies in the Slovak social security system are outlined by Bodnárová (1999). It concerns, e.g. small difference between the official minimal wage and living minimum, easily accessible various forms of support, opportunities to combine various forms of social allowances, which altogether can be sufficient for Roma with lower living ambitions.

[44] We can hardly expect more active social approach from communes with hundreds of poor house holds under the present financial and personal capacities of local self-governments.

[45] For example,in Veľká Ida in eastern Slovakia (Štark, 1998).

vant cases, the monthly distribution of social payments should be reconsidered and distributed every week, as some households spend the received cash during the first few days after delivery, suffering throughout the rest of the period.[46]

3.11. Housing

For socio-economically deprived Roma households, it is almost impossible to meet their housing needs without external help. Roma—who own minimal property, are unemployed and live on social allowances—have minimal opportunities to save enough money or receive loans. The majority of these households are financially excluded from these possibilities and the standard financial options are not accessible to them (building societies, mortgages, etc.). The higher cost of housing that emerged following the deregulation of the real estate market has worsened the housing situation of the Roma. The pressure for their relocation or their voluntary retreat from expensive locations has lead to their concentration in marginal localities or unsuitable areas on the outskirts of towns and cities.[47]

The poor housing conditions and rapid population growth of the Roma have forced local self-governments to act (e.g. Lučenec, Martin, Spišká Nová Ves). The minimal local and state resources available have allowed for the construction of an insufficient number of new houses. They have consisted mainly of various forms of simple, smaller housing units, fulfilling basic housing standards. In order to satisfy Roma housing needs, inexpensive building materials have been used, as well as movable housing units or wooden houses. In some cases, these housing projects attempted to respect the specific needs of the Roma population, but in other cases new housing was not co-ordinated with local Roma requests and did not properly address the needs of the local community. For example, Roma in Čičava (in eastern Slovakia) were not satisfied with the new social housing in small cabins.[48] The most suitable technologies, forms of financing and the involvement of Roma are being developed only now.

Many local governments have developed projects for the improvement of the living environment in Roma settlements (including improved drinking water, sewage and gas). Communes can receive subsidies from the State Environmental Fund. Bringing these services to isolated Roma settlements is an extremely expensive investment. Nevertheless, the poor finances of local administration is used as an excuse to ignore the abysmal living conditions in some Roma settlements. Even simple, inexpensive solutions could improve their dismal standard of living (fixing roads and wells, collecting waste, improved access to public transport).

A further problem is the fact that Roma settlements were often built on land that did not belong to them, without building permission or planning documentation. Under such

---

[46] It could also diminish the role of Roma usurers. Poorer Roma households have problems with long-term planning of households expenditures, so they borrow money from usurers. They have to return this money after receiving social benefits.

[47] Some problems with relocations, segregation are outlined, e.g. in Říčan (1998).

[48] Pravda (1999) 14 August.

conditions, substantial improvement of these settlements is restricted by legal constraints. Issues of land ownership, planning and the depreciation of Roma housing facilities are sensitive issues among the majority population, which also suffers from housing shortages.

3.12. Cultural institutions

A number of minority cultural institutions (theatres and museums that often function as minority departments of Slovak institutions) are financed by the state through regional state administrations. The state also subsidises other important minority cultural institutions (cultural associations, media, cultural events). Between 1995 and 1998, state financing in this area stagnated, and in some cases many of these institutions did not receive already approved resources.[49] Local self-governments cover the costs of local cultural institutions like libraries and local museums. They also support local art groups, folk ensembles and cultural festivals, and create the possibility for different types of cultural activities. Many of the local cultural institutions are festering due to the poor condition of many local government budgets, but minority communities have their own cultural associations that oversee a wide range of activities.

The activities of local self-governments serve the needs of Slovaks and Hungarians in particular (these two groups usually form a majority in local councils and have a strong history of co-operating with local governments). Local self-governments and local activists can request state support for local cultural activities from the Pro-Slovakia Cultural Fund, but the resources of this state fund are very limited. In many ethnically heterogeneous communities, the cultural activities of all local groups receive support. One of the best cases of such local co-operation can be found in the town of Levoča and its local elementary art school, where talented Roma children study music, painting and drama. This initiative is also supported by foreign resources and provides good opportunities for Roma children to advance in education.

Case Study 3. Ruthenian Revival

The problem: Ruthenians suffered strong Ukrainisation under the communist regime. Ruthenians wanted to revitalise their identity through an association for cultural, educational and religious needs.

The actors involved: 'Ruthenian Revival' Association, Greek Catholic Church, World Congress of Ruthenians.

The issue proceeding: All Ruthenians were made Ukrainians by an official declaration in the late 1940s. Forced 'Ukrainisation' started in 1952 with massive state support for Ukrainian infrastructure. This policy led to the closure of the Ruthenian school network (almost 250 elementary schools), the banning of the Greek Catholic Church in favour of the Russian Orthodox Church, and collectivisation of agriculture. This solution was refused (i.e. Ruthenians turned to Slovak schools and the Roman Catholic Church). Miraculously, after almost 50 years, the

---

[49] According to: 'Správa k implementácii Rámcového dohovoru Rady Európy na ochranu národnostných menšín v Slovenskej republike za MK SR', 1999. In fact it was not stagnation. Due to inflation it was a remarkable decrease of state expenditures spent for minority culture.

small Ruthenian minority in Slovakia survived. Ruthenian-sponsored initiatives to improve their position have played a crucial role in supporting their interests and cultural associations, with the Ruthenian Revival Association as its key 'umbrella'. (Another organisation also formed in 1989 is the Association of Ruthenian Intelligentsia in Slovakia.) The Ruthenian Revival has its centre in Pre_ov; it has its own local and regional branches, especially in northeastern Slovakia. In Bratislavia, Ruthenian representatives develop wide-ranging activities in building the position of its minority in comparison to other minority communities in Slovakia. There are difficulties due to some conflicts with Ukrainian minority representatives.

The results: The Ruthenian Revival Association, in co-operation with other Ruthenian associations, strengthened the minority's position within Slovak society. They developed good ties with local government in their subsequent districts and municipalities. Their activities have helped the revival of Ruthenian identity in the whole of Central Europe, especially in the field of Ruthenian language. Ruthenians are represented in the Council of the Slovak Republic for National Minorities. Teaching in the Ruthenian language began again, as well as teachers' training. The Theatre of Alexander Duchnovìè (Divadlo Alexandra Duchnovìèa) began to give performances in Ruthenian. Slovak Public Television broadcast special programmes only in Ruthenian. The debate and initiatives in 1999-2000 address problems with broadcasting in Ruthenian on Slovak Radio (public) and Ruthenian as a liturgical language.

Source: 'Sixth Congress and Changes in Leadership of Ruthenian Revival' (1999) *Narodny Novinky* (in Ruthenian), No. 24-26, pp 1-2.

3.13. Nongovernmental organisations

A major source of support for minority groups has come from the 'third sector'. This sphere has attracted numerous active citizens, often dissatisfied with political developments and the political culture in Slovakia. They are sensitive to various local problems that have not been dealt with effectively, mostly due to the lack of resources and limited capacities of local administrations. The voluntary sector initiates various projects targeted at minority communities in the fields of education, culture and living environments, and uses resources from various donors. Local governments usually co-operate with these voluntary organisations and often co-finance third-sector projects in their localities, or offer other forms of support for their activities (office space, facilities, services, etc.).

4. Conclusions

4.1. Participation

Effective work to improve the situation of minority communities is not possible without the direct involvement of and co-operation with minority groups and their leaders. All policies that aim to address minority issues efficiently must be organised in co-operation with local authorities. Local public administration cannot operate in a schematic way without any sensitivity to specific local features.

More participatory forms of government at the local level should be applied that can lead to solutions acceptable for both minority and majority populations. Various formal and informal minority advisory bodies should co-operate with local public administration institutions, partly as a training field for future minority leaders. Local public administration should be able to co-operate and support multi-faceted activities with private and third-sector actors willing to act in favour of minorities.

4.2. Decentralisation and deconcentration

Because of its important role in meeting minority needs, the power, autonomy, financial base and personal capacities of local public administration must be expanded. Public administration reform should reduce the overly strong position of state administration. The regional level of government should be introduced and the administrative-territorial division rethought.

4.3. Local finances

Local self-governments should be given the freedom to make decisions without financial impediments so they can address minority issues. Expenditures can be controlled and directed to the relevant fields by local councils including fields also covered by the state administration. Municipal resources can be combined with private finances in the formation of new legal entities, and municipalities can combine their resources in various forms in intermunicipal associations.

4.4. Flexible local state administration

The competencies of local state administration must be organised in a more flexible and co-operative way. State administration should retreat from its bureaucratic and passive position, based on the uniform application of particular policies or the distribution of allowances to minorities through district offices, according to rules assigned by the central government. Suitable evaluation procedures should address project administration, creating opportunities for their correction and reshaping. The atmosphere of dependency in some minority communities, policies based on 'giving' and not on 'working together', should be revised. Local minority communities are diverse and are interested in different issues. The success of many policies depends on the identification of suitable participants and their will to participate.

4.5. Strong local self-government

A stronger role, more power and more resources should be granted to local self-governments. They can be more effective than state institutions and are better able to design locally appropriate social and housing policies. The selective, direct and deliverable distribution of social allowances requires decentralisation and reorganisation. Because this type of distribution depends on local information, local self-governments should play a much more active role.

4.6. Professionalism

In local public administration, a better trained staff would ideally cope with minority issues. They should be trained in communication, negotiation, developing and sustaining co-oper-ation with minority communities and their leaders, and in understanding the specific fea-tures and needs of minorities. Special training has to address local mayors and councilors representing minorities as well. The professional work addressing minority needs should include the preparation of high-quality strategies, as well as efficient administrative prac-tices. Special, better-aimed and well-designed programmes and allowances should be quick-ly implemented to address concrete needs (e.g. planned housing allowances).

4.7. The value of diversity

The various ethnic groups living in Slovakia should be better informed about each other's specific features, history, co-existence, rights and responsibilities within society. The school system should prepare specialists addressing minority problems at the local level (e.g. social workers, teachers, specialists in minority culture). Initiatives targeting Roma edu-cation should be reconsidered according to the interests of local Roma communities, including specific forms of adult training (both in Romany and Slovak languages).

4.8. Active employment policies

Local administrations should formulate their own strategies for 'equal employment oppor-tunities' in the public sector (including local bureaucracies and the police). The institu-tions of public administration and private companies should define fields for preferential treatment ('positive action') for particular minorities or should strictly respect the appli-cation of equal opportunities to improve the chances of minority population in employ-ment (including actions against discrimination in the labour market). Initiatives that penalise employers refusing to employ Roma and reward employers with a particular per-centage of Roma employees (for example, through lower taxation and better access to public contracts) should be considered.

　　The existence of an active employment policy based on co-operation between local self-governments and labour offices should be protected. More co-operation should be required between allowance givers and receivers in the local community, which can be organised effectively by local self-governments. The training of the unemployed for continuous employment should be organised according to local needs. A special fund for the support of Roma businesses should be created that could help to improve access to credit for Roma entrepreneurs and create workplaces for the Roma in particular regions and localities.

4.9. Contracting of municipal services

The contracting of municipal services and public projects to companies employing relatively high numbers of Roma workers provides a means of employment protection. In the private sector the support of Roma employment is limited and should be reconsidered. In the public sector the number of Roma employees in public administration should be increased, including offices responsible for the most sensitive issues for the Roma (social security, labour offices, health services and general public administration). Such a policy would improve communication and develop trust between minority and majority communities.

4.10. Land, ownership and living conditions

Public administration should initiate the clarification of the ownership rights over the land and housing of the Roma population. Planning documentation should be prepared especially for poorer settlements with the participation of local minority communities. The location of new Roma housing only in local, compact, built environments and discriminatory practices on the land and real estate market should be deterred. Housing problems, especially those of Roma households, can be solved only by combining the activities and resources of the state, local self-government and minority population (including self-help). Special programs should address isolated Roma settlements. Local self-government can play a crucial co-ordinating role in numerous activities addressing the living environment of minorities at the local level.

Further reading

Bačová, Viera (1996) Etnická identita a historické zmeny (Ethnic identity and historical changes), Bratislava: Veda.

Bakker, Edwin (1997) *Minority Conflicts in Slovakia and Hungary*, Capelle a/d Ijssel: Labyrinth Publications.

Brusis, Martin (1997) 'Ethnic Rift in the Context of Post-Communist Transformation: The Case of the Slovak Republic', *International Journal on Group Rights*, Vol. 5, No. 1, pp. 3-32.

Bordás, Sándor and Hunčík Péter (1999) *SPON–Systém prognózovania ohnísk nap%otia* (EWS - Early warning system), Dunajská Streda and Bratislava: Vydavateľstvo NAP Kiadó and Sándor Márai Foundation.

Hunčík, Peter (1999) 'Maďarská menšina ve Slovenské republice' (Hungarian minority in Slovak Republic), in: Gabal, Ivan et al., *Etnické menšiny ve střední Evropi* (Ethnic minorities in Central Europe), Praha: G plus G, pp. 204-218.

Kusý, Miroslav (1998) *Čo s našimi Maďarmi* (What about our Hungarians), Bratislava: Kalligram.

Mann, Arne B. (ed.) (1992) *Unknown Romanies*, Bratislava: Ister Science Press.

Mesežnikov, Grigorij, Michal Ivantyšyn and Tom Nicholson (eds.) (1999) *Slovakia 1998-1999. A Global Report on the State of Society*, Bratislava: Institute for Public Affairs.

Šutaj, Štefan and Milan Olejník (1998) 'Slovak Report', in: J. Kranz and H. Kupper (eds.) *Law and Practice of Central European Countries in the Field of National Minorities Protection after 1989.*,Warsaw: Center for International Relations, pp. 269-321.

Zeľová, Alena (ed.) (1994) *Etnické minority na Slovensku v procesoch sociálnych premien* (Ethnic minorities in Slovakia under the processes of social changes), Bratislava: Veda.

A State to Build, A Nation to Form:
Ethno-policy in Ukraine

Viktor Stepanenko

Contents

A State to Build, A Nation to Form:
Ethno-policy in Ukraine

Viktor Stepanenko

Abstract

This chapter will analyse relations between the Ukrainian state and ethnic groups living within its borders by looking at the strengths and weaknesses of the country's policy on minority issues. The Chapter will also attempt to recommend improvements in Ukrainian ethnic policy. Unlike most countries of Central and Eastern Europe, Ukraine does not have a stable and developed historical tradition of independent statehood, and thus it has a less clearly defined national identity than some of its neighbours. As a result, the process of democratic state-building is inextricably linked with the process of nation-building. The overlap of these two processes is the source of various political ambiguities, which have created a disadvantageous situation for certain minority groups.

The government's responses to recent challenges to its authority have produced several ambiguous policies. The fear of secessionist movements has significantly slowed down the reform of public administration decentralisation, as well as the introduction of self-governance at the local level. For example, some members of the Russian ethnic minority have perceived recent efforts to strengthen the status of Ukrainian as the official state language as being unfriendly to minorities and discriminatory against those seeking public work.

Meanwhile, a group of Crimean Tatars, most of whom are re-settling in Ukraine after past deportation to Uzbekistan, have become more politicised in response to their perception that the government is not doing enough for them. Tatars have complained that they have not received sufficient support in re-settling, and that the process of acquiring citizenship has excluded many of them from participation in elections.

Other minority issues need to be addressed in Ukraine as well, and they can probably be best handled at the local level. As this chapter will attempt to show, one of the greatest current weaknesses in Ukraine's existing policy on minorities is a centrist approach. By leaving local authorities with only limited funding and decision-making powers, the policy eliminates a potential effective tool for ensuring minority rights.

1. Introduction

1.1. The roots of ethnic diversity

In contrast to Russia and the majority of Central European and Baltic states, Ukraine does not possess a stable or developed historical tradition of independent statehood. Until now, Ukraine has only enjoyed two brief periods of independence in the modern era: for a few years after the Cossack rebellion of 1648, and under a succession of weak governments between 1917 and 1921.[1] Ukraine occupies a position on the border between Central and Eastern Europe and Russia. By virtue of this geographical location, and its historical development, the country is a crossroad of political, cultural, historical, ethnic and religious influences between the east (Russia) and west—and between the south (Turkey, the Balkans) and the north (the Baltics and Scandinavia).

One of the most important demographic features of Ukraine is its broad range of ethnic groups. There are more than 130 minority ethnic groups residing in the country, representing 28% of the total population. Thus, Ukraine accommodates a wide range of cultural, linguistic and religious diversity. According to the results of the 1989 census,[2] Ukraine's population is 51.4 million, of which Ukrainian nationals make up about 72% (37.4 million). Russians are the second major ethnic group, making up more than one-fifth of Ukraine's population (11.3 million).

Other major ethnic groups—each making up less than 1% of the population—include Jews, Belarussians, Moldovans, Crimean Tatars,[3] Bulgarians, Poles, Hungarians and Romanians. Minorities whose total population within Ukraine is between 50,000 and 100,000 consist of Greeks, Volga (or Kazan) Tatars, Armenians and Germans. Even smaller groups include the Roma, Gagauz, Georgian, Chuvash, Uzbek, Mordvin, Slovak, Czech, Bashkir, Latvian, Lithuanian and Estonian peoples. These groups represent an extremely colourful picture of linguistic, cultural and religious diversity. (See Table I.)

It should be stressed that ethnic Ukrainians themselves do not form a homogenous community. Their identity varies due to the diverse historical heritage of different parts of the country. Factors in variations of ethnic Ukrainians include:

---

[1] Taras Kuzio (1992) *Ukraine. The Unfinished Revolution,* London: Alliance Publishers, p. 7.

[2] Apart from the statistics on the Crimean Tatars all the data is from the latest 1989 Soviet census 'Natsional'nyi sostav naseleniia SSSR' (The national composition of the USSR) (1991) Moscow, Finansy i Statistika, pp. 134-136.

[3] According to the statistics of the State Committee for Nationalities of the ARC on 1 October 1996. See: Buznytsky et al. (1997) 'Stability and Integration in the Autonomous Republic of Crimea: The Role of International Community', Kiev: International Renaissance Foundation, pp. 10-11.

Table I. The Largest Ethnic Minorities in Ukraine and their Main Characteristics

Nationality	Number (in thousands) and per cent of total	Character of distribution (compact or dispersed)	Type of distribution (city or village)	Religion	Region(s) of living
Russians	11,355 (22.1%)	Dispersed, but regionally concentrated	More than 80 per cent live in cities and industrial regions	Russian Orthodox	East (Donbass), south, Crimea
Jews	486 (0.9%)	Dispersed	Overwhelming majority is urban population	Judaism	Cities and towns (Odessa, Kiev, Kharkiv, etc.)
Bela-russians	440 (0.8%)	Predominantly dispersed	Predominantly urban with a share of rural population	Greek Catholic/ Russian Orthodox	Rural popula-tion in north-west regions (Polissya and Volyn)
Moldovans	324 (0.6%)	Predominantly compact residence	Predominantly in rural areas	Orthodox	Southwest (Odessa region)
Crimean Tatars	260 (0.5%)	Compact residence	Predominantly in rural areas	Islam	Crimea
Bulgarians	233 (0.45%)	Compact residence	Predominantly in rural areas	Orthodox and Catholic	Southwest (Odessa and Kherson regions)
Poles	219 (0.4%)	Dispersed, but regionally concentrated	Predominantly in urban areas	Catholic	Northwest regions (Polissya and Volyn)
Hungarians	163 (0.3%)	Compact residence	Predominantly in rural areas	Catholic and Protestant	Trans-Carpathian region
Romanians	134.7 (0.26%)	Compact residence	Predominantly in rural areas	Orthodox	Bukovyna (Chernivtsi region)
Greeks	98.6 (0.19%)	Compact residence	Urban and rural population	Orthodox	South (Odessa, Zaporiszhya regions)
Germans	51 (0.10%)	Predominantly compact residence	Predominantly in rural areas	Protestant	South and Trans-Carpathian region
Roma	47.9 (0.09%)	Predominantly compact residence	Urban and rural population		Trans-Carpathian region and southeast

· The main polarities are the strongly nationalist-oriented western part of the coun-
  try, on the one hand, and the 'Russified' Southeast, on the other.
· The main language used in the Southeast, especially in the cities, is Russian, while
  Ukrainian is dominant in the western area.
· Divisions include the Ukrainian (Greek) Catholic Church, which has historically
  been dominant in the west; the Russian Orthodox Church; the Ukrainian
  Autocephalous Orthodox Church; and the Ukrainian Orthodox Church, which
  succeeded from the Moscow patriarchate in 1992.

It should be noted that, due to socio-political and cultural factors in the development
of a historically divided Ukrainian society, the political cultures of the eastern and western parts of the country are different. The eastern regions of the country accommodate a
large Russian population and traditions of Soviet-Russian administration are stronger,
whereas in the western regions, Ukrainians form the majority and a more liberal national consciousness has developed.

1.2. Socio-historical background

The roots of Ukrainian nationalism stem from the beginning of the 20TH century, when
Ukrainian intellectuals agitated for an independent state. The struggle for independence
succeeded in 1917, when the Bolshevik Revolution broke up the Russian Empire. Ukraine
had a brief and anarchic period of independence beginning in 1917, at which time the
Ukrainian People's Republic was proclaimed in Kiev. In 1918, the new state adopted the
law on national-personal autonomy,[4] which provided a legal avenue for ethnic minorities to establish their autonomies. These plans were never implemented, however, because
Ukraine was one of the first countries to be forcibly seized by Russia as the Bolsheviks
asserted their power. Successive political and military attempts to restore the independent status of Ukraine failed, and in 1922, most of Ukraine became part of the USSR as
one of Soviet republics. (Certain western parts of Ukraine did not join the USSR then,
because at that time they belonged to Poland, Romania and Czechoslovakia.)

From the late 1920s, the Soviet leadership repressed both the Ukrainian community
at large and its minorities. The Stalinist regime, claiming to pursue the political goals of
collectivisation and the struggle against a 'class enemy', created a deadly famine in
Ukraine—with the aim of crushing the independent peasantry and the last vestiges of
Ukrainian nationalism. More Ukrainians died during the 1932-33 man-made famine than
during the Second World War. From that time to the middle of the 1980s, the best representatives of the Ukrainian intelligentsia were assassinated or deported to Siberia on the
basis of political accusations of being 'bourgeois nationalists'.

Various ethnic groups were expelled from Ukraine to remote parts of Central Asia and
eastern regions of Russia. During and after the war, almost 450,000 ethnic Germans and
about 200,000 Crimean Tatars, as well as more than 38,000 Crimean Greeks, Bulgarians

---

[4] National-personal autonomy refers to the concept of self-government for minorities.

and Armenians,[5] were deported from eastern Ukraine to Central Asian regions of the USSR and Siberia. Under Nazi occupation during the war, Jewish and Roma minorities were exterminated en-masse in western Ukraine. In Babiy Yar, now part of Kiev, about 100,000 Jews, Roma and other people were assassinated by Nazis.

In the postwar period, nationality policy in Ukraine and the rest of the former Soviet Union was strongly centralised in the hands of the Communist Party apparatus. Despite the fact that the Ukrainians were the official titular nation and the prevailing ethnic majority in the former Ukrainian Soviet Socialist Republic, they, and other non-Russian nationalities, were subjected to 'internationalist policies'. The ultimate goal of these policies was the merger (*slijanie*) of different ethnic groups in order to form a new historical community of '*Soviet people*'. At the same time, social and political upward mobility in the Soviet Union was informally linked to ethnic origin. The famous fifth point of Soviet passports declared the ethnic origin of the bearer. Ethnicity was often the reason for hidden discrimination, particularly towards Jews. Typically, there was a traditional minority network in places with a high concentration of minorities—like Hungarian and Romanian schools in Trans-Carpathia, and Gagauz and Bulgarian schools in Odeska oblast. But educational policy during the postwar era served as the main tool in implementing 'internationalist policy'. During the postwar period, Russification severely impacted non-Russian Slavs, Ukrainians and Belarussians.

The declaration of an independent Ukrainian state in 1991, and the ratification of the Constitution in 1996, were the final steps in the quest for Ukrainian independence. In order to foster greater support for independent Ukraine among national and ethnic minorities, the Declaration on State Sovereignty of Ukraine, as well as the Declaration of the Rights of Nationalities of Ukraine (November 1991), included provisions to protect minority rights. Soon after, a Law on National Minorities in Ukraine (1992) was adopted.

During the first years of independence, Ukrainian lawmakers aimed at achieving broad support for statehood among the populace by adopting the concept of a '*civic nation*', which would include all citizens, regardless of their ethnic origin. In 1996, with the adoption of the new Constitution, came the ratification of the political and legal framework for development of the 'civic nation'. The constitution defines this concept as 'the Ukrainian people—citizens of Ukraine of all nationalities'.

2. Recent Policy Challenges

Ethnic policy in Ukraine faces three major challenges:
1. The issues of state decentralisation and territorial autonomy for minority groups. (This is especially important with regard to Crimean Autonomy and the rights of the Crimean Tatars.)
2. The linguistic rights of the Russian-speaking population of Ukraine.

---

[5] Y. Belukha (ed.) (1999) *Deportovani krymski tatary, bolgary, virmeny, greky, nimtsi. Zbirnyk dokumentiv (1941-1998)*, Kiev: Abris, p. 3.

3. Issues related to policy and legal provisions for immigrants and refugees coming
   into Ukraine.

These challenges set the stage for current state-ethnic relations in Ukraine, and determine the main trends in ethno-policy[6] and power-sharing. Ukrainian policy-makers view
these challenges in the context of the dilemma over political priority: the desire to create
an inclusive multi-ethnic state versus the desire to promote Ukrainian national identity.

The unresolved issue of state decentralisation—including the complex question of territorial autonomy for minority groups—demands territorial-administrative reform, along
with profound reforms in local government. These changes must include an alteration of
the traditional, strongly centralised model of policy-making. There is a need for institutionalised power-sharing that considers the interests of minorities as stake-holders. Such
a strategy corresponds to the model of an inclusive, multi-ethnic state.

The dilemma of Ukraine's task of nation-state building is also revealed in the unset-
tled problem of the language rights of the country's Russian-speaking population. The
problem has already generated dangerous tensions between central and local authorities.
One controversial case involved legal precedents for local governments' decisions on a
declaration of Russian as a second official local language, in the eastern Ukrainian localities of Kharkiv, Lugansk and Luganska oblast in 1998-1999.

The growing legal and socio-economic problems of refugees and immigrants, especially illegal immigrants, reveal the absence of a clearly elaborated state migration policy—as well as a lack of co-ordination between central and local authorities in dealing
with these issues. The limited autonomy of local self-governments means that local policy on immigrants and refugees is likely to be ineffective. Meanwhile, the central authorities demonstrate their inability in dealing with migrants' problems and in initiating real
political efforts on prevention of human trafficking at the international level.

2.1. The perspective on territorial autonomy

In the range of internationally recognised means for implementing special minority rights,
only the right to territorial autonomy is not provided under current Ukrainian legislation.[7] The ambitious proclamations of the Declaration of the Rights of Nationalities of
Ukraine of 1991, in which the Ukrainian state guaranteed 'the right of all nationalities to
preserving their traditional settlements' and promised 'to provide an existence of national administrative units', were not included in the Law on National Minorities (1992) or
in the 1996 Constitution.

Claims for various degrees of territorial autonomy by various ethnic groups living
in compact areas are apparently considered to be a threat to a unitary state in Ukraine.
From the state's perspective, the main problem with territorial autonomy is the absence

---

[6] Ethno-policy is a term used to refer policies towards national and ethnic minorities in Ukraine,
and does not include policies towards religious and other minorities.

[7] Crimea is not a case of *national territorial* autonomy; Crimean autonomy is based on the *administrative-territorial* principle.

of legislative guarantees to prevent the kind of separatism that could potentially threaten the country's territorial integrity.[8] In regions with compact national minorities, the issue of power decentralisation can be turned into a question of extending the minority's right of local self-governance to the point where it becomes a right to territorial autonomy. This is exactly the question that arose when voters initiated local referendums on autonomy.

Case Study 1. Territorial Autonomy

Issue: The right of ethnic minorities regarding territorial autonomy.

Subjects studied: 1) national organisations of ethnic Hungarians in Trans-Carpathia; 2) local self-governments of the Beregovskiy district and Zakarpatska (Trans-Carpathia) oblast—the Beregivskiy district council, the Zakarpatska oblast council; 3) the Ukrainian government.

Proceedings of the case: On 1 December 1991 a local referendum on the creation of the Hungarian autonomous unit in Beregivskiy district took place. A total of 82% of the voters supported the idea of autonomy. On 25 April 1992 a plenary meeting of the district council approved the draft of law 'On a Hungarian Autonomous Unit'. The central authorities simply ignored the referendum and the draft law that followed it. Since that time, the issue of a Hungarian autonomous unit has been repressed by the central government and kept out of the national media. However, the national organisations of ethnic Hungarians have not dropped the idea.

The issue of national territorial autonomy came up in the last elections, when some candidates said they favoured the idea. But given the current political climate in Ukraine, efforts aimed at the peaceful creation of national territorial autonomy seem unlikely to succeed.

Lessons: 1) Inconsistency in legislation and the lack of certainty with respect to minority rights can create dangerous tensions between local and central authorities. 2) The central authorities' strategy of simply ignoring the issue pushes the conflict into a latent stage. Such an approach can only further tensions and ensure that the issue does not disappear until it is appropriately addressed.

Sources: Mykhailo Tovt (1997) 'Problemy Ugorskoi natsionalnoi menshyny u suchasniy Ukraini' Kiev: Nova Polityka, Vol. 3, pp. 24-28; J. Marcsuk (1999) 'Az autonomia nem utopia', *Karpati Igaz Szo*, 26 June.

Local referendums in 1991—in the Bolgradskiy district of Odeska oblast and in the Beregivskiy district of the Zakarpatska oblast (Trans-Carpathia)—supported the idea of national territorial units in these areas. However, central authorities simply ignored the results of the local initiatives taken by ethnic minorities—Bulgarians and Gagauzes in the first case and Hungarians in the second. The contradiction between the promising Declaration of the Rights of Nationalities of 1991, which fed minorities' aspirations on territorial autonomy, and current legislation on minorities, which does not mention autonomy, may create a dangerous clash of rights and interests of different groups in Ukraine.

---

[8] Political decisions and practical measures on decentralisation in the exercise of state power in favour of extending a level of regional self-governance (while preserving state unity) is one of the most significant and problematic issues in the post-communist transformation in Ukraine.

According to state law, Ukraine is a unitary state, composed of the Autonomous Republic of Crimea and 24 territorial administrative units, or *oblasts* (regions). Thus, the only case of autonomy is in Crimea, but its autonomy is administrative, not national. Since 1991, when the state rejected the initiatives of Hungarian and Bulgarian-Gagauz minorities to establish national territorial units, the idea of national-territorial autonomy was also raised in the political movement of the Crimean Tatars. Aside from these instances, there have been no other visibly significant political manifestations on the issue of national-territorial autonomy from Ukraine's other ethnic minorities. The Russian minority is, however, particularly active in claiming rights to cultural autonomy, with special emphasis on linguistic rights.

In terms of local self-government, the rights of minorities are satisfied in local communities where they constitute the majority of voters. This is the case with Hungarians in the Beregivskiy district of Transcarpathia, Romanians in rural areas of Bukovyna and Bulgarians in the Bolgradskiy district of Odeska oblast. In these locations, the ethnic minorities have been able to elect a majority in their local self-governments.

2.1.1. A special case: Crimean Administrative Autonomy

The Autonomous Republic of Crimea (ARC) enjoys administrative autonomy within the territorial structure of Ukraine. The Crimean case represents a 'reverse' ratio in the majority-minority relationship in Ukraine: Ukrainians in Crimea are an ethnic minority, making up only 25% of the peninsula's population, while the Russian majority is 63%. The demographic situation in Crimea is also complicated by the process of active repatriation of formerly deported nations apart from Crimean Tatars, including Armenians, Bulgarians, Greeks, Germans, Crimchaks, Karaims and other peoples.

The history of political and ethnic relations in Crimea is complex and turbulent. In the 16TH and 17TH centuries, the Crimean peninsula belonged to the Crimean Khanate. As a result of Russo-Turkish wars, it was annexed by the Russian empire in 1792. The Soviet power was established in Crimea in 1921, with the creation of the Crimean Autonomous Soviet Socialist Republic (Crimean ASSR), part of Soviet Russia. During the early years of the Crimean ASSR, Crimean Tatars, who made up 25% of the Crimean population in the 1926 census, enjoyed a high level of national cultural autonomy. This relative autonomy came to an end in late 1927, when a 'struggle against bourgeois nationalism', country-wide collectivisation and an anti-religious campaign led to mass political repression against the Tatar intelligentsia and Muslim clergy. During and after World War II, the Crimean Tatars—as well as small numbers of Bulgarians, Armenians, Greeks, Germans, Crimchaks and Karaims—were accused of having collaborated with Nazi Germany, and then forcibly deported to Central Asia and eastern regions of Russia. The new settlers moving to the peninsula, which was considered a desirable place to live, were mostly ethnic Russians. Crimean administrative territorial autonomy was abolished in 1946.

In 1954, administration of Crimea was officially transferred from Russia to the Ukrainian Soviet Republic. Therefore, when Ukraine declared independence in 1991, Crimea automatically became a part of the new state. The new and uncertain position of the Russian postwar immigrants and their descendants, a socio-economic crisis and other factors, compounded by a mass return of Crimean Tatars, created a volatile clash of expectations among the different ethnic groups inhabiting Crimea. The territorial status of the peninsula also turned into one of the more difficult issues in Russian-Ukrainian inter-state debates over the post-Soviet legacy. The Ukrainian leadership's decision to restore the autonomous status of Crimea and hold a referendum on Crimean autonomy helped defuse the situation.

After a lengthy negotiation process between the Ukrainian and Crimean governments, the 1996 Constitution of Ukraine defined the main political and legislative regulations for the autonomous status of the Republic of Crimea. In accordance with the Ukrainian Constitution, the Constitution of the Autonomous Republic of Crimea was adopted by the Crimean parliament in October 1998, and approved by the *Verkhovna Rada* (national legislature) of Ukraine in December 1998.

The Crimean Constitution generally adheres to principles of minority protection contained in the Constitution of Ukraine. One major difference, however, is that the Crimean Constitution gives special status to the Russian language. Although Ukrainian is recognised as the state language, and the Crimean Republic guarantees protection for the Tatar language, the Crimean Constitution classifies Russian as 'the language of the majority', which functions as the language of inter-ethnic communication in the public sphere. This provision has a discriminatory effect towards Tatar and Ukrainian. The use of these languages for public matters is only allowed if it is acceptable for all interested parties. The Crimean Constitution does, however, guarantee the right of all citizens to be educated in their mother tongue.

The Crimean Constitution has been strongly criticised by the leaders of the Crimean Tatars. They are dissatisfied with the Constitution because:

1. It does not recognise the Crimean Tatars as one of the indigenous peoples of Crimea.
2. It does not legitimise the *Kurultay* (National Assembly) and the *Mejlis*—the elected representative bodies of the Crimean Tatars.
3. It does not ensure the effective representation of the Crimean Tatars as integral members of the power structure in Crimea.

Indeed, the Crimean Constitution does not provide any guaranteed quotas for political representation of minorities in the Crimean legislature. According to the Constitution, a person elected to the Crimean Parliament must be a Ukrainian citizen who has lived in the country for no less than five years. Because the Crimean Tatar population is mostly recent returnees, about a half of the adult Tatar population were not Ukrainian citizens by the beginning of 1998.[9] Even by the middle of 2000, an estimated 14,000 to 20,000 adult Tatar returnees, including 13,700 from Uzbekistan, were still considered to be de-jure stateless people, according to UNHCR data.[10] Although more Crimean Tatars are receiving citizenship, many still do not meet residence requirements, so that the whole Crimean Tatar minority of around 260,000 people could conceivably be legally represented by a mere 150,000 eligible voters.

Thus, the Constitution of the Autonomous Republic of Crimea falls short in enshrin-

---

[9] From an interview with a leader of the Crimean Tatars, Mustafa Dszamilyov, *Nezavisimost,* 20 January 1998

[10] UNHCR office in Ukraine. Online. Internet: http://www.un.kiev.ua.

ing the political rights of Crimean Tatars. This situation will likely increase tensions between the Tatars and Crimean authorities, and also between Tatars and the Ukrainian central authorities. This problem, along with the Ukrainian majority's strategic interrelation with the largest ethnic minority—Russians—poses the greatest threat to peaceful ethnic relations in Ukraine.

At the same time, the case of Crimean autonomy proves the effectiveness of accommodating and power-sharing strategies in dealing with separatist trends.[11] Crimean autonomy plays a significant role as a *legal and institutional precedent* in the development of public administration reform in Ukraine.

2.1.2. *Politicisation of the Crimean Tatars*

It is an axiom that government neglect or discriminatory policies toward ethnic minorities leads to ethnic mobilisation and the politicisation of those minorities. This can be witnessed in the Ukraine, where there is a growing political mobilisation of Crimean Tatars, who have returned en-masse from Central Asia and Siberia more than 45 years after their exile. The repatriates have found insufficient provisions for their adaptation process and have experienced a high level of unemployment. These factors created a strong economic impetus for political mobilisation and self-organisation by the Tatar community.

To some extent, both the Crimean and the Ukrainian governments were unprepared for the scale and pace of the Tatars' repatriation movement. Authorities had hoped for an organised and gradual return of the formerly deported people. There were plans to prepare housing and greater social infrastructure for re-settlers. But things happened more quickly than officials expected.

By the end of 1992, about 190,000 Crimean Tatars had resettled in Crimea of their own accord. This influx of people has generated enormous problems for central and local governments. The radical change of the ethnic situation in Crimea has also generated serious tensions between the existing local population, who are mostly ethnic Russians, and the incoming Tatars. Crimean authorities are often guilty of both tacit and explicit discrimination towards Tatars.

All of these factors have encouraged Crimean Tatars to create their own political and governmental structures at all levels. (The issue of the Crimean Tatars' local self-governmental structures are presented in further detail below.) In fact, political mobilisation of the Crimean Tatars began with the repatriation process in 1991. The main aims of the Tatars' political organisations are to achieve political privileges for the Crimean Tatars, based on their historical status as an indigenous people, and to establish the Tatars' national-territorial autonomy in Crimea.

The Crimean Tatar case, which has the potential to lead to open ethnic conflict, involves the clash of the interests of different ethnic groups. The aspirations and claims of the politically mobilised ethnic minority can only be realised within limits before they begin to violate the rights of other ethnic groups.

---

[11] See also: *Ethnic Conflict and Migration in Europe. First Report of the Ethnobarometer Programme* (1999) CSS-CEMES, pp. 53-81.

2.2. Linguistic Rights of the Russian Minority

The interaction of ethnic Ukrainians with the Russian minority—which makes up 81% of the non-ethnically Ukrainian population—is a politically sensitive and strategic issue for the stability and unity of the state. Historic, religious and linguistic affinity between Ukrainians and Russians have forced this issue to the forefront of domestic politics.

About 63% of Ukraine's ethnic Russians live in Crimea. Elsewhere, the central, and especially the western, regions of the country are overwhelmingly Ukrainian in terms of ethnic and linguistic composition. Nonetheless, the Russian language plays a major role in everyday communication in the cities of central Ukraine, including the capital, Kiev.

The official status of Russian as the second state language in Ukraine is one of most problematic policy issues at both the central and local levels. This issue is not only important to ethnic Russians, but also to *'Ukrainian Russophones'*. Many ethnic Ukrainians have assimilated the Russian language, due to a policy of 'Russification' that began under the tsars and continued in the Soviet regime.

Although many Ukrainians might prefer a *'one state, one language'* ideology, the country is in fact bilingual, and Russian may actually be the dominant language. Nonetheless, according to the current Law on Languages, Ukrainian is the only official language at the political and legislative level.[12] Ukrainian alone was granted official language status, while Ukrainian, Russian and other languages were proclaimed the languages of 'inter-ethnic communication'. Though Russian was not given distinct status, a free usage of Russian and other national languages is guaranteed.

Practical application of the law places stronger emphasis on the implementation of Ukrainian in all spheres of public life, particularly in education. As a consequence of this so-called 'policy of Ukrainisation', the ratio of Russian to Ukrainian schools was changed in favour of the latter during the early years of independence. According to data from the Ministry of Education, during the first four years of Ukrainian independence, the number of pupils who studied in Ukrainian increased from 45 to 56.5%.[13] According to government data from 1998, 65% of students in Ukrainian secondary schools studied in Ukrainian and 34.1% studied in Russian.[14]

However, Ukrainisation has not occurred as rapidly as some authorities had hoped, in part because of the way Ukraine's population is distributed. The majority of students studying in Ukrainian live in rural Ukraine, in western and central parts of the country. While in Crimea, where about 25% of ethnic Ukrainians live, 98.1% of the students study in Russian. A similar situation prevails in the eastern and southern regions of Ukraine. Furthermore, the effectiveness of Ukrainian instruction for Ukrainisation is not clear. Many children who study in Ukrainian schools in central, eastern and southern Ukraine prefer

---

[12] The Law on Languages in Ukraine was adopted in 1989 (before state independence was won).
[13] M. Zgurovskyi (1995) 'Educational issues at the parliamentary meeting', Kiev: *Osvita*, 22 February.
[14] The Bulletin of the State Committee on Nationalities and Migration of Ukraine (1999) p. 110.

to communicate with each other and their families in Russian. This is particularly true for senior pupils in the Ukrainian capital, Kiev.[15]

Despite its inconsistent results, the policy of Ukrainisation produced strong criticism and resistance from the representatives of the Russian-speaking community. Though the law guarantees citizens the right to use their national languages, Russians demanded that their language share equal footing with Ukrainian as Ukraine's second official language.

The debate over the use of the Russian language—and, implicitly, the linguistic rights of Ukraine's Russian minority—has already been actively explored in two presidential election campaigns. In 1994, three-quarters of the Ukrainian-speaking community supported Leonid Kravchuk. Meanwhile, three-quarters of the Russian-speaking community backed the eventual winner, Leonid Kuchma. As Andrew Wilson concludes, 'of all elections in 1990-1994, the presidential elections of the summer of 1994 showed the polarisation between Ukrainian historical regions most sharply'.[16] In the parliamentary election of 1998, eight political parties actively used the language issue in their political agendas. The relative success of one of them—the Communist Party—demonstrated that the unresolved issue of the linguistic rights of Russian-speakers may augur an uncertain destiny for the democratic transformation of Ukraine and the existence of its present borders.

2.3. Migration

As elsewhere in modern Europe, external migration has recently become a demographic factor in Ukraine's inter-ethnic relations. Though the number of immigrants entering the country is almost equal to the level of emigration,[17] migration has changed the country's ethnic composition. While most Germans and Jews[18] have left Ukraine since the mid-1980s, there is large-scale immigration of formerly deported ethnic groups, especially Crimean Tatars.

The growing legal and socio-economic problems caused by the influx of illegal immigrants, deported people and refugees reveals the absence of a clearly elaborated state migration policy. It is also obvious that there is a lack of co-ordination between central and local authorities in dealing with these issues. The situation has produced tension among the population of a country that was essentially closed to the outside world a short time ago.

The prospect of EU enlargement, and the new visa regimes it will bring to Ukraine's immediate neighbours, could further aggravate tensions surrounding migration. Illegal

---

[15] Larisa Masenko (1999) *Mova i polityka*, Kiev: Soniashnyk, p.145.

[16] Andrew Wilson (1997) *Ukrainian Nationalism in the 1990s*, Cambridge: Cambridge University Press, p.145.

[17] M. Shulga (ed.) (1998) *Vyvchennia vplyvu zovnishnioi migratsii 1991-1996 na zminy etnichnogo skladu naselennia Ukrainy ta ii regioniv*, Kiev: International Organization for Migration, p. 52.

[18] Among all the ethnic groups of Ukraine, Germans and Jews show the highest index of emigration (the ratio of external emigrants of given ethnic group to its total number). In all, 14,400 Germans out of 37,800 left the country in 1991-1996. And 350,000 Jewish people emigrated in the period between 1984-1995. Ibid., p. 61.

immigrants and refugees, who used to consider the Ukraine a stopping point on the way west, will find it harder to leave the country. These migrants could create a substantial financial burden for Ukraine, and there is no clear legal provision for EU assistance with this problem.

It is possible to distinguish three main flows of immigrants into the country:

1. *Repatriation of Crimean Tatars and other deported peoples.* This is the most significant source of immigration into the Ukraine. Apart from the Crimean Tatars, returnees include Armenians, Bulgarians, Greeks, Germans, Crimchaks, Karaims and other peoples of the Crimea. Active repatriation began when the Supreme Soviet of the USSR adopted the Declaration of 14 November 1989, which recognised the repressive acts against the deported peoples and removed the obstacles to their return. Since the late 1980s, more than 250,000 formerly deported people or their descendants have returned to Crimea, and immigrants now constitute about 10% of the population of the peninsula. The massive wave of returnees has created enormous socio-economic difficulties for both central and Crimean authorities. This has not stopped the Ukrainian government from supporting repatriation and allocating budgetary resources for the process—though local authorities are still overburdened.

2. *Refugees from the former Soviet Union.* Since 1991, Ukraine has assimilated about 150,000 ethnic Ukrainians, Russians, Armenians and people from other ethnic groups within the former Soviet republics.[19] The socio-economic problems these refugees face are exacerbated by the ambiguity in the Ukrainian laws on immigrants and refugees. Many of these people do not fit into any of the four judicial categories for migrants in need of assistance.[20] This is especially a problem for ethnic Ukrainians, who are either fleeing ethnic conflict or were denied citizenship in the Baltics or other parts of the former Soviet Union. Further, even those who do manage to qualify as refugees have only received limited government support.

3. *Refugees from South Asia, the Middle East and Africa.* As much as 85% of the refugees from these regions are Afghans, and the rest are citizens from about 20 African and Asian countries. The first officially registered refugees from this category, mostly Afghans, were former students who applied for refugee status after the breakdown of the USSR. Experts estimate that there are about 3,000 people from this group who are currently registered as refugees, while there are at least 15,000 undocumented migrants, most of whom are concentrated in Kiev.[21]

Due to its location, Ukraine has also become a destination for numerous illegal immigrants, many of whom consider the country a gateway to the west. Insufficient Ukrainian laws regarding immigrants, and an unwillingness of central and local authorities to deal with the problem, has resulted in a huge growth in illegal immigration. There is, however, considerable discrepancy between official and actual data on the situation. According

---

[19] Olena Malinovska (1998) 'Bizhentsi v Ukraini', Kiev: *Problemy migratsii,* Vol. 2, p. 3.

[20] According to national legislation, these four legal categories are as follows: 'a person seeking asylum', 'refugee', 'migrant' and 'deported person'.

[21] *Ethnic Conflict and Migration in Europe. First Report of the Ethnobarometer Programme* (1999) CSS-CEMES, p. 202.

to the experts' estimates, the total number of illegal immigrants and persons with indefinite status varies between 70,000 and 500,000.[22]

Ukrainian officials admit that they lack a clear migration policy.[23] The laws are inadequate, there are complex bureaucratic procedures for registration—and there is a weak and under-funded system for immigration control and statistical registration. Although a law on refugees was adopted in 1993, its implementation only began in March 1996, with the first officially recognised documents for refugees. Until then, inexperienced local officials were forced to make decisions about refugees, without clear legislative guidance. Experts suggest that the social status of refugees would improve if there was a simpler registration procedure at the local level, coupled with stronger controls on entry into the country.[24]

Thus, in summary, Ukraine's ethno-policy since 1991 has faced three major challenges: (1) territorial autonomy for minority groups, (2) the linguistic rights of the Russian-speaking population and issues related to immigrants, and (3) refugees entering Ukraine.

Efforts to establish territorial autonomy by Hungarian and Gagauzes in 1991 were unsuccessful, and claims for autonomy by various ethnic groups living in compact areas are generally low on Ukraine's political agenda. The only exception is the Crimean Tatars, who have organised and increased their political voice. But the state still seems to consider any claims for territorial autonomy by ethnic groups as a potential threat that could lead to separatism and eventually threaten the country's territorial integrity.

Given current political circumstances, minorities with compact residence could benefit by working toward local government reform. By pressing for much needed decentralisation, and thereby empowering local governments, minorities with compact localised populations can achieve a higher level of self governance. This is particularly the case for Hungarians in the Beregivskiy district of Trans-Carpathia, Romanians in rural Bukovyna and Bulgarians in Odeska oblast, who constitute the majority in their local communities.

The Ukrainian government did achieve some success in using power-sharing strategies to defuse potential separatist trends by establishing Crimean territorial-administrative autonomy. But, because the Crimean Constitution does not do enough toward recognition of the Crimean Tatars, that group has become more politicised. The case of the Crimean Tatars, involves competing interests between different ethnic groups. Therefore, the aspirations of the politically mobilised Tatars can only be realised to a certain extent without violating the rights of other groups.

The quest for language rights among the Russian speaking population of the country is another potential source of conflict in Ukraine. The problem has already generated tensions between the central government and some local authorities, who have sought to give the Russian language official legal status. Attempts by the government to encourage 'Ukrainisation' have been unsuccessful, because they ignore the realities of the country's population distribution.

---

[22] M. Shulga (ed.) (1998) *Vyvchennia vplyvu zovnishnioi migratsii 1991-1996*, p. 47.

[23] A. Belyaev, Vice-Head of the State Committee on the Defence of the State Border of Ukraine (1998) 'U nas nelegalami zanimaiutsia vse po chut'-chut', *Den,* 9 September.

[24] S. Pirozhkov, A. Ruchka, L. Aza (1998) 'Bizhentsi v Ukraini: sotsiologichnyi portret', *Sociologia: teoria, motody, marketing,* Vol. 1-2, p. 183.

3. A Difficult Bargain: Legal Instruments and Institutions Promoting the Rights of Minorities

While the Ukrainian state has done well to achieve relative stability and avoid openly violent conflicts, efforts on the part of ethnic minorities to preserve their identities have been one of the most sensitive political issues in Ukraine. Some of the policies aimed at promoting Ukrainian language and culture have had discriminatory effects on minority members.[25] This section will look at the existing international and Ukrainian legal instruments affecting minority issues in the country, and analyse the successes or failures of these measures.

3.1. Process of European integration: influence of international law

The Ukrainian political leadership has officially proclaimed a policy of seeking strategic integration into Euro-Atlantic structures. The government has already taken steps in this direction, including membership in the Council of Europe, participation in the OSCE, a partnership co-operation agreement with the EU and a special charter on partnership with NATO. At the same, however, Ukrainian foreign policy also seeks a strategic partnership with Russia. This somewhat inconsistent foreign policy reflects geo-political ambivalence of the Ukrainian political elite and the population at large. Surveys indicate that the western regions of the country traditionally show prevailing western orientation, while the more populated eastern and southern regions demonstrate a strong socio-political and cultural affiliation with Russia.[26]

From the perspective of ethnic minorities, Ukraine's membership in the Council of Europe and other international obligations are considered helpful channels for the protection of basic rights. Russian minority political activists, for example, take advantage of the opportunities afforded by Council of Europe membership as a tool for international advocacy of their cultural-linguistic identity rights.[27]

As a member of the Council of Europe, Ukraine is obligated to ratify the main statutes of this organisation by specified dates. The Framework Convention for the Protection of National Minorities was ratified by the Parliament in 1997. The European Charter for Regional or Minority Languages was ratified at the end of 1999, but, in a controversial decision, the Constitutional Court annulled this ratification on procedural grounds.

---

[25] The Law on Languages in Ukraine introduced a preference to Ukrainian language; the Law on the Freedom of Conscience and Religion introduced an administrative procedure to register non-native religious organizations both at the central and the local levels.

[26] V. Vorona (ed.) (1999) *Ukrainske suspilstvo: monotoring sotsialnykh zmin (1994-1999)*, Kiev: Institute Sociologii, p. 187.

[27] Interview with a political activist of the Russian community and Ukrainian MP V. Alekseev. *Kievskie Vedomosti* (2000) 4 September.

3.1.1. Framework Convention for the Protection of National Minorities (FCNM)
Ukraine signed the Framework Convention for the Protection of National Minorities in September 1995. When Parliament ratified it in 1997, the minority provisions of the convention became part of national legislation.

Joining the Convention has prompted several pro-minority activities, which were outlined in the materials for the report,[28] on the implementation of legal provisions of the Convention that Ukraine submitted to the Council of Europe. The report cited progress in improving relations with Crimean Tatars, including the April 1999 presidential decree creating the Council of Representatives of Crimean Tatars.

The report also noted progress in self-organising activities of ethnic minorities at both the regional and national levels. The Association of National-Cultural Communities and Societies of the Crimea, the Confederation of National-Cultural Communities of Western Ukraine and the Association of National-Cultural Communities of Odeska oblast were created. The second All-Ukrainian Congress of National Communities of Ukraine was conducted in 1999. The All-Ukrainian Congresses, and meetings of Jews, Greeks, Germans, Poles and Crimean Tatars of Ukraine, were conducted by national societies of these ethnic minorities.

The report also pointed out some failures related to the implementation of minority rights. It admits that socio-economic issues relevant to deported peoples of Crimea are unresolved, and only 51% of returnees are provided with satisfactory housing. The report cited instances of discrimination and ethnic intolerance, including anti-Semitic publications.

3.1.2. European Charter for Regional or Minority Languages
The European Charter for Regional or Minority Languages includes several state obligations designed to guarantee the use of minority languages in education, legal and administrative proceedings, the media and other areas of daily life.

Ukraine signed the Charter in 1996, though the Ukrainian Parliament only ratified it in December 1999, following much debate. Ukrainian nationalists opposed ratification, claiming the Charter would promote the dominance of Russian language and culture. According to member of Parliament Mykhaylo Kovach, a Hungarian, even representatives of the State Committee for Nationalities supported an anti-minority position in the debates over ratification.[29]

This victory for minority rights was short-lived, however. The endorsement of the Charter for Regional or Minority Languages was repealed in the summer of 2000, when the Constitutional Court ruled that Parliament breached the ratification procedure. It seems apparent that the court's decision was a political one, designed to foster exclusionary language policies.

The Constitutional Court's repeal of ratification of the Charter, and the new trend in language policy, were strongly criticised by representatives of the Russian ethnic community, who consider the decision illegitmate and purely political. The decision set a dangerous legal precedent, which casts ambiguity on the Charter's ratification, and its legitimacy in Ukraine.

---

[28] State Committee on Nationalities and Migration (1999) *Evropeiskiy orientyr etnonatsionalnoi polityky Ukrainy,* Bulletin, Vol. 3.

[29] M. Kovacs (1999) 'Szavazas elotti vita a Nemzetisegi es regionalis Nyelvek Europai Chartajarol', *Karpati Igaz Szo,* 12 June, (an official regional newspaper in Hungarian in Ukraine).

3.2. Bilateral treaties

Bilateral international agreements, particularly with neighbouring countries, can be considered an important method to internalise minority rights legislation. Since independence, the Ukrainian government has concluded such agreements with Hungary,[30] Poland, the Republic of Moldova and Lithuania. Bilateral treaties with Russia and Romania, ratified in 1997, are particularly important because of the complex relations between Ukraine and these neighbouring countries. The treaties involve the protection of respective minorities' rights, including the right to cultural autonomy.

Ukrainian experience demonstrates that implementation of bilateral treaties strengthens international trust and contributes to regional stability in Central and Eastern Europe. In the framework of the treaties, representatives of Ukraine and its neighbouring countries, meet annually to discuss concerns of ethnic minorities. The practical results of the bilateral interrelations for Ukraine are: mutual regular intergovernmental monitoring of minority rights implementation; the development of inter-border regional co-operation; facilitating of economic support of ethnic minorities abroad by their kin-states; and development of cultural and educational initiatives, which aim at provision of minority cultural autonomy.

3.3. Constitutional and internal legislative guarantees

The 1996 Constitution is the source of the most important rights and guarantees for minorities. This includes the right of legal equality, the prohibition of discrimination and the right to develop minority culture and preserve ethnic identity. The Constitution also provides for protection against hate crimes.

According to Article 10 of the Constitution, the official language is Ukrainian. The same article also guarantees the free development, use and protection of Russian and other languages of the minorities of Ukraine. However, the Russian community of Ukraine is dissatisfied with the unofficial status of Russian and the debate over whether to make it an official language is one of the most serious inter-ethnic issues in the country.

The Constitution confirms state support for the development of ethnic minorities, and obliges local authorities in places of compact minority residence to ensure the implementation of national and regional programs for minorities' national and cultural development. The document also includes the prohibition of discrimination, including 'positive discrimination', or affirmative action.

3.3.1. Declaration of the Rights of Nationalities of Ukraine—1991
The first major document regulating the principles of Ukraine's ethno-policy, the Declaration of the Rights of Nationalities of Ukraine, was adopted by Parliament on 1 November 1991. It proclaimed the equality of all people and ethnic groups in Ukraine—

---

[30] 'The agreement signed in 1991 was praised by some Hungarian leaders as a model for other countries to follow'—quoted in M. Opalski (ed.) (1996) 'Ethnic Minority Rights in Central Eastern Europe', Ottawa, p. 35.

and helped the new government gain broad support. When a popular referendum on Ukrainian independence was held a month later, voters overwhelmingly backed the idea, even in regions in which ethnic minorities were concentrated. In some districts where ethnic Romanian and Moldovanian populations are predominant, over 90% of the electorate voted in favour of Ukrainian independence.[31]

Though the Declaration does not provide mechanisms for the implementation of minority rights, it still preserves its significance as one of the first politically important documents and as a guarantee of state obligations toward minorities.

3.3.2. Law on National Minorities in Ukraine—1992

This law guarantees minorities the right to national and cultural autonomy, including rights to: form associations, receive education in their native language, practice their religion, use national symbols, commemorate minority holidays and develop national traditions.

The law guarantees that, in regions where a minority group predominates, their language can be used in tandem with the official state language of Ukrainian for all institutions and government bodies. These provisions have been mostly implemented: Hungarian and Ukrainian are the languages used by public institutions in some Trans-Carpathian regions; Romanian is used in 'ethnic Romanian' regions of Bukovyna; and Russian is broadly and predominantly used in government and public institutions in eastern and southern Ukraine and in Crimea.[32]

The law provides for the political rights of minorities by guaranteeing equality of the individual rights of the persons belonging to ethnic minorities rather than by guaranteeing the minorities' collective rights. Ukrainian legislation does not provide special norms for political representation of ethnic minorities, such as electoral quotas. Although there are some provisions which can help territorially concentrated groups—like Hungarians and Russians—gain minority representation in central and local government, these measures do not benefit dispersed groups, like Crimean Tatars and Roma.

The Law on National Minorities in Ukraine allows minorities to participate in government through their associations—which can nominate candidates for central and local elections. However, there is some ambiguity in the implementation of this right, because it was not mentioned in the recent law on local self-government.

The law implies that the interests and needs of ethnic minorities are also represented through advisory bodies, which consult with the government on minority issues. However, these bodies can only advise, and lack the necessary authority to provide for true political involvement of minorities in the decision-making process.

3.3.3. Law on Citizenship of Ukraine

The Law on Citizenship was adopted in 1991, and it ensures the equality of all permanently residing citizens before the law, regardless of their ethnic, cultural, linguist or religious identity. The inclusive character of the law was based on the so-called 'zero-option'

---

[31] Interview with Ivan Gnatushyn, Head of the Chernivtsi local state administration. *Uryadovyj Kurjer* (1995) 5 August.

[32] Interview with Olexander Efremov, the Head of Luganska oblast state administration. *Zerkalo nedeli* (2000) 29 August.

approach, which *automatically* granted Ukrainian citizenship to citizens of the former USSR who permanently resided in Ukraine at the moment of the declaration of independence.

Naturalisation for Ukrainian citizenship demands five years of continuous legal residence and renunciation of foreign citizenship. This legal norm affected deported people who had returned and established their residence in Ukraine and the process of acquiring citizenship has excluded many of them from participating in elections. Progress was recently made in this respect, due to a 1999 agreement between Ukraine and Uzbekistan that simplified the procedure of renunciation of Uzbekistan citizenship for Tatars seeking to become Ukrainian citizens.

3.3.4. Law on Local Government in Ukraine—1997

The Constitution and the Law on Local Government of 1997 legitimise the local territorial community as the subject of local governance. The law does not provide any special regulations regarding possible ethno-cultural specificity of these territorial communities. But it does provide a powerful tool for minorities who are concentrated in one region, and make up the local voting majority.

The law grants local governments specific rights in facilitating a renaissance of national-cultural traditions and in providing broad possibilities for education in the mother tongue of local people. The local government manages the communal property of its district, but the issues of control over local budget revenues and of the separation of power between decentralised government and the local state administration are not clearly elaborated in the law.

3.3.5. Law on Education

The Law on Education guarantees the right of minorities to education in their mother tongue.

In the 1998-99 school year, 13% of all state schools in Ukraine offered instruction in the ethnic minorities' language of choice. 11.6% of the secondary schools in Ukraine are bilingual. Russian is taught as a subject in 90% of all state secondary schools. Since the Soviet period, minority schools have been created in regions where Ukraine's ethnic minorities are situated, in accordance with the decisions of local administrations and the wishes of the local populations.

Implementation of educational policy has remained highly centralised and it still places stronger emphasis on the affirmation of the Ukrainian language. Education policy follows the dubious premise of establishing correspondence between the language of instruction and the ethnic composition of the region. This policy has a discriminatory effect with respect to ethnic Russians, Ukrainian Russophones and some highly Russified ethnic minorities—such as Jews and Belarussians.

Hungarians or Romanians are not particularly affected by this nationalising educational policy. However, their representatives still express concern about recent tendencies to strengthen the centralised, *'top-down'* approach of educational policy towards minorities, which they say does not take into account the traditions of relative educational autonomy.

3.3.6. *The Constitution of the Autonomous Republic of Crimea*

Because of its special provision for the Russian language, the Crimean Constitution has a certain discriminatory effect towards other ethnic minorities of Crimea, mainly Ukrainians and Crimean Tatars. There are only three schools in Crimea that use Ukrainian language for instruction and nine Crimean Tatars' schools, even though Crimean Tatars make up about 10% of the Crimean population.

Other serious shortcomings in the Crimean Constitution include its neglect of political and representative rights of the Crimean Tatar population and the legislative refusal to recognise the Crimean Tatars as one of the indigenous peoples of the Crimea.

The exclusive character of the Crimean Constitution is likely to increase tensions—both locally and with the Ukrainian central authorities.

3.4. *State Programmes*

There are a number of special state programmes intended to be realised in the sphere of current ethno-policy in Ukraine, including:

· The National Programme for the Renaissance and Development of Education of Ethnic Minorities for 1994-2000;
· The National Programme for the Development of Cultures of Ethnic Minorities by 2000;
· The National Programme on the Adaptation and Integration in Ukrainian Society of Crimean Tatars and Other Deported Peoples;
· The 'Ukrainian Language' Programme.

These programmes are elaborated by the government and ratified by the Parliament. Implementation is financed through the state budget, though the government seeks additional financial support from other sources. This particularly relates to the implementation of the programme on the adaptation of deported peoples, where international support is sought. The main implementing governmental agency is the State Committee on Nationalities and Migration. Ethnic minorities can advise on the elaboration and implementation of these state programmes through the involvement of the Council of Representatives of Civic Associations of National Minorities.

3.5. *Central Institutions*

During the past ten years, various institutions have been set up to design and implement policies regarding minorities. This section provides an overview of those institutions.

3.5.1. *Constitutional Court*

Control over the effective implementation of various guarantees of rights is exercised by the Constitutional Court of Ukraine and by courts of general jurisdiction. However, the country's judicial system is still not fully independent, and its control upon governmental agencies is insufficiently developed. The central government's influence over the Constitutional Court, particularly in the sphere of ethno-politics, has prompted minority activists to complain that the Court acts as a tool for the government's goal of Ukrainisation. The Court struck down the Ukraine Parliament's endorsement of the Charter for Regional or Minority Languages on the grounds that there were procedural flaws in the vote. It seems obvious, however, that the court's decision was a political one, designed to foster exclusionary language policies.

The Constitutional Court's bias was also apparent in another recent ruling on the use of state language in government institutions and educational process in Ukraine. This case appeared to be a reaction to decisions by some local governments in eastern Ukraine to give Russian the status of official language. In its 14 December 1999 ruling, the Constitutional Court declared Ukrainian to be the state language and the obligatory means of communication in governmental institutions for the whole territory of Ukraine. By this ruling, Ukrainian was also defined as the language of instruction in all educational institutions, though the court permitted other languages to be studied concurrently with Ukrainian.

3.5.2. Committee of Human Rights, National Minorities and International Relations in the Verkhovna Rada (Parliament) of Ukraine

This committee is the main body specialising in minority rights provision in the national legislature. The Committee elaborates and supervises legislative initiatives on minority issues. Members of the Committee are usually representatives of ethnic minorities, and are often the activists on behalf of their national communities.

3.5.3. The Parliamentary Commissioner of Human Rights (Ombudsman)

In January 1998, the Ukrainian president signed a law creating the Parliamentary Commissioner on Human Rights, a constitutionally-mandated independent human rights ombudsman. The Parliament elected Nina Karpachova as the first ombudsman in April 1998.

By law, the ombudsman can initiate investigations into implementation of human rights by any public/governmental institution. However, the law created a weak position with limited enforcement power. The Commissioner of Human Rights can, however, provide the government with recommendations to amend existing laws or practices.

Although the issues of minority rights are still not the focus of the work of the Commissioner on Human Rights, the ombudsman was involved in the inter-governmental debate over Russian-language issues. Responding to criticisms of the Ukrainian government's plans for wider use of the Ukrainian language, Nina Karpachova said that she had not received a single complaint of discrimination against the Russian language since a Ukrainian-Russian human rights agreement took effect in 1999. She also stated that ethnic Russians in Ukraine are afforded many cultural and linguistic protections,[33] and com-

---

[33] Quoted in: P. Byrne (2000) Ukraine, Russia clash over language. Kiev: *Kyiv Post*, 24 February.

plained that 'there is not a single school, theatre, library, newspaper, magazine or TV program for millions of Ukrainians residing in Russia'.[34]

It seems that the ombudsman's office is not entirely independent, and highly sensitive issues of ethnic minorities are interpreted in a political way. This fact indicates a lack of development of democratic traditions in the country.

3.5.4. State Committee for Nationalities and Migration

The State Committee is a central executive institution dealing with national minority rights, issues related to the Ukrainian diaspora and migration. The committee has regional branches attached to regional governmental executives. The mandate of this committee is to design and implement activities to prevent ethnic conflicts, and to elaborate national ethno-policy. It also has a role of co-ordination between various activities of the state in promoting inter-ethnic peace.

The Committee has often been criticised by representatives of ethnic communities for its bureaucratic and 'declarative' approach toward minority issues. Ethnic minority leaders charge that having a committee, instead of a full ministry, for minority rights—and lumping ethnic and migration issues together—transgresses the Law on Minorities. They add that this Committee's existence is evidence of the simplistic approach taken by the state towards minorities and migration.

3.5.5. Council of Representatives of Civic Associations of National Minorities

The Council is an advisory body to the central government, composed of 25 representatives from minority organisations that have countrywide status. The Council takes part in elaboration of legislative initiatives and in implementation of state programs on minority issues, but it can only make recommendations.

Despite its purely advisory character, the Committee plays an important role in providing a channel of communication and co-ordination between the government and minority organisations, and between minorities themselves. The opportunity for minority representatives to participate in governmental meetings on minority issues increases transparency of state policy in this field. The role of the Committee can be substantially increased by giving it the function of a 'minority audit commission', which would be allowed to monitor state policy on minority issues, observe implementation of minority rights provisions and offer legally binding expertise on evaluation of state ethno-policy. Minorities therefore have a weak position vis-à-vis the Ukrainian state, as their role is limited in political decision-making, and their representative body enjoys only a consultative role in the policy process.

---

[34] Ibid.

4. Implementation of Ethno-policy at the Local Level

The system of public administration in Ukraine involves two verticals of power—the appointed executive branch and the elected legislative and self-governmental branches. The relationship between these two verticals is rather complicated, particularly at the local level. At the top of the executive vertical, the president appoints his representatives at the regional and district levels. The *gubernators*, or heads of local state administration, who are often appointed on the basis of loyalty to the president, have the real power in the regions and are mainly accountable to the president and the Cabinet of Ministers.

The local state administrations are also formally accountable to the elected local councils. But issues of this accountability, as well as of authority delegation, are ambiguous and undeveloped in national legislation. In fact, the Ukrainian system has a strongly centralised executive vertical, from 'top to bottom', which is often justified as being modelled after the French system. In truth, the country's recent experience with an omnipotent Communist Party structure is probably the main inspiration behind the current system.

The system of self-government involves an elected council at the municipal level. The deputies, and leaders, of these councils are elected for a four-year term by community residents. The citizens also elect the deputies of district and regional councils, but the leaders of these bodies are elected by the council deputies. Deputies of the self-governmening councils elect their own executive bodies, which often delegate authority to parallel executive structures of the appointed local state administration. Control of the local budget, which consists of local and state contributions, is even more complicated and vague under current legislation.

The elected local self-government formulates and suggests the local agenda of the budget, and the appointed local executives are the implementing agencies, which control practical decision-making. In addition, local state administrations are fully responsible for implementation of state programs at the regional level. This means that the appointed local state administrations are in charge of implementing both state or local policies pertaining to minorities. According to the law, the local self-governments officially have wide opportunities to conduct local ethno-policy, but their role is substantially diminished by the usually limited local budgets.

4.1. State involvement in local ethno-policy issues

The experience of post-communist transition in Ukraine involves a profound transformation of the traditional model of 'top-down' policy-making. This process implies a reform in the interaction between the central authorities and local communities in every sphere, including inter-ethnic relations. Though the traditional scheme of centrally-planned policy-making is still politically and psychologically strong in Ukraine, the process of democratic decentralisation of power has begun.

When discussing 'local government' in Ukraine, unless otherwise specified, we mean the system which combines the institutions of the state local administration (local executives) and the local self-governmental agencies. The principal question is: who is the main actor in conducting ethno-policy at the local level? The answer, as we will try to demonstrate, very much depends on the concrete cases, regions and issues involved. In general, the centralised approach still prevails in Ukraine.

Though fully effective local self-government in Ukraine is still only an ideal,[35] the Constitution and the 1997 Law on Local Self-Government provide norms, principles and forms of direct governance by territorial communities at the municipal level. While these laws do not expressly provide for ethno-cultural specificity in self-government, the law does guarantee local self-governments the right to facilitate a renaissance of national-cultural traditions, as well as allowing broad opportunities for education in the local mother tongue. Unfortunately, as mentioned above, the budgets of local self-governments are small and poorly regulated. This is a serious shortcoming for the implementation of local initiatives concerning minority needs.

The inherent contradiction in ethno-policy in Ukraine is that the central state is still the main actor in this policy at the local level, but the state is interested in building a Ukrainian nation-state.[36] In the Ukrainian context, this apparent conflict of interest substantially reduces the possibility of power-sharing with ethnic minorities, particularly from the perspective of national-territorial autonomy for some ethnic groups.

Nationalist Ukrainian politicians justify this contradiction by arguing that it is the best approach to counter the threat to a unitary Ukrainian state from a developing economic crisis, on the one hand, and increasing political rights of indigenous peoples of Ukraine, on the other.[37] From this perspective, dominant in Ukrainian political discourse, even if ethnic issues appear locally, they have state significance, and therefore must be settled from the point of view of the state's interests. As a result, the implementation of ethno-policy at the local level can be highly complex.

4.2. Main actors and mechanisms of ethno-policy implementation

The mechanism for implementing ethno-policy at the local level, the main actors in this implementation and their relationship may vary in different cases. Nevertheless, it is possible to describe the most typical scheme of implementation of ethno-policy at the local level in Ukraine.

The main state executive institution in the sphere of ethno-policy is the State Committee of Ukraine on Nationalities and Migration. Attached to the Committee is an advisory body, the Council of Representatives of Civic Association of National Minorities of Ukraine,

---

[35] Among the most difficult issues that are still not properly regulated in the current legislation and are crucial for a true working system of local self-governance are: the problem of local taxation and budget, the issue of separation of power with the state local administrations, which represent executive power at the district and regional levels, the issues of control upon property and its division at the local level.

[36] It does not mean that the unitary state model is incompatible with the policy of democratic accommodation of ethnic differences. We are referring only to the concrete case, in which the tradition of administrative policy-making is still politically and psychologically strong.

[37] V. Dashkevich (1996) 'Chy pogrozhuie sumnyi dosvid Avstro-Ugorzhyny Ukraini?', Kiev: *Viche*, Vol. 12, p. 79.

which fulfills a mostly representative role. State ethno-policy is mainly articulated through state programs. The Committee implements its policy through the system of its regional representation at the local level. The Committee departments are incorporated into the structure of the state local administration. In the more ethnically heterogeneous regions, the second vice deputy of the head of local state administration is usually responsible for the sphere of inter-ethnic relations.

Minority education policy is controlled and implemented by the Ministry of Education, through its own executive bodies at the local level—which include oblast, district and municipal departments of education.

The practical functions of the State Committee on Nationalities, and its regional executive branches, are often reduced to supervision of local executive administrations in conducting ethno-policy—along with attempts to co-ordinate the ethno-policy activity of executive bodies, self-government institutions and national cultural societies. The Committee also provides assistance to the departments of local government that are responsible for conducting inter-ethnic policy in the regions.

National cultural societies of minorities tend to become the representative bodies of ethnic minorities in their interaction with central and local state agencies.[38] Even more importantly, countywide organisations of ethnic Hungarians, Jews, Crimean Tartars, Germans and other ethnic communities become the basic form of self-organisation, and often play the role of ethnic self-government in these communities.

A typical, centrally dictated approach to ethnic issues is described by the following case study on the support of the Karaims.[39] In this more representative case, bureaucratic difficulties have led to the failure of the 'centralised strategy'.

Case Study 2. Financing Minority Education: A Failed Project

The problem: Karaims are becoming an extinct ethnic group, and they need measures to protect their national cultural identity.

The actors involved: 1) National cultural association of Karaims 'Krymkaraylar'; 2) the State Committee of Nationalities; 3) the local authorities of the Crimea.

The issue proceedings and failed strategy: In 1995 the Karaims' national cultural association 'Krymkaraylar' submitted a program for the protection of the historical and cultural legacy of Karaims, and support of their ethno-social development, to the State Committee (then the Ministry) of Nationalities. Based on this proposed program, the Cabinet of Ministers ordered seven ministries to prepare projects concerning the issue. The projects prepared involved the creation of classes with Karaim-language instruction, the preparation of the Karaim cadres, restoration of Karaim libraries and even the restitution of the Karaim cultural and art relics taken from the Crimea to Russia.

---

[38] V. Rebkalo et al. (1996) Ethno-national Processes in Modern Ukraine, Kiev, p. 43.

[39] Karaims are one of ancient indigenous peoples of the Crimea. The Karaim language belongs to the Turkish language group. Their religion is Karaimism, based on the Old Testament. Karaims are becoming an extinct ethnic group, which is currently numbered at 2,602 persons, living in the territory of the former USSR, according to the 1989 census. In 1989, 1,404 Karaims lived in the Crimea, but according to newer data, the number of the Crimean Karaims was reduced to 800 by 1996.

It was supposed that the project would begin in 1998 and would be financed by Crimean local authorities. However, the expenditure on the Karaim project was not adopted by the Crimean government, mainly because of lack of funding. Furthermore, the project was still not approved by the Ukrainian central authorities because of the time-consuming bureaucratic procedures and the change of government. Consideration of the entire project had to begin again. And even if the programme is adopted by the government, it has to be approved by the Parliament of Ukraine.

Lesson: Inefficiency of the state's 'centralised' strategy, lack of co-ordination between central and local authorities and the lack of political will in dealing with the minorities issues prevented important ethno-policy from being implemented.

Source: Ukraina moloda (1998) 16 June.

The Karaims' case proves that centralised management of inter-ethnic issues is losing its effectiveness. The problem is simply that this approach lacks one crucial traditional factor: sufficient centralised state subsidies, which can be controlled and distributed at the regional level.

Despite this weakness, the political and psychological inertia of thinking that only the centre can settle the problems of ethnic minorities is still strong. The situation could also be taken as an indication that the issues of ethnic minorities are of marginal importance in state and local policy, especially in budgeting issues. In the opinion of the leaders of ethnic communities, the argument of lack of financial resources becomes a sort of official justification for the situation.

The experience of the German community in Ukraine is an example of ethnic self-organisation and self-government that effectively deals with concrete issues of local policy.[40] The German agencies of self-determination in Ukraine include the Association of Germans of Ukraine, German Youth of Ukraine, the *Volksrat* (People's Council) of Ukrainian Germans and its executive structure, '*Volksparlament*'.

These institutions of ethnic Germans successfully co-ordinate their efforts in local policy with local self-governments of the regions where ethnic Germans live: Trans-Carpathia, the Odeska oblast and the Crimea. In co-ordination with the Federal Republic of Germany and German national societies of Ukraine, the regional state administration of Odeska oblast deals with four projects designed to create job opportunities in the village of Kudryavska, a settlement of German migrants. The German case, however, is exceptional due to the better organisation and mobilisation of this minority group relative to other groups and the financial support of the German state for ethnic Germans abroad.

As can be seen from the comparison of these two cases, without adequate financing, the promise of self-government as outlined in the 1997 Law, is an empty promise indeed.

---

[40] A. Belyakov (2000) 'Integration processes of ethnic and so-called Russian Germans in Ukraine', LGI database. Online. Internet: http://www.osi.hu/lgi/ethnic.

4.3. Representation of minorities in local government

While the Law on Local Self-Government gives ethnic minorities living compactly the opportunity to elect their own representatives to the bodies of local self-government, some officials see the situation as a potential threat to multi-ethnic local communities. If one ethnic group gains local control, it could encourage 'positive discrimination' to the benefit its own members, at the expense of other ethnic groups. In other words, 'the issues of local policy and its commissions can not be dependent on the nationality of the mayor of a city, but they should be strictly regulated by the law'.[41]

Current legislation is meant to prevent this situation by providing sufficient opportunities for representation of minorities in the governmental structures of all levels. In general, certain academic studies confirm that the legislation is working. The authors of a 1996 survey concluded that 'the official characteristics of nationality of the heads of local self-government involved in the study mostly corresponds to the ethnic composition of the country'.[42]

The level of involvement and the index of representation[43] of ethnic minorities in the representative bodies—at all levels, from local village councils up to the *Verkhovna Rada* of Ukraine (excluding the Republic of Crimea[44])—are represented in Table 2. According to the index of representation, Russians, Belarussians, Jews, Poles, Germans, Kazan Tatars and some other ethnic groups are underrepresented in the structures of representative power, while the percentage of Ukrainians, Moldovans, Hungarians, Romanians and Bulgarians in regional and local self-government exceed their share in the ethnic composition of the country. These statistics demonstrate that the ethnic groups that live compactly have some advantage in governmental representation in comparison with the groups that are predominantly dispersed.

The low representation of Russians does not appear to be the result of open discrimination against them, but rather can be explained by several factors, including the phenomenon of 'shifting identity'. (Many individuals who previously identified themselves as Russians now identify themselves as Ukrainian.) The surveyors discovered that some ethnic Ukrainians who occupied high positions in the state and administrative structures in the former Soviet Union indicated their nationality as Russian during the Soviet period, perhaps because they perceived this identity would assist in upward mobility under the previous policy of Russification. The same people now, during Ukrainisation, identify themselves as Ukrainians.[45]

---

[41] I. Prokopchuk (1998) 'The Issues of Self-Government in Odessa Region', *Golos Ukrainy*, 26 November.

[42] Y. Saenko, A. Tkachuk et al. (1997) *Local Self-Government in Ukraine: Problems and Perspectives*, Kiev.

[43] The ratio between a percentage of total number of deputies of a given ethnic group and its percent in the ethnic composition of Ukraine

[44] The complex case of the Crimea and the facts of open discriminatory policy towards ethnic minorities, particularly Crimean Tatars will be demonstrated next.

[45] Ibid.

Table 2. The Ethnic Characteristics of the Deputies of Ukraine (March 1998)*

Nationality	Number	Per cent of total number of deputies 162,445=100 per cent	Per cent of the ethnic composition of Ukraine and index of representation
Ukrainians	147,126	90.5	72–1.26
Russians	9,900	6.1	22.1–0.28
Moldovians	1,123	0.7	0.6–1.17
Bulgarians	998	0.6	0.45–1.33
Hungarians	711	0.44	0.3–1.47
Romanians	586	0.36	0.26–1.38
Belarussians	532	0.33	0.8–0.4
Poles	434	0.27	0.4–0.67
Greeks	316	0.19	0.19–1
Jews	181	0.11	0.9–0.12
Gagauzes	95	0.05	0.062–0.8
Azerbaijani	54	0.033	0.07–0.47
Germans	53	0.033	0.10–0.33
Armenians	42	0.026	0.10–0.26
Kazan Tatars	29	0.02	0.17–0.12
Total	162,445	100	100–1

Source: Statistical account of the Secretariat of the *Verkhovna Rada* of Ukraine on 29 March 1998; M. Tomenko (1998) 'Ukrayinskyi parlamentarizm' (The Ukrainian parliamentarianism) Kiev: *Khronika 2000*, Vol. 27-28, pp. 239-240.

Note: Apart from the representatives of ethnic groups indicated in the table, the deputy corps of Ukraine include: 29 Albanians, 25 Georgians, 19 Czechs, 13 Latvians, 12 Uzbeks, 12 Tadjiks, 11 Lithuanians, 9 Kazakhs, 9 Turkmens, 8 Mordvins, 7 Osetins, 6 Chuvash, 5 Slovaks, 5 Chechens, 5 Udmurts, 5 Roma, 4 Lezgins, 3 Avars, 3 Crimean Tatars, 2 Bashkirs, 2 Estonians, 2 Koreans, 2 Dagestanis, 2 Turks, 2 Tabasarans, as well as one Swede, Ingush, Marian, Assirian, Tuwin, Komi, Cherkess, Agul, Finn, Ujgur and Kirgiz.

The national composition of some territorial communities, in which ethnic minorities are numerically dominant, gives a legal advantage for these national minorities to be proportionally represented in institutions of local self-government, particularly at the level of village and district councils. The phenomenon of 'ethnic' district and village councils can already by observed in Ukraine. Thus, in the local elections of 1994 in Bolgradskyi district, Odeska oblast, Gagauzes were elected in 11 village councils from 17 councils in the district.[46]

---

[46] P. Nadolishnij (1998) *Ethno-national Factor of Administrative Reform in Ukraine*, Kiev, p. 140.

However, there are more blatant signs of open discriminatory politics with respect to minorities. According to the statistics presented by Mustafa Dzsamilyov, a leader of the Crimean Tatars, at the third *Kurultay* (National Assembly) in 1996, the Tatars, who make 10% of the Crimean population, only had 0.5% representation in the bodies of executive power and were practically absent from Crimean self-governmental structures.[47]

4.4. Political organisation of minorities

Ukrainian independence was accompanied by the growth of ethnic self-awareness among Ukrainians and other ethnic groups resident in the country. As self-awareness was translated into a desire for activism, there was considerable growth in the number of national societies and associations. According to official statistics, as of 1 November 1999,[48] 429 national cultural societies and civic associations, including 25 organisations with countrywide status, have been registered. The number of national societies has almost doubled between 1995 and the end of 1999.

Most of these national societies of ethnic minorities declared themselves as cultural associations, whose main purpose was the realisation of minority rights to cultural autonomy. In most cases, however, this legal aim was not converted into the political context, and these associations were not politicised. Exceptions include the case of the Rusyn cultural society, (described in the case study below), ethnically based parties of the Hungarian minority and the Crimean Tartar National Movement.

Perhaps one reason why so few associations became political organisations was the successful 'open' strategy of the democratic political parties and movements of Ukraine in the early 1990s. Groups like the Popular Movement of Ukraine (*Rukh*), facilitated, to some extent, the political and civic integration of the different democratically oriented parts of society, including minority groups, around the idea of democratic reforms.

Case Study 3. Moderating Extremism

The problem: The development of a cultural society into a political organisation promoting an extremist, destabilising message.

The actors involved: 1) the Society of Carpathian Rusyns; 2) local authorities of Sub-Carpathia; 3) Ukrainian central authorities.

The issue proceedings: The Society of Carpathian Rusyns, founded in 1990 as 'a regional cultural educational society', came forward with a declaration of regional independence of Trans-Carpathia in 1990. The leaders of the Society formed the 'Government of Trans-Carpathian Rus' in 1993, with the political aim of restoring the 1938 borders between Ukraine and (former) Czechoslovakia. Radical political forces in Slovakia and Hungary supported the movement. Due to indifference from the local government and noninterference by Ukrainian cen-

---

[47] V. Vyzgrin (1998) 'Crimean Tatars: Discrimination and the consequences of smouldering conflict' *Problemy migratsii*, Vol. 2.

[48] State Committee on Nationalities and Migration (1999) *Evropeiskiy orientyr etnonatsionalnoi polityky Ukrainy*, Bulletin, Vol. 3., p. 20.

tral authorities, the 'Rusyn issue', which was apparently initiated by a 'cultural society' with about 200 members, quickly grew beyond its regional borders and united extremist political forces in a movement that threatened regional stability and security.

The strategy used to address the problem: Because the Rusyn political arguments were mostly drawn from unorthodox interpretations of history, language and identity of the Trans-Carpathians, a number of scientific conferences were organised by local and central authorities, with the aim of providing counter-arguments. The tension was mostly defused by the mid-1990s. However, it seems that a more effective settlement of the 'Rusyn issue' involves removing motives for destabilisation by developing inter-regional economic co-operation among neighbouring countries in the region.

The result: Because of the Rusyns' political manifestation, well-intentioned plans for social and economic development of the Trans-Carpathian Ukraine through increased regional autonomy were partly discredited. These ideas are still perceived by central Ukrainian authorities with a dose of suspicion. Ultimately, the development of the local self-government in the region was hampered.

Nevertheless, motivations still exist for the political organisation of minorities. The Ukrainian experience proves that:

1. The issues of culture, education, ethno-cultural development and, especially, minorities linguistic rights, are extremely important and can be easily politicised.
2. Unresolved ethnic issues inevitably lead to active political mobilisation of ethnic groups. In particular, the processes of ethnic mobilisation and self-organisation of German and Crimean Tatars' have resulted in the creation of parallel systems of government for these ethnic communities.

The controversial issues of local self-government (through local *mejlises*, or councils) of Crimean Tatars is particularly interesting. Acting unilaterally, the Crimean Tatars have established 250 local mejlises, which function as a system of parallel self-governmental and executive bodies of Tatar government at the local level. The mejlises were mostly created as the result of the inability or unwillingness of central and, above all, local authorities to deal with the difficult issues facing Crimean Tatars. The mejlises were also a reaction to the local authorities' open, and hidden, discrimination towards Tatars. (See Section 2.) The mejlises at all levels are unrecognised by state and local authorities, though the authorities do not forbid or interfere with mejlises activities. These bodies are therefore exclusively for the self-government of one ethnic community. In their structure and principle, the local mejlises are elected bodies. They deal with the whole spectrum of everyday issues affecting Tatars. Depending on the issue, a local mejlise may resolve the problem by dealing with official administrative structures of the same level—or the mejlise could pass the issue on to a higher meljise, who can deal with officially recognised authorities on a higher level.[49]

---

[49] D. Ablyamitov (1994) 'The Bodies of National Self-Government of Crimean Tatars', *Local and Regional Self-government of Ukraine*, Kiev, Vol. 4 (9), p. 42.

Mejlises do more than the official local government in dealing with the specific needs of the ethnic community. Furthermore, they can act as mediators between official government structures and Tatars. One possible drawback of this practice is that the existence of a 'parallel' local government can reinforce the isolation of Tatars in multi-cultural Crimea and have an effect of 'self-ghettoisation' of this ethnic group.

The increasing political mobilisation of the Crimean Tatars, who now openly declare the achievement of territorial autonomy in the Crimea as the objective of their political movement, is a classic example of unresolved ethnic issues leading to political mobilisation of minority groups. Another such example is the politicisation of the issue of linguistic rights of Russians living in Ukraine.

4.5. Financial issues in the field of minority protection

Financial support of ethnic minorities is one of the biggest problems in the field of minority protection in Ukraine. Financing the special needs of minority groups often receives low priority in state and local budgets. In fact, the very principle of financial support for ethnic minorities is now debated at the official level in Ukraine. This spending, and some other so-called 'mandatory expenditures' implied by current legislation, are put in doubt by the state's inability to fulfill its obligations because of the regular budget deficit.

The situation is similar at the local level. Schools for ethnic minorities and public cultural institutions used by national societies are financed through the existing state infrastructure, and new needs and initiatives can hardly be covered by tiny local budgets. The local government is generally responsible for the co-ordination and facilitation of projects initiated by national societies, which are largely self-financed. Significant financial support for some national societies, such as German, Jewish, Hungarian and others is provided by government and private organisations in their kin-states.[50] International donor organisations and institutions also provide financial support for ethnic minority initiatives.

As we have pointed out, the structures of local self-government are not well developed and the important issue of financial independence is not entirely regulated by current legislation. Further, even when local governments do finance the special needs of minorities, the distribution of funding is often not carried out in the legally prescribed manner.

---

[50] However, there are also some problems with financial assistance from abroad. As one of the leader of the ethnic Hungarian community admits, '"external" financial and economic support of Hungarian organisations of Ukraine due to different reasons (including the lack of transparency and information on financing, different systems of accountability, discrepancy in the tax and custom rules etc.) often turns into a personal profitable business for local 'activists' and foreign "bureaucrats"'. See: Mykhaylo Tovt (1997) 'The Problems of the Hungarian Minority in a Contemporary Ukraine', Kiev: *Nova Polityka,* Vol. 3, p. 27.

4.6. Minority education

Beginning in December 1991, the Ukrainian state launched a state policy on education, requiring that all schools, including those with minority languages, follow state guidelines. The current law on education also proclaims state control over educational institutions of all types, including minority and private schools.

Most of the minority schools in Ukraine are public schools. Many of these schools were established in minority regions during the Soviet period, in accordance with the decisions of local administrations and the wishes of the local populations. Since 1991, a network of minority national schools has been developed, in part because of the considerable increase in the number of Sunday and private schools organised by minority national societies. But the policy towards national schools has remained centralised. There is a single state curriculum for all schools. The only difference between Ukrainian schools and schools for national minorities is the language of instruction and the courses on native language and literature.[51]

A positive development in education with respect to minority needs is the emergence of Sunday schools for minorities, organised by their national societies. According to official statistics, in 1993 there were 26 minority Sunday schools, and by 1998 there were twice that amount.[52] The increase of these schools indicates that minority organisations are becoming a positive force in minority education policy, and that they can influence the decision-making process at the local level. As a result of successful partnerships between local governments and national societies, advanced schools (*gymnasiums* and *lycees*) for minorities have recently been established. One gymnasium with Bulgarian-language instruction was opened in Odessa oblast and two Romanian gymnasiums and a lycee opened in Chernivtsi oblast.[53] Since independence, four gymnasiums with Hungarian-language instruction were added to the existing 50 Hungarian schools. Three of the Hungarian gymnasiums were founded by the Trans-Carpathian Reformist Church. The first nongovernmental high school for national minorities, the Zakarpatskyi pedagogical institute, was also founded in Beregovo, Trans-Carpathia.

Despite this progress, representatives of ethnic communities are worried by the recent trend toward strengthening the centralised 'top-down' approach in educational policy for minorities. A project on ethnic education policy, prepared by the Ministry of Education in 1997, called for more study in Ukrainian, and for the preparation of exams in Ukrainian.

---

[51] The state programme 'Education: Ukraine of the 21ST Century', adopted at the First All-Ukrainian Congress of Teachers in 1992.

[52] V. Troszynskyi (1997) 'Poshuky zgody' (The search for consent), *Viche,* Vol. 10, p. 41.

[53] According to Ukrainian official figures in respect of Romanian minority, there are 104 schools with Romanian language of instruction (there are schools in practically all Romanian villages). Romanian pedagogical cadres study at the departments of the Chernivtsi and Uszhorod universities and in Chernivtsi pedagogical college. In comparison, 66,000 officially registered and about 200,000 'unofficial' Ukrainians of Romania have the possibility to attend only one a 'half-Ukrainian' lycee (40% of classes are with Ukrainian language of instruction) and 70 schools with the Ukrainian classes (Interview with the Head of the Department of the State Committee on Nationalities of Ukraine, A. Popko (1998) *Ukrainske slovo,* 5 March.

Representatives of ethnic minorities, particularly the Hungarian and Romanian groups, say the new policy, which had not even been put forward for discussion among the representatives of ethnic minority groups, does not take into account their traditions of relative educational autonomy.

Another obstacle to minority-language education, enforced through Ukrainian-language requirements, is a shortage of dictionaries and textbooks for teaching Ukrainian to minority-language speakers. Some observers consider the delay in materials to be a masked attempt by the Ministry of Education to indirectly push national minorities toward enrolment into schools offering instruction in the Ukrainian language.[54]

Another inter-ethnic sticking point is the issue of Russian-language schools. While Russians constitute about 22% of the national population, about half the schools in the Soviet Ukraine were Russian—in the period from 1970 until the late 1980s—because many ethnic Ukrainians consider Russian their native language. The new educational policy of Ukrainisation has resulted in an increase in Ukrainian schools and a decrease in Russian ones. The reasoning given by authorities is that there should be a correspondence between ethnic composition and educational structure.

During the first four years of independence, the number of students studying in Ukrainian increased from 45% to 56.5%.[55] Although the changes often involved a mere change in a school's title—particularly in the regions of eastern and southern Ukraine—it brought strong criticism from the Russian community and a considerable number of Ukrainians in traditionally 'Russian' regions of the country.[56]

The Ukrainian handling of school language policy is an example of a centralised approach to ethno-policy that does not take into consideration regional, historical and cultural specificity. This has lead to growing tensions between the central government and minority populations.

4.7. Local policy on socio-economic and cultural empowering of the Roma community

The socio-economic crisis affecting the whole population of the country has had the most severe impact on the Roma community. The problems of the Roma in Ukraine are similar to problems of their ethnic counterparts in other countries. These include unemployment, illiteracy, a high child mortality rate, a higher incidence of diseases from unsanitary conditions and infectious diseases and and social isolation and exclusion, which exacerbate the difficulty of obtaining minimal social benefits.

Official statistical data on the Roma population of Ukraine—numbering about 48,000, according to the 1989 population census—does not correspond to current reality. The European Roma Rights Center estimates that 55,000 Roma live in Ukraine. Roma groups themselves believe that the real figure is at least twice this. The discrepancy in data is characteristic of the neglect and poor understanding that typifies the situation of the Roma in Ukraine.

---

[54] Kuksa, V. (1999) 'Minorities Would Be Keen to Learn Ukrainian...', *Den*, 3 March.

[55] M. Zgurovskyi (1995) 'The High Mission of the Ukrainian Teachers', *Osvita*, 15 June.

[56] *My Motherland* (1998) 17 June.

The first major attempt to support the socio-economic empowerment of Roma communities was the Integrated Rural Community Development Program, elaborated by the
Renaissance Foundation and the Carpathian Foundation in 1996. The principal aim of
the program was to facilitate co-ordination and partnership between local government,
civic organisations, NGOs and private business structures in socio-economic development of communities.[57] Further attempts to empower Roma communities are ongoing.
A first, symbolic, achievement has been the election of the first Roma representative to a
local council of Uzhgorod in Trans-Carpathia.

5. Conclusions and Recommendations

Since 1991, an inclusive nationality policy has been combined with the visible articulation of a policy that supports an ethnic Ukrainian state. Contradictory decisions on administrative Ukrainisation were made at the beginning of the 1990s; conversely, during the
same period advanced legislation on minority rights was adopted. Official political movements—which involved attempts to form a democratic, social and legal state and a 'civic
nation'—were accompanied by a trend toward neglect of minority rights. This ambiguity in the nation-state-building strategy can be explained by the unresolved political conflict between the desire to creating an inclusive, multi-ethnic state and the desire to promote a Ukrainian national identity.

Other reasons for both a negligent state policy on minorities and an ambiguous nation-
state-building strategy include:
1. the lack of developed democratic traditions among democratic institutions;
2. limited democratic local self-government; and
3. minimal public participation in the decision-making process by all of citizenry,
   including minorities.

With this political and legal backdrop in mind, the following policy recommendations
are proposed for a number of key issue areas relevant to the situation of minority groups
in Ukraine.

5.1. Legal framework for minority protection

National legislation on minority rights is approaching accepted international legal norms
and agreements in the sphere of human and minority rights. However, numerous ambiguities and shortcomings in the legal framework in this sphere are:
   · The limited legal possibilities for direct political participation by minorities in deci-
     sion-making at both national and local levels, particularly with regard to the issues
     concerning their own interests.
   · The absence of legal provisions for collective and socio-economic rights of minori-
     ties.

---

[57] A. Sofyj (2000) *'Partnership'* LGI database. Online. Internet: http://www.osi.hu/lgi/ethnic.

- The lack of systematic links between legal positions on minorities, and inconsistencies within the corpus of relevant laws.
- An unsatisfactory implementation of minority legislation which is dependent largely on political consensus at both national and local levels.[58] Recently, there have also been some worrying trends that can best be characterised as willful neglect, by central and local authorities, of the pressing issues surrounding minority rights.

Without question, greater legislative clarity on issues of concern to minorities, including minority language education, rights to cultural and/or territorial autonomy, citizenship issues, the status and rights granted to Ukraine's large immigrant communities and other relevant topics is crucial. To that end, the numerous contradictions between the 1991 Declaration of the Rights of Nationalities and current legislation on minorities should be resolved.

5.2. Decentralisation and public administration reform

Institutional reform also implies the search for an optimal model—ranging from a unitary state to a federative state with significant local self-governance, up to territorial autonomy for some ethnic minorities. However, a fear of territorial separatism is still predominant in Ukrainian political discourse. The unresolved dilemmas within Ukrainian state-building hinder the process of the implementation of minority rights, as well as institutional and administrative reforms.

Even in the present climate of unfinished administrative reforms, Ukraine's experience shows that a local ethno-policy performed by local self-government is more effective than the traditional, centralised approach. As public opinion illustrates, the local level can be a bridge in building trust between state and minority interests. Local action can provide better opportunities for minorities to satisfy their own needs themselves through self-governmental participation. Public administration structures must be given the appropriate authority and financial autonomy necessary to meet the needs of local ethnic communities.

5.3. Political participation

In the Ukrainian context, the policy of accommodation implies the political and participatory empowerment of ethnic minorities and broadening their level of involvement in the political decision-making process, both at the central and local levels of government. The aforementioned 'top-down' administrative approach in dealing with the issues of ethnic minorities still prevails in Ukraine. The state strategy on ethno-policy in Ukraine treats ethnic communities, and their organisations, as the objects of influences—rather than full-fledged partners in shaping and conducting ethno-policy. Ukraine's transition process

---

[58] However, this is not a specific 'Ukrainian case', but rather it proves a common trend in a post-communist transformation. Particularly, participants of the LGI workshop 'Local Governance in Multi-ethnic Communities of Central and Eastern Europe' point out that 'there is the tension in the transition period between the imperative of the rule of law, and the realisation that law operates within a broader social and political context—in which the law is not always implemented'.

could be enhanced by encouraging the establishment of local civil society through community development and self-organisation of independent groups, including minorities.

- There must be constant participation of minority representative councils in the process of local policy-making, particularly in regard to policy concerning the interests of ethnic minorities in multi-ethnic communities.
- Regular public hearings on minority issues, and other feedback methods, must be employed, to ensure that local policy is transparent and accountable for local people, particularly for the minority groups.
- 'Hot issues' of inter-community relations, such as the language regime in local schools, must be settled through negotiations. The participation of minority community representatives in the negotiations is a crucial condition.

5.4. Cultural autonomy

Ukraine's experience in dealing with inter-ethnic issues demonstrates that:

- The issues of culture, education, ethno-cultural development and linguistic rights are emotionally charged and can be easily politicised.
- Unresolved ethnic issues and neglect of these issues by central and local authorities, can readily lead to active political mobilisation of ethnic groups. Most notably, the processes of ethnic mobilisation and self-organisation of ethnic German and Crimean Tatar communities have resulted in the creation of so-called 'parallel systems of government' in these communities.
- Inter-regional and international co-operation in the border regions should be developed and economic links with neighbouring countries whose minorities are living in Ukraine should be strengthened. The establishment of Ukrainian-Hungarian, Ukrainian-Romanian and Ukrainian-Polish local co-operation, initiated by local communities and co-ordinated by local governments of neighbouring countries, can be mentioned as successful examples.

The controversial issue of the linguistic rights of minorities (particularly the large Russian minority) must be resolved. A new law on languages is being developed, and this could do much to solve the problem—but only if the law eschews the principal of Ukrainisation.

- The new law should be based on the principles of equality of the two main languages of the country, and on the inalienable right of free language identification.
- The European Charter for Regional and Minority Languages should be ratified.

Further efforts to protect the cultural autonomy of minority groups can include symbolic (and inexpensive) measures that demonstrate the local authorities' commitment to minorities' needs. Such measures can include:

- listing street names in two main languages;
- conducting cultural festivals for ethnic minorities;
- facilitating the work of national-cultural societies by providing accommodations for their activities, granting local taxation privileges or reducing their payments for communal expenses;

- facilitating the organisation of Sunday schools for minorities, as well as other cultural and educational events;
- employing all legal possibilities for displaying ethnic symbols in local municipalities in which ethnic minorities are dominant.

5.5. Public finances

Clear and predictable rules for financing cultural initiatives and organisations must be implemented. More specifically:
- Both local and central governments must provide physical space and transparent rules for the distribution of subsidies.
- Legal and transparent forms of control and accountability on distribution of funds for minority cultural initiatives must be achieved by allowing for an independent minority audit by authoritative members of local minority communities.
- More funding is needed for returning peoples such as the Crimean Tartars and others, in order to build permanent housing, basic infrastructure, adequate education services, sufficient heath care and promote employment among these immigrant populations.

5.6. Education

To date, Ukraine's highly centralised education policy has in many cases been used as an instrument of 'Ukrainisation'. This does not bode well for minority cultural protection and for positive inter-ethnic relations. The policy of Ukrainisation is incompatible with adequate protection for minority rights to education in their mother tongue. Equally important, the development of Ukraine's education system in a way compatible with minority rights is hindered by the high degree of centralisation of education policy.
- A bottom-up, decentralised policy approach is necessary to improve both majority and minority education.
- Policy decisions affecting school curricula, the employment of teachers, teachers' salaries, school maintenance and other relevant education issues should be made at the local level, or in greater co-operation with local authorities.

5.7. Capacity-building

- Best practices at the national and international levels should be studied.
- Training courses and seminars on multi-ethnic management and conflict prevention strategies should be organised for local officials. A school on municipal management—part of which can be multi-ethnic issues—was opened in Sudak, on the initiative of local self-government. This is the first serious achievement in this direction.
- Special training programs and regular meetings of state officials and minority organisations may serve as confidence-building measures between majority and minority communities and may serve to undermine the current attitude among government officials that state security interests are inherently contradicted by the interests of minority groups.

In conclusion, it should be noted that some 'success stories' of self-governmental man-agement of ethnic issues—particularly in the Trans-Carpathia, Chernivtsi and Odessa regions—are partly founded on maintenance of local traditions, together with the every-day practice of inter-ethnic tolerance. Ukraine is mercifully still free of serious ethnic con-flict—not because of, but rather despite, the dominant centralised approach to ethnic issues.

Further reading

Bennett, Robert (1993) *Local Government in the New Europe,* London: Belhaven.

CSS-CEMES (1999)*Ethnic Conflict and Migration in Europe. First Report of the Ethnobarometer Programme,* pp.53-105, 193-211.

Kymlicka, Will (1996) *Multicultural Citisenship. A Liberal Theory of Minority Rights,* Oxford: Clarendon Press.

Nadolishnij, Petro (1998) *Ethno-natsionalnyi factor administratyvnoi reformy v Ukraini* (Ethno-National Factor of Administrative Reform in Ukraine), Kiev: UADU, Academy of Public Administration at the office of the President of Ukraine.

Saenko, Yuriy et al. (1997) *Mistseve samovriduvannia v Ukraini: problemy i prognozy* (Local self-gov-ernment in Ukraine: problems and forecast), Kiev: Instutut Sotsiologii.

Stepanenko,Viktor ([[) *Managing Multi-ethnicity in a Newly Independent State: Ethno-policy in Ukraine after 1991.*

Suksi, M. (ed.) (1998) *Autonomy: Applications and Implications,* The Hague: Kluwer.

Wilson, Andrew (1997) *Ukrainian Nationalism in the 1990s,* Cambridge: Cambridge University Press.

PART THREE

GLOSSARY OF TERMS,
BIBLIOGRAPHY
AND
INDICES

GLOSSARY OF TERMS

Accountability:	Sometimes distinguished from responsibility. One actor is accountable to another if the latter may sanction and forbid his or her actions. Chains of responsibility run downward by delegation, chains of accountability run upwards. Accountability is a concept closely linked to good governance.
Acculturation:	The process whereby an individual or group acquires the cultural characterstics of another through cultural contact. Acculturation is a one-way process, in which one culture absorbs another, and is to be distinguished from the two-way process of assimilation, in which homogeneity results from changes in both.
Active Employment Policies:	Policies aimed at increasing employment of long-term unemployed job-seekers. AEPs also represent an effort to create realistic opportunities for those whose access to the labour market is limited and to use public tenders preferentially to ensure the employment of job seekers with 'job placement difficulties'. AEPs involve government action, not only regulations and incentives.
Affirmative Action/ Positive Discrimination:	Public and private sector policies designed to incorporate racial and ethnic minority group citizens and women into a variety of political, social, educational and economic institutions. The aim is to compensate for past discrimination or historical disadvantage. These policies have been adopted in a large number of democracies, but the term is usually applied to the United States, where the policy has been the subject of considerable debate.
Arbitrariness:	The exercise of power is called arbitrary when no legitimate reason can be given for its use which has weight for anyone other than the person who exercises it. A power applied through law is not arbitrary. The instruments and culture of democracy are notionally the most effective means of curbing arbitrariness and making the state responsive to the aspirations of citizens.

Assimilation:

A two-way process of cultural homogenisation in which different groups come to resemble one another more closely. Assimilation aims at the creation of a common ethnic identity through the merging of cultural and other differences.

Autonomy:

Living under one's own laws or control over one's own actions. Autonomy of the individual is to be distinguished from autonomy of the state, of regions, groups or institutions. Types of autonomy with particular importance for minorities include: administrative, cultural, political and territorial.

Bottom-Up Policies:

Policy measures or programmes initiated at the local or community level that can have a broader impact at the regional or state level.

Bureaucracy:

A concept crystallised in the early nineteenth century used to refer to 'rule by officials'. Various slants have been attached to the definition depending on whether the collective body of individuals or the institutions of such rule should be the centre of attention. Its use has since been extended to cover the administration by trained professionals not just of the state but of all large organisations and is often used as a synonym for 'large organisation' that is resistant to change.

Central/Local Relations:

In analysing central-local relations within a state's administration, the following key points should be considered: the scope and variety of the functions administered by the centre, localities and special agencies; the number and size of different local units and their relationships with one another horizontally and vertically; their relative shares of public revenues; the constitutional status of the various actors; and the political, economic and administrative controls over local units available to the centre or its agents.

Centre of Government
Institutions:

Core executive units of government. Depending on the prevailing constitutional system, these can be either the President's or Prime Minister's Office, or a combination of both. (Term introduced by the OECD Public Management Service.)

Citizenship:

The term denotes the full and responsible membership of an individual in a state. In social science it has been used primarily to denote the status of individuals in the development of modern nation-states. Citizenship refers to rights which a state confers upon certain or all individuals in a territory over which it has control. Conditions of citizenship are determined within each state in accordance with its own legal provisions. Citizenship denotes a relationship between an individual and a state by which the individual owes allegiance and the state owes protection.

Civil Society:

A broad definition is appropriate for the purposes of this book—the whole range of civic action independent of formal political institutions. Civil society thus includes cultural and recreational groups and associations, religious organisations, economic relations, labour unions and other activities not owned or directly controlled by the state. It should be noted, however, that civil society and the state are not necessarily in opposition to one another but, ideally, should complement one another.

Clientelism:

The term used to describe informal power relations between individuals or groups in unequal positions, based on the exchange of benefits. Persons or groups of higher status (patrons) take advantage of their authority and resources to protect and benefit those with inferior status (clients). Clientelism has been particularly noticeable in transitional societies, undergoing rapid modernisation.

Consociational
Democracy:

As the principal alternative to the more familiar majoritarian or Westminster-style type of democracy, consociational democracy is particularly suitable for the governance of plural societies that are deeply divided by religious, ideological, linguistic, regional, cultural, racial or ethnic differences and which form clearly separate segments. Its four basic principles are: executive power-sharing in the form of a grand coalition government; proportional representation; community autonomy; and minority veto.

Corruption:

The use of the resources of public office for improper ends.

Council of Europe (CoE):

The Council of Europe was founded in 1949 as a European Organisation for intergovernmental and parliamentary cooperation. Its statutory principles are pluralist democracy, respect for human rights and the rule of law. It has over 40 member states.

Cultural Reproduction:

A means by which communities achieve continuity, self-recognition and are recognised by others as self-sustaining. Examples of tools of cultural reproduction are spoken and written language, symbols (such as flags), myths, memories, religious practices, rituals, written and oral histories.

Decentralisation:

A system of governmental organisation that involves placing actual decision-making in the hands of units outside of the centre of power, either geographically or organisationally. The dispersal of authority and implementation from a central government to more specific jurisdiction, agencies or locations.

Deconcentration:

The decentralisation of central government ministries. Deconcentration with authority means that regional branches of central government offices are created with limited ability to make independent decisions. Deconcentration without authority occurs when regional offices are created with no independent capacity for decision-making. All deviations from normal practice must be approved by the centre.

Democracy:
Derived from the Greek *demos* (people) and *kratia* (rule or authority), hence 'rule by the people'. Although the root meaning is simple, both 'rule by' and 'people' have been interpreted in markedly different ways.

Discrimination:
Any distinction, exclusion, restriction or preference related to ethnicity, race, religion, gender, socio-economic status or other means of differentiation which has the purpose or effect of nullifying or impairing the recognition, enjoyment or exercise, on an equal footing, of all rights and freedoms. Discrimination can be practiced by individuals, groups or institutions.

Dual Subordination:
System of local-central government relations in which the local self-governing authority is subject to the control of both the local political party administration and to the control of the next level of public administration.

Dual System of Local Government:
System in which local self-governing authorities are institutionally separated from state administration institutions; the state administration does not have a representative at local self-governing authorities.

Equal Opportunity Policy:
A concept closely linked to affirmative action and which aims at the attainment of a representative public service (bureaucracy) depending largely on the extent to which various groups in society have equal access to employment in the public service. It includes government programs that promote equal opportunities for segments of the population which historically have been underrepresented.

Ethnic Group:
A concept which is both controversial and difficult to define but most theorists agree that an ethnic group is self-aware and possesses some degree of coherence and solidarity, and is composed of people united by common interests, common real or perceived origin and historical memory.

European Union (EU):
First established as an organisation of economic co-operation in 1951 between six European countries. After fifty years and four waves of accession, the EU today has fifteen member states and is preparing for a fifth enlargement towards Eastern Europe. The EU's main institutions are: the Council of Ministers, the European Commission, the Committee of Permanent Representatives, the European Court of Justice and the European Parliament. Over the past fifteen years, political issues and broader integration have become increasingly important.

Federalism:
The constitutional division of power between a central or national government and a series of subnational governments. Federal systems accommodate both regional diversity and political unity.

Fiscal Decentralisation:
The division of public expenditure and revenue between levels of government, and the discretion given to regional and local governments to determine their budgets by levying taxes and fees and allocating resources.

Fused System of Local Government:	System in which a representative of the state administration either directs or is part of the executive body of local self-governing authorities.
Globalisation:	At a minimum, globalisation can be described as primarily an economic process in which the globe is rapidly becoming a single, fused economic unit, driven partially by the formation of regional trading blocs, but increasingly across the globe. This is made possible by the current communications and information technology. In addition, efforts to bring more orderly and reliable responses to social and political issues that go beyond capacities of states join this economic process.
In-Service Training:	Training of officials that have already worked for a certain period in the Administration, with the purpose of improving their capacities or as part of a promotion system.
Initial Training/ Pre-Service Training:	Training directed at those aspiring to be civil servants. If this training is directed at civil servants that have been recruited but have not yet taken up their position in the administration, the term 'post-entry initial training' is also used.
Integration:	A social, economic and political process through which distinct identities of various groups are preserved and respected to a certain degree, but are brought into mainstream society. To be distinguished from marginalisation, segregation, acculturation and complete assimilation.
Inter-Cultural Education:	A type of education in which pupils from different backgrounds are taught in the same classroom or system, and are able to learn about each other's as well as their own culture and history, in the language of the majority or in mixed schools administered in the language of the majority.
Legitimacy:	A concept denoting one or more aspects of the lawfulness of a regime, its representatives and their 'commands'. It is a quality derived not from formal laws or decrees but from social acceptance (or acceptability) and appropriateness. It has become central to debates over how and whether rulership, government or power is validly exercised, and about the extent, grounds and sources of such validity.
Minority:	There are no internationally agreed definitions of what constitutes a minority, but it is generally acknowledged that it is not for the state to determine who is a minority. Most often, minorities are identified by both subjective and objective criteria, including self-identification with the group, national, racial, ethnic, linguistic and religious elements which distinguish the minority from other population groups in a country.
Minority Self- Government (MSG):	Institutions established in Hungary to protect the cultural autonomy of minorities. MSGs are elected by minorities who have a right of consent over issues that are of primary concern to them, such as culture,

education, languages and the media. On other matters that directly affect them, they are given consultative rights. These bodies may also establish and maintain cultural and educational institutions. MSGs exists at both local and national levels.

Marginalisation:

The state of being excluded from social, economic, political and other spheres of mainstream society, on grounds of race, religion, ethnicity, gender, culture or other distinction.

Multi-Cultural Education:

Multi-culturalism highlights pluralism and the need for separate 'spaces' within which groups can develop their own culture. Multi-cultural education implies a need for teaching in minorities' own languages, cultures and histories, potentially in separate environments.

Multi-Culturalism:

A concept that highlights pluralism and the need for separate 'spaces' within which groups can develop their own culture. A term originally used in the 1970s to discuss the incorporation of immigrants into Western European countries and the United States.

Multi-Ethnicity:

A concept which explicitly rejects the idea of full acculturation and assumes that different ethnic and language groups will live in the same state and sustain their different languages and cultures. Recognition of multi-ethnicity demands a level of sensitivity and accommodation by all groups to the demands of the others. In political terms, this means a degree of power sharing, along the lines of consociationalism.

Nation-State:

A fusion of two dissimilar principles, the one political and territorial, the other historical and cultural. The 'state' element signifies the modern, rational, autonomous state that came to fruition in the early modern period in Europe. The 'nation', defined as a named human community with a myth of common ancestry, historical memories and standardised mass culture, possessing a single territory, includes elements of ethnic cultural and 'civic' features. The great majority of so-called nation-states are poly-ethnic in composition. The homogeneous nation-state remains a powerful, though no longer universal, political ideal.

Nationalism:

A political doctrine and sentiment that suggests that the legitimate political unit is coextensive with the national unit. On this theory, legitimacy and political propriety are violated if some members of a given nationality are incorporated in political units dominated by other nationalities, or if their own unit has an excessive number of members drawn from other nationalities.

Official Language:

The language used by the state and agents of the state for government purposes and in its communication with citizens. The designation of the majority language as the only 'official' language often excludes minority individuals and groups from the public sphere and often makes the relationship between minorities and government officials and institutions more difficult.

Ombudsman/
Ombudsperson:

An official authorised by statute to investigate complaints from citizens about improper, unfair or discriminatory treatment by public servants and state authorities. He or she reports to the legislature and is independent of the political executive and the bureaucracy. In general terms, the Ombudsperson stands as an impartial intermediary between the bureaucracy and the individual citizen.

OSCE:

Organisation of Security and Cooperation in Europe. Created originally as the Conference for Security and Cooperation in Europe (CSCE) in the early 1970s as a forum for dialogue and negotiation between East and West in the Cold war period. The CSCE functioned as a conference of 35 States until 1990. Today the OSCE has 53 Participating States from Central Asia to North America. Areas of activity include questions related to security in Europe, cooperation in economics, science and technology, environment and humanitarian and other fields.

Parallel Bureaucracy:

A system in which the state administration is 'shadowed' and controlled by the administration of the leading political party at most or all levels of the hierarchy.

Parliamentary System
of Government:

A system in which the government derives its mandate solely from the parliament. There may be a separate presidential office, the incumbent of which is indirectly elected or appointed.

Political Participation:

The act of taking part in the formulation, passage or implementation of public policies. This broad definition applies to the activities of any person, whether an elected politician, a government official or an ordinary citizen, who is active in any way in the production of policy within any type of political system. Some scholars add that participation must be voluntary and genuine.

Politicisation of
Public Administration:

System of management of public administration in which appointments, recruitment and dismissal of civil servants is dependent mainly on their political affiliation rather than on professional competence. The degree to which an administration is politicised is determined both by the hierarchical level down to which political motives are the predominant element in the recruitment, promotion and dismissal process, and by the degree to which political motives influence these decisions.

Presidential System
of Government:

A system in which the president appoints and heads the government.

Public Administration:

Institutional arrangements for the provision of public services, incorporating the complex of agencies, authorities and enterprises, the formal rule structures, mixes of instruments and conventions of behaviour which describe the organisational means of service delivery.

Public Policy:	A purposive course of action taken by public persons, groups or the government within a given field addressing some problem or matter of public concern.
Public Services:	Services and goods provided to the public to meet different social needs that cannot be delivered by individual efforts. Traditionally, public services were provided by community institutions; in modern societies, they are provided by the state, and in post-industrial societies they are provided by the state, the private sector and non-profit organisations.
Public Sector:	That part of the political economy controlled or funded by the government—national, state, provincial or municipal.
Racism:	An ideology proposing a hierarchy of groups based on racial characteristics that legitimises exclusion of and discrimination against racial groups perceived as inferior. Racism as a doctrine makes an association between race and social, cultural and moral worth.
Regionalisation:	A concept referring to the creation of a new level in a state's territorial organisation. Regional institutions can vary widely in terms of bodies, responsibilities and powers, but they are always superimposed on existing local institutions. They can be defined broadly, including regions that are merely subordinate levels of the central government, or narrowly, whereby the only expression of regionalisation is the region as a territorial authority.
Rule of Law:	A political ideal to which a state's constitutional arrangements should give effect. At its most basic, the concept merely implies a preference for law and order as opposed to anarchy and strife. Generally, the concept implies also what is sometimes called the principle of legality: that government must be conducted according to law. Most formulations of the concept go even further and include a moral or political content in order to guarantee that fundamental values are not infringed.
Secession:	The act of leaving a federation or confederation. For the purposes of this book, the term is often used with reference to fears of central governments of secession by territorially compact minorities
Segregation:	The establishment by law or by custom of separate institutions of education, separate facilities of leisure and recreation, and perhaps even separate kinds and places of work, for people belonging to different groups, usually defined in terms of race, caste or ethnicity. Integration aims at reversing segregation.
Self-Determination:	A doctrine justifying the autonomy and independence of an individual or group conceived as possessing a distinctive identity and free-will. Inherent ambiguities in the term include the question of who exactly constitutes the 'self' (e.g—the national) and to what degree the self can 'determine' its status, condition or future (i.e.—whether it automatically extends to full territorial independence).

Self-Government: A condition in which an individual or collectivity manages his/her own affairs and resources, and is solely responsible for his/her actions and destiny. More narrowly, a doctrine commending the virtues of autonomy or living according to one's distinctive 'inner rhythms', which require freedom from external constraints.

Semi-Presidential System
of Government: A system of government which has a dual executive, based on different electoral mandates. The system has a directly elected president as well as a government dependent upon the support of the parliament.

Separatism: A movement that takes as its starting point the principle of self-determination of peoples, and the opinion that sovereignty over a given territory is only legitimate when it results from the consensus of those people living within that territory. Separatists generally regard the state as an institution of national self-organisation, and therefore ethnic homogeneity and cultural consensus become ideological elements for the political and territorial separation based on these criteria.

Sovereignty: The condition of exercising supreme authority. A sovereign may be an individual person or a collective identity. In the modern era, a term generally applied to states. 'State sovereignty' can be defined as either legal or political freedom from external control. In recent years, the nature of state sovereignty has changed as states are increasingly integrated in supranational organisations.

State: In its modern definition as a form of political association was generally agreed upon in the nineteenth century, though the term still eludes specific definition. States have a distinct territorial character, sovereign authority from both an internal and external standpoint, resources of physical power at their disposal, a legal personality, and are distinguished by bonds among their members. Without question, contemporary forces, such as globalisation are changing the nature of the state, its boundaries and the relationship between states and citizens.

Statutory Instruments: The rules, regulations and orders made by the executive under designated legislative authority.

Subsidiarity: Principle stating that decisions should be taken at the lowest appropriate level. Subsidiarity is commonly argued to be the best form of governance to address minority/majority issues.

Territoriality: An emotional or passionate connection or bond with a particular territory or 'homeland'. Territoriality is a powerful component of national identity, and its presence or absence is sometimes used to distinguish between 'nations' and 'ethnic groups'.

Top-Down Policies: Policies or policy programmes designed an initiated by the central government—i.e., state-directed policies. Top-down policies are implemented but do not originate at the local level.

Transparency:

The duty of those responsible for the management of resources to report, openly and fully, on their intended and actual use of those resources. Without transparency, there can be no true accountability.

Unitary System of
Government:

A unitary government is characterised by a single level of government for the entire country. There are no regional or local governments acting independently of the national government. The national government usually delegates specific powers to locally constituted bodies or functionaries who are responsible to the national government for their action. The most emulated example of this form of government is the French system.

United Nations (UN):

Formally established in October 1945, in the aftermath of the Second World War, when its basic constitutive instrument, the UN Charter, entered into force for the 51 founder states. The UN is comprised of special agencies, funds and programmes and among its central organs are: the General Assembly, Security Council, Secretariat, International Court of Justice, and the Economic and Social Council (ECOSOC).

Xenophobia:

A psychological concept describing certain persons' disposition to fear or abhor other persons or groups perceived as outsiders.

Glossary Sources:

James E. Anderson (1997) *Public Policymaking*, Third Edition, New York: Houghton Mufflin Company.

Richard M. Bird, Robert D. Ebel, Christine I. Wallich (eds.) (1999) *Decentralization of the Socialist State*, World Bank Regional and Sectoral Studies, Second Edition.

Vernon Bogdanor (ed.) (1997) *The Blackwell Encyclopedia of Political Science*, Oxford: Blackwell Publishers.

'Central and Eastern Europe Skills-Exchange Workshop Series', Minority Rights Group International.

'Compendium of Activities' (2001) UNDP Programme for Accountability and Transparency, January.

Kenneth Davey (2000) 'Fiscal Decentralisation', *Local Government Brief*, Budapest, LGI, September.

Daniel Kaufman, Aart Kraay, Pablo Zoido-Loboton (2001) 'Governance Matters: From Measurement to Action', *Local Government Brief*, Budapest, LGI, January.

John McGarry and Brendan O'Leary (eds.) (1993) *The Politics of Ethnic Conflict Regulation: Case Studies of Protracted Ethnic Conflicts*, Routledge: London.

J.Oloka-Onyango (1999) 'Globalisation in the Context of Increased Incidents of Racism, Racial Discrimination and Xenophobia', Working paper submitted to the Sub-Commission, E.CN.4/1999/Sub-Com 2/8.

'Regionalisation and its Effect on Local Self-Government' ([ ])Report by the Steering Committee on Local and Regional Authorities (CDLR), Local and Regional Authorities in Europe, No. 64, Council of Europe Publishing.

Roger Scruton (ed.) (1982) *A Dictionary of Political Thought,* London: Macmillan Press.

BIBLIOGRAPHY

George Schöpflin ·· *Minorites and Democracy*

Abrams, Bradley F. (1995) 'Morality, Wisdom and Revision: the Czech Expulsion of the Sudeten Germans', *East European Politics and Societies*, Vol.9, No.2, pp. 234-255.

Altermatt, Urs (1997) *Nationalismus in Europa*, Zürich: Verlag Neue Zürcher Zeitung.

Anderson, Benedict (1991) *Imagined Communities*, 2nd edition, London: Verso.

Arendt, Hannah (1958) *The Origins of Totalitarianism*, London: Allen and Unwin.

Armstrong, John (1982) *Nations before Nationalism*, Chapel Hill NC: University of North Carolina Press.

Aspeslagh, Robert, Hans Renner, Hans van der Meulen (eds.) (1994) *Im historischen Würgegriff: die Beziehungen zwischen Ungarn und der Slowakei in der Vergangenheit, Gegenwart und Zukunft*, Baden-Baden: Nomos Verlag.

Balázs, Zoltán (1998) *Modern hatalomelméletek*, Budapest: Korona.

Banac, Ivo (1984) *The National Question in Yugoslavia*, Cornell: Cornell University Press.

Barany, Zoltan (1996) 'Living on the Edge: the East European Roma in Postcommunist Politics and Societies', in: Drobizheva, Leokadia et al. (eds.) *Ethnic conflict in the Post-Soviet World*, Armonk NY: M.E.Sharpe.

Barth, Fredrik (ed.) (1969) *Ethnic Groups and Boundaries: the Social Organisation of Culture Difference*, Bergen/Oslo: Universitetsforlaget.

Bauman, Zygmunt (1987) *Legislators and Interpreters*, Cambridge: Polity.

Bauman, Zygmunt (1994) 'After the Patronage State: a Model in Search of Class Interests', in: Christopher Bryant and Edmund Mokrzycki (eds.) *The New Great Transformation*, London: Routledge. pp.14-35.

Bauman, Zygmunt (1997) 'Intellectuals in East-Central Europe: Continuity and Change' *East European Politics and Societies*, Vol.1, No.2, pp.162-186.

Bauman, Zygmunt (1998) *Globalization: the Human Consequences*, Cambridge: Polity.

Beck, Ulrich, Anthony Giddens and Scott Lash (1994) *Reflexive Modernisation: Politics, Tradition and Aesthetics in the Modern Social Order*, Cambridge: Polity.

Berger, Peter (1998) 'A globalis kultura negy arca', *2000*, August-September 1998. pp. 16-20.

Berger, Peter (1967) *The Sacred Canopy: Elements of a Sociological Theory of Religion*, New York: Doubleday.

Berger, Peter and Thomas Luckman (1991) *The Social Construction of Reality: a Treatise in the Sociology of Knowledge*, London: Penguin.

Berlin, Isaiah (1990) 'The Bent Twig: On the Rise of Nationalism', *The Crooked Timber of Humanity*, London: John Murray.

Billig, Michael (1995) *Banal Nationalism*, London: SAGE.

Bíró Zoltán & József Lőrincz (eds.) (2000) 'Szeklerland in Transition: Essays in Cultural Anthropology', Miercurea Ciuc: ProPrint.

Boia, Lucian (1997) *Istorie si mit in constiinta romaneasca,* Bucharest: Humanitas.

Bourdieu, Pierre (1992) *Language and Symbolic Power,* Cambridge: Polity.

Bourdieu, Pierre (1993) *The Field of Cultural Production,* Cambridge: Polity.

Boyarin, Jonathan (ed.) (1994) *Remapping Memory: the Politics of TimeSpace,* Minneapolis: University of Minneapolis Press.

Cassirer, Ernst (1946) *Language and Myth,* New York: Dover.

Cassirer, Ernst (1946, 1974) *The Myth of the State,* New Haven, London: Yale University Press.

Cesarani, David and Mary Fulbrook (eds.) (1996) Citizenship, Nationality and Migration in Europe, London: Routledge.

Connor, Walker (1994) *Ethnonationalism: the Quest for Understanding,* Princeton NJ: Princeton University Press.

Coupe, Laurence (1997) *Myth,* London: Routledge.

Craciun, Maria and Ovidiu Ghitta (eds.) (1995) *Ethnicity and Religion in Central and Eastern Europe,* Cluj: Cluj University Press.

Donnan, Hastings and Thomas M. Wilson (1999) *Borders: Frontiers of Identity, Nation and State,* Oxford: Berg.

Douglas, Mary (1975) *Implicit Meanings,* London: Routledge.

Douglas, Mary (1986) *How Institutions Think,* Syracuse NY: Syracuse University Press.

Douglas, Mary (1996) *Thought Styles: Critical Essays on Good Taste,* London: SAGE.

Dunleavy, Patrick and Brendan O'Leary (1987) *Theories of the State: the Politics of Liberal Democracy,* London: Macmillan.

Durkheim, Emile, (1995)*The Elementary Forms of Religious Life,* New York: Free Press.

Eliade, Mircea (1954) *The Myth of the Eternal Return: Cosmos and History,* London: Penguin.

Elias, Norbert (1982) *The Civilizing Process: State Formation & Civilization,* Oxford: Blackwell.

Elias, Norbert (1991) *The Symbol Theory,* London: SAGE.

Elias, Norbert (1992) *Time: an Essay,* Oxford: Blackwell.

Fukuyama, Francis (1995) *Trust: The Social Virtues and the Creation Prosperity,* London: Hamish Hamilton.

Gellner, Ernest (1988) *Plough, Sword and Book: the Structure of Human History,* London: Collins Harvill.

Gellner, Ernest (1992) *Reason and Culture: the Historic Role of Rationality and Rationalism,* Oxford: Blackwell.

Gellner, Ernest (1991) 'Islam and Marxism: some comparisons' *International Affairs* 67:1, pp. 1-6.

Gellner, Ernest (1994) *Conditions of Liberty: Civil Society and its Rivals,* London: Hamish Hamilton.

Gellner, Ernest (1995) *Nations and Nationalism,* Oxford: Blackwell.

Giddens, Anthony (1990) *The Consequences of Modernity,* Cambridge: Polity.

Giddens, Anthony (1999) *Runaway World: How Globalisation is Reshaping Our Lives,* London: Profile.

Glenny, Misha (1999) *The Balkans 1804-1999: Nationalism, War and the Great Powers,* London: Granta.

Gombár, Csaba et al. (eds.) (1997) *És mi lesz, ha nem lesz? Tanulmányok az államról a 20. század végén,* Budapest: Helikon for Korridor.

Hall, John (1994) *Coercion and Consent,* Cambridge: Polity.

Hall, John (ed.) (1995) *Civil Society: Theory, History, Comparison,* Cambridge: Polity.

Hankiss, Elemér (1997) *Az emberi kaland: egy civilizáció-elmélet vázlata,* Budapest: Helikon.

Hankiss, Elemér (1999) *Proletár reneszánsz: tanulmányok az európai civilizációról és a magyar társadalomról,* Budapest: Helikon.

Hirschman, Albert O. (1970).*Exit, Voice and Loyalty: Responses to Decline in Firms, Organizations and States,* Cambridge MA: Harvard University Press.

Hobsbawm, Eric (1990) *Nations and Nationalism since 1780,* Cambridge: Cambridge University Press.

Hobsbawm, Eric and Terence Ranger (eds.) (1983) *The Invention of Tradition*, Cambridge: Cambridge University Press.

Holquist, Michael (1990) *Dialogism: Bakhtin and his World*, London: Routledge.

Holy, Ladislav (1996) *The Little Czech Nation and the Great Czech Nation: National Identity and the Post-communist Social Transformation*, Cambridge: Cambridge University Press.

Horowitz, Donald (1985) *Ethnic Groups in Conflict*, Berkeley: University of California Press.

Hosking, Geoffrey and George Schöpflin (eds.) (1997) *Myths and Nationhood*, London: Hurst.

Hroch, Miroslav (1985) *Social Preconditions of National Revival in Europe*, Cambridge: Cambridge University Press.

Ignatieff, Michael (1994) *Blood and Belonging : Journeys into the New Nationalism*, London: Verso.

Ignatieff, Michael (1996) 'Nationalism and Toleration', in: Richard Caplan and John Feffer, *Europe's New Nationalism: States and Minorities in Conflict*, New York: Oxford University Press.

Jowitt, Ken (1992) *New World Disorder: the Leninist Extinction*, Berkeley: University of California Press.

Judah, Tim (1997) *The Serbs: History, Myth and the Destruction of Yugoslavia*, London: Yale University Press.

KAM (1995) *Változásban? Elemzések a romániai magyar társadalomról*, Miercurea-Ciuc: ProPrint.

KAM (1996) *Egy más mellett élés: a magyar-román, a magyar-cigaáy kapcsolatokról*, Miercurea-Ciuc: ProPrint.

Kapferer, Bruce (1987) *Legends of People, Myths of State*, Washington: Smithsonian Institute Press.

Keane, John (1993) 'Nations, Nationalism and the European Citizen', *Filosovski Vestnik/Acta Philosophica*, (Ljubljana) Vol. 14, No. 2, 1993, pp. 35-56.

Kedourie, Elie (1960).*Nationalism*, London: Hutchinson.

Kemp, Walter (1999) *Nationalism and Communism in Eastern Europe and the Soviet Union: a Basic Contradiction*, London: Macmillan.

Kertzer, David I. (1988) *Ritual, Politics and Power*, New Haven CT: Yale University Press.

Koselleck, Reinhart (1997) 'The Temporalisation of Concepts', *Finnish Yearbook of Political Thought* Vol. 1, Jyväskylä: SoPhi, pp. 16-24.

Kuhn, Thomas (1962) *The Structure of Scientific Revolutions*, Chicago: University of Chicago Press.

Lal, Deepak (1998) *Unintended Consequences: the Impact of Factor Endowments, Culture, and Politics on Long-Run Economic Performance*, Cambridge MA: MIT Press.

Lauristin, Marju and Peeter Vihalemm ((1997) *Return to the Western World: Cultural and Political Perspectives on the Estonian Post-communist Transition*, Tartu: Tartu University Press.

Leff, Carol Skalnik (1988) *National Conflict in Czechoslovakia: the Making and Remaking of a State 1918-1987*, Princeton: Princeton University Press.

Lijphart, Arendt (1968) *The Politics of Accommodation*, Berkeley: University of California Press.

Mach, Zdzislaw (1993) *Symbols, Conflict and Identity*, Albany NY: SUNY Press.

McCrone, David (1998) *The Sociology of Nationalism*, London: Routledge.

Macdonald, Sharon (ed.) (1993) *Inside European Identities: Ethnography in Western Europe*, Oxford: Berg.

McGarry, John and Brendan O'Leary (eds.) (1992) *The Politics of Ethnic Conflict Regulation*, London: Routledge.

McNeill, W.H. (1964) *Europe's Steppe Frontier*, Chicago: University of Chicago Press.

McNeill, W.H. (1983) *The Pursuit of Power*, Oxford: Blackwell.

Mann, Michael (1993) *The Sources of Power: The Rise of Class and Nation-States 1760-1914*, Cambridge: Cambridge University Press.

Mann, Michael (1995) 'A Political Theory of Nationalism and its Excesses', in: Sukumar Periwal (ed.) *Notions of Nationalism*, Budapest: Central European University Press, pp. 44-64.

Markusse, Jan D. (1998) 'Ethnonationalism in Western Europe: Alto Adige as an Example of a Consociational Solution of Ethnic Conflict', in: Anna Krasteva (ed.) *Communities and Identities,* Sofia: Petekston. [ISBN 954-457-100-3]

Mastnak, Tomaz (1996) 'Fascists, Liberals and Anti-Nationalism' in Caplan, Richard & John Feffer, *Europe's New Nationalism: States and Minorities in Conflict,* Oxford: Oxford University Press, pp. 59-74.

Mayerfeld Bell, Michael and Michael Gardiner (eds.) (1998) *Bakhtin and the Human Sciences: No Last Words* London: SAGE.

Miller, David (1995) *On Nationality,* Oxford: OUP.

Motyl, Alexander (1999) *Revolutions, Nations, Empires: Conceptual Limits and Theoretical Possibilities,* New York: Columbia University Press.

Musil, Jiri (ed.) (1995) *The End of Czechoslovakia,* Budapest: Central European University Press.

Noiriel, Gerard (1996) *The French Melting Pot: Immigration, Citizenship and National Identity,* trans. Geoffroy de Laforcade, Minneapolis: University of Minnesota Press.

Offe, Claus (1994) *Der Tunnel am Ende des Lichts: Erkundungen der politischen Transformation im Neuen Osten,* Frankfurt/Main: Campus.

Offe, Claus (1996) *Modernity and the State: East, West,* Cambridge: Polity.

Offe, Claus (1998) 'Agenda, Agency and Aims of Central East European Transitions', in: Stefano Bianchini and George Schöpflin (eds.) *State Building in the Balkans: Dilemmas on the Eve of the 21st Century,* Ravenna: Longo. [ISBN 88-8063-172-1]

Ollila, Anne (ed.) (1999) *Historical Perspectives on Memory,* Helsinki: SHS.

Orridge, A.W. (1981) 'Varieties of Nationalism', in: Leonard Tivey (ed.) *The Nation-State: the formation of modern politics,* Oxford: Martin Robertson. pp. 39-58.

Pecican, Ovidiu and Enikö Magyari-Vincze (eds.) (1997) *Transition in Central and Eastern Europe,* Cluj: Cluj University Press.

Periwal, Sukumar (ed.) (1995) *Notions of Nationalism,* Budapest: Central European University Press.

Pierré-Caps, Stéphane (1995) *La Multination: L'avenir des minorités en Europe Centrale et Orientale,* Paris: Odile Jacob.

Pléh, Csaba (1996) 'A narratívumok mint a pszichológiai koherenciateremtés eszközei' [Narratives as instruments for creating psychological coherence] *Holmi* ,Vol. 8, No. 2, February 1996, pp. 265-282.

Puntscher Riekmann, Sonja (1998) *Die kommissarische Neuordnung Europas: das Dispositive der Integration,* Vienna: Springer.

Pusic, Vesna (1994) 'Dictatorship with Democratic Legitimation: Democracy versus Nation', *East European Politics and Societies,* Vol. 8, No. 3.

Rothschild, Joseph (1981) *Ethnopolitics: a Conceptual Framework,* New York: Columbia University Press.

Schöpflin, George (1993) *Politics in Eastern Europe 1945-1992,* Oxford: Blackwell.

Schöpflin, George (2000) *Nations, Identity, Power,* London: Hurst.

Schöpflin, George and Nancy Wood (eds.) (1989) *In Search of Central Europe,* Cambridge: Polity.

Schöpflin, George (with Geoffrey Hosking) (1997) *Myths and Nationhood* including 'A Taxonomy of Myths and their Functions', London: Hurst.

Scott, James C. (1998) *Seeing like a State: How Certain Schemes to Improve the Human Condition Have Failed,* New Haven: Yale University Press.

Sekelj, Laslo (1993) *Yugoslavia: the Process of Disintegration,* New York: Columbia University Press.

Shafir, Michael (1985) *Romania: Politics, Economics and Society,* London: Pinter.

Shoup, Paul (1968) *Communism in the Yugoslav National Question,* New York: Columbia University Press.

Siedentop, Larry (2000) *Democracy in Europe,* London: Penguin.

Silber, Laura and Alan Little (1995) *The Death of Yugoslavia,* London: Penguin.

Simic, Andrei (1973) *The Peasant Urbanites: a Study of Rural-Urban Mobility in Serbia*, New York: Seminar Press.

Simpson, David (1993) *Romanticism, Nationalism and the Revolt against Theory*, Chicago: Chicago University Press.

Smith, Anthony (1986) *The Ethnic Origins of Nations*, Oxford: Blackwell.

Smith, Anthony (1998) *Nationalism and Modernism: a critical survey of recent theories of nations and nationalism*, London: Routledge.

Steiner, George (1984) *Antigones*, Oxford: OUP.

Szporluk, Roman (1988) *Communism and Nationalism: Karl Marx versus Friedrich List*, Oxford: Oxford University Press.

Sztompka, Piotr (1991) 'The Intangibles and Imponderables of the Transition to Democracy', *Studies in Comparative Communism*, 24:3, September.

Szűcs, Jenő (1988) *Vázlat Európa három történeti régiójáról*, Budapest: Magvető; partially translated as 'Three Historical Regions of Europe', in: John Keane (ed.) *Civil Society and the State*, London: Verso, pp. 291-332.

Tamir, Yael (1993) *Liberal Nationalism*, Princeton: Princeton University Press.

Tilly, Charles (ed.) (1975) *The Formation of the National State in Western Europe*, Princeton NJ: Princeton University Press.

Urry, John (2000) *Sociology beyond Societies: Mobilities for the Twenty-first Century*, London: Routledge.

van Istendael, Geert (1994) *A belga labirintus avagy a formátlanság bája* (The Belgian labyrinth or the charms of formlessness), Budapest: Gondolat.

Verdery, Katherine (1991) *National Ideology under Socialism: Identity and Cultural Politics in Ceausescu's Romania*, Berkeley CA: University of California Press.

Walas, Teresa (1995) *Stereotypes and Nations*, Cracow: International Cultural Centre.

Weber, Eugen (1977) *Peasants into Frenchmen: the Modernization of Rural France 1870-1914*, London: Chatto.

Weber, Max (1958) *'Politik als Beruf' Gesammelte Politische Schriften*, 2ND edition, Tübingen: Mohr Verlag. pp.493-548.

Zartman, William (ed.) (1995) *Collapsed States: The Disintegration and Restoration of Legitimate Authority*, Boulder and London: Lynne Rienner Publishers.

Tony Verheijen ·· Public Administration Reform: A Mixed Picture

Bennett, R. (1994) *Local Government in the New Europe*, New York: Belhaven Press.

Coulson, A. (1995) *Local Government in Eastern Europe*, Cheltenham: Edward Elgar Publishers.

Feldbrugge, F.J.M. (ed.) (1987) *The Distinctiveness of Soviet Law*, Dordrecht: Martinus Nijhoff Publishers.

Fournier, J. (1998) 'Governance and European Integration, Reliable Public Administration', in: *Preparing Public Administrations for the European Administrative Space*, Paris: OECD, SIGMA Papers: No. 23.

Hesse, J. J. (1993) 'From Transformation to Modernization: Administrative Change in Central and Eastern Europe', *Public Administration*, Vol. 71, No. 1/2.

Hesse, J. J. (1998) 'Rebuilding the State, Administrative Reform in Central and Eastern Europe', in: *Preparing Public Administrations for the European Administrative Space*. Paris: OECD, SIGMA Papers: No. 23.

International IDEA (1997) *Democracy in Romania*, Stockholm.

Jabes, J. and M. Vintar (eds.) (1996) *Public Administration in Transition*, Bratislava: NISPAcee.

Jabes, J. (ed.) (1997) *Developing Organisations and Changing Attitudes, Public Administration in Central and Eastern Europe,* Bratislava: NISPAcee.

Jabes, J. (1998) *Professionalisation of Public Servants in Central and Eastern Europe,* Bratislava: NISPAcee.

Jabes, J. and J. Caddy (eds.) (2000) *Improving Relations between Public Administration and Citizens,* Bratislava: NISPAcee.

Josza, G. (1988 and 1989) 'Das reformprojekt Gorbatschows im ramen des Politbürokratischen Systems', *Köln: Berichte des Bundesinstituts für Ostwissenschaftliche und Internationale Studien,* No. 43 (1988) and No. 6 (1989).

Kotchegura, A. (1998) 'The Political Regime and the Civil Service in Present Day Russia', paper presented at the NISPAcee Annual Conference, Prague, 18-20 March 1998.

Meyer-Sahling, J. (2000) 'East meets West: Adapting Western Frameworks for the Study of Politico-Administrative Relations to Post-Communist Settings', unpublished paper, London: LSE.

Verheijen, T., and A. Dimitrova (1996) 'Private Interests and Public Administration: the Central and East European Experience', *International Review of Administrative Sciences,* No. 62, pp. 197-218.

Verheijen, T. (1995) *Constitutional Pillars for New Democracies,* Leiden: DSWO Press.

Verheijen, T. and D. Coombes (1998) *Innovations in Public Management, Experiences from East and West Europe,* Aldershot: Edward Elgar Publishers.

Verheijen, T. (1999) *Civil Service Systems in Central and Eastern Europe,* Aldershot: Edward Elgar Publishers.

Patrick Thornberry ·· *An Unfinished Story of Minority Rights*

Alston, P., M. Bustelo and J. Heenan (eds.) (1999) *The EU and Human Rights,* Oxford: Oxford University Press.

Alston, P. and J. Crawford (eds.) (2000) *The Future of UN Human Rights Treaty Monitoring,* Cambridge: Cambridge University Press.

Asad, T. (1997) 'On Torture, or Cruel, Inhuman and Degrading Treatment', in R. A. Wilson (ed.) *Human Rights, Culture and Context,* London and Chicago: Pluto Press.

Barbieri, M. (1999) 'Group Rights and the Muslim Diaspora', *Human Rights Quarterly* 21, pp. 907-26.

Benoit-Rohmer, F. (1996) *The Minority Question in Europe: Texts and Commentary,* Strasbourg: Council of Europe Publishing.

Biscoe, A. (1999) 'The European Union and Minority Nations', in: P. Cumper and S. Wheatley (eds.) *Minority Rights in the 'New' Europe',* The Hague: Martinus Nijhoff Publishers.

Bloed, A. and P. van Dijk (eds.) (1999) *Protection of Minority Rights through Bilateral Treaties: The Case of Central and Eastern Europe,* The Hague: Kluwer Law International.

Bobbio, N. (1996) *The Age of Rights,* Cambridge: Polity Press.

Brownlie, I. (1992) *Basic Documents on Human Rights,* Oxford: Clarendon Press, 3RD edition.

Dimitrov, N. (1999) *The Framework Convention,* Skojpe and Melbourne: Matica Makedonska.

Eagleton, T. (2000) *The Idea of Culture,* Oxford: Blackwell Publishers, 2000.

Eide, A. (1993) *Possible Ways and Means of Facilitating the Peaceful and Constructive Solution of Problems Involving Minorities,* UN Doc. E/CN.4/Sub.2/1993/34, section II.

Estebanez, M. Amor Martin (1996) *International Organisations and Minority Protection in Europe,* Turko/Abo: Abo Akademi University.

Framework Convention for the Protection of National Minorities. Online, Internet: http://www.human-rights.coe.int/Minorities/index.htm

Framework Convention for the Protection of National Minorities: Collected Texts (1999) Strasbourg: Council of Europe Publishing.

Geertz, C. (2000) *Available Light*, Princeton: Princeton University Press.

Gilbert, G. (1999) 'Minority Rights under the Council of Europe', in: P. Cumper and S. Wheatley (eds.) *Minority Rights in the 'New' Europe'*, The Hague: Martinus Nijhoff Publishers.

Gilbert, G. (1996) 'The Council of Europe and Minority Rights', *Human Rights Quarterly* 18.

Green, L. (1994) 'Internal Minorities and their Rights', in: J. Baker (ed.) *Group Rights*, Toronto, Buffalo, London: Toronto University Press.

Hoffman, R. (1999) 'A Presentation of the Framework Convention...and its Contribution to the Protection of Minority Languages', in: *Implementation of the European Charter for Regional or Minority Languages.* Strasbourg: Council of Europe.

Human Rights: Status of International Instruments (1987) New York: United Nations.

Jacobs, F. G. and R. C. A. White (1996) *The European Convention on Human Rights,* Oxford: Clarendon Press, 2ND edition, chapter 22.

Kymlicka, W. (ed.) (1995) *The Rights of Minority Cultures,* Oxford: Oxford University Press.

Lund Recommendations on the Effective Participation of National Minorities in Public Life. Online, Internet: http://www.osce.org/hcnm/documents/lund.htm.

Marks, S. (1997) 'The End of History? Reflections on Some International Theses,' 3 *E.J.I.L.*

Mertus, J. (1997) 'The Dayton Peace Accords: Lessons from the Past and for the Future', in: P. Cumper and S. Wheatley (eds.) *Minority Rights in the 'New' Europe'*, The Hague: Martinus Nijhoff Publishers.

'Minority Education Rights' (1996/7) International Journal on Minority and Group Rights, Special Issue, Vol. 4, No. 2.

'Minority Language Rights and the Oslo Recommendations' (1999) International Journal on Minority and Group Rights, Vol. 6, No. 3.

Mutua, Makauwa (2000) 'Politics and Human Rights: An Essential Symbiosis', in: M. Byers (ed.) *The Role of Law in International Politics,* Oxford: Oxford University Press.

Online, Internet: CEI Website. See: http://www.ceinet.org/minority.htm.

Online, Internet: European Commission Website, 'Economic Restructuring and Development in Southeastern Europe.' See: http://www.seerecon.org/KeyDocuments.

OSCE High Commissioner on National Minorities, *Report on The Linguistic Rights of Persons Belonging to National Minorities in the OSCE Area,* The Hague, March 1999.

OSCE High Commissioner on National Minorities, *Report on the Situation of Roma and Sinti in the OSCE Area,* The Hague, April 2000.

Pettit, P. (1997) *Republicanism: A Theory of Freedom and Government,* Oxford: Oxford University Press.

Preece, Jackson J. (1998) *National Minorities and the European Nation-States System,* Oxford: Clarendon Press.

Report on the Linguistic Rights of Persons belonging to National Minorities in the OSCE Area (1999) The Hague: OSCE High Commissioner on National Minorities, March.

Report on the Situation of the Roma and Sinti in the OSCE Area (2000) The Hague: OSCE High Commissioner on National Minorities, April.

Second Report on France, European Commission against Racism and Intolerance (ECRI) Council of Europe Doc. CRI (2000) 31.

Special issue dedicated to minority education rights, especially The Hague Recommendations, of the International Journal on Minority and Group Rights, Volume 4, No. 2 (1996/97).

Special issue dedicated to minority language rights, especially the Oslo Recommondations, of the International Journal on Minority and Group Rights, Volume 6, No. 3 (1999).

Spiliopoulou-Akermark, A. (1997) *Justifications of Minority Protection in International Law.* Uppsala: Iustus Forlag.

Suksi, M. (ed.) (1998) *Autonomy: Applications and Implications*, The Hague: Kluwer.

Taylor, C. (1991) *The Ethics of Authenticity*. Cambridge, Mass and London: Harvard University Press.

Thornberry, P. (1999) 'In the Strongroom of Vocabulary', in: P. Cumper and S. Wheatley (eds.) *Minority Rights in the 'New' Europe'*, The Hague: Martinus Nijhoff Publishers.

Thornberry, P. and M. Amor Martin Estebanez, (1994) *The Council of Europe and Minorities*, Strasbourg: Council of Europe, 1994.

Universal Declaration of Human Rights. Online, Internet: http://www.un.org/Overview/rights.html.

Elena Gyurova ·· *Emerging Multi-ethnic Policies in Bulgaria: A Central – Local Perspective*

Documents and Statistics

National Statistical Institute of Bulgaria (1994) *Results of the 1992 Census Vol.I. Demographic Characteristics*, Sofia: NSI.

Central Commission for Local Elections (1999) *Bulletin on the Results of the Local Elections Held on 16 October 1999 and on 23 October 1999. Vol.I. General Results*, Sofia: CCLE.

Bulgarian Council of Ministers (CM), Documents on the Establishment of Consultative Bodies and the Adoption of Programmes on Ethnic Minority Issues, 1994-1999: CM's Resolution No. 267/30.06.1994 for Interdepartmental Council on Ethnic Issues at the CM; CM's Decree No. 123/14.06.1995 on the National Council on Social and Demographic Issues at CM; CM's Decree No. 449/4.12.1997 on the National Council on Ethnic and Demographic Issues at the CM; CM's Resolution No. 163/30.01.1997 on the Programme on Solving Problems of the Roma in the Republic of Bulgaria; CM's Resolution of 22.04.1999 on the Framework Programme for the Equal Integration of the Roma in Bulgarian Society.

Decision of the Council of Ministers No. 36/9.02.1998 on the Adoption of a Strategy for the Establishment of a Modern Administrative System of the Republic of Bulgaria and the Declaration of the Government on the Strategy.

State Gazette, No. 106 / 3 December 1999, Council of Ministers' Decree No. 208/ 22 Nov. 1999, National Regional Development Plan for the period 2000-2006.

State Gazette, No 26 / 11 March 1999, Regional Development Act.

Books

Georgiev, J., I. Tomova, K. Kanev and M. Grekova (1993) *The Ethnocultural Situation in Bulgaria*, Sofia: The Archive of the International Centre for Minority Studies and Intercultural Relations (ICMSIR).

Krasteva, Anna. (ed.) (1998) *Societies and Identities in Bulgaria*, Sofia: Petekston.

Raichev, A., K. Kolev, A. Bundjolov and L. Dimova (2000) *Social Stratification in Bulgaria*, Sofia: Fridrich Ebert Foundation, Social-Democratic Institute, LIK.

Tomova, Ilona (1995) *The Gypsies in the Transition Period*, Sofia: ICMSIR.

Zheliazkova, A. (ed.) (1994) and (1997) *Interrelations of Compatibility and Incompatibility between the Christians and the Muslims in Bulgaria*, Sofia: ICMSIR.

Journals and Periodicals

Bedrov, I. (2000) 'Discrimination in Public Food Establishments is a Violation of Public Order', Sofia: *Etnoreporter*, No. 1, p. 14.

Emerson, Martin (1999) 'Roma Education in Eastern and Central Europe: Some Personal Reflections', *European Journal of Intercultural Studies*, Vol. 10, No. 2, pp. 201-206.

'Fifteen Months and a Half: Step by Step to Consensus' (1999) Sofia: *Etnoreporter*, No. 2, pp. 36-38.

Jecheva, M. (1998) 'Will Integration be able to Fight the Accumulated Effect of the Disadvantaged Position', Sofia: *Etnoreporter*, No. 4, pp. 4-6.

Kandeva, E. (1998) 'Reforms in the Public Administration and the Modern State', Sofia: *Parliamentary Democracy*, No. 8, pp. 4-21.

Kyuranov, Deian (1998) 'Integration Today: An Attempt at Systematic Theses', Sofia: *Etnoreporter*, No. 4, pp. 13-14.

'Public Administration and the Democratic Process' (1998) Sofia: *Parliamentary Democracy*, Special Issue. Publications of the Institute for Political and Legal Studies.

Schöpflin, George (1998) 'Citizenship, Ethnicity and Cultural Reproduction', Sofia: *Etnoreporter*, No. 1, pp. 36-40; No. 2, pp. 6-10.

Stefanova, M. (1998) 'The Model of Local Government in Bulgaria', Sofia: *Parliamentary Democracy*, No. 8. pp. 22-37.

Todorov, E. and M. Velikova (1999) 'A TV Programme Standing on Its Own (for Now)', Sofia: *Etnoreporter*, No. 5, pp. 51-52.

Reports

Committee for the Defence of Minority Rights (CDMR) (1994) *Minority Groups in Bulgaria in a Human Rights Context*, Sofia: CDMR.

Regular Report of the European Commission on the Progress of Bulgaria in the Accession Process to the EU (1999) From the Internet Site of EC.

A collection of reports from the conference, 'Parliamentarism and Contemporary Self-Government in Bulgaria' (1999) Sofia: USAID, LGI.

The World Bank (1999) *Bulgaria. Poverty During the Transition Report,* No. 18411, Executive Summary, Sofia: The World Bank Mission in Bulgaria.

The World Bank (1999) *Entering the 21st Century, World Development Report 1999-2000. Summary*, Washington DC: The World Bank.

UNDP (1999) *National Report on Human Development in Bulgaria 1999*, part I, 'Regional Differences: A Burden or a Chance', Sofia: UNDP

European Commission Against Racism and Intolerance (ECRI) (2000) *State Reports. The Second Report from Bulgaria*, submitted on 18 June 1999, Strasbourg: Council of Europe.

Human Rights Project NGO (1999) *Annual Report for 1998*, Sofia: Human Rights Project NGO.

Magazine and Newspaper Articles

'An interview with R. Rusinov from Human Rights Project NGO' (1999) *Why not?* No. 10, Sofia: CEGA.

Human Rights Project Bulletin (1998) Focus. Special issue. No. 10.

Kostov, P. (1999) 'Shall We Let the Law Eat Us Alive?' *Drom Dromendar*, Vol. 5, No. 6, November.

'Human Rights – Enforceable or Only Guaranteed' (2000) *Pari*, 4 February.

Laura Laubeová ·· *The Fiction of Ethnic Homegeneity Minorities in the Czech Republic*

Documents and Statistics

'National Employment Plan' (1999) *Sociální Politika,* No. 6.

1999 Country Reports on Human Rights Practices—Czech Republic (2000) Bureau of Democracy, Human Rights and Labor, U.S. Department of State, February 25

Act No. 326 of 30 November 1999, on Residence of Aliens in the Territory of the Czech Republic

'Analysis of the Beginning, Present Situation and Possibilities of Solving the Problems of Inhabitants of Maticni street', Final Report (1999) Prah–Ustí nad Labem: R Mosty–Socioklub, 30 April.

Bratinka Report. See in this bibliography, Report on the Situation of the Romany Community in the Czech Republic and Government Measures Assisting its Integration in Society.

Concluding Observations on the Czech Republic (1998) Committee on Elimination of Racial Discrimination (CERD), 19 March.

Communiqué of the Federal Ministry of Foreign Affairs No. 416/1992 Coll., on adoption of the Agreement between the Czech and Slovak Federative Republic and Poland on Good Neighbor Relations, Solidarity and Friendly Co-operation.

Communiqué of the Ministry of Foreign Affairs No. 521/1992 Coll., on adoption of the Agreement between the Czech and Slovak Federative Republic and the Federative Republic of Germany on Good Neighbor Relations and Friendly Co-operation.

Communiqué of the Ministry of Foreign Affairs No. 235/1993 Coll., on adoption of the Agreement between the Czech Republic and Slovakia on Good Neighborliness, Friendly Relations and Co-operation.

Communiqué of the Ministry of Foreign Affairs No. 96/1998 Coll., Framework Convention for the Protection of National Minorities.

Government Resolution No. 84/1994, on adoption of the Agreement between the Government of the Czech Republic and the Government of Poland on Cross-Border Cooperation.

Czech Helsinki Committee, *Report on Human Rights in CR in 1997.*

Czech Helsinki Committee, *Report on Human Rights in CR in 1998 and in 1999.*

Documentation Centre for Human Rights, 'Situace romské menšiny v ČR v letech 1998-1999' (Situation of Romany Minority in the CR in 1998-1999), a written statement provided to the researcher), 28 June 1999.

European Commission against Racism and Intolerance (ECRI), *Country by Country Approach, Report on the Czech Republic,* CRI (97) 50, 1997.

European Commission against Racism and Intolerance (ECRI): *Second report on the Czech Republic,* CRI 4, 2000.

Ethnic makeup of the Czech population. Basic information from final results of the 1991 public census. Prague, 1993.

Informace o plnění zásad stanovených Rámcovou úmluvou o ochraně národních menšin (Information on compliance with the Framework Convention for the Protection of National Minorities, Office of the Government of CR) 1 April 1999.

Informace o zprávě o plnění závazků plynoucích z Mezinárodní úmluvy o odstranění všech forem rasové diskriminace (Information on Report on implementation of the International Convention on Elimination of all forms of Racial Discrimination), Office of the Government of CR, 4 November 1999.

Law No. 508/1921 Coll., Treaty between Leading Powers Allied and Associated and Czechoslovakia signed in Saint-Germain-en-Laye on 10 September 1919.

Law No. 121/1920 Coll., which introduces the Constitutional Act of the Czechoslovak Republic.

Law No. 122/1920 Coll., based on Article 129 of the Constitution which sets out principles of language rights in the Czechoslovak Republic.

Law No. 144/1968 Coll., on status of national minorities in Czechoslovak Socialist Republic.

Law No. 23/1991 Coll., which introduces the Charter of Fundamental Rights and Freedoms as a constitutional law of the Czech and Slovak Federative Republic.

National Programme for the Preparation of the Czech Republic for Membership in the European Union, June 1999, Online, Internet: http:// www.czech.cz.

Návrh koncepce politiky vlády vůči příslušníkům romské komunity, napomáhající jejich integraci do společnosti a následné dokumenty rozpracovávající dané teze a koncepci (Draft Policy of the Czech Government towards the Romany community supporting their integration into society, Office of the Government of CR, April 1994), and related Government Resolution: Usnesení vlády ČR č. 279, 7 April 1999 o koncepci politiky vlády vůči příslušníkům romské komunity, napomáhající jejich integraci do společnosti.

Opatření na řešení problematiky zaměstnanosti osob obtížně umístitelných na trhu práce se zřetelem na příslušníky romské komunity, včetně usnesení vlády č. 640 ze dne 23.6.1999, MPSV (Measures to address the employment of persons with job placement difficulties with special regard to the Roma community, incl. government resolution of 23 June 1999), Ministry of Labour.

Programové prohlášení vlády ČR (Policy statement of the Czech Government), 1999.

Reforma verejne spravy (Public Administration Reform).

Report of Human Rights in the CR in 1998, Office of the Government of CR, 1 April 1999.

Report of Human Rights in the CR in 1999, Draft version.

Report on the Situation of the Romany Community in the Czech Republic and Government Measures Assisting its Integration in Society, Office of Minister without portfolio, The Czech Republic Government Office, Prague, 29 October 1997. The so-called Bratinka Report, includes the Government Resolution No. 686/97.

Resolution of the Government of the Czech Republic from 19 March 1998, No. 192 on Report on State Strategy in Punishing Criminal Offenses Motivated by Racism and Xenophobia or Committed by Supporters of Extremist Groups.

Statistical Yearbook of the Czech Republic 1993, Prague 1993, pp. 412-413.

United States Information Service: 1998 Country Reports on Human Rights Practices - Czech Republic.

Usnesení vlády CR ze dne 9.9. 1998 č. 589 o jmenování vládního zmocněnce pro lidská práva (Resolution of the Czech Government on nominating of the Human Rights Commissioner).

Ústavní zákon č. 1/1993 Sb, Ústava ČR, Hlava sedmá - Územní samospráva (Constitutional Law, Part 7–Territorial self-government).

Zpráva o plnění úkolů vyplývajících z usnesení vlády č. 686/1997 o situaci romské komunity v ČR. Informace pro schůzi vlády a usnesení vlády č. 643 ze 30. září 1998 (Report on implementing the resolution 686/1997 on situation of Romany community in CR, Office of the Government of CR, 30 September 1998).

Zpráva o rozpracování a aktivním postupu při uskutečňování dosud přijatých opatření ve vztahu k romské komunitě. Informace pro schůzi vlády ČR, 4. ledna 1999 (Report on elaborating and active policy in implementing measures related to Romany Community, Office of the Government of CR, 4 January 1999).

Books

Čanek, David (1996) *Národ, národnost menšiny a rasismus*, Praha: ISE.
Davidová, Eva (1995) *Cesty Romů*, Olomouc: UJEP.
Fraser, Agnus (1998) *Cikáni*, NLN, Praha.
Frištenská, Hana, Sulitka, Andrej (1995) *Průvodce právy příslušníků národnostních menšin v ČR*, Praha: Demokratická aliance Slovákov v ČR.
Gabal, Ivan (1999) *Etnické menšiny ve střední Evropě*, Praha: G plus G.
Modood, T. and P. Werbner (1989) *The Politics of Multiculturalism in the New Europe*.
Pekárek, Pavel (1997) *Romové–reflexe problému*, Praha: Pastelka.
Socioklub (1999), *Romové v České Republice (Roma in the Czech Republic)*, Prague: Socioklub.

Interviews

Body, Ladislav, Advisor to the Minister of Labour, 7 July 1999.
Davidova, Eva, 8 May 1999.
Goral, Ladislav, 23 June 1999.
Hejkrlíková, Jana, Rom member of the Interministerial Commission for Romany Affairs, 15 June 1999.
Holcová, Helena, Member of the team preparing the Government Conception towards Roma, 7 July 1999.
Holomek, Karel, Rom activist, 14 May 1999 and 29 June 1999.
Horáková, Milada, Research Institute of Labour and Social affairs, 7 July 1999.
Jiřincová, Helena, New School Foundation, 8 July 1999.
Kaplan, Petr, Ministry of Labour, 10 June 1999 and 7 July 1999.
Koskova, Alena, Council of the Pardubice Municipality, 24 June 1999.
Mitraš, Jaroslav, Rom employee, Ministry of Interior, 3 May 1999.
Moro, Jan, Rom member of a commission at the Ministry of Labour, 7 July 1999.
Pasova, Hilda, Rom social worker, 15 April 1999.
Pilař, Jiří and Marta Teplá, Ministry of Education, 29 June 1999 (informal debate at a conference break).
Sekyt, Viktor, Interministerial Commission for Romany Affairs, 1 April 1999, 11 June 1999 and 29 July 1999.
Sivák, Milan, Rom assistant in Most, 24 April 1999.
Šiškova, Tatjana, Sociologist, 22 June 1999.
Tancošova, Albína, Ministry of Education, 4 April 1999.
Tomášková, Petra, Czech Helsinki Committee,17 June 1999.
Turková, Jarmila, Legal Counsel, 22 June 1999.
Vávra, Libor, President of the Union of Judges, 2 July 1999.
Víšek, Petr, Ministry of Labour and Social Affairs, 11 June 1999.

Jenő Kaltenbach ·· *From Paper to Practice in Hungary:*
The Protection and Involvement of Minorities in Governance

Documents

Az országgyűlési képviselők választásáról szóló 1989. évi XXXIV. Törvény (Law on Elections).
A helyi önkormányzatokról szóló 1990.évi LXV. Törvény (Local Government Act).
Az állampolgári jogok országgyűlési biztosáról szóló 1993. évi LIX. Törvény (Act on the Parliamentary Commissioner of Human Rights).

A nemzeti és etnikai kisebbségek jogairól szóló 1993. évi LXXVII. Törvény (Minority Act).

A közoktatásról szóló 1993. évi LXXIX. Törvény (Act on Public Education).

National Curricula Plan, 130/1995 (X.26) 1998. Relevant from 1st of September 1998.

Ministerial Act about the State Normatives for Local Governments, National and Ethnic Supplementary Normatives... 1/1997(I.28) PM-BM.

Mid-term strategy to increase the life conditions of Gypsy population - Governmental Act 1093/1997 (VII.29.).

Ministerial Act on the Child Care and School Education of National and Ethnic Minorities (32/1997. (XI. 5.).

J/3670 Report on the Situation of National and Ethnic Minorities in the Hungarian Republic, Dr. Vastagh Pál, Minister of Justice, January 1997.

J/5524 Beszámoló a nemzeti és etnikai kisebbségi jogok országgyűlési biztosáról 1997 (Annual Report of the Parliamentary Commissioner for the Rights of National and Ethnic Minorities) 1 January-31 December 1997, Budapest.

J/859 Beszámoló a nemzeti és etnikai kisebbségi jogok országgyűlési biztosáról 1998 (Annual Report of the Parliamentary Commissioner for the Rights of National and Ethnic Minorities) 1 January-31 December 1998, Budapest.

J/2259 Beszámoló a nemzeti és etnikai kisebbségi jogok országgyűlési biztosáról 1999 (Annual Report of the Parliamentary Commissioner for the Rights of National and Ethnic Minorities, 1 January-31 December 1999, Budapest.

Report of the Government of the Republic of Hungary to the National Assembly on the situation of the national and ethnic minorities living in the Republic of Hungary, Hungarian Government Report No. J/3670 (Budapest: Office of the Prime Minister 1997).

Bilateral Treaties

1991 Declaration of the principles of co-operation between the Hungarian Republic and the Ukrainian Soviet Socialist Republic in the area of national minority rights

1991 Agreement for the good neighbour policy and the basis of co-operation between the Hungarian Republic and Ukraine

1992 Agreement for ensuring special rights for the Slovenian national minority in the territory of the Hungarian Republic and for the Hungarian national community in the Slovenian Republic

1992 Treaty of friendship and co-operation between the Hungarian Republic and the Slovenian Republic

1992 Treaty between the Hungarian Republic and the Croatian Republic on friendly ties and co-operation

1992 Treaty between the Hungarian Republic and the German Federal Republic on friendly co-operation and European partnership

1992 A joint declaration between the Hungarian Republic and the German Federal Republic on the German minority in Hungary and support for German to be taught as a foreign language

1995 Treaty between the Hungarian Republic and the Croatian Republic on protection of the Croat minority in Hungary and the Hungarian minority in Croatia

1995 Treaty between the Hungarian Republic and the Slovak Republic on good neighbour policy and friendly co-operation

1996 Treaty between the Hungarian Republic and Romania on understanding, co-operation and good neighbour policy

372   DIVERSITY IN ACTION ·· PART III

Books

Csefkó, Ferenc and Ilona Kovács Pálné (1999) *Kisebbségi Önkormányzatok Magyarországon* (Minority Self-Governments in Hungary) Budapest: Osiris Kiadó.
Office for National and Ethnic Minorities (1999) *Kisebbségek Magyarországon* (Minorities in Hungary) Budapest.
Representation and Participation of Minorities Budapest, 15-16 October 2000, Conference materials, published by the Parliamentary Commissioners Office, Council of Europe, MRG Int. Budapest.
Kovács, Dr. Péter (1996) *International Law and Minority Protection*, Budapest: Osiris.
Kertesi, Gábor and Gábor Kézdi (1996) 'Cigány tanulók az általános iskolában. Helyzetfelmérés és egy cigány oktatási koncepció vázlata' (Roma pupils in elementary schools: report and draft concept on the education of the Roma), in: *Cigányok és iskola,* Budapest: Educatio Press.
Puporka, L. and Zs. Zádori (1999) 'The Health Status of Roma in Hungary', Washington DC: The World Bank.
Hungarian Helsinki Committee (1999) 'Report on the Situation of Minorities in Hungary, September.

Articles

Harsányi, Eszter and Péter Radó (1997) 'Cigány tanulók a magyar iskolában' (Roma pupils in public education in Hungary) *Educatio,* spring.
Kemény, István (1997) 'A magyarországi roma (cigány) népességről két felmérés tükrében (On the Hungarian Roma population in the light of two surveys), *Magyar Tudomány,* No. 6.
'A jog lehetőségei és korlátai' (From the prohibition of negative discrimination to positive discrimination, the possibilities and limits of law) (1999) *Indok.*
Havas, Kemény and Kertesi (1998) 'Relative gypsy in the ring of classification', *Kritika,* No. 2.
Kemény, I (1997) 'The Roma (gypsy) population of Hungary', *Magyar Tudomány,* No. 6.
Kertesi, G. (1995) 'Gypsy children in the school, gypsy adoults on the labour market' (Cigány gyerekek az iskolában, cigány felnottek a munkaeropiacon), *Közgazdasági Szemle,* No. 1.
Kertesi, G. (1994) 'The Labour Market Situation of the Gypsy Minority in Hungary' Japan Project on Employment Policies for Transition in Hungary, Working Paper 14, Budapest.
Ladanyi, J.(1993) 'Patterns of Residential Segregation and the Gypsy Minority in Budapest', *International Journal of Urban and Regional Research.* Vol. 17. No.1. pp. 30-41.
Riba, I. (1999) 'Minority Self-Governments in Hungary' *The Hungarian Quarterly,* Volume 40.

Piotr Bajda, Magdalena Syposz and Dariusz Wojakowsksi ··
Equality in Law, Protection in Fact:
Minority Law and Practice in Poland

Adamczuk, L. (1997) *Wyznania religijne. Stowarzyszenia narodowosciowe i etniczne w Polsce 1993-1996* (Religion and National and Ethnic Associations in Poland 1993-1996), Warsaw, pp.169-184.
Antoszewski, A. and R. Herbuta (1998) *Leksykon Politologii* (Lexicon of political science), Wroclaw, pp. 498-499.
Babinski, G. (1997) *Pogranicze Polsko-Ukrainskie,* Kraków.
Bachmann (1999) *Polska Kaczka – Europejski Staw. Szanse i Pulapki Polskiej Polityki Europejskiej* (Polish duck – European pond. Chances and traps of Polish European policy), Warsaw, pp. 99-111.
Dziennik Ustaw (Journal of Law) of 1993, No. 7, item 34.

Eberhard, P. (1996) *Miedzy Rosja a Niemcami. Przemiany narodowosciowe w Europie Srodkowo-Wschodniej w XX w* (Between Russia and Germany. Nationalities changes in Central East Europe in 20ᵀᴴ century), Warsaw, p. 102-107.

European Commission Against Racism and Intolerance (2000) *Second Report on Poland*, June.

'Gminy lokalne, sejmiki partyjne' (Gminas are in local committee hands while powiats and voivodship councils are in the in hands of political parties), *Rzeczpospolita*, No. 250, 24-25 October 1998, p. 3.

Information Concerning the Education of Children and Youths of Roma Origin in Poland, OSCE Human Dimension Implementation Meeting, October 2000, document 267.

Jagielski, J. (1998) *Obywatelstwo polskie. Zagadnienia podstawowe* (Polish citizenship. Basic issues), Warsaw, p. 34.

Johannes, B. (1996) 'Podwójne obywatelstwo – szansa czy bariera we wspólpracy polsko-niemieckiej?' (Dual Citizenship: a Chance or Obstacle on the Road to Polish-German Cooperation?), in: P. Bajda, (ed.) *Obywatelstwo w Europie Srodkowo-Wschodniej* (Citizenship in Central-East Europe), Warsaw, p. 72.

Kamusella, T. (1996) 'Asserting minority rights in Poland', *Transition*, Vol. 2, No. 3, p. 17.

Klimkiewicz, B. (1999) *Participation of National and Ethnic Minorities in the Public Sphere: Recommendations for Poland*, Open Society Institute, p. 6.

Kranz, J. (ed) (1998) *Law and Practice of Central European Countries in the Field of National Minorities Protection after 1989*. Center for International Relations.

'Lech Wałęsa do wyborców w sprawie mniejszosci' (Lech Walesa's letter to electors on minorities), *Gazeta Wyborcza*, No. 6, 15 May 1989, p. 1.

Liegois, P. and N. Gheorghe (1997) *Roma/Gypsies: A European Minority*, Minority Rights Group.

Lodzinski, S. (1992) *Aktywnosc spoleczno-polityczna i dzialanosc kulturalno-oswiatowa mniejszosci narodowych w Polsce w okresie 1989-1992* (Social, political, cultural and education activity of national minorities in Poland between 1989-1992), Biuro Studiów i Ekspertyz Kancelarii Sejmu, Pakiet IP – 19M, Warsaw, p. 27.

Lodzinski, S. (1989) 'Repatriacja osób narodowosci lub pochodzenia polskiego w latach 1989-1997. Problemy prawne i instytucjonalne' (Rapatriation of persons with Polish orgins or Polish nationality between 1989-1997. Institutional and legal issues), in: *Repatriacja osób narodowosci polskiej lub pochodzenia polskiego w latach 1989-1997*, Biuro Studiów i Ekspertyz Kancelarii Sejmu, Informacje i opinie, pakiet IP – 76S, Warsaw, p. 9.

Lodzinski, S. (2000) The Policy of Multi-culturalism in Poland in 1990s (national minorities and immigrants). Legal solutions and social perceptions. Paper presented at World Conference Against Racism Regional Seminar, Warsaw, July 2000.

Lodzinski, S. (1998) 'The Protection of National Minorities in Poland: Law and Practice after 1989', in: J. Kranz, *Law and Practice of Central Europe Countries in the Field of National Minorities Protection after 1989*, Warsaw, p. 156.

Lodzinski, S. and P. Bajda (1995) *Ochrona praw osób nalezacych do mniejszosci narodowych* (Protection of persons belonging to national minorities), Warsaw, p. 164.

Malikowski, M. (1997) 'Polish-Ukrainian Relationship in the Province of Przemysl in the Period of Political Transformation', in: M. S. Szczepanski (ed.) Ethnic Minorities and Ethnic Majority. Sociological Studies of Ethnic Relations in Poland, Katowice, pp. 203-223

Maziarski, W. 'Sleepily, silently, threateningly', *Gazeta Wyborcza*, 5-6 September 1998, pp. 16-19.

Ministerstwo Edukacji Narodowej, Informacja o sytuacji edukacyjnej mniejszosci narodowych w Rzeczpospolitej Polskiej (Ministry of Education, Information paper on education situation of national minorities in Republic of Poland), Warsaw, 1994, table 1.

Minorities and the Media in Central and Eastern Europe Workshop Report (1999) London: Minority Rights Group.

Mniejszosci Narodowe w Polsce – Informator 1994 (National Minorities in Poland in 1994) (1995) Warsaw, pp. 93-94.

Ogólne Zalozenia Reformy Ustrojowej Panstwa (General Guidelines on the Reform of the Political System in Poland) (1998) Warsaw, p. 19 and appendix 2.

Powiat's Self Government Act, *Dziennik Ustaw*, No 91, position 576, 5 June 1998.

Regional Self Government Act, *Dziennik Ustaw*, No 91, position 578, 5 June 1998.

Sadowski, A. (1991) *Great and Little Nation. Belarussians in Poland*. Krakow: Nomos, pp. 121-122.

Sadowski, A. (1995) *Polish-Belarussian Borderland. Identity of its Inhabitants*. Bialystok: TransHumana.

Self-Government Act, *Dziennik Ustaw*, No. 34, position 198, 17 May 1990.

Szczepalski, Marek S. (1996) 'People without Local Homeland and the Regional Education', in: T. Lewowicki, B. Grabowska (eds.) *Borderland Communities. Multiculturalism. Education*, Cieszyn: Uniwersytet Slaski, pp. 167-170.

Szmeja, M. (1998) 'Historical and Social Underpinnings of Development of German Minority and Silesian Nation in Poland', Warsaw: *Studia Socjologiczne*, No 4 (151), p. 55.

Tefelski, M. (1995) 'Press on the Borderland', in: A. Sadowski (ed.) *Eastern Borderland from the Perspective of Sociology*, Bialystok: TransHumana, p. 217-228.

Thornberry, P. (1997) 'Contemporary Legal Standards on Minority Rights', in: Minority Rights Group (ed.) *World Directory of Minorities*.

Tyma, P. (1999) *Raport: Dostep Mniejszosci Narodowych do Mediow Publicznych w Polsce*. (Report on access of national minorities to public media in Poland).

Wodz, K. (ed.) (1993) *'Ours' and 'Aliens' in Upper Silesia*, Katowice: Uniwersytet Slaski.

Wodz, K.(ed.) (1995) *Regional Identity—Regional Consciousness: The Upper Silesian Experience*, Katowice: Uniwersytet Slaski.

Wodz, J. (ed.) (1990) *Upper Silesia from the Upper-Silesians' Point of View*, Katowice: Uniwersytet Slaski.

Wodz, K. and P. Wroblewski (1997) *Social World of Silesians. Reconstruction of the Common Consciousness*. Katowice: Uniwersytet Slaski.

World Directory of Minorities (1997) London: Minority Rights Group.

István Horváth and Alexandra Scacco ··
From the Unitary to the Pluralistic: Fine-tuning Minority Policy in Romania

Bereschi, Zsuzsa (2000) Adviser on International Relations to the President of the DAHR, interview, October.

Constantinescu, M. (1992) *Constitucia Romãniei– comentatã ci adnotatã*, Regia autonomã 'Monitorul Oficial', Bucharest, p.7.

Crampton, R. J. (1994) *Eastern Europe in the Twentieth Century*, London and New York: Routledge, p. 108.

Dunay, P. (1997) 'Hungarian-Romanian relations: A Changed Paradigm', in: Monika Wohlfeld (ed.) *The Effects of Enlargement on Bilateral Relations Between Central and Eastern Europe*, Paris: Institute for Security Studies.

Durandin, C. (1995) *Historire des Roumains*, Librarie Artheme Fayard.

Gallagher, T. (1999) *Democracy and Nationalism in Romania: 1989-1998*, Bucharest: All Educational, p. 1.

Gurr, T. (1993) *Minorities at Risk: A Global View of Ethnopolitical Conflicts*, United States Institute of Peace Research.

Habermas, J. (1994) 'Citizenship and National Identity', in: B. van Steenbergen (ed.) *The Condition of Citizenship*, London: Sage Publications, pp. 20-35.

Hetcher, M. ([ ]) *Internal Colonialism: The Celtic Fringe in British national Development, 1536-1966.* London: Routledge.

Horváth, I. (1999) 'Multiculturalism in Romania: Alternative or Evasion', in: Culic, Horváth and Stan (eds.) *Reflections on Differences. Focus on Romania,* Brussels: IPIS, pp. 1-12.

LGI Decentralisaton Volume 3, 'Local Governments in the CEE and CIS- An Anthology of Descriptive Papers: Romania', p.18. Work in Progress.

Livezeanu, I. (1995) *Cultural Politics in Greater Romania: Regionalism, Nation Building and Ethnic Struggle, 1918-1930,* Ithica: Cornell University Press.

Oprescu, D. (1999) 'Politici publice pentru minorit__ile nationale din România', in: *Sfera Politicii,* no. 66, January 1999, pp. 13-18.

Radocea, A. (1995) 'Structura etnic_ a popula_iei României _i evolu_ia ei în ultimele decenii', in: *Recens_mântul popula_iei _i locuin_elor din 7 Ianuaria 1992. Structura etnic__i confesional_ a popula_iei* Comisia Na_ional_ pentru Statistic_, pp. VII-LXXI.

Recensământul populatiei si locuintelor din 7 ianuarie 1992. Structura etnică si confesională a populatiei. Bucuresti, 1995, Comisia Natională pentru Statistică.

Report on the Application of Romania for Membership of the Council of Europe, 19 July 1993, Doc. 6901, paragraphs 44 and 59.

Romanian Constitution. Online, Internet: www.uniwuerzburg.de/law/ro00000_.html

The Legislative and Institutional Framework for the National Minorities of Romania (1994) Bucharest: Romanian Institute for Human Rights.

Kymlicka, W. (1995) *Multicultural Citizenship: A Liberal Theory of Minority Rights,* Oxford University Press.

Varga, E. Á. (1998) 'A romániai magyarság föbb demográfiai jellemzöi az 1992 évi népszámlálás eredményei alapjá', in: Varga, *Fejezetek a jelenkor Erdély népesedéstörténetéböl,* Budapest: Püski, pp. 260-276.

Verdery, Katherine (1991) *National Ideology under socialism: Identity and Cultural Politics in Ceasusescu's Romania.* Berkeley and Los Angeles: University of California Press.

Weber, R. (1997) 'The protection of national minorities in Romania: a matter of political will and wisdom', in: Kranz and Küpper (eds.) *Law and Practice of Central European Countries in the Field of National Minorities Protection After 1989,* Warsaw: Center for International Relations, pp. 199-268.

World Directory of Minorities (1997) Minority Rights Group, pp. 240-244.

Zamfir, E. and Zamfir, C: Tiganii. (1993) *Intre ignorare si îngrijorare Editura Alternative.* See also: Miroiu A. (ed.) (1998) *Invatamântul românesc azi. Studiu de diagnoza.* Polirom, pp. 141-144.

Ján Buček ·· *Responding to Diversity: Solutions at the Local Level in Slovakia*

Documents and statistics

Alternatívny návrh usporiadania samosprávy vyšších územných celkov (Alternative proposal of organisation of higher units of self-government), Office of the Government of the Slovak Republic, July 2000.

Ministry of Culture of the Slovak Republic. *Činnosti sekcie menšinových kultúr Ministerstva Kultúry Slovenskej Republiky v oblasti menšinovej politiky za 1. Štvrťrok 1999.* (Activities of Minority Cultures Section of Ministry of Culture of the Slovak Republic during first quarter of 1999. According to information of Section of Minority Cultures of Ministry of Culture from 2 July 1999), Online: http://www.culture.gov.sk.

Statistical Census 1991 (Sčítanie ľudu, domov a bytov 1991), Statistical Office of the Slovak Republic (1991) Bratislava.

Statistical Yearbook of the Slovak Republic 1992, Bratislava: Statistical Office of the Slovak Republic.

Statistical Yearbook of the Slovak Republic 1998, Bratislava: Statistical Office of the Slovak Republic and Bratislava: Veda.

Municipal election in Slovak Republic 18.-19. November 1994, Bratislava: Statistical Office of the Slovak Republic (in Slovak).

Municipal election in Slovak Republic 18.-19. December 1998, Bratislava: Statistical Office of the Slovak Republic, (in Slovak).

Institute of Information and Forecasting in Education (UIP MŠ SR) (1997) *Sieť škôl spracovaná podľa sumárnych výkazov z Ústavu informácií a prognóz školstva k 15.9.1997 za školský rok 1997/98* (School network elaborated according to records of Institute of Information and Forecasting in Education to 15.9.1997 for school year 1997/1998), Elaborated by K. Ondrášová,

Ministry of Culture of the Slovak Republic (1999) *Správa k implementácii Rámcového dohovoru Rady Európy na ochranu národnostných menšín v Slovenskej republike za MK SR.* (Report to implementation of the Global Agreement of the Council of Europe on minority protection in Slovak Republic on behalf of Ministry of Culture of the Slovak Republic), News of Ministry of Culture of the Slovak Republic, 30 March 1999, Online: http://www.culture.gov.sk.

Čič, M., et al. (1997) *Komentár k Ústave Slovenskej Republiky* (Commentary to the Constitution of the Slovak Republic, Martin (Matica Slovenská).

Stratégia reformy verejnej správy v Slovenskej Republike (Strategy of Public Administration Reform in the Slovak Republic). Verejná Správa, Vol. 54, No. 22-25, Supplement.

United Nations Development Programme. *Národná správa o ľudskom rozvoji - Slovensko 1998* (National Report on Human Development Slovakia - 1998). UNDP, 1998.

Zákon č.141/1961 Z.z. o trestnom konaní súdnom v platnom znení (Act No. 141/1961 Coll. on the Penal Court Proceedings (Penal Code) as amended).

Zákon č. 346/1990 Zb. o voľbách do orgánov samosprávy obcí v úplnom znení zákona č. 233/1998 Z.z. a č. 331/1998 Z.z. (Act No. 346/1990 Coll. Municipal Election Act, in full version of Act No. 233/1998 and Act No. 331/1998 Coll.).

Zákon č. 369/1990 Z.z. o obecnom zriadení (v platnom znení) (Act No. 369/1990 The Communities Act).

Zákon č. 138/1991 Z.z. o majetku obcí v platnom znení (Act No. 138/1991 on Municipal Property as amended).

Zákon č. 254/1991 Z.z. o Slovenskej televízii (v platnom znení) (Act No 254/1991 Coll. on Slovak Television as amended).

Zákon č. 255/1991 Z.Z. o Slovenskom rozhlase (v platnom znení) (Act No 255/1991 Coll. on Slovak Radio as amended).

Zákon č. 191/1994 Z.z. o označovaní obcí v jazyku národnostných menšín (Act No. 191/1994 Coll. on Municipal Topographical Indications in Minority Languages).

Zákon č. 154/1994 Z.z. o matrikách (Act No. 154/1994 Coll. on Registry Offices as amended by Act No. 222/1996 on the Organisation of Local State Administration).

Zákon č. 270/1995 Z.z. o štátnom jazyku Slovenskej republiky (Act No. 270/1995 Coll. on the State Language of the Slovak Republic as amended).

Zákon č. 221/1996 Z.z. o územnom a správnom usporiadaní Slovenskej republiky (Act No. 221/1996 on Territorial and Administrative Division of the Slovak Republic).

Zákon č. 222/1996 Z.z. o organizácii miestnej štátnej správy v platnom znení (Act No. 222/1996 Coll. on Organisation of Local State Administration as amended).

Zákon č. 184/1999 Z.z. o používaní jazykov národnostných menšín (Act No. 184/1999 on the Use of Minority Languages).

Zákon č. 301/1999 Z.z. o štátnej správe v školstve a školske samospráve (Act No. 301/1999 on State Administration in Education and School Self-government).

Books

Bačová, Viera (1996) *Etnická identita a historické zmeny* (Ethnic identity and historical changes), Bratislava: Veda.

Bakker, Edwin (1997) *Minority Conflicts in Slovakia and Hungary*, Capelle a/d Ijssel: Labyrint Publication.

Berčík, Peter (1998) *Financovanie miestnych samospráv v Slovenskej Republike* (Financing local self-governments in the Slovak Republic), Banská Bystrica and Bratislava: Matej Bel University and Local Self-Government Assistance Centre.

Čierna-Lantayová, Dagmar (1992) *Podoby Česko-Slovensko-Maďarského vzťahu 1938-1949* (Aspects of the Czechoslovak-Hungary Relation in the years 1938-1949), Bratislava: Veda.

Horowitz, Donald L. (1985) *Ethnic Groups in Conflict*, Berkeley: University of California Press.

Hrabko, Juraj (1999) *Referendum v Štúrove* (Referendum in Stúrovo), Bratislava: Kalligram.

Chmel, Rudolf (1996) *Moja maďarská otázka* (My Hungarian Question), Bratislava: Kalligram.

Janics, Kálmán (1994) *Roky bez domoviny* (Years without homeland), Budapest: Puski.

Podolák, Peter (1998) *Národnostné menšiny v Slovenskej Republike z hľadiska demografického vývoja* (National minorities in the Slovak Republic—from demographic development point of view), Martin: Matica Slovenská.

Říčan, Pavel (1998) *S Romy žít budeme—jde o to jak* (We will live with Romanies—The question is how?), Praha: Portál.

Zeľová, Alena (ed.) (1994) *Etnické minority na Slovensku v procesoch sociálnych premien* (Ethnic minorities in Slovakia under the processes of social changes). Bratislava: Veda.

Articles and reports

Bačová, Viera and Alena Zeľová (1993) 'Etnické menšiny na Slovensku' (Ethnic minorities in Slovakia), *Sociológia*, 25, 4-5, pp. 417-431.

Bačová, Viera, Mária Homišinová and Marc-Phillipe Cooper (1994) 'Problémy verejnej správy na Slovensku vzhľadom na národnostne zmiešané oblasti' (Problems of Public Administration in Slovakia with respect to nationaly mixed areas), *Sociológia*, 26, 5-6, 447-454.

Bodnárová, Bernardína (1999) 'Sociálna politika' (Social Policy), in: G. Mesežnikov and M. Ivantyšyn, (eds.) *Slovensko 1998-1999–Súhrnná správa o stave spoloènosti* (*Slovakia 1998-1999. A Global Report on the State of Society*), Bratislava: Inštitút pre verejné otázky, pp. 515-538.

Brusis, Martin (1997) 'Ethnic Rift in the Context of Post-Communist Transformation: The Case of the Slovak Republic', *International Journal on Group Rights*, Vol. 5, No. 1, pp. 3-32.

Buček, Ján (1997) 'Size categories of municipalities and local self-government finances in Slovakia', *Acta Universitatis Carolinae Prague*, *Geographica*, 32, Supplementum, pp. 297-305.

Clark, Gordon L. (1984) 'A Theory of Local Autonomy', *Annals of American Association of Geographers*, 74, 2, pp. 195-208

Dostál, Ondrej (1996) 'Menšiny' (Minorities), in: Martin Bútora and Peter Hunčík (eds.) *Slovensko 1995—Súhrnná správa o stave spoločnosti*, Bratislava: Nadácia Sándora Máraiho, pp. 51-60.

Dostál, Ondrej (1998) 'Národnostné menšiny' (National minorities), in: Martin Bútora and Michal Ivantyšyn (eds.) *Slovensko 1997—Súhrnná správa o stave spoločnosti a trendoch na rok 1998*, Bratislava: Inštitút pre verejné otázky, pp. 155-170.

Gabzilová, Soňa (1994) 'Menšinové školstvo v Slovenskej Republike po novembri 1989' (Minority schooling in Slovak Republic after November 1989), *Slovenská štatistika a demografia*, Vol. 4, No. 4, pp. 45-57.

Gecelovský, Vladimír (1992) 'Právne normy týkajúce sa Rómov a ich aplikácia v Gemeri 1918-1938' (Legal norms concerning Roma and their application in Gemer 1918-1938), in: Arne B. Mann (ed.) *Unknown Romanies*, Bratislava: Ister Science Press, pp. 79-89.

Hunčík, Peter (1999) 'Maďarská menšina ve Slovenské republice' (Hungarian minority in Slovak Republic), in: Ivan Gabal et al., *Etnické menšiny ve střední Evropi* (Ethnic minorities in Central Europe), Praha: G plus G. pp. 204-218.

Jurová, Anna (1992) 'Riešenie rómskej problematiky na Slovensku po druhej svetovej vojne' (The solution of Romany Problems in Slovakia after the Second World War), in: Arne B. Mann (ed.) *Unknown Romanies*, Bratislava: Ister Science Press, pp. 91-102.

Kollárová, Zuzana (1992) 'K vývoju rómskej society na Spiši do roku 1945' (On the development of the Romany community in the Spiš District up to 1945), in: Arne B. Mann (ed.) *Unknown Romanies*, Bratislava: Ister Science Press, pp. 61-72.

Krivý, Vladimír (1997) 'Regióny' (Regions), in: Martin Bútora and Michal Ivantyšyn (eds.) *Slovensko 1997—Súhrnná správa o stave spoločnosti a trendoch na rok 1998,* Bratislava: Inštitút pre verejné otázky, pp. 315-332.

Kusý, Miroslav. (1999), Ľudské a menšinové práva' (Human and Minority Rights), in: Grigorij Mesežnikov and Michal Ivantyšyn (eds.) *Slovensko 1998-1999—Súhrnná správa o stave spoločnosti. (Slovakia 1998-1999 A Global Report on the State of Society),* Bratislava: Inštitút pre verejné otázky, pp. 173-190.

Lukáč, Pavol and Rudolf Chmel, Ivo Samson and Alexander Duleba (1999) Vzťahy Slovenska so susednými štátmi, Nemeckom a Ruskom (Slovakia's relations with neighbouring countries, Germany and Russia), in: Grigorij Mesežnikov and Michal Ivantyšyn (eds.) *Slovensko 1998-1999 —Súhrnná správa o stave spoločnosti. (Slovakia 1998-1999 A Global Report on the State of Society),* Bratislava: Inštitút pre verejné otázky. pp.333-374.

Magocsi, Paul R. (1992a) 'Carpathian Ruthenians: current state and future perspectives' (in Slovak). *Slovak Ethnology,* 40, 2, pp. 183-192.

Magocsi, Paul R. (1992b) 'Odpoveď' (Answer on comments published in No. 2), *Slovak Ethnology,* 40, 3, pp. 317-322.

Nemec, Juraj; Peter Berčík and Peter Kukliš (2000) 'Local Government in Slovakia', in: T. Horváth, (ed.) *Decentralization: Experiments and Reforms,* Budapest: OSI/LGI, pp. 297-342.

Plichtová, Jana (1993) 'Czechoslovakia as a multi-cultural state in the context of the region 1918-1992', in: Minority Rights Group and TWEEC (ed.) *Minorities in Central and Eastern Europe,* London: Minority Rights Group, pp. 11-18.

Safran, William (1994) 'Non-separatist policies regarding ethnic minorities: positive approach and ambiguous consequences', *International Political Science Review,* Vol. 15, No. 1, pp.61-80.

Salner, Peter (1998) 'Jews in Slovak urban civil society', in: Elena Mannová (ed.) *Urban civil ociety in Slovakia 1900 to 1989,* Bratislava: AEP, pp. 137-146 (in Slovak).

Sándor, Eleonóra (1996) Slovensko-maďarská základná zmluva (Slovak-Hungarian Basic Treaty), in: Bútora, Martin. and Peter Hunčík (eds.) *Slovensko 1995—Súhrnná správa o stave spolocnosti,* Bratislava: Nadácia Sándora Máraiho, pp. 45-50.

Smooha, Sammy (1982) 'Existing and alternative policy toward the Arabs in Israel', *Ethnic and Racial Studies,* Vol. 5, pp. 71-98.

Šujanová, Silvia (1999) 'Framework Convention for the Protection of National Minorities in the Context of the Slovak Republic', Bratislava: Citizens and Democracy Foundation, Minority Rights Group–Slovakia.

Šutaj, Štefan, and Milan Olejník (1998) 'Slovak Report', in: Kranz and Kupper (eds.) *Law and Practice of Central European Countries in the Field of National Minorities Protection after 1989,* Warsaw: Center for International Relations, pp. 269-321.

Vašečka, Michal (1999) 'Romovia' (Romanies), in: Mesežnikov and Ivantyšyn, *Slovensko 1998-1999— Súhrnná správa o stave spoločnosti,* Bratislava: Inštitút pre verejné otázky, pp. 757-776.

Zartman, I. William (1995) 'Dynamics and Constraints in Negotiations in Internal Conflicts,' In: Zartman, I. William (ed.) *Elusive Peace—Negotiations an End to Civil Wars,* Washington D.C.: The Brookings Institution, pp. 3-29.

Zubriczký, Gabriel (1998) 'Segregácia rómskeho obyvateľstva vo vidieckych obciach Slovenska' (Segregation of Romany population in Rural Settlements of Slovakia), *Geographica: Acta Facultatis Rerum Naturalium Universtiatis Comenianae*, No. 41, pp. 113-121.

Newspaper/magazine articles

Ash, T. G. (1999) 'Aj voda nás tlačí na západ, tvrdí premiér dočasnej vlády, ktorá chce vytvoriť štát menom Rusínsko' (Water also moved us on the west, asserts Prime Minister of interim government, which want to create state with the name Ruthenia), *Magazín SME*, 17 April, p. 2.

Bančanský, A. (1999) 'Starosta Ňagova popiera diskrimináciu' (Mayor of Ňagov refuses discrimination), *PRAVDA*, 23 March, p. 2.

Beňová, J. (1999) 'Spája ich domov, rozdeľujú extrémne názory' (They are joined together on home, devided by extreme opinions), *PRÁCA*, 30 April, p. 24.

Borszék, P. (1998) 'Svitanie nad getom odstrčenách' (Dawn over the ghetto of excluded), *PRÁCA*, 7 November, p. 3.

Čerčanská, K. (1999) 'Ombudsman nie je staršiakom' (Ombudsman is not a spook), *PRÁCA*, 17 June, p. 22.

Drozd, J. (1998) 'Koho budu voliť Rómovia' (For whom will vote Roma), *Národná Obroda*, 31 January 1998, p. 7.

Duleba, A. (1997) 'Rusínska' otázka' (Ruthenian' Question), *OS - Fórum Občianskej Spoločnosti*, No. 2, pp. 46-50.

Ďurková, K. (2000) 'Problém Slovenska nie je etnický - rozhovor s Péterom Hunčíkom' (The problem of Slovakia is not ethnic - Interview with Péter Hunčík), *Domino Fórum*, Vol. 9, No. 43, pp. 4-5.

Gaál, L. (2000) 'Kto potrebuje komárňanskú župu' (Who needs Komárno region), *SME* (taken from Uj Szó), 14 October, p. 6.

Gáfriková, O. (1999) 'Súhlas na ratifikáciu Európskej charty miestnej samosprávy' (The consent with ratification of European charter of Local Self-government). *Obecné Noviny*, No.47, 16 November, p.5.

Hospodárske Noviny (1999) 'Problém takmer jako snehová guľa' (The problem almost like a snowball), 17 December, p. 3.

Hospodárske Noviny (1999) 'Kanadská podpora projektu pre Rómov' (Canadian support for Roma project), 8 June.

Hospodárske Noviny (1999) 'Naliehavým problémom i úroveň bývania' (Housing situation also pressing problem), 15 July.

Hrubovčák, J. (2000) 'S Rómami nemáme žiadne problémy' (We have no problems with Roma), *Obecné noviny*, No. 3, p. 20.

Kačáni, D. (1999) 'Stratégia Vlády Slovenskej Republiky na riešenie problémov Rómskej národnostnej menšiny' (Strategy of the Government of the Slovak Republic for solving Roma national minority

Kotian, R. (2000) 'Rómsky krok správnym smerom' (Roma step in right direction), *SME*, 24 October 2000, pp. 6.

Krajčovič, M. (1997) 'Jedenásť Rómov čistí Trnavu' (Eleven Romanies is cleaning Trnava), *SPP - Poradca Stavebníka*, 11-12, p.201.

Kusý, M. (2000) 'Zdroje maďarských nárokov na vlastnú župu' (The origins of Hungarian requirements for own region). *SME*, 18 October, p. 6.

Magdolenová, K. (1998) 'Človek v rómskej koži' (A man in Roma skin), *SME Magazín*, 10 October, pp. 4.

Magdolenová, K. (1998) 'V sobotu posvätili prvé pastoračné centrum pre Rómov na Slovensku' (First pastoral centre for Romanies in Slovakia was sacrified in Saturday), SME, 17 August, p. 3.

Narodny Novinky (1999) 6ᵀᴴ Congress and changes in leadership of Ruthenian Revival (in Ruthenian) No. 24-26, pp 1-3.

Obecné Noviny (1998) 'Ako to bolo v parlamente' (How it was in the parliament), No. 31-32, 28 July, pp. 4-7.

Olach, B. (1999) 'Riešenie problémov závisí najmä od vzťahu väčšiny k menšine' (Solution depends on the relation of majority to minority—Reports on round table meeting in Čilistov 16 March 1999 dealing with Romanies in Slovakia), Obecné Noviny, No.18, p. 6; No.19, p.14; No.20, pp. 6-7; (No. 21), p. 15.

Piecka, J. (1999) 'Žarnovická cesta spolupráce s Romami' (Žarnovica way in co-operation with Romanies), Obecné noviny, 9, 47, p. 8.

Prekopová, O. (1999a) 'Z Rómov nebudú gadžovia' (Romanies will not be 'gadžo'), Pravda, 3 March, p. 2.

Prekopová, O. (1999b) 'Lacnejšie bývanie' (Cheaper housing), Pravda, 26 June 1999, p. 2.

Praca (1999) 'Vyriešia bytovú otázky Rómov?' (Do they resolve the Roma housing issue?). 11 August, p. 4.

Pravda (1999) 'Rómske deti o sexe' (Roma children education about sex), 12 March, p.2.

Pravda (1999) 'Bagrom na odpadky' (Waste refusal by a dredge), 10 April, p. 3.

Pravda (1999) 'Rómsky problém' (The Roma problem), 24 April, p. 3.

Pravda (1999) 'Z juhu neemigrujú' (They do not emigree for the south), 8 July, p.2.

Pravda (1999) 'Program hotový' (The Program is prepared), 22 July, http://www.pravda.sk.

Pravda (1999) 'Budúcnosť Rómskych osád' (The future of Roma settlements), 23 July, http://www.pravda.sk.

Pravda (1999) 'Nezáujem o byty' (Houses without interest), 14 August , p. 5.

Pravda (1999) 'Väčšina v chatrčiach' (Majority in shacks), 24 January, http://www.pravda.sk.

Sisak, M. (1997) 'Rusíni nie sú Ukrajinci a naopak' (Ruthenians are not Ukrainians and vice versa), OS - Fórum Občianskej Spoločnosti, No. 2, pp. 37-39.

SME (1998) 'Seden fakúlt UK ponúka možnosť prihlásenia sa občanom rómskej národnosti' (Seven faculties of Comenius University offer chance for additonal application), 15 April, p. 2.

SME (1998) 'RIS je presvedčená o diskriminácii Romov, vládny splnomocennec oponuje, že len v istých oblastiach' (RIS is assured on discrimination of Roma, governmental plenipotentiary refuse it), 21 October, p. 3.

SME (1998) 'V Jelšave odmietajú udeľovat trvalé bydlisko prichádzajúcim Rómom, aj keď tým porušujú zákon' (Refusing to give permanent living to coming Roma in Jelšava, although it is against the law), 28 November, p. 3.

SME (1998) 'Podľa M. Baláža vznik rómskej samosprávy časť obyvateľov Prievidze víta' (Part of Prievidza citizens welcome formation of Roma self-government), 7 October, p. 2.

SME (1999) 'Kanaďan českého pôvodu učí slovenských Rómov žiť a pracovať (Canadian of Czech origin is teaching Slovak Romanies to live and work), 7 January, p.3.

SME (1999) 'Rusínske oddelenie na Prešovskej univerzite' (Ruthenian department of Presov University), 20 April, p. 3.

SME (1999) 'Návrh zákona o používaní jazykov národnostných menšín podľa SMK' (Proposal of the Act on Use of Languages of National Minorities According to Slovak Hungarian Coalition). 14 June, p. 5.

SME (1999) 'Tento mesiac by mala byť dokončená nová koncepcia riešenia rómskej problematiky' (This month a new strategy for solving of Roma issue should be finished), 24 June, p. 3.

SME (1999) Starosta košického Lunik IX nechce aby sídlisko bolo centrum ľudského odpadu' (Mayor of Košice Lunik IX does not want this settlement to be a centre of 'human waste), 13 June, p. 1.

Štark, L. (1998) Sociálne dávky formou osobitného príjemcu' (Social payments in form of specific recipient), *Verejná Správa*, No. 9, p.7.

Tóth, I. (1998) 'Práca a byty—základný predpoklad' (Labour and housing—basic requirement), *Verejná Správa*, No. 25, p. 18.

Új Szó (1999) 'Új ház 23 nap alatt' (House built in 23 days), 12 August, Régióink p. IV.

Višváder, P. (1998) 'Predídeme principu účelových koalícii' (We avoid the principle of functional coalitions), *Obecné Noviny*, No. 44, 27 October, pp. 8-9.

Victor Stepanenko ·· *A State to Build, A Nation to Form Ethno-policy in Ukraine*

Documents and statistics

The Organization of the United Nations: Universal Declaration of Human Rights.

The Council of Europe: Framework Convention for the Protection of National Minorities.

The Council of Europe: European Chapter for Regional and Linguistic Minorities.

The Council of Europe: European Chapter of Local Self-Government

The Constitution of Ukraine (adopted on 28 June 1996).

The Constitution of the Autonomous Republic of Crimea (adopted on 21 October 1998).

The Declaration of the Rights of Nationalities of Ukraine.

The Law of Ukraine 'On National Minorities in Ukraine'.

The Law of Ukraine 'On Languages in Ukrainian SSR'.

The Law of Ukraine 'On Education'.

The Law of Ukraine 'On Local Self-Government in Ukraine.'

The Concept of the Development of National Minorities of Ukraine.

The State Programme 'Education: Ukraine of the 21-st century' (adopted at the 1-st all-Ukrainian congress of teachers in 1992).

The Report of the State Committee of Ukraine on Nationalities and Migration on 1998.

The national composition of the USSR on the data of All-Union population census of 1989. Moscow, 1991: Finansy i Statistika.

Books

Anderson, Benedict (1983) *Imagined Communities. Reflections on the Origin and Spread of Nationalism*, London:Verso.

Beiner, Reiner (ed.) (1995) *Theorizing Citizenship*, Albany: State University of New York Press.

Bennett, Robert (1993) *Local Government in the New Europe*, London: Belhaven.

Buznytsky, Yuriy, et al. (1997) *Stability and Integration in the Autonomous Republic of Crimea: The Role of International Community*, Kyiv: International Renaissance Foundation.

Dente, Bruno and Francesco Kjellberg (eds.) (1988) *The Dynamics of Institutional Change in Local Government: Reorganization in Western Democracies*, London:Sage.

Gellner, Ernest (1983) *Nations and Nationalism*, Oxford: Basil Blackwell.

Guibernau, Montserrat (1996) *Nationalisms. The Nation-State and Nationalism in the Twentieth Century*, Cambridge: Polity Press.

Hall, John A., (ed.) (1995) *Civil Society: Theory, History and Comparison,* Cambridge: Polity Press.

Helton, Arthur et al. (1996) *Crimean Tatars: Repatriation and Conflict Prevention,* New York: OSI, Forced Migration Project.

Jacob, Betty M. et al. (eds.) (1993) *Democracy and Local Governance. Ten empirical studies,* Honolulu, Hawaii: Matsunaga Institute for Peace, University of Hawaii.

Kuzio,Taras (1992) *Ukraine. The Unfinished Revolution,* London: Alliance Publishers.

Kymlicka, Will (1996) *Multicultural Citisenship. A Liberal Theory of Minority Rights,* Oxford: Clarendon Press.

Leonova, Alla (1998) *Ethno-cultural Policy of Ukraine,* Kiev: The Ministry of Culture of Ukraine.

Lijphart, Arend (1975) *The Politics of Accommodation. Pluralism and Democracy in the Netherlands,* 2ND ed., Berkeley: University of California Press.

Malenkovich, Vladimir (1997) 'The prospects of the development of Russian and Ukrainian culture in Ukraine', in: *The Dialogue between Russian and Ukrainian Cultures in Ukraine,* Kiev: The Society of Russian Culture in Ukraine.

Nadolishnij, Petro (1998) *Ethno-national Factor of Administrative Reform in Ukraine,* Kyiv: Academy of Public Administration at the Office of the President of Ukraine.

Nikityuk, Viktor (1996) *Status of Ethno-national Minorities,* Kyiv: Estet.

Opalski, Magda and Piotr Dutkiewich (ed.) (1996) *Ethnic Minority Rights in Central Eastern Europe,* Ottawa: Canadian Human Rights Foundation.

Pieklo, Jan et al. (1995) *Conflict or Co-operation. The Media and Minority Problems,* Krakow: Znak Foundation for Christian Culture.

Rebkalo, Valerij et al.(1996) *Ethno-national Processes in Modern Ukraine,* Kiev: Academy of Public Administration at the Office of the President of Ukraine.

Saenko Yuriy et al. (1997) *Local Self-government in Ukraine: Problems and Perspectives,* Kyiv: Institute of Sociology of National Academy of Sciences of Ukraine.

Shulga, Mylola (ed.) (1998) *The study of influence of external migration of 1991-1996 on the changes of ethnic structure of the population of Ukraine and its regions,* Kiev: International Organization for Migration.

Smith, Anthony D. (1991) *National Identity,* London: Penguin.

Wilson, Andrew (1997) *Ukrainian nationalism in the 1990s,* Cambridge: Cambridge University Press.

Articles and reports

Ablyamitov, Dszulvern (1994) 'The bodies of national self-government of Crimean Tatars', *Local and Regional Self-government of Ukraine,* Vol. 4 (9), pp. 40-43.

Arel, Dominique (1995) 'Language Politics in Independent Ukraine: Towards One or Two State Languages?', *Nationalities Papers,* Vol. 23, No 3, pp. 597-622.

Britchenko, Petro (1998) 'The implementation of international standards of protection of national minorities in Ukraine', *Yuridicheskiy Vestnik,* Vol. 4, pp. 100-102.

Goncharenko, Sergyi (1994) 'The Problem of the Content of Education', Poltava, Ukraine: *Post-Metodika,* No. 2, pp. 2-3.

Malinovska, Olena (1998) 'The Refuges in Ukraine', *The Problems of Migration,* Vol. 2, pp. 2-13.

Mishanych, Oleksa (1996) 'Rusynism in a political test-tube', *Viche,* No. 11, pp. 91-102.

Naiman, O. (1997) 'National Minorities of Ukraine: situation, problems and perspectives', in: *'Ethno-national Development in Ukraine and the Situation of Ukrainians in Diaspora', Materials of the International conference in Chernivtsi.* Chernivtsi, 22-25 June, Vol.2, pp. 287-292.

Offe, Klaus (1996) 'Ethno-Politics in East European Transitions', Moscow: *Polis,* No. 2, pp. 27-45.

Pavlenko, Valentina (2000) 'My Motherland—the newspaper of ethnic minorities in Ukraine' LGI database (http://www.osi.hu/lgi/ethnic).

Pidgrushnyi, Georgij (1995) 'Secondary Schools in Ukraine', Kyiv: *Rozbudova derzhavy*, No. 7-8, pp. 62-64.

Schoplin, George (1991) 'National Identity in Soviet Union and East Central Europe', *Ethnic and Racial Studies*, Vol. 14, No. 1, pp. 3-14.

Tomenko, Mylola (1998) 'The Ukrainian Parliamentarianism', *Khronika 2000*, Vol. 27-28, pp. 232-247.

Tovt, Mikhay (1997) 'The problems of the Hungarian minority in conteporary Ukraine,' *Nova Polityka* Vol. 3.

Troszynskyi, Volodymyr (1997) 'The Search for Consent', *Viche*, Vol. 10, pp.31-44.

Udovenko, Gennadiy (1997) 'Report of the Minister of Foreign Affairs at the meeting of the Council of regions of Ukraine', *Polityka i Chas*, No. 7, pp. 3-8.

Vyzgrin, Valeriy (1998) 'Crimean Tatars: Discrimination and the consequences of smouldering conflict', *The Problems of Migration*, Vol. 2, pp. 34-44.

Wilson, Andrew (1995) 'The Donbas between Ukraine and Russia: The Use of History in Political Disputes', *Journal of Contemporary History*, Vol. 30, pp. 265-289.

(Newspaper/magazine articles

'To attention of the President' (The letter of the leaders of the national societies of Ukraine to the President of Ukraine) (1996) *Vseukrainskie Vedomosti*, 16 October.

Grabar, M. (1999) 'The Kyiv Budget', *Holos Ukrainy*, 23-29 April.

Popesku, I. (1996) 'A Person in the State', *Golos Ukrainy*, 3 December.

'Unrully Child. A Survey of Ukraine' (1994) *Economist*, 7 May, pp. 3-18.

Vovkanych, S. and S.Tsapok (1996) 'Do National and Regional Vectors always combine together?', *Chas/Time*, 26 April.

Zgurovskyi, M. (1995) 'Educational issues at the parliamentary meeting', *Osvita*, 22 February.

Zgurovskyi, M. (1995) 'The High Mission of the Ukrainian Teachers', *Osvita*, 15 June.

Interview with the leader of the Crimean Tatars Mustafa Dszamilyov, *Nezavisimost*, 20 January 1998.

Interview with Ivan Gnatushyn, the Head of Chernivtsi local state administration, *Uryadovyj Kurjer*, 5 August 1995.

Interview with Petro Ovcharenko, Head of the Department of ethno-national processes at the State Committee of Nationalities and Migration, *Open World*, Review of IRF (Soros Foundation in Ukraine), August-October 1998, pp. 10-11.

385

INDEX OF TERMS

Index of Minority Groups

Armenians 101, 102, 110, 118, 123, 176, 177, 208, 245, 247, 313, 316, 321
Bashkirs 310
Belarussians 310, 313, 327
Bulgarians 170f, 176, 177, 190, 278, 310, 312, 313, 315, 316, 321, 340
Bulgarian Muslims 100, 101, 102, 125
Chinese 141
Chuvash 310
Crimchaks 310, 316, 321
Crimean Tatars 309, 310, 312, 313, 316, 317-318, 320-321, 322, 324, 326, 327, 328, 337, 338, 339, 344, 345
Croatians 140, 176, 278
Czechs 208, 276, 310
Estonians 310
Gagauz 101, 310, 313, 315, 316, 322
Georgians 310
Germans: 140, 141, 176, 207, 216-217, 219, 224, 225, 229, 230, 244, 246, 247, 276, 320
autonomy, 209, 210, 344
education, 227-228
expulsion of, 140, 142f, 175, 208, 251, 312
kin-state and, 139, 215, 339
political mobilisation, 338
representation/participation, 198, 210, 214, 221, 222-224, 256, 324
Greeks 101, 102, 140, 170f, 176, 177, 190, 208, 245, 310, 312, 321, 324
Hungarians: 15, 140, 141, 150, 244, 246, 278, 279, 280, 282, 310, 313, 339
autonomy, 252, 256, 266, 267, 322
education, 143, 251, 266-268, 271, 295-298, 327, 340-341
language, 11, 12, 245, 276, 288, 297-299, 326

political mobilisation, 252-253, 256, 315-316
representation/participation, 256, 259, 260, 263, 283-284, 291, 292
Jews 101, 102, 120, 123, 140, 146, 154, 170f, 175, 208, 209, 210, 216, 244, 245, 247, 276, 277, 310, 313, 320, 324, 327, 339
Karaims 208, 310, 316, 321
Kashubs 208
Latvians 310
Lipovans 244
Lithuanians 208, 215, 219, 224, 228, 229, 310
Macedonians 101, 109, 110, 116, 208
Moldovans 310, 326
Mordvins 310
Moravians 276
Poles 140, 141f, 176, 245, 276, 310, 324, 344
Roma: 15, 50-51, 100, 109, 142-143, 174, 176-177, 207-208, 245, 279, 280, 313
criminalisation of, 142
discrimination against, 107, 155, 174, 180, 192, 195, 196, 209, 216, 252, 256, 278, 279, 288;
education, 121, 142-143, 146, 147f, 152-154, 159-160, 167-168, 188-189, 190-3, 214-215, 229, 268-269, 271, 295-297, 302;
employment, 123, 299;
experts, 107, 149;
integration, 103, 111, 158-159, 161-162, 181, 184, 233;
media and, 123, 264;
political mobilisation, 110, 252-253, 283-285, 293;
political participation, 116, 181, 198, 223, 258-259, 261, 264, 290, 291, 293;
public services, 124, 199;